THE NEWCASTLE UPON TYNE BACH CHOIR
Celebrating a Century of Singing, 1915–2015

THE NEWCASTLE UPON TYNE BACH CHOIR

Celebrating a Century of Singing, 1915–2015

CHRISTINE BORTHWICK • ERIC CROSS
ROY LARGE • PHILIP OWEN

LINE CLEAR EDITIONS

Line Clear Editions
5 Devon Road, Hersham, Surrey, KT12 5RB

First published 2016

Designed, edited, indexed and set in 11 on 14 point Monotype Imprint by J. George Timcke

ISBN 978-1-784562-95-3

Published in association with Fast-Print Publishing

An environmentally friendly book
printed and bound in England
by www.printondemand-worldwide.com

Lord Mayor's Chamber

Civic Centre, Newcastle upon Tyne, NE1 8QA

Newcastle upon Tyne Bach Choir Centenary Celebrations 2015

I am very pleased and honoured to pen this greeting from the city of Newcastle upon Tyne on the occasion of your centenary year. As someone who has been associated with the University over a period of years, I am well aware of the contribution you have made to the musical diversity of our city, from your conception in 1915, to promote the Bach cantatas, to your current more diverse output, much beloved of our city's music lovers.

I feel that the choir is a true musical asset to our historic musical heritage and you have grown under the patronage of the University and the guidance of Dr Cross over a period of years.

On behalf of the city may I wish you all a very happy centenary year and a successful future.

Lord Mayor
Councillor Ian Graham

Contents

Foreword

HAD you been asleep for a hundred years or more, you could well wake up one morning about now and believe that some new form of musical pursuit had been invented, or at any rate newly discovered. For choral singing, it would appear, has been reborn. Readers of this book will certainly know differently, and, if not beforehand, they most certainly will afterwards.

As a child, at the close of the Second World War, I heard chapels, churches and drill halls resounding with the sound of choirs letting rip – though that would be in the nicest of musical manners, of course.

For most choirs it would suffice to offer up, at fairly regular intervals, what might be regarded as the 'big three': Haydn's *Creation*, Mendelssohn's *Elijah* and, of course, Handel's *Messiah*, with the odd foray into Stainer's *Crucifixion* and Maunder's *Olivet to Calvary*. This book of the history of the Newcastle Bach Choir, however, makes extraordinary reading about a group of enthusiasts and far-seeing musicians who made up programmes of works that would not be discovered by most others of supposedly serious intent until several decades later. It is a tribute to some remarkable people who have nurtured a wonderful choir through to the present day, creating a history of which so many can be justly proud.

It has given me great pleasure to make this tribute to friends and colleagues, and I wish the Choir ever greater strengths for the next fifty – no, the next hundred – years.

Singing is good for you, and this is the proof of it.

THOMAS ALLEN
London, September 2015

Preface

THE Newcastle upon Tyne Bach Choir was born into a world in crisis. The Great War was less than a year old, and the establishment in England of an institution dedicated to performances of music by a German composer was fraught with unique emotional, political and practical difficulties. Its founder, the musicologist William Gillies Whittaker, and his band of loyal pioneers would be justly proud to know that their creation has survived and prospered for so long.

In anticipation of the centenary in November 2015 the choir considered how best to celebrate this unique event in its history. The concept of a book arose from those discussions and a team was assembled to give it practical reality.

All the contributors to this book have strong links with the choir. Christine Borthwick, a flautist, her husband Antony (violin), sister-in-law Margaret (flute) and brother-in-law Michael (cello) were regular members of the Tyneside Chamber Orchestra which accompanied many of its concerts. She completed a Ph.D. thesis on the life and work of W. G. Whittaker in 2007. Eric Cross, initially a member of the bass line in the late 1970s and now Professor of Music and Culture and Dean of Cultural Affairs at Newcastle University, has been the choir's musical director since 1984. Roy Large, formerly Senior Lecturer in music at St Mary's College, Fenham, has long-standing familial links beginning with his grandfather Wilson, who was a tenor and office-holder from 1919, and his mother, Greta, who was in the choir for over sixty years. He has recently been working on a study of Bach choirs in the United Kingdom. Philip Owen, a former Health Service consultant radiologist and Senior Lecturer at Newcastle University Medical School, has been a member of the tenor line of the choir since the early 1970s.

We should like to thank the Committee of the Newcastle Bach Choir for their support and encouragement and our publisher George Timcke for his professional expertise and calm guidance in bringing the work to fruition. We are grateful to His Worship, Councillor Ian Graham, Lord Mayor of Newcastle upon Tyne, for his warm and generous greeting. We also acknowledge the support that our President, Sir Thomas Allen, has given to the choir over many years and wish to thank him for providing the foreword to this book. The contributors have expressed their individual and personal acknowledgements within the chapters that follow. Photographic credits are given in the captions for the figures. Those uncredited are from the choir's archives.

CHRISTINE BORTHWICK   ERIC CROSS   ROY LARGE   PHILIP OWEN

September 2015

Abbreviations

ACCS Armstrong College Choral Society
ARCM Associate of the Royal College of Music
ARCO Associate of the Royal College of Organists
ATCL Associate of Trinity College London
B.Mus. Bachelor of Music
BMS British Music Society
D.Mus. Doctor of Music
FRCO Fellow of the Royal college of Organists
ISM Incorporated Society of Musicians
L.Mus. Licentiate of Music
LCM London College of Music
LRAM Licentiate of the Royal Academy of Music
LTCL Licentiate of Trinity College London
Mus.Bac. Bachelor of Music (*Musicae Baccalaureus*)
Mus.Doc. Doctor of Music (*Musicae Doctor*)
NEMT North of England Musical Tournament
NFMS National Federation of Music Societies
NLPS Newcastle Literary and Philosophical Society
   (now the 'Lit & Phil')
PRS Performing Rights Society
RCM Royal College of Music
SNAM Scottish National Academy of Music

PART ONE

Whittaker and his Choir

Chapter 1
The Founder: William Gillies Whittaker (1876–1944)

Philip Owen

Fig. 1 William Gillies Whittaker *c.*1925.
Courtesy Newcastle City Libraries.

WILLIAM GILLIES WHITTAKER, popularly known in his time as 'WGW', was born on 23 July 1876 at 17 Clarence Crescent in the Newcastle parish of All Saints. His father was John Whittaker and his mother Mary Jane Gillies. John Whittaker hailed from the Cumbrian village of Little Corby, which is near the modern community of Warwick Bridge. John's mother, Mary Ann Whittaker, also had her roots in that area, but John's father was not named on his birth certificate.

At the time of his marriage John was clerk to an earthenware manufacturer in Newcastle (the Maling Pottery), but he also later became clerk to the Byker and Heaton Burial Board.

Mary Jane Gillies had her roots firmly in the Northumbrian town of Hexham. On her paternal side she was descended from Andrew Gillies through his son William. They were tobacconists, of the well-known firm of Gillies & Smith based in St Mary's Chare (known locally as Back Street). Mary's mother, Susanna Walton, was descended from Henry Walton, who was the schoolmaster at the Sub-scription School and actuary for the Tindale Ward Savings Bank.

William Gillies Whittaker had two younger siblings: John Henry (b.18 October 1880), who died of rheumatic fever at the age of seven, and Lily (b.3 August 1888), who later married, had two children and settled in Edinburgh. The Whittaker family were Liberals and staunch Methodists who attended Brunswick Place Methodist chapel in central Newcastle. At about the time of Lily's birth they were living at 31 Cardigan Terrace, Heaton, but by 1901 they had moved to 18 Heaton Grove, where his parents and sister were still living in 1911.

Whittaker's early education in Newcastle was at the Clarence Street Wesleyan Day School, which he attended from 1882 to 1887 and where he learned to read tonic sol-fa. He showed some early musical interest, playing the piccolo in a local fife and drum band. In 1885, aged nine, he began pianoforte lessons with a strict lady who rapped his knuckles when he made errors. He made his first (reluctant) public performance at the keyboard in Alnmouth in 1886, and while still at school became a pupil of John Nicholson, the former organist of Hexham Abbey. He seems to have been prone to accidents, and once broke his right arm. In later life the injury affected his posture at the conducting rostrum and led to his rejection from the services in the First World War. His father, John, was quite musical and followed his son's career with intense pride. He passed on his abstinence from alcohol to his son.

Whittaker won a Corporation exhibition scholarship in 1892 and entered the College of Physical Science and Arts in Newcastle (later Armstrong College of Durham University), with the aim of pursuing a scientific career. That year he was appointed accompanist to the Armstrong College Choral Society under Charles Sanford Terry (who later became professor of history at Aberdeen). Whittaker later acknowledged Terry's seminal influence on his subsequent musical career. He completed two years of a science course, but his interests and abilities clearly lay in other directions. He began to study for a Durham B.Mus., specializing in the organ (taking lessons from the Newcastle organist William Rea) and singing. His studies were supplemented by a number of holiday courses in

London, in which he studied musical theory under Dr G. F. Huntley and singing under Kate Emil Behnke, Frederic Austin and others. His daughter Mary recalled him telling her that he set himself a punishing fourteen-hour daily schedule of organ and piano practice, but this prodigious effort cannot be verified.

In 1894, at the age of eighteen, in order to fund his music studies, he became an organist at St George's Presbyterian Church, Jesmond, on an annual salary of £15, before taking up a similar post at St Paul's Presbyterian Church, South Shields, at an enhanced annual fee of £35. He joined the Armstrong College Choral Society, soon becoming its accompanist and eventually its conductor. In 1895 he joined the Gateshead Choral Society (from 1899 onwards the Newcastle and Gateshead Choral Union), initially as a bass but finally as a tenor under the conductorship of James Preston (see fig. 2). There he gained knowledge of choral training techniques. In 1897 he was elected to membership of the Incorporated Society of Musicians and the following year passed the ARCO examination.

Fig. 2 James M. Preston, from the programme for the Newcastle Musical Tournament of 1919. *Courtesy Newcastle City Libraries.*

Whittaker was a successful student, and in 1898, at the age of twenty-two, was selected to join the teaching staff of Armstrong College. His first appointment was as instructor in music, at which time he was also appointed honorary conductor of the Armstrong College Choral Society. Works performed by it under his leadership included music by Bach (*My spirit was in heaviness*), Byrd (one of the three Masses), Brahms (*Nänie*), Goetz (*Naenia* and *Hiawatha*), Holst (*The Cloud Messenger*, the *Hymn to Dionysos* and *Hymns from the Rig Veda*) and Debussy (*The Blessed Damosel*). Eventually he was promoted to lecturer and finally to reader. He gained the FRCO diploma in 1901, and the following year, after two failed entries, the Durham B.Mus. Characteristically he then threw himself into studying for the D.Mus. It was, however, to take until 1921 before he was awarded this degree, largely because of a clash between his modern approaches to harmony and the ultra-conservative orthodoxy of the examining body.

Fig. 3 Sir Henry Hadow, from the programme for the Newcastle Musical Tournament of 1919. *Courtesy Newcastle City Libraries.*

In 1901 a young musician, Edgar Leslie Bainton, came to Newcastle to teach pianoforte and composition at the Newcastle Conservatoire of Music. Bainton was to have a profound influence on Whittaker's career, and they became great friends and musical soulmates. In 1902 William Henry Hadow of Worcester College, Oxford (see fig. 3), gave the first of many subsequent lectures on musical subjects at the Newcastle Literary and Philosophical Society that greatly stimulated Whittaker.

From 1904 to 1912 Whittaker was a part-time lecturer at the Newcastle Education Committee's pupil–teacher centre, and from 1906 until 1920 part-time singing master (on a salary of £40) at the Central Newcastle High School, where he contributed articles to the school magazine.

On 27 July 1903, at the age of twenty-six, Whittaker married 34-year-old Clara Watkins at the Park Terrace Presbyterian Church in Gateshead, County Durham. At the time of their marriage he was living with his parents at 18 Heaton Grove, Newcastle, and Clara with her parents at 13 Woodbine Place, Gateshead. Whittaker was recorded as a teacher of music, and although Clara's occupation was not given we know from the 1901 census that she was also a music teacher. Both William and Clara's fathers were classified as commercial clerks. Clara's father, Thomas Watkins, was born in Alnwick (the son of a farmer from Belford), and she was born in Westoe (near South Shields), where the Watkins family lived at 19 Saville Street. On her birth certificate her father was described as a master mariner, but subsequent censuses reveal his declining fortunes, and by 1911 he was a charting clerk. The Watkins family moved to Gateshead in the 1880s. Whittaker's best man at the wedding was John William Bullerwell, senior lecturer in physics at Armstrong College. Bullerwell was a keen musician, and like the groom a collector of northern folk songs. He was also treasurer of the Choral and Orchestral Society of the University and would later be closely associated with the Newcastle Bach Choir from its foundation. They remained lifelong friends.

The Whittakers eventually set up home at 4 Granville Gardens in the pleasant and prosperous Newcastle suburb of Jesmond, where they were living in 1911. They had two daughters, Clara Margaret (b.9 March 1905), who was known within the family as Clarrie, to distinguish her from her mother, and Mary Gillies (b.22 May 1906). Both daughters attended the Central Newcastle High School, Clara from 1910 and Mary between 1911 and 1923.

It was tacitly assumed that both daughters would have musical careers, and they were therefore taught to play instruments, Clarrie the cello and Mary the violin. However, Clarrie studied European languages and later became a secretary. Mary alone followed the preordained path, and attended the Royal College of Music in London from September 1923 until July 1928, qualifying as an ARCM.

Mary described her father as

a human volcano . . . leaping up and down stairs, always two or three steps at a time, black mop of hair flying, big red moustache bristling; bursting into the dining room at odd moments to gulp down a glass of milk and soda water, always kept in readiness on the sideboard.

He was a vegetarian and a teetotaller, and insisted that his family should be too; he read the daily newspapers throughout meals; would not have a telephone; did not have a car; worked from 7.30 a.m. to 3.30 a.m., regarding sleep as a waste of time; did not suffer fools gladly and told them so. Most of his music teaching took place in the family home. His dedication to music and his various eccentricities impacted on the family, and his long-suffering wife went to extraordinary lengths to ensure that his dietary obsession did not undermine his health. The doorbell was constantly ringing, and the lack of a telephone and transport meant that his wife was frequently delivering – usually on foot – messages to colleagues and pupils. Mary recounted that

his appearance was one of [my mother's] despairs, for he always seemed to insist on the wrong article of clothing to combine with the right one, and in any case, the extra huge manuscript-size pockets especially ordered to be inserted inside every jacket and overcoat, and always full to overflowing, caused him to take on a singularly peculiar shape.

The annual task of spring-cleaning the music room was entrusted only to Mrs Whittaker, who had to ensure that every scrap of paper and every book was meticulously replaced on the 'miles' of bookshelves.

Family holidays, fondly remembered, were spent at a succession of rented cottages. One of those retreats was at Deanham, close to Wallington Hall (home of the Trevelyans) and in the shadow of Shaftoe Crags, about 18 miles north-west of Newcastle. The other holiday home was at Boghead, near Whitfield, some 30 miles west of Newcastle, where the girls could run wild while their father worked in isolation in an old corrugated-iron army hut in the garden. Mary rather fancifully located Boghead in 'the Northumbrian hills', but although in Northumberland it is actually in the north Pennines. Sadly, Clara Whittaker became increasingly deaf, and this placed an enormous additional strain on her generous and self-effacing support for her husband. It was most probably also a catalyst in the eventual decline of their marriage.

At about this time, Whittaker had an adult French piano pupil by the name of T. J. Guéritte, who was working as a civil engineer in Newcastle. Guéritte was well connected in contemporary French musical circles, being a friend of Debussy and Ravel. He brought Ravel to Newcastle and introduced Whittaker to him.

In 1908 Whittaker became conductor of the Whitley Bay and District Choral Society (at £20 per annum) while continuing his activities with the growing and increasingly successful Armstrong College Choral Society. He also continued with his own singing lessons under several well-known teachers, and was clearly quite good, for it was suggested that he might take up an operatic career.

William Henry Hadow was appointed principal of Armstrong College in 1909. He was a talented musician and a gifted public speaker, uncompromising in his opinions but generally encouraging and helpful to Whittaker's musical activities with the College Choral Society.

With his professional life becoming ever busier, Whittaker resigned his post as organist at St Paul's, South Shields, in July 1910. It was about this time that he conducted a Newcastle performance of part of Gustav Holst's *Hymns from the Rig Veda*. Holst had been a friend of Ralph Vaughan Williams from their days as students at the Royal College of Music, and they and Whittaker became lifelong friends. Holst's daughter, Imogen, recalled first meeting Whittaker at her parent's home in Barnes in 1913: 'He seemed to me to be immensely tall and energetic. I can remember my father's obvious delight at having him with us, and during the next few years I could recognise the particular excitement in his voice whenever he told us, "Will is coming!"'

Whittaker and Holst were engagingly frank when criticizing each other's music, but it was always done in an affectionate manner. Their friendship extended to walking tours, on which they were accompanied by Vaughan Williams and Balfour Gardiner. Mary recalled her father, Holst and Vaughan Williams setting out on a walking tour in 1913 in the Northumbrian hills, 'knapsacks on backs, staying at wayside inns'. It was during that fourteen-day holiday that Holst encouraged Whittaker to take up writing music.

Whittaker became part of the teaching staff of the Newcastle Conservatoire alongside Edgar Bainton, George R. Dodds, H. Yeaman Dodds, the violinist Alfred Wall, the conductor J. E. Hutchinson and the cathedral organist William Ellis. They introduced British music by Holst, Bax, Vaughan Williams and others, and the Conservatoire had a major influence on the musical life of the region.

In 1913, while on holiday, Whittaker read an English edition of Schweitzer's *Bach*, in which the author had formulated the notion of singing Bach cantatas at home for pure enjoyment. In 1914 the Armstrong College Choral Society presented him with a large number of Bach-Gesellschaft-Ausgabe scores of the works of J. S. Bach, and he promptly invited students and pupils to join him each week to sing Bach's cantatas around the piano at his home. Those early days are well described by Edgar Crowe, a founding member of the choir:

> With a full muster of two to a part, as a beginning, [you] struggled along zealously, if not always accurately, while if your co-partner, sharer of your life's joys and sorrows, happened to be absent, a little practice in solo singing was yours – much to your satisfaction, of course! I have known members conceal their feelings so well, however, that a directly opposite impression might have been obtained by the casual observer. Dr Whittaker 'orchestrated' at the piano . . . and sang, impartially, tenor, bass, and fragments of the other parts when occasion called for such assistance (and this was by no means infrequent) besides doing a little conducting in his spare moments. . . . It was arduous but exhilarating work and it was due to this thorough grounding that we finally acquired some knowledge of the Bach idiom and a true appreciation of his greatness as a composer.

Bainton suggested to Whittaker that 'we were selfish people to sing all these cantatas for our own exclusive benefit, and that we should give some of them in public'.

During a singing lesson with Frederic Austin in 1914, Whittaker mentioned that he had written some folk song settings, and subsequently sent Austin copies of the scores. Austin was very impressed with them, showed them around the musical cognoscenti of London, arranged for them to be published, and invited Whittaker to conduct performances in the capital.

In the summer of 1914 Whittaker, his wife and two daughters were in the middle of a tour of Germany and Belgium when war clouds broke. They were very fortunate to escape. Their friend Edgar Bainton was not so lucky: he and his wife, on a Wagner pilgrimage to the Bayreuth Festival, were arrested, and Edgar spent the duration of the First World War in an internment camp at Ruhleben, near Berlin. More about that episode can be read in Ethel Bainton's biography in Chapter 4. On his return to Newcastle, Whittaker mounted a 'grand war relief music festival' at the St James's Park football ground, where a massed choir and orchestra of 1,250 performed choruses by Handel, Elgar and Stanford.

Whittaker had taken note of Bainton's comments about offering the domestic performances of Bach's cantatas to a wider audience, but was constrained by the absence of a good local tenor. He eventually discovered one in the person of John

Vine, a former Durham pitman. His first meeting with the young tenor is described in detail in Vine's biography in Chapter 8. This discovery was the ultimate catalyst to Whittaker's most notable choral creation, the founding of the Newcastle upon Tyne Bach Choir in 1915. Bach's choral works were virtually unknown in the United Kingdom at the time, and it was a courageous venture in the atmosphere of strong anti-German sentiments during the First World War. The initial aim was to perform Bach's cantatas employing vocal and instrumental resources as close as possible to those of the composer. Percy Lovell, a subsequent conductor of the choir, said that Whittaker 'was well ahead of his time since the swing towards so-called "authenticity" in Baroque style was still decades in the future'. There were several initial practical problems to overcome. Many cantatas were not published in English, so Whittaker had to make his own translations; and orchestral parts were not obtainable, so they had to be copied out by enthusiastic members of the choir. Walter Shewell Corder, a Quaker, amateur antiquarian and partner in the Tyneside firm of Williamson & Corder (gelatine and glue manufacturers), inaugurated a guarantee fund to enable them to continue. The first performance was made on 27 November 1915, with a choir of twenty-four vocalists, at the Newcastle Central High School for Girls. A detailed and eloquent account of the early Bach Choir under Whittaker can be found in Chapter 2.

The war had a profound and negative impact on the Armstrong College Choral Society. With many of the men having been called up for military service, Whittaker was confined to conducting an all-women's choir for the duration of the war.

He became conductor of the Newcastle and Gateshead Choral Union in 1918, and began to restore its fortunes, which had also been severely affected by the war years. Works performed under his leadership included pieces by Elgar, Parry (*Voces clamantium*), Bridge (*Lament* and *A Prayer*), Byrd (the four-part Mass), Bach (the motet *Be not afraid*), S. S. Wesley (*Let us lift up our heart*), Vaughan Williams (*Fantasia on a Theme by Thomas Tallis*), Holst (*The Cloud Messenger*) and Bainton (*Before Sunrise*).

On 29 September 1919, to celebrate the armistice at the end of the war, a concert took place at the St James's Park football ground, featuring massed choirs, bands and an orchestra that Whittaker conducted. A similar concert was arranged for the following year at the same venue, for which the excellent St Hilda's and Spencer's Steel Works Bands were hired to play (see fig. 4). The concert included specially commissioned pieces by Bainton (*Song of Freedom and Joy*) and Holst (*Two Psalms*), which their composers conducted. Whittaker conducted some of his own works, as well as music by Stanford (*The Last Post*), Grainger (*We Have Fed our Sea for a Thousand Years*) and various choruses by Handel.

Fig. 4 At the Newcastle and District Festival Choir concert at St James's Park football ground, 18 July 1920. *Left to right*: W. G. Whittaker, James Oliver (conductor of St Hilda's Colliery Band), Edgar Bainton, Gustav Holst. *Courtesy Royal College of Music.*

The year 1919 was a landmark in the history of the Newcastle Bach Choir, when William Ellis was appointed organist at Newcastle Cathedral and the choir's first honorary organist. His contributions to the choir are recorded in his biography in Chapter 9. In that year Hadow left Armstrong College.

During 1919 Whittaker, Edgar Bainton, William Ellis, Alfred Wall and George R. and Yeaman Dodds started the North of England Musical Competition Tournament, which was to have an enriching and nurturing influence on local musical life. (See fig. 5.) This in turn led to Whittaker's being appointed to the Glasgow festival in 1920 and set in train his subsequent high international demand as an adjudicator. In July that year Whittaker and friends were contemplating one of their regular walking holidays, but Whittaker became overenthusiastic, resulting in the following pained response from Gustav Holst:

Fig. 5 From the programme for the North of England Musical Tournament, June 1920. *Back row*: Alfred H. Wall, H. Yeaman Dodds, Edgar Bainton. *Front row*: William Ellis, George R. Dodds, William Gillies Whittaker. *Courtesy Newcastle City Libraries*.

Balfour [Gardiner] and I had planned a nice gentle fat middle aged tour for you – Thaxted, Cambridge, Oxford, Burford, Bibury, Ashampstead. And then you come along with your 600 mile record stunt! NO. I can't do it. I haven't a byke [*sic*] or the energy or the will.

In 1920 Whittaker founded the Armstrong College Orchestral Society, and also that year was offered a university appointment elsewhere (unknown); but he turned it down when some local donors gave Armstrong College a sum of money to develop music.

Over the years the Whittaker household entertained many leading contemporary composers and musicians. The composer and writer H. Orsmond Anderton records a visit he made in 1920 to Whittaker's home. 'I was shown into his study with a big piano and lined with books. . . . We had a pleasant chat, during which his sincere and cordial nature delighted me, as well as his keen and eager interest in his artistic work.'

During his life, Whittaker edited the Bach Cantata series with English texts by Charles Sanford Terry. The culmination of this work and his magnum opus, *The Cantatas of J. S. Bach* (in two volumes), was published posthumously by the Oxford University Press in 1959.

Whittaker had an abiding interest in folk music. There are apocryphal stories of him cycling to the far recesses of the region, wearing the ill-fitting jackets described above by his daughter, pockets filled with manuscript paper on which to record what he had heard. He wrote many choral arrangements of folk songs for the Armstrong College Choral Society, publishing *North Country Folk Songs* in 1915 and *North Countrie Ballads, Songs and Pipe-Tunes* in 1921. Gustav Holst commented that he found it hard to teach his London singers the correct Geordie accent! *The Musical Times* of 1 January 1930 said that his folk song arrangements were so original in conception and technique that they deserved to rank as creations rather than transcriptions. Among the best known of his folk arrangements are 'Blow the wind southerly', 'Bonny at morn', 'Ma bonny lad', 'The Keel Row', 'The waters of Tyne', 'Billy Boy' and 'Bobby Shaftoe'. Many of his folk compositions were later performed and recorded by leading artists such as Kathleen Ferrier. He also had a great love of the Northumbrian small pipes, writing with humour that

> They are more suitable for the fireside than the open air: their tone is a charming cross between the oboe and the clarinet. . . . The small bellows . . . held between the right arm and the body . . . allows the player to smoke while playing.

On one occasion he took a German visitor to hear a local exponent of the small pipes. The visitor said, 'Are you telling me that peasants in your district sing these songs? If so, the English must be the most musical race in the world!' To which Whittaker replied: 'Who told you they aren't?'

Among his most popular compositions were *A Lyke-Wake Dirge* (written to commemorate the men of Armstrong College who had died in the First World War), *The Celestial Sphere*, his setting of Psalm 139, and *Among the Northumbrian Hills* (a work stimulated by his many wanderings in the wild scenery of his native county and which he dedicated to Gustav Holst; see fig. 6). Whittaker was awarded Carnegie prizes for *Among the Northumbrian Hills* in 1921 and for *A Lyke-Wake Dirge* in 1924. His long-time friend George R. Dodds described him as 'a natural, sociable, jolly friend, full of good fellowship and a fondness for a joke or a good

Fig. 6 The postcard from Gustav Holst to W. G. Whittaker, 24 May 1921.
Courtesy University of Glasgow Library, Special Collections.

story', who despite his success was 'utterly unspoilt: simple of character, entirely unselfish, and with a helping hand for any who [sought] his co-operation'.

On 28 June 1921 the University of Durham conferred on him an honorary D.Mus. Also that year the French Ministry of Education made him an Officier d'Académie de France for his propaganda work in the interest of modern French music. Gustav Holst believed that Newcastle upon Tyne consistently undervalued Whittaker's work, writing: 'I hope the Doctorate will make its due effect on your benighted Village and bring [the] good luck and comfort that is so long overdue.' In September of that year Holst's work *The Hymn of Jesus* was performed at the Three Choirs Festival in Hereford, after which Whittaker, Holst and Vaughan Williams embarked on a walking tour of the surrounding countryside. Whittaker recorded the event in a series of informal photographs, but sadly he does not appear in any of the pictures.

In 1921 Whittaker began to give lectures to the Workers' Educational Association (WEA). In subsequent years the Bach Choir gave a number of concerts for the organization in the mining town of Ashington.

In the summer of 1923 Whittaker conducted performances of his own compositions in a 'Northumbrian pageant' held at the Newcastle Theatre Royal, at which Bach Choir members (discreetly) took part.

Between July 1923 and January 1924 he undertook a world tour examining for the Associated Board of the Royal Schools of Music in Australia and the USA, with Professor Percival Driver as his co-examiner on the Australian leg. While crossing the Pacific, Whittaker wrote the score for *The Celestial Sphere*, which he dedicated to a fellow passenger. Details of the tour are covered extensively by Christine Borthwick.* During his year of absence the Newcastle Bach Choir was conducted by Edgar Bainton.

On his return from the overseas tour Whittaker discovered that the Bach Choir and the Choral Union were in deep financial difficulties. The Bach Choir was rescued by the guarantee fund that had been inaugurated by Walter Shewell Corder in 1918.

Whittaker became involved with the Oxford University Press, and through this association developed friendships with Hubert Foss and Edmund Fellowes. Fellowes had rediscovered the score of William Byrd's Great Service in the library at Durham Cathedral and subsequently edited it. In May 1924, at St Nicholas's Cathedral in Newcastle, the Bach Choir gave the first performance of the Great Service in more than 300 years. Foss persuaded Whittaker to repeat the concert in London on two subsequent occasions in November that year. A particularly fruitful result of Whittaker's collaboration with OUP was the highly acclaimed *Clarendon Song Books* series published in 1931.

Whittaker joined the Central Advisory Committee of the British Broadcasting Corporation in 1925.

Poor attendances at some of his more adventurous Bach Choir concerts were noted by music critics in the local press. These comments and a realization that he was not going to secure a chair of music at Armstrong College bred personal discontent. Holst, writing to him in 1926, said: 'As for AC [Armstrong College] I used up all my bad language long ago.'

Around this time, with his two daughters away from home (Mary was at the Royal College of Music in London and Clarrie was studying abroad), Whittaker began to take stock of his increasingly unhappy marriage and made an unsuccessful application for a post in London.

Whittaker had a strong relationship with Clarrie, with whom he corresponded regularly. She joined him in France during a solitary motoring holiday that he took

* Mary Christine Borthwick, '"In the Swim": The Life and Musical Achievements of William Gillies Whittaker (1876–1944)'. Ph.D. thesis, University of Durham, 2007.

in Italy in 1926. That year there was a possibility of a chair at Liverpool University, but it never materialized.

After the Bach Choir's tour of Germany in July 1927 Whittaker returned to the Continent a few weeks later for a touring holiday with Clarrie, during which they visited Germany, Austria and Hungary. During the autumn he was Alsop Visiting Lecturer at Liverpool University. That year he resigned as conductor of the Choral Union and was succeeded by his friend George R. Dodds.

Whittaker lectured at a summer school at Cornell University in 1928, and enjoyed a motoring tour of the Adirondacks, also visiting Canadian relatives and Walter and Ella Clapperton at McGill University in Montreal. He was offered the professorship of music at Cornell, but for personal reasons rejected it (a decision that he would later come to regret). Also that year he delivered three lectures at the Royal Institution.

In 1928, after nearly thirty years at Armstrong College, Whittaker was appointed the first Gardiner Professor of Music at Glasgow University and first principal of the Scottish National Academy of Music (SNAM); see fig. 7. This was a defining moment in the Whittakers' personal relationship – a sad period in their lives that has been described in detail by Christine Borthwick.*

Whittaker moved to Glasgow and took up residence at 60 Cleveden Drive, a University-owned property in a pleasant residential area not far from the Botanic Gardens and the university complex. Clara moved to London to join her daughter Mary, who was working there as a music teacher and living at 13 Fairfax Road, Hampstead. By 1930 the family home in Jesmond was occupied by Joan and Oscar Brunstrom but was still in the possession of the Whittakers.

The Newcastle Bach Choir continued to rehearse for concerts under the guidance of its assistant conductor, Joseph Robinson. Whittaker returned to conduct the performances until his final concert with the choir on 30 May 1930.

At the time of Whittaker's appointment in Scotland, Glasgow University conferred on him an honorary MA degree and Edinburgh University an honorary Mus.Doc. On arrival in Glasgow he found SNAM in disarray. It had no endowments, poorly paid and poorly-qualified peripatetic teachers, and students who were interested only in paper qualifications. Whittaker set about trying to remedy these problems. His greatest difficulties, however, were with the governors of SNAM, who were insular, introspective and highly resistant to change. A young local musician, Erik Chisholm, was also to prove a constant source of irritation, and he and Whittaker developed a mutual antipathy. A full and balanced account of their personal and professional rivalries has been given elsewhere by Christine

* See p. 16n.

Borthwick.* A particular source of friction with the governors was Whittaker's reintroduction of opera and the inauguration of a successful annual Opera Week. Within SNAM Whittaker created a highly regarded Diploma in Musical Education for which he brought in new teachers such as Annie Lawton and later Ernest Potts from Newcastle. Within the university he expanded the teaching of music to degree standard (introducing B.Mus. and D.Mus. degrees), and after some initial resistance raised the standard of musicianship in the University Orchestral Society.

Fig. 7 Whittaker conducting the orchestra of the Scottish National Academy of Music. *Courtesy Scottish National Academy of Music.*

In 1931 Whittaker was made a fellow of the Royal College of Music, and in 1934 became president of the Incorporated Society of Musicians.

He inaugurated a small Bach Cantata Choir within the National Academy to continue his Newcastle traditions. Entry to the choir required a very high standard of sight-reading ability, and Whittaker was proud of their performances, which he regarded as better than any he had achieved before. By 1936 he had conducted all

* See p. 16n.

of Bach's cantatas, and later recounted his achievements in 'A Pilgrimage through the Church Cantatas of J. S. Bach', which was published in the *Musical Times* of May to July 1936.

In 1936 Mary and Clarrie Whittaker both announced that they were to be married. On 21 August 1936 Mary married Edward Percy Pollitzer at the Willesden register office in London. Clarrie and Whittaker were both witnesses at the ceremony. A fuller account of Mary Whittaker's life is given in her biography in Chapter 10.

Fig. 8 Whittaker in 1936. *Courtesy University of Glasgow Archives Services (ref. GB0248 UP1/407/1).*

Clarrie's fiancé, Marcel Le Guyon, was an engineer employed by the same firm as Clarrie. Marcel was born in 1903 in Perros Guirec in Brittany, the son of Pierre Guyon, a railway engineer. Unfortunately for the young couple, Madame Guyon, who was a staunch Roman Catholic, objected to the marriage, and it was some years before they were finally united.

As an antidote to the turmoil of his new professional life, Whittaker undertook many motoring holidays in Europe during the 1930s. Never a man of half measures, he applied to these trips all the enthusiasm and detailed planning that characterized his daily work. Inevitably they had some musical or other cultural focus, and he exploited his many international contacts to facilitate the ventures. Whenever possible he tried to arrange for daughter Clarrie to join him for all or part of the holiday. He had a particular love of Scandinavia, which became his preferred destination in the late 1930s until the rise of the National Socialist (Nazi) Party made visiting Germany increasingly difficult. Wonderful descriptions of these holidays have been quoted by Christine Borthwick.*

Whittaker began to encounter more problems with the governors of SNAM in his attempts to revise the curricula and introduce new teaching methods. The saga is recounted by Nicholas Webber† and in greater detail by Christine Borthwick. At the end of September 1938 he felt unable to continue, and asked to be relieved of his Academy appointment. Unfortunately his two appointments were inextricably linked by Scottish parliamentary statute, and this caused problems with his university chair, whose functions he continued to undertake in a 'temporary' capacity.

In 1939 Whittaker was begged to resume his duties at the Academy, which surprisingly he did, but he laid down stringent terms. That year it became clear that war in Europe was inevitable, and he visited Clarrie and Marcel in Paris for Christmas. In June, Clarrie made a strenuous and ultimately successful escape to England, while Marcel, meanwhile, was drafted into the French army.

But there were further problems brewing in Glasgow in relation to the appointment of an Academy vice-principal, which was made in Whittker's absence and without consultation. Fortunately, compulsory retirement age was approaching, and Whittaker formally departed in 1941, Glasgow University conferring on him the honorary degree of Doctor of Laws to mark the occasion.

In 1941 Marcel Guyon escaped with the remnants of the French army via Spain and joined the Free French forces of General Charles de Gaulle in London. On 31 May 1941 Clarrie married Marcel at the register office in Barnet, Hertfordshire, and Whittaker was one of the witnesses. At the time of the marriage the couple were living at 30 Bohun Grove, East Barnet, and Marcel had the rank of lieu-

* See p. 16n.
† Nicholas Webber, 'Facets of Whittaker. 1. The man.' W. G. Whittaker Centenary Festival anniversary brochure, 1977. See also p. 16n.

tenant. Marcel went on to serve as an engineer with the First Regiment of Artillery of the Free French Forces (terre 1re Dfl/RA), finally attaining the rank of captain. The regiment fought against Rommel's Axis forces in North Africa at the Battles of Bir Hakim (1941) and El Alamein (1942) before moving to fight in France and in the Alps. Clarrie and Marcel had no children, and, in keeping with many marriages that took place under the stress of war, it did not last. Clarrie eventually had a successful career with the Standard Electric Company and settled in New York, where she lived for a time at 228 East 36th Street, in a fashionable part of Manhattan. According to US social security records she died in New York on 4 December 1999, aged ninety-four. She did not remarry.

In 1941 Edward and Mary Pollitzer celebrated the birth of their firstborn, Jonathan, by commissioning the world-renowned sculptor Jacob Epstein to produce a bronze of William Gillies Whittaker's head. Epstein named it *The Viking*, and it was to preside over the family dining-room for many years.

After his retirement Whittaker took on the role of musical director to the Scottish Command of the Entertainments National Service Association (ENSA). He seems to have spent a large amount of his time organizing concerts, rehearsing and conducting performances, and indexing the vast gramophone record collection. But his health was rapidly deteriorating; he was losing weight, stooping and exhibiting a variety of debilitating neurological symptoms in his arms and legs. Nevertheless, outside of his duties for ENSA he read widely, gave lectures, wrote articles, and completed the manuscript of his *Music and Books*. He conducted a concert at St Nicholas's Cathedral, Newcastle, in December 1943, and attended the Fenham Teacher Training College in February 1944 to prepare examination papers for the summer examinations. During these visits he was briefly reunited with many old friends for the last time.

His final duty for ENSA took him to the Orkney Islands, to officiate at the islands' musical festivals. In keeping with his personal traditions he did not spare himself. On Tuesday, 29 June 1944, he delivered a lecture in Kirkwall about five Russian composers. Over the next few days he adjudicated at preliminary rounds in Kirkwall, Stromness and Hoy. On Sunday, 2 July, he adjudicated at the competition finals and conducted a concert of massed choirs and orchestras of HM Forces in the Garrison Theatre in Stromness. A contemporary account by his long-time friend H. Croft Jackson, organist at St Magnus Cathedral, Kirkwall, states: 'I was deeply shocked at his physical appearance. He was obviously ill, yet was carrying on for the love of his life's cause.' His appearance was compatible with his serious underlying conditions of stomach cancer and *diabetes mellitus*. He became acutely unwell, and was detained at the Standing Stones Hotel in

Stenness, where he was found dead in his room at 7.25 a.m. on Wednesday, 5 July, 1944. He was sixty-eight.

Clara Whittaker outlived her husband, and died at the age of eighty-eight on 6 March 1956, at her new home, 6a Marryat Road, Wimbledon, not far from the home of her daughter Mary.

In 1963 Mary and Edward Pollitzer presented Whittaker's working library, together with various personal and edited manuscripts and more than two hundred letters from Gustav Holst, to the University of Glasgow.

For the centenary of Whittaker's birth in 1976, members of the family established the Whittaker Centenary Fund to promote a better awareness of the man and his music. As part of this organization, Jonathan Pollitzer created Viking Publications, which he ran from 3 Pembroke Gardens, London, where he lived with his mother and sister. A number of concerts took place in Newcastle and Glasgow to celebrate the centenary year.

Mary and Edward Pollitzer later divorced, and Mary moved to Goddards Green, Kent, where she lived at 'The Oast House', Cranbrook.

Edward Pollitzer died on 6 December 1988, aged seventy-seven, and Mary on 2 April 2003, aged ninety-six. Jonathan died suddenly on 22 May 2003, aged sixty-one, only seven weeks after his mother's death.

At the time of writing (2015), W. G. Whittaker has been dead for seventy-one years. Although some of his musical compositions have long since been forgotten, the author and many of his generation fondly remember singing his settings of Northumbrian folk songs as children. Memories of his sincerity, passion and boundless energy have survived in numerous contemporary records and personal recollections. Foremost among the enduring legacies of this great man is the Newcastle upon Tyne Bach Choir, now in its centenary year. The rest of this book pays tribute to the history of the choir and its achievements.

Chapter 2
Whittaker's Bach Choir (1915–1930)

Christine Borthwick

Be sensitive, very sensitive, to the temper of your singers, feel their pulse continually, achieve your results through them, by understanding them. . . . If any member proves impervious to general remarks . . . arrange for a word or two in private, or even a short rehearsal on his own. Get him to look upon it in the light of a gratuitous lesson given out of a spirit of friendship.

W. G. Whittaker, *Hints to Choral Conductors*

Fig. 9 William Gillies Whittaker *c*.1915. Family photograph. *Author's collection.*

THE Newcastle upon Tyne Bach Choir has now in 2015 reached its centenary year, an achievement that inevitably throws the spotlight on its hugely talented and enterprising founder, William Gillies Whittaker ('WGW'). An outline of his life has been given in Chapter 1.

The Bach Choir really was an outstanding phenomenon. Whittaker admitted only singers capable of accurate sight-singing, and coupled this with a required dedication to turn up for all rehearsals. He was an exacting man searching for performance authenticity, using fewer singers and thinner orchestras at a time when this approach was very much in its infancy. Whittaker earned a lasting reputation for his superb training of the choir he created, an excellent instrument that permitted him to become the first English conductor to perform all of Bach's church cantatas – a 'pilgrimage' as he called it. He performed eighty-two cantatas with the Newcastle Bach Choir and the remainder in Glasgow, where, as principal of the Scottish Academy of Music and a professor at the university, he founded another Bach Cantata Choir. In this chapter, which covers the first fifteen years of the Newcastle Bach Choir's history, various people associated with the choir are named; biographies of many of them will be found in Chapters 3–11. The subsequent history of the choir is recounted in Chapters 12 and 13. Percy Lovell, one of Whittaker's successors, described him as 'that great man, W. G. Whittaker', and listed his achievements in Newcastle in a lecture to the Newcastle Literary and Philosophical Society (NLPS) in 1993:

> 'Bach and British' was Whittaker's motto for the Bach Choir. He certainly was a key figure in the Bach revival – which had been gaining momentum all through the nineteenth century. The Cantatas were still mostly unknown and unsung in this country 75 years ago. . . . Whittaker led a personal crusade by performing many of these works in Newcastle, editing and publishing others and making many lovely movements available for schools and amateurs.

The Origin of the Choir

WHITTAKER was thirty-eight when he founded the choir in 1914, immediately after the outbreak of war. This move could probably be regarded as a vital career step on his part as he sought to fill the sudden vacuum in local musical activities that had been precipitated by the conflict and at the same time take the lead as a local choral conductor.

Central to his intellectual development was the NLPS, its musical collection and its visiting lecturers, among them Mary Wakefield, Arnold Dolmetsch, John Radcliff and Ebenezer Prout. Cecil Sharp addressed the society in 1909 on 'Folk Songs', a subject that so inspired Whittaker that he produced the first of his own north-country folk song arrangements the following year. Another lecturer, Rutland Boughton, became a close friend. Membership of other musical organizations such as the Incorporated Society of Musicians and the Musical League brought him into contact with native composers such as Elgar, its president, and Frederick Delius, its vice-president, and with Vaughan Williams, Granville Bantock, Gustav Holst and Balfour Gardiner.

Whittaker was a protégé of J. B. Clark (see fig. 10), a local businessman and organist (and later father-in-law of the composer Elisabeth Lutyens). Clark was secretary of the Newcastle and Gateshead Choral Union, and took a fatherly interest in Whittaker's career.

Fig. 10 James B. Clark, from the programme for the Newcastle Musical Tournament of 1919. *Courtesy Newcastle City Libraries.*

When James Preston resigned from the Choral Union in 1908, Clark selected Henry Coward, one of the most distinguished choir trainers in the country, to replace him. Owing to his heavy workload, Clark asked Whittaker to give classes in sight-reading for the Choral Union and to deputize for Coward on occasion. On becoming official assistant conductor of the Choral Union in 1908, Whittaker, now a lecturer at Armstrong College, was able to give up his organist's post.

Although Coward was deeply influential on Whittaker as a choral trainer, others also helped to forge his musical outlook, such as Edgar Bainton (of the Newcastle Conservatoire), the singer Frederic Austin, who helped to promote his folk song arrangements, Henry Hadow, principal of Armstrong College and a former visiting lecturer at the NLPS (see fig. 3), and Charles Sanford Terry (fig. 11). Terry, a history lecturer, who founded the Choral Society at Armstrong College, was known for his interest in Bach. When Terry left for Aberdeen, Whittaker took over as lecturer at Armstrong College.

Though Whittaker was later delighted to find himself, in his own words, 'in the swim' with all the leading British musicians of the day, he possessed another facet to his personality which projected him into the top ranks of working musicians and undoubtedly had a huge effect on the success of the Bach Choir: this was a desire to be at the cutting edge of contemporary music. This he pursued not only in his own compositions but in the direction of other modern British and French composers.

A red-letter day and a turning-point in his career arrived when he conducted Charles Kennedy Scott's splendid Oriana Choir in a set of his own folk song arrangements at one of the most ambitious Balfour Gardiner concerts at the Queen's Hall with the London Symphony Orchestra. Gardiner entertained all the participants (who included many major composers and musical personalities) to dinner at Pagani's afterwards, where Holst exclaimed to Whittaker: 'You are one of us now. You must come up more frequently.' Whittaker took these comments to heart, and a friendship between the two men endured until Holst's death in 1934.

During the summer of 1914, Whittaker and his wife travelled to Switzerland for one of their yearly 'musical pilgrimages' to the continent. On reaching Strasbourg they learned that Germany had declared war on Russia and that the army had been called up. It was impossible to get on to the crowded trains. With great difficulty and resourcefulness Whittaker obtained a lift to Basle and then to Lucerne, whence, after being trapped for three weeks, they eventually reached home. Many British musicians were in Germany at the time; the Baintons, on their way to the Bayreuth Festival, boarded their train only to be arrested and interned immediately. Women were released after three months, but men, including Bainton, were kept for the duration at the Ruhleben camp in Spandau, near Berlin. Ethel Bainton, once a student of Edgar Bainton, returned home, reopened the Conservatoire and kept it going throughout the war, asking Whittaker to join the staff to help with advanced students.

At home, many choirs and associations folded as men left for the front. The sudden departure of Bainton, the conductor of the only permanent city orchestra (the Newcastle Philharmonic Orchestra), conductor of the Harmonic Choir and organizer of frequent and regular concerts at the Conservatoire, left a vacuum in musical life in Newcastle. Whittaker was, by reason of an injury to his arm sustained in childhood, judged unfit for military service when he tried to enlist. (His unsuccessful attempt to enlist is recounted in Chapter 1.) So, with the excellent experience that he had gained as a choral trainer with the Choral Union and with his own choir and orchestra at Armstrong College, Whittaker was now ready for his new venture.

Whittaker's Love of Bach's Music

WHITTAKER, writing in one of his *Collected Essays*, said he first developed a love of Bach as he 'indulged in tea-time duets' with his piano teacher John Nicholson and they played an arrangement of Bach's Fugue in G major for organ. He confessed that 'this began one of the ruling passions of my life, the worship of Bach'. In his essay 'A Pilgrimage through the Church Cantatas of J. S. Bach', Whittaker described his reasons for founding the Bach Choir as 'the story of a journey which few men have been privileged to undertake' in the hope that it would 'set some eager minds on a similar adventure'. While in his post as organist at St Paul's Presbyterian Church, South Shields, Whittaker conducted Bach's Cantata No. 106, *God's time is the best* (*Gottes Zeit ist die allerbeste Zeit*).

From this date, he admitted, 'the vocal music of Bach first began to fascinate', and he endeavoured to perform as many cantatas as possible. With a frustrating shortage of available editions with English words he was largely ignorant of the repertory and its concomitant detail. He bought what second-hand copies he could afford, without original German texts and containing much that was 'incomprehensible'. Later he wrote that 'without the words one cannot possibly grasp the meaning of the music or understand Bach's methods'.

The Influence of Charles Sanford Terry

THE name of Charles Sanford Terry has already been mentioned in connection with Whittaker's formative musical years. In addition to the choral life of Armstrong

Fig. 11 Charles Sanford Terry, no date. *From Mirror of Music 1947 Vol. 1 Plate 53.*

College, Terry's most significant influence was, however, the development of his research into Bach's music. His first writings to appear were three volumes on *Bach's Chorales*. A copy of the first volume, dedicated to Ivor Atkins and published by the Cambridge University Press in October 1915, was sent 'With the Author's Compliments' to Whittaker, who obviously pored over the publication making copious notes in the margins (see fig. 12). Alison Shiel, an honorary research fellow in music at Aberdeen University (where Terry was professor of history) and currently accompanist to the Newcastle Bach Choir, noted that the link between Terry's academic research and the move towards greater authenticity in performances of Bach was fittingly summed up in Whittaker's own words:

> Professor Terry's amazing erudition and enviable intimacy with the vast bulk of the entire publications of the Bachgesellschaft, and his enthusiasm and under-standing, are a trumpet call to professional and amateur musicians to explore

these thousands of pages and turn their silent staves into living sound. . . .
Scholarship has pointed the way: let the practical musician follow.

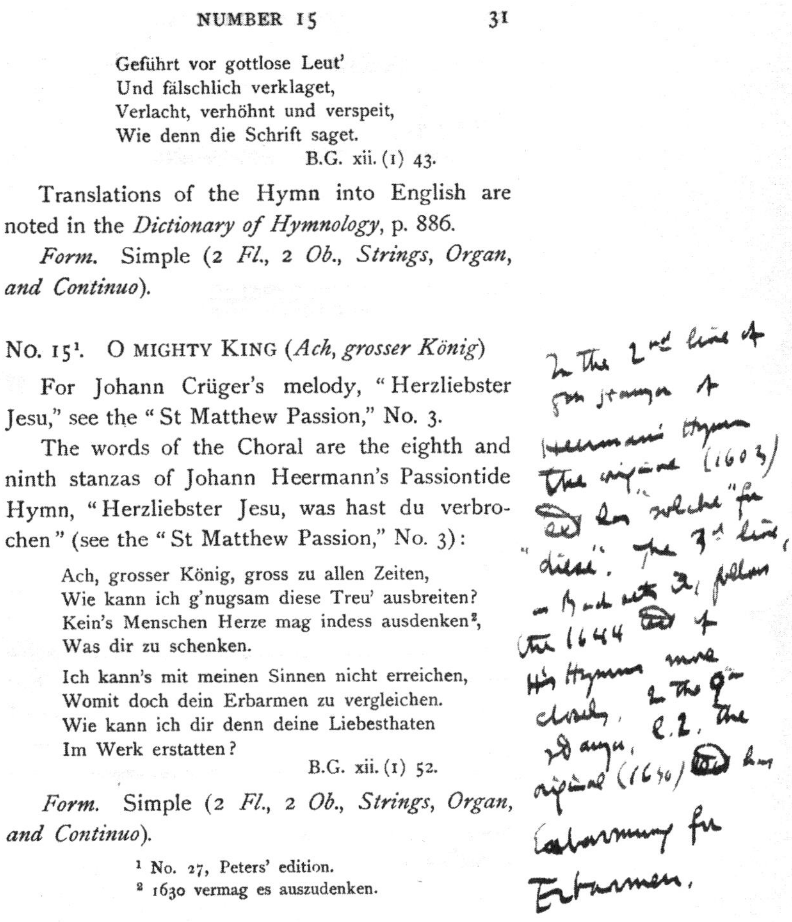

NUMBER 15   **31**

> Geführt vor gottlose Leut'
> Und fälschlich verklaget,
> Verlacht, verhöhnt und verspeit,
> Wie denn die Schrift saget.
> B.G. xii. (1) 43.

Translations of the Hymn into English are noted in the *Dictionary of Hymnology*, p. 886.

Form. Simple (2 *Fl.*, 2 *Ob.*, *Strings, Organ, and Continuo*).

NO. 15[1]. O MIGHTY KING (*Ach, grosser König*)

For Johann Crüger's melody, "Herzliebster Jesu," see the "St Matthew Passion," No. 3.

The words of the Choral are the eighth and ninth stanzas of Johann Heermann's Passiontide Hymn, "Herzliebster Jesu, was hast du verbrochen" (see the "St Matthew Passion," No. 3):

> Ach, grosser König, gross zu allen Zeiten,
> Wie kann ich g'nugsam diese Treu' ausbreiten?
> Kein's Menschen Herze mag indess ausdenken[2],
> Was dir zu schenken.

> Ich kann's mit meinen Sinnen nicht erreichen,
> Womit doch dein Erbarmen zu vergleichen.
> Wie kann ich dir denn deine Liebesthaten
> Im Werk erstatten?
> B.G. xii. (1) 52.

Form. Simple (2 *Fl.*, 2 *Ob.*, *Strings, Organ, and Continuo*).

[1] No. 27, Peters' edition.
[2] 1630 vermag es auszudenken.

Fig. 12 From W. G. Whittaker's own copy of C. S. Terry, *Bach's Chorales* (1915). *Author's collection.*

The Beginnings of the Newcastle Bach Choir

IN 1913, when holidaying on a farm, Whittaker read Newman's English edition of Schweitzer's *Bach* and immediately adopted the writer's suggestion of singing Bach cantatas at home, posting invitations for weekly meetings to a dozen friends and pupils. This 'study circle' (a term adopted by Percy Scholes, Whittaker's friend and a strong proponent of musical education) analysed and sang cantatas with two pianists and some string players. The group, composed of Rutherford School pupils and other pupils and friends, met during that summer term; all were excellent sight-readers. They took all the published cantatas in numerical order, with everyone singing the solos, singers dropping out whenever a part went out of their range. Bainton urged Whittaker to have these informal sessions made more public, but Whittaker was diffident about such a venture. By the end of the summer of 1914, however, war had broken out and everything about musical life in Newcastle had changed. With Bainton interned at Ruhleben and many choirs closed, Whittaker acknowledged 'the scarcity of musical life in the city' and formed the Newcastle Bach Choir, though he felt he had everything to learn.

Alfred Wall, leader of Whittaker's orchestra at Armstrong College and a teacher at the Conservatoire, doubted that the necessary soloists could be found for the enterprise; Whittaker retorted that he would 'grow them'. Ernest Potts, a good local baritone and a friend from their schooldays, 'sang Bach superbly', according to Whittaker, and was still available, as were good soprano and contralto soloists. The matter was solved completely when a former pitman, John Vine, wrote to Whittaker asking for singing lessons. A superb pianist and a strong sight-reader, Vine 'fairly bubbled over with enthusiasm'; but, most important, he possessed a splendid voice. Whittaker wrote: 'thus John Vine made the Newcastle Bach Choir possible'. The teaching practices of Potts, and also George R. Dodds and his brother Yeaman, turned out singer after singer capable of doing justice to Bach. More soloists joined the ranks of the choir.

At the beginning Whittaker tried to recreate a Bach-sized choir, restricted to twenty-four singers in order to maintain a perfect balance between singers and orchestra, allotting an equal number of singers to each part. When a bout of influenza ravaged the ranks of his singers, he decided to increase their numbers to forty. But he raised the standard of sight-singing for entrants and kept reserves waiting to join, which had a salutary effect on 'slackers'. He filled choral parts with copious directions (see fig. 13), of general force and gradations, to be effected immediately, using 'an army of copyists . . . volunteers from the choir'. He rehearsed all duets and trios chorally, claiming that, as most soloists were unreliable in their counting, one rehearsal on the day of the concert was not enough. Band parts were 'impossibly flawed'; so, writing out the parts himself, all details were compared with the Bach-Gesellschaft. Ideas of authenticity, particularly with regard to dynamics, were also influenced by his friendship with Arnold Dolmetsch, whose seminal treatise, *The Interpretation of the Music of the XVIIth and XVIIIth Centuries*, was published in 1915, at the very time that Whittaker was launching

Fig. 13 From W. G. Whittaker's own score of the B Minor Mass.
Author's collection.

his new choir. At the outset Whittaker decided to perform the cantatas in English. At first he used available translations, but later he wrote his own texts, which were not direct translations of the original German words.

Whittaker resigned the conductorship of his Tynemouth choir to concentrate on his new venture, and, helped by the secretary of the Conservatoire, Beatrice Turnbull, produced an information sheet in October 1915, headed 'Bach Perform-ances'. Outlining the choir's aims and aspirations, he included an order form for tickets. It was also resolved to give concerts in November, February and March in an effort to compensate for the closure of musical societies due to the war. Only string accompaniments could be provided, because of difficulties in finding players and a shortage of funds. The performances would be given in the Central Newcastle High School for girls, by permission of Miss Hiley, the headmistress, who valued Whittaker as a staff member.

The first concert, which took place on the afternoon of 27 November 1915, featured three church cantatas: No. 2, *Ah! God in mercy look from Heaven* (*Ach Gott, vom Himmel sieh darein*), No. 68, *God so loved the world* (*Also hat Gott die Welt geliebt*), with an 'impressive fugal chorus', and No. 140, *Sleepers, wake* (*Wachet auf, ruft uns die Stimme*), for chorus, with a 'familiar chorale' at the end. Also performed was Cantata No. 53, *Strike, then, longed-for hour* (*Schlage doch, gewünschte Stunde*), an alto aria then attributed to Bach but now to Melchior Hoff-mann. Alfred Wall played Bach's Violin Concerto in E major and Mrs George Dodds, Robina Burn, John Vine and Ernest Potts sang well as soloists.

On 5 February 1916 the choir sang Cantatas No. 10, *My soul doth magnify the Lord* (*Meine Seele erhebt den Herren*), No. 38, *From depths of woe I call on Thee* (*Aus tiefer Not schrei ich zu dir*), and No. 104, *Thou guide of Israel* (*Du Hirte Israel, höre*), and the eight-part motet *Come Jesu, come* (*Komm, Jesu, komm*). Ethel Bainton played Bach's Clavier Concerto in D minor. Critics were on the whole appreciative of the performances.

At the last concert of the season, on 25 March, Cantata No. 61, *Come, Redeemer of our race* (*Nun komm, der Heiden Heiland*), the eight-part motet *The spirit also helpeth us* (*Der Geist hilft*) and the solo cantata No. 56, *I will my cross with gladness carry* (*Ich will den Kreuzstab gerne tragen*), performed by Potts, were given, with Annie Eckford of the Conservatoire giving a 'refined and sensitive performance of the *Italian Concerto* and also playing in the Concerto in D minor for two violins. The concert concluded with Cantata No. 4, *Christ lay in death's dark prison* (*Christ lag in Todes Banden*). Whittaker was delighted, and noted that 'the hall was packed and appreciation was so great that we added an extra concert of British music'.

At this time Whittaker made a personal commitment to perform all 198 of Bach's church cantatas. He estimated that he performed about seventy of them in Newcastle. (An examination of the programmes and his lists indicates that he may have forgotten one or two, such as No. 88, which was sung in 1926. In fact fifteen cantatas are unaccounted for, as far as the lists included in Whittaker's autobiography are concerned.) Whittaker rarely repeated a cantata in Newcastle (Nos. 4, 27, 53, 56 and 133 being exceptions), and some cantatas were performed elsewhere (No. 190 by the Armstrong College Choral Society (ACCS) and Nos. 19, 34, and 151 in London in 1922). His performances were backed up by painstaking research, including visits to Bach's birthplace at Eisenach (during which he explored Bach's residences, his manuscripts and the history of the extended family of Bach), and by his intimate knowledge of the works as reflected in his erudite writings on the subject. Whittaker guaranteed success with his choir by relying on strict forms of audition: 'making sure that no one was admitted who could not read a Bach aria at sight'.

There were other stalwarts on whom he depended, such as his Rutherford College colleague, Robert Peel, who sang as a tenor in the choir with John Harding. George R. Dodds and John Vine also sang as additional tenors in a Byrd mass; indeed, commitment was essential for all members. Whittaker's cousin from Hexham, Archibald S. Gillies, once sang in the basses, hoping vainly that his cousin would encourage his talent as a singer. Disillusioned, according to his daughter, Edna Gillies, he soon left the choir.

At its outset, the new choir was beset with problems. As war took its toll, the numbers of men in both choir and orchestra began to dwindle, engendering a sense of instability among the choral members. Beatrice Turnbull had to inform subscribers in 1916 that the choir was in immediate jeopardy owing to the exodus of male choristers. On the other hand, attendance by the public was buoyant, so that a larger hall than the one then available at the High School needed to be found. Music soared in price, but with a stroke of luck Whittaker heard that a large quantity of sold-off Breitkopf stock was available very cheaply. Borrowing £25, the choir bought an immense number of vocal scores of the cantatas, retailing them at 4d. a copy, a purchase that served the choir for years.

In this second season Whittaker introduced cantatas that required oboes d'amore and flute. Local players only possessed high-pitched instruments, and hiring was fraught with the difficulties of different fingering systems. James Causley Windram, bandmaster at the local army barracks, saved the situation. According to Whittaker: 'we borrowed an oboe d'amore from London'. Windram's brother, William Charles, a boy in the band, 'rigged it up with elastic, string, & all manner of gadgets, to make it agree with the system to which he was accustomed, & played an obbligato in a manner I have rarely heard surpassed'. Windram gave valuable advice on instruments, including high trumpets, and performed himself.

Included in the programme of 4 November 1916 was Cantata No. 115, *Rise, my soul, be well prepared* (*Mache dich, mein Geist, bereit*), the Brandenburg Concerto No. 5 in D, the Suite in B minor for flute and strings, and Cantata No. 116, *O Jesu Christ, thou prince of peace* (*Du Friedefürst, Herr Jesu Christ*). The choir sang 'with commendable sustained power and greater smoothness than of yore'. The programme carried an 'in memoriam' note for Second Lieutenant Walter Roan of the Durham Light Infantry, a student of Armstrong College who had been accompanist to the Bach Choir during September and November 1915 and had fallen in action on 29 September 1916.

The next concert, on 2 December 1916, was given in a room 'now hardly large enough to hold the audience', and an upright piano replaced the former grand piano, being 'more in keeping in tone and power'. There were more instrumental works: Ethel Bainton played Bach's Clavier Concerto in F minor and Alfred Wall the Violin Concerto in A minor. The choir sang Cantata No. 12, *Wailing, crying* (*Weinen, Klagen, Sorgen, Zagen*), the eight-part motet *Be not afraid* (*Fürchte dich nicht*), and Cantata No. 70, *Watch ye, pray ye* (*Wachet! betet! betet! wachet!*). Arthur Laycock, a well-known virtuoso cornet player from the St Hilda's Colliery Band, South Shields, made possible the performance of certain cantatas with trumpet, and his playing was much admired.

Whittaker was surrounded by a coterie of supportive and loyal members, such as Lance Hughes and John Harding, who constituted a nucleus that carried out all the detailed work of running the concerts and relieved Whittaker of many logistical responsibilities. Hughes penned the note announcing the transfer of concerts in February to a larger venue, the Central Hall, Westgate Road, opposite the Tyne Theatre – a move calculated to make possible the choir's first performance of Bach's St John Passion. In May a concert of British music, including Holst's *The Cloud Messenger*, could now accommodate a larger audience, which made financial sense. Owing to the difficulties caused by the war, however, the St John Passion, performed on 31 March 1917, was the last Bach concert by the choir for more than a year.

A Pioneer of British Music

WHITTAKER loved modern music, whether British, French or German, but also appreciated performing the rediscovered old English music that was being published by the Carnegie Trust. In May of the first season of the Bach Choir he included an 'extra concert' of British music, chronologically ordered, in aid of the Lord Mayor's War Relief Fund, with soloists John Vine and Annie Eckford, accompanist Edna Steele, and James ('Jimmie') Mark playing the violin. Byrd's five-part Mass, Purcell's Violin Sonata in G Minor and William Babell's Violin Sonata in B flat were performed. Later came Bainton's *Sunset at Sea*, Vaughan Williams's *Five Mystical Songs*, Delius's *On Craig Dhu* and choral folk song arrangements by Bantock, Holst (his setting of the Hampshire folk song 'I sowed the seeds of love', dedicated 'to W. G. Whittaker and his singers'), Boughton and Whittaker himself, along with piano music by Benjamin Dale, Percy Grainger and Balfour Gardiner.

On 19 May 1917 the Bach Choir performed Holst's *The Cloud Messenger*. There were madrigals by Farmer, Gibbons, Weelkes and Wilbye (in four, five and eight parts), and choral settings and folk tunes by Grainger and Vaughan Williams, as well as trios by Bax and Dunhill for violin, viola and piano.

With men disappearing to war, financial support drained away, causing doubts whether the concerts could survive, since costs were increasing 'in all directions'. Walter Corder, the honorary secretary, volunteered to organize a guarantee fund to ensure the continuance of the concerts. The names of those who had sent the 'recommended maximum sum of three guineas' to Mr Corder for the guarantee fund were recorded in the local press.

Next season's first concert was delayed until 15 December 1917, when no cantatas or motets were performed, 'because of the difficulty of keeping permanent & adequate tenor & bass lines together at present', and a Christmas concert was given. Carol collections such as *The Monster Book of Carols for Church and Home* (Walter Scott Publishing Co. Ltd, 1912) and *The English Carol Book* by Percy Dearmer and Martin Shaw of 1913 encouraged the practice of carol-singing, emulating Holst's similar practice at Thaxted. Whittaker produced an exciting programme of British Christmas music, including items by William Byrd and John Attey, Richard Dering's motet *Quem vidistis pastores*, Vaughan Williams's *Fantasia on Christmas Carols*, and a second performance of Benjamin Dale's *Before the Paling of the Stars*. There were modern British carols: Whittaker's four manuscript arrangements of traditional carols preceded Bainton's *Song of the Virgin Mother*, Holst's 'Of one that is so fair and bright' (also in manuscript) and Walford Davies's *O little town of Bethlehem*. Frank Bridge's settings of 'Sally in our Alley' and 'Cherry Ripe' and Grainger's *Molly on the Shore*, *Mock Morris* (for string band), *Handel in the Strand* (*Clog Dance*) (for strings and piano), *My Robin is to the Greenwood Gone* and *Colonial Song* were 'happy and exhilarating pieces'.

Walter Clapperton sang solos with orchestral accompaniment, including Frederic Austin's *The Twelve Days of Christmas*.

On 23 March 1918 a 'second concert of British Music' was given. It featured modern English compositions including Bainton's *Humoreske: The Vindictive Staircase* (to words by W. W. Gibson). Madrigals by Gibbons, Morley, Wilbye and Weelkes, and choral folk song settings by Holst, Bantock, Grainger and Vaughan Williams were performed. Annie Lawton was the soloist in Bantock's *The Seal Woman's Croon* and Grainger's *Brigg Fair*. North-country sea shanties (from R. R. Terry's manuscript 'Collection of Sea Songs and Shanties') were also sung. Whittaker contributed two choral arrangements: 'Have ye seen owt, o'ma bonny lad?' and 'Billy Boy'. Annie Eckford and Alfred Wall gave two violin sonatas in A by Philip Gibbs (1699–1788) and John Ireland's newly-composed Second Violin Sonata.

A Return to Bach

IT was more than a year since Whittaker had given any Bach concerts. A projected St Matthew Passion had been abandoned because of the difficulty of keeping adequate tenor and bass lines, but now it was decided to perform more cantatas. Parts were written out by volunteers for an extra Bach concert on the 'sunny afternoon of 25 May' in 1918, when Crüger's unaccompanied chorale *Deck thee, O my soul, with gladness*, followed by the relevant Bach cantata, No. 180, *Soul, array thyself with gladness* (*Schmücke dich, o liebe Seele*), was heard by a good audience. Whittaker thought the cantata was 'one of the most constantly blissful of the series'. Cantata No. 106, *God's time is the best* (*Gottes Zeit ist die allerbeste Zeit*), was one of Bach's most popular and perfect.

Next came Cantata No. 198, *Laß, Fürstin, laß noch einen Strahl*. Originally a secular cantata, a *Trauerode* (funeral ode) for Queen Christiane Eberhardine, it was performed on this occasion as *Rebuke me not* in words by J. M. Diack that bore no relation to the original German. Whittaker made 'careful substitutions' in the orchestra, since in his opinion Bach's demands could be met only by 'specialists in old instruments'. The parts originally written for two violas da gamba were played on cellos and the two parts originally written for lutes were played on the piano. The parts for strings, oboes d'amore and transverse flutes were played on the appropriate instruments.

The German name of Bach in the programme had caused anger in Newcastle. A letter under the pseudonym 'Citizen' was sent to the editor of the *North Mail* under the heading 'German Atrocities', objecting to Whittaker's practice of performing works by Bach. The writer, horrified by accounts of the ill-treatment of British prisoners of war by a German sea captain, agreed with the comments of a London coroner who called for 'the extermination of the Hun race' and asked for Whittaker to be stopped: 'I care not who the master may be. I consider it an insult to the citizens of Newcastle that such performances should be allowed.' Whittaker replied that the Bach Choir had performed the music of thirty British composers in the last three years, eighteen of whom were still living, and that he agreed with Alexander Mackenzie, principal of the Royal Academy of Music, who had recently explained that performing Bach was a supreme necessity at this time. What had this composer to do with the war? He had been dead for over a century and a half.

The Bach Choir prospectus, confined by a paper shortage to only a few lines, announced the clearing of the Bach Choir's debt by 'a few friends', the establishment of the guarantee fund, and the need for more public support. Holst wrote to Whittaker on 4 June 1918: 'Congratulations on the BC success. £30 worth of JSB at 4d. each ! Ye Gods!!'

The armistice that ended the fighting in the First World War was signed on 11 November 1918. The war was over and the choir became a fully-fledged society with six recitals per session, of which four would be cantata programmes. The first post-war concert was held on 16 November. Cantata No. 44, *You will they put under ban* (*Sie werden euch in den Bann tun*), opened the concert. Whittaker described the work as uncompromisingly grim. Cantata No. 182, *King of Heaven, be thou welcome* (*Himmelskönig, sei willkommen*), contained some elaborate violin writing, played by Alfred Wall, and a part for flute à bec played on modern instruments by S. Middleton (Leeds Symphony Orchestra) and Wall. Whittaker chose this work as suitable for introducing Bach to audiences, with the imagery in its 'curving, descending passages in the obbligato flute and voice' and the way in which the 'buoyancy of the *Schlufscher* leaves one with the happiest of impressions'.

The Bach Choir in Peacetime

WHEN Bainton returned in December 1918 to resume musical life in the city, Whittaker was forty-two. He was soon to be appointed conductor of the Choral Union and had sustained the ACCS throughout the war, but, with the many new attractions that followed the end of the conflict, it was going to be a struggle to keep the Bach Choir going. The question of where to hold the concerts had still not been satisfactorily resolved. Subscribers disliked the Central Hall, so a new venue was selected: this was the Westgate Hall, a large Methodist Church hall at the top of Westgate Road where 'accommodation . . . is ample and comfortable, and the Hall contains a three manual organ'. It was now obvious that, though the singing of Bach cantatas was the *raison d'être* of the Bach Choir, it would never attract large audiences. Henceforward Whittaker ensured that British music concerts both financially sustained the Bach Choir and allowed it to win a reputation worthy of the choir's attainments. Nevertheless, the organization of the Bach Choir had become a delicate balancing act. Sometimes he combined Bach performances with other elements of the choir's repertory; for example, on Saturday 21 December 1918 he gave a short preliminary lecture at 2.45 p.m. followed by a programme of Christmas music from the Christmas Oratorio and Cantata No. 133, *In thee do I rejoice* (*Ich freue mich in dir*), for Christmas Tuesday, using four solo voices and only 'an extended chorale on a large scale' from the choir. The introduction, interludes and coda were supplied by the orchestra (with oboes d'amore). Music by Byrd and Walford Davies preceded Holst's *Choral Fantasia on Traditional Carols*, which Holst himself described as 'poor stuff anyway and not worth doing'. Frederic Austin's very popular *The Twelve Days of Christmas* was performed again 'by popular request', together with four carols by Charles Kennedy Scott, from a nativity play, and Vaughan Williams's *Wassail Song*.

Alfred Wall's Carnegie Award-winning Piano Quartet received its first performance at the concert, led by the composer, with Eckford as pianist. This performance probably prompted Whittaker to begin to hold chamber music concerts in the Westgate Hall, since the venue, which was unsuited to choral concerts because of its layout, was appropriate for chamber music recitals.

Whittaker, perhaps self-indulgently, took steps to instigate a series of such recitals there, under Bach Choir auspices. There would have been a great demand for them initially, the Newcastle-upon-Tyne Chamber Music Society having being closed for the duration of the war. Walter Corder had offered to finance the series, and 'longed for Chamber Music concerts that differed from those given by the Chamber Music Society, without fashion and evening dress'. Whittaker, in personal contact with the artists, selected interesting programmes, and, with the exception of a Beethoven festival, ensured that a British work was included in each concert. This gave him a certain degree of influence with the composers whom he encouraged in this way, and many were attracted to take part in Bach Choir choral concerts.

Meanwhile, as far as Bach cantatas were concerned, by 1918 Whittaker had performed all the cantatas available with English translations (or all with accompaniments that were financially possible), and now embarked on using the German editions from the choir's large stock of music. It has already been noted that Whittaker considered it of paramount importance that the audience understood every nuance of the text. C. S. Terry provided some translations, but often Whittaker produced his own. In supplying the words, Whittaker attempted to 'fit the words in such a way as to bring out Bach's faithful interpretation of his text'. This could be testing, as he maintained, 'not only on account of the difficulty of translating from one language to another, but because some of the expressions of the hymn jar somewhat upon our present-day tastes'.

Cantatas in St Nicholas's Cathedral

THE challenge of finding more opportunities to perform Bach cantatas was solved to a certain extent in 1919 when organist William Ellis, previously assistant organist at Durham Cathedral, became organist at St Nicholas's Cathedral, Newcastle. Ellis was keen to invite the Bach Choir to participate in recitals at the cathedral. This opened up opportunities, but it proved to be something of a curate's egg for Whittaker, because the collections taken never covered expenses, even with a largely amateur orchestra; moreover, the building was 'a heart-breaking place acoustically'. The singers could hear neither their neighbours nor other lines. Nevertheless Whittaker loved performing in the 'fine choir of the fourteenth-century building', for its 'right surroundings' gave him 'great satisfaction'. At the first recital, on 24 May 1919, the chorale *Schmücke dich*, followed by Ellis's playing of the chorale prelude on that chorale, was preceded by the eight-part unaccompanied motet *Sing ye to the Lord* (*Singet dem Herrn*). With demobilization well under way, Potts returned to sing the solo cantata No. 56, *I will my cross with gladness carry* (*Ich will den Kreuzstab gerne tragen*). Whittaker implemented a policy of performing the solo church cantatas, fearing that, with no chorus or large orchestra, they would never be revealed to the general musical public, and he was sure that the best atmosphere for them was in church. The orchestra was led by Alfred Wall.

On 12 April 1919, Cantata No. 158, *May peace be with you* (*Der Friede sei mit dir*), the last Weimar solo cantata, was performed in the Westgate Hall. Whittaker believed that Bach's motets were intended to be accompanied by an organ and to be sung by a larger choir than the cantatas called for: up to sixty voices. With an organ now available, Whittaker included the motets *Praise the Lord, O ye heathen* (*Lobet den Herrn, alle Heiden*) and *Sing ye to the Lord* (*Singet dem Herrn ein neues Lied*) in the concert, as well as the secular cantata No. 203, *Amore traditore*

(*Treacherous love*), and the chorus 'Give welcome' from the secular cantata No. 207, *United discords of vibrating strings (Vereinigte Zwietracht der wechselnden Saiten)*. Mark and Eckford performed Bach's F minor violin sonata and Eckford the Partita No. 2 in C minor for clavier. Songs and arias followed, including 'Edifying thoughts of a smoker' from the Anna Magdalena book, sung by baritone Walter Clapperton (then at the Royal College of Music and described by the *North Mail* as having 'a very rich voice' – see Chapter 8). Also featured was an aria from *Phoebus and Pan*.

A contemporary press report pointed out that, though the singing was 'as good as always', the sopranos and contraltos were hardly strong enough to balance the tenor and basses. Having already tried three venues for the Bach Choir, Whittaker was all too aware of the relevance of this assessment, admitting that even now there was 'not one acoustically fitted for its purpose'.

The 1918/19 season ended with three more cantatas, performed in the Westgate Hall on 31 May 1919: No. 93, *He who relies on God's compassion (Wer nur den lieben Gott läßt walten)*, No. 131, *Out of the darkness (Aus der Tiefen rufe ich, Herr, zu dir)*, and No. 176, *Man's heart is stubborn (Es ist ein trotzig und verzagt Ding)*, which employed two oboes and an oboe da caccia. The strings played the Brandenburg Concerto No. 3. The finances of the Bach Choir were precarious, and were cushioned to a great extent by loyal local supporters such as Walter and Percy Corder, W. Deans Forster and F. J. Culley, and James B. Clark.

A Permanent Home: Concerts in the King's Hall

THE move to the Central Hall caused many subscribers to threaten to resign because of the discomfort there. Although the Westgate Hall was modestly comfortable, its acoustics were impossible for choral performances. Whittaker now decided to use the King's Hall at Armstrong College for Bach Choir concerts, because of its size and character. This handsome panelled room, which was hung with portraits and graced by a large and a small balcony, was ideal for the purpose. The Council of Armstrong College willingly gave its permission, and the venue is still used by the choir today. Chamber concerts would continue at the Westgate Hall and cantata recitals at the cathedral. Cantata No. 167, *Ye mortals extol the love of the Father (Ihr Menschen, rühmet Gottes Liebe)*, was given at St Nicholas's on 29 November 1919. In No. 73, *Lord, as thou wilt (Herr, wie du willt, so schick's mit mir)*, which was probably written with a horn obbligato, Bach had transferred the part to organ manual, with the continuo played by the organ pedal. Also performed was Cantata No. 3, *O God, how many pains of heart* (*Ach Gott, wie manches Herzeleid*).

The first complete performance of Bach's St Matthew Passion by the choir took place on 27 March 1920 in the King's Hall, Part I in the afternoon and Part II in the evening, with a choir of forty, twenty-two strings and the requisite woodwind, using the Elgar/Atkins edition, uncut to retain 'the flawless unity of the work'. The choirs were suffering from 'unavoidable absenteeism' owing to a flu epidemic, which is probably why Whittaker included a choral group from Rutherford Girls' School to sing as the ripieno chorus.

A week beforehand, true to his 'music appreciation' principles, Whittaker, assisted by the Bach Choir and Potts, had lectured on the work for the Church Musicians' Union in the Connaught Hall. The *Yorkshire Post* explained that Whittaker's forces were exactly the same as those used at Leipzig, and published an article by Whittaker on the imperative of using a small choir. The *Newcastle Journal* wrote that Whittaker's interpretation of the Passion was 'obviously intended . . . as a service rather than a performance'. Whittaker reinforced this impression by requesting that applause be withheld until the end.

Despite a total audience of sixty in the fifth season, there was a loss of £45; so it was decided to raise admission charges slightly. The chamber concerts had resulted in a loss of £22. Whittaker appealed for more subscribers for both types of concert. He remained concerned that the cantata concerts were unsatisfactory, owing to the cathedral's acoustics. Income from the concerts barely covered expenses. Rehearsals continued to take place at the Conservatoire and in the hall of the Central High School, and concerts were given at the King's Hall and in the cathedral.

A cantata concert was given in the cathedral on 6 November 1920. Cantata No. 8, *God in Heaven, when comes my ending?* (*Liebster Gott, wenn werd ich sterben?*), was performed. No. 26, *Ah how fleeting* (*Ach wie flüchtig, ach wie nichtig*), compares man's life to a mist that appears and disappears; containing the longest aria in all Bach's church music, it required virtuoso singing. By contrast, No. 67, *Hold in remembrance Jesus Christ* (*Halt im Gedächtnis Jesum Christ*), included what Whittaker described as 'one of the most remarkable numbers in the cantatas'. Whittaker referred to it as a scena for bass with SAT chorus, flute, two oboes d'amore and strings. The soloists, Jane Fleming, Annie Lawton, Tom Purvis and Ernest Potts, and the choir sang, totally out of sight, from the Lady Chapel. Attendance at the concert was meagre.

On 18 December 1920, in 'a sparkling performance', all three Christmas sections of the Christmas Oratorio (Nos. 1, 2 and 3) were sung to an appreciative audience. Then the Brandenburg Concerto No. 2 in F was played. On 8 January 1921 the rest of the Christmas Oratorio (the New Year sections) were given before 'a rather thin audience'. The soloists, Hendry and Purvis, had given 'a good account'. Mrs George Dodds needed to 'make a determined effort to overcome the distressing vibrato which frequently prevents one from knowing what note she is singing'.

At a cathedral concert on 7 May 1921 the choir performed a Bach motet in eight parts and a series of unaccompanied chorales. William Ellis played a number of Bach's organ chorale preludes.

Holst and *The Hymn of Jesus*

AT the Westgate Hall on 22 February 1919, a concert was given featuring Byrd's ground for strings, *When the Leaves bee Greene*, Rutland Boughton's choral folk song variations, *William and Margaret*, Walford Davies's *Solemn Melody* for strings and organ, Balfour Gardiner's *News from Whydah* (which had been conducted in Newcastle by Bainton in 1912), and Goossens's *By the Tarn* and his *Rhapsody* for cello and piano played by Hetty Page. A first Newcastle performance of Purcell's *Dido and Aeneas* preceded piano pieces by Gerald Tyrwhitt (Lord Berners). The concert was well attended.

The first choral concert of the fifth season on the afternoon of Saturday, 20 December 1919 took place in the King's Hall before a large audience, with Lawton and Hendry as soloists. Walford Davies's *Six Pastorals* were played; then followed Holst's *St Paul's Suite* for string orchestra. Dowland's *Lachrimae, or Seaven Teares* followed, along with Bantock's *Hebridean Folk Songs*, Boyce's Suite for String Orchestra and sea shanties by R. R. Terry and Vaughan Williams. Christmas items ended the concert: Herbert Howells's *Here is the little door*, Vaughan Williams's *Fantasia on Christmas Carols* and some traditional carols. The *Yorkshire Post* also mentioned that 'two carols by Mr W. G. Whittaker were charmingly sung by Miss Lawton'. At this concert, Wilson Large, a printer, joined the tenor section, his firm soon taking on the printing of all subsequent Bach Choir programmes. At the next choral concert of British music in the King's Hall, on 7 February 1920, Bainton, as guest pianist, played Frank Bridge's *Four Characteristic Pieces* and the Capriccio No. 2 in F sharp minor. Cyril Scott's *Danse Nègre*, John Ireland's *Rhapsody*, *Decorations* and *Four Preludes* followed; and Percy Grainger's *The Sussex Mummers' Christmas Carol* and *Shepherd's Hey* were so well received that Bainton gave them an encore. Works by Wilbye, Morley and Dowland were sung, together with a group of folk songs, including Balfour Gardiner's 'The

Three Ravens' and 'The hunt is up', and two arrangements by Whittaker that had won prizes in a competition organized by Hugh Roberton of the Glasgow Orpheus Choir: 'The Captain's Lady' and 'The Deil's awa''.

Encouraged by Holst, Whittaker plucked up courage to invite Balfour Gardiner to be a guest at the next Bach Choir concert on 20 November 1920. Gardiner travelled north that day for a concert centred on many of his own unaccompanied vocal works. Gardiner had arranged publication of Whittaker's folk song arrangements in 1914 to enable Whittaker to conduct at a concert of British music in the Royal Albert Hall with Kennedy Scott's Oriana Madrigal Choir. One other item was Granville Bantock's *The Death Croon*, sung by Lawton with a six-part chorus *bouche fermée*. Whittaker also played, accompanying Carl Fuchs in cello solos, including Bach's Sonata in G for cello and piano. *The Death Croon* was thought to be the most effective work on the programme, and had been 'most exquisitely rendered' by Lawton. Gardiner showed his gratitude to Whittaker by dedicating to him a group of five piano pieces published in 1922 under the general title of *Shenandoah* and including one called 'Jesmond' in honour of Whittaker's home district.

Whittaker had recently introduced a new event, the 'social function' or reception, given by the British Music Society (BMS) for musical guests to Newcastle. Gardiner was entertained that afternoon at the Pen & Palette Club, which acted as a forum for the arts in Newcastle, giving hospitality to many artists, writers and musicians visiting the city.

Holst visited Newcastle on 5 March 1921 to conduct his *The Hymn of Jesus*. He had conducted the work with the Oxford Bach Choir on 13 June 1920 and in Cambridge in February. He sent the programme of the Cambridge performance for Whittaker's perusal and arrived the evening before the concert to rehearse the choir. Whittaker had another appointment, leaving his deputy, Joseph Robinson, in charge for the evening. Afterwards Robinson told Whittaker that Holst tried the work through once, said nothing, and continued to look at his score. The choir wondered what was going to happen. Writing later Whittaker recorded that

> Holst then put his arm through that of the assistant, led him aside and said: 'What does one do with a choir when it is perfect?' 'You are joking, Mr Holst.' 'Not in the slightest. I've never heard anything like this before. The choir is simply perfect; everything is exactly what I want, I can't tell them anything. What am I to do?' 'Well, just take it through once more.'

The Hymn of Jesus both opened and closed the concert. A group of singers from the ACCS formed the semi-chorus. A local music critic wrote: 'Much of the music is frankly revolutionary, daringly dissonant, and uncompromisingly uncomfortable. Of enjoyment, it gave us none, yet one could not feel altogether unappreciative of its sheer audacity.' Holst had allowed Whittaker to rescore *The Hymn of Jesus* for a smaller orchestra. He was taken to Tilley's Restaurant afterwards for a BMS reception. Back at home he wrote to Whittaker; his letter is reproduced as fig. 14.

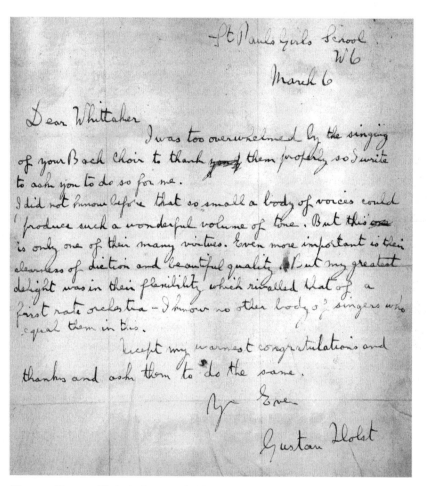

Fig. 14 Gustav Holst's letter of March 1921, after the performance of
The Hymn of Jesus. Newcastle Bach Choir archive.

After the performance of *The Hymn of Jesus* in March 1921 there was an invitation (presumably from Holst) for the choir to repeat the work in London, but, since a larger choir was required, this had been regretfully declined. The idea of a trip to London was irresistible to Whittaker, however, and shortly afterwards the

Newcastle Journal announced that the Bach Choir was to visit London soon after Christmas to give a series of Bach cantatas.

Early in 1921 Whittaker met someone who was to be a regular guest performer with the Bach Choir and visitor to his home – the young pianist, Harriet Cohen. Both were participants in the spring of 1921 in one of Dan Godfrey's concerts at Bournemouth. Whittaker conducted his *Prelude to 'The Choephoroe'*; and Cohen, who had become established as an exponent of Bach's keyboard works, played his Clavier Concerto in D minor. Although their personal accounts of their first meeting in Bournemouth differ, the result was that Cohen was invited to Newcastle to play with the Bach Choir.

On 5 November 1921, Cohen played the Clavier Concerto in D minor with the Bach Choir to a capacity audience. She also played Bax's unpublished Second Piano Sonata in one movement and gave an encore of a Scarlatti sonata in D. The choir sang Bach's Cantatas No. 23, *Thou very God and David's Son* (*Du wahrer Gott und Davids Sohn*), and No. 27, *Who knows how near my latter ending* (*Wer weiß, wie nahe mir mein Ende?*). The motet in eight parts *The Spirit also helpeth us* (previously sung in 1915) was also sung. After this, Cohen returned almost yearly to play at Armstrong College, feeling gratitude towards Whittaker. 'He, as it were, opened up the north of England to me.'

Percy Grainger, Myra Hess and Harold Bauer had all played Bach in London from the beginning of the century, but it was Harold Samuel (who performed Bach's *Goldberg Variations* there in 1898) who from 1919 led the trend towards all-Bach piano recitals. Whittaker was a great admirer of this genre of music performance, wrote Bach transcriptions himself, and, despite his desire for authenticity in his own choral concerts, found nothing wrong in playing Bach's solo keyboard music on the piano.

At the next cantata recital, which was held in St Nicholas's on 26 November 1921, the Weimar cantata for Sexagesima, No. 18, *As the rain and snow fall* (*Gleichwie der Regen und Schnee vom Himmel fällt*), scored for chorus, STB soloists and orchestra (with four lines of violas, two flutes à bec, bassoon and bassi) was performed, as well as Cantata No. 19, *There arose a great strife* (*Es erhub sich ein Streit*), which begins dramatically with a rapid fugal subject in the opening chorus depicting St Michael casting out the dragon. At a 'Christmas and New Year concert' of British music on 17 December 1921, Olive Tomlinson played Grainger's *The Sussex Mummers' Christmas Carol*, Ireland's *Merry Andrew* and Balfour Gardiner's *Noël*. John Vine sang Bax's *A Christmas Carol*, Balfour Gardiner's *Winter Songs* (including 'When icicles hang'), Cyril Rootham's *Noël*, Stanford's *The Winds of Bethlehem*, Walford Davies's *O little town of Bethlehem*, songs by

Berners, Whittaker and Noble-Vine, and carols arranged by Vaughan Williams, as well as traditional carols. The choir also gave a second performance of Benjamin Dale's *Before the Paling of the Stars* and Bach's motet in eight parts for New Year's Day, *Sing ye to the Lord*.

Towards an Authentic Orchestra

WHITTAKER found 1922 'a notable year for the choir, even though it brought one devastating experience'. He was referring first to the Bach Choir's trip to London, when their magical singing earned them a high opinion in the capital, and secondly to the disturbing change in Holst's personality that had been evident during the composer's visit to Newcastle in November. Although Holst had issued the invitation, it was his former pupil, Jane Joseph, who organized the visit. The Bach Choir raised money to reimburse working people among its ranks, many of whom were in 'a state of high excitement', having never previously visited London. Whittaker's piano pupils and choir members copied out the parts, taking many hours, and Whittaker wrote out continuo parts from figured bass. It was probably he who elaborated a simple invitation from Holst for the choir to sing in London to the status of a 'festival'. Whittaker planned the orchestra, advised by Holst, engaging eighteen orchestral players including Anthony Collins (leader), Bernard Shore (viola), Albert Fransella (flute), Léon Goossens and J. Macdonagh (oboes and oboes d'amore) and, as first trumpet, the Yorkshire musician Mark Hemingway.

On Wednesday, 22 February 1922, the Bach Choir sang first in the Aeolian Hall at 8.15 p.m. to a full house (see fig. 15). Henry Wood, Holst and Vaughan Williams were in the large and appreciative audience. Whittaker began with three church cantatas, all sung previously in Newcastle: No. 3, *O God, how many pains of heart* (*Ach Gott, wie manches Herzeleid*), No. 19, *There arose a great strife* (*Es erhub sich ein Streit*, and No. 34, *O fire everlasting* (*O ewiges Feuer, o Ursprung der Liebe*). The Bach Choir also sang the eight-part motet *The Spirit also helpeth us*, and the orchestra performed the *Ouverture* in D. The soloists were Dorothy Silk, Margaret Champneys, Steuart Wilson and Clive Carey – 'a fine team', as Whittaker described them, and 'all skilled Bach singers'. Dorothy Silk, with Gerald Cooper at the harpsichord, sang songs from the Schemelli book, 'with exquisite feeling'. The choir sang almost without flaw: 'the volume of tone was astonishing, and the soft passages beautifully done'. Edgar Crowe had written on 10 February in the *Chronicle* that high praise for the choir had come from Vaughan Williams, Holst and Balfour Gardiner.

This was the first time that London critics had been exposed to the Newcastle Bach Choir, and their response was effusive. One recorded that the choir was 'clearly an institution to be reckoned with' and that they had sung with 'admirable precision and expressiveness'. Another critic found them 'admirably disciplined'. *The Times* considered that they had 'fulfilled expectations from the first and ended by surpassing them'. The *Musical Times* commented on the accuracy of their pitch. The *Sunday Times* critic reviewed the first concert and found that, for such a small choir, 'their range of dramatic resource [had been] remarkable', attained by 'perfect steadiness, clarity and balance of the parts'.

The *Christian Science Monitor* of Boston, Mass., summed up: 'this small, compact body of singers, with ringing northern voices and the flexibility, precision, and fire of an orchestra, came as a revelation. . . . Dr Whittaker conducted without a baton, and his folk respond as readily to the slightest as to the most emphatic movements of his hands.' Herbert Thompson in the *Yorkshire Post* admired the crisp verbal attack and the balance of tone, but noticed a lack of resonance in the basses. At the second concert, held the following day at St Margaret's, Westminster, Whittaker conducted the eight-part motets *Sing ye to the Lord* and *Come, Jesus, come*. The solo harpsichordist, Violet Gordon Woodhouse, performed the Partita No. 5, along with preludes and fugues and other solos. Woodhouse, who played the harpsichord and the clavichord, was a forerunner in popularizing the use of authentic instruments. The same soloists sang at the third concert, in St Michael's, Cornhill, on Friday 24 February. Whittaker described the scene in a newspaper account:

> Three hours before we began there was a crowd outside. For an hour before we commenced, the building was packed with as many people as it would hold. They were jammed right up the aisle; they were sitting on the steps of the platform from which I conducted. If I swayed an inch, I bumped into human bodies. The church grew hotter and hotter. The flutes and oboes sharpened so much that Dr Harold Darke, the organist, had to transpose the figured bass part up a semitone during the last hour.

The Bach Choir sang three cantatas: No. 4, *Christ lay in Death's dark prison* (*Christ lag in Todes Banden*), No. 8, *God in Heaven, when comes my ending?* (*Liebster Gott, wenn werd ich sterben?*), and No. 26, *Ah, how fleeting* (*Ach wie flüchtig, ach wie nichtig*). For the first time the choir sang Cantata No. 151, *Comfort sweet, my Jesu comes* (*Süßer Trost, mein Jesus kömmt*). This adoration of the Christ, for the third day of the Feast of the Nativity, was distinctive, Whittaker writing: 'to the soprano, is allotted one of the most supremely beautiful arias in the whole range

Fig. 15 The choir in the Aeolian Hall, London, for the London Bach Festival, February 1922. *Courtesy Newcastle City Libraries.*

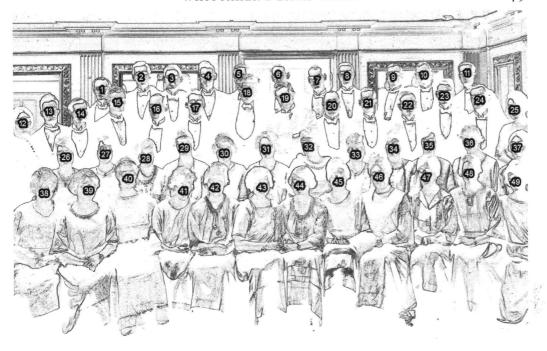

1. John Bell Cartner, tenor
2. James Alexander Benson, tenor
3. James Fairley Pedelty, tenor
4. William Bean, tenor
5. John Harding, tenor
7. Edward Thomas Stewart, bass
8. Joseph Robinson, bass
9. Henry Stanley Todd, bass
10. Ernest George Robinson, bass
11. George Alfred Bocock, bass
13. William Wilson Large, tenor
14. Lancelot Swindale Hughes, tenor
15. James Webster, tenor
16. John Storey Hebron, tenor
17. Stewart Edington Hattle, tenor
18. William Gillies Whittaker, conductor
19. Walter Shewell Corder, secretary to the guarantors

20. Nathaniel Keys, bass
21. Isaac Winter, bass
22. James Osborne Richardson, bass
24. Matthew Bambrough, bass
25. Olive Tomlinson, accompanist
26. Ailsa Blair, soprano
27. Florence Railton, soprano
28. Gladys Strachan, soprano
38. Ruby Ireland, soprano
39. Daisy Ireland, soprano
40. Jane Walton Fleming, soprano
41. Alice Beryl Cresswell, soprano
44. Ethel Frances Bainton, soprano
45. Alice Michaelina Havelock, contralto
46. Ethel Jane Browne, contralto
49. Isabella Rochester, contralto

Annotation by Philip Owen

of the cantatas.' Against a flauto traverso arabesque, this aria was 'melting in its exquisite tenderness'. *The Times* described how many of the audience stood for two hours, and reported the first cantata as 'exhilarating to listen to'. When at rehearsal, Carey, a baritone, had found the bass solo in *Christ lag in Todesbanden* out of his range, Whittaker asked the choir to sing the number chorally at the concert, so it 'sounded as if it were being sung by a colossal bass, & no-one was more delighted than Carey himself'. Some choir members stayed on in London, joining Dorothy Silk in the fourth and last of a series of 'old music' concerts that she was giving in the Steinway Hall, with soloists Norah Dawnay, Norman Stone and Clive Carey, and Harold Darke as organist. Bach Choir members were entertained afterwards at a 'beano' by Morley College students, and Mrs Gordon Woodhouse brought her clavichord. The Bach Choir gave a rousing rendering of Holst's rollicking chorus 'Bring us in good ale' and the sea shanty 'Billy Boy', which, sung in the vernacular, 'both bewildered and pleased the London students'.

Walter Corder related how, when he tried to thank Vaughan Williams, the composer replied: 'No, it is we who are indebted to Newcastle. This week has been a perfect revelation to us. We have never realised till now what Bach could really mean.' Corder described how, at St Michael's: 'For two hours the crowded audience, largely of necessity, standing in discomfort, listened with profound attention and in reverent silence.'

According to Edgar Crowe, the Bach Choir returned in the small hours, only to be 'plunged' next evening by Whittaker into a rehearsal of the B Minor Mass for their choral concert on 18 March.

Bach's B Minor Mass, perhaps regarded by Whittaker as a metaphorical conclusion to the festival, presented the next challenge for the Bach Choir. Whittaker lectured on the work with Bach Choir illustrations on 11 March, the performance taking place on 18 March 1922, given by forty voices for the four- and eight-part choruses, ten extra sopranos in the five-part, and ten extra altos in the Sanctus. Though the Mass had been sung twice 'on the grand scale' by the Choral Union, it was surely the first performance in Britain by such a small choir.

The audience 'overflowed into all the corridors', enthusiasts standing throughout the long performance. Wall and Hemingway played their obbligato parts exquisitely, one local critic claiming that the performance marked 'the highest water-mark of the society's work'. Afterwards the Bach Choir adopted a regular three-year cycle alternating the Mass and the two Passions.

In 1921 another 'peace music festival', a hang-over from the armistice celebrations of 1919, had been held in Newcastle, followed by a further festival in 1922. Whittaker participated on Sunday 9 April, with the Bach Choir and the remnants of the wartime Newcastle upon Tyne and District Festival Choir, in a 'grand concert' in the Palace Theatre with Arthur Laycock, a well-known cornet player, and the St Hilda's Colliery Band conducted by Oliver. The programme, however, was not one that could satisfy an audience of such diverse taste, the Bach Choir performing Cantata No. 190, *Sing ye to the Lord* (*Singet dem Herrn ein neues Lied*), and the motet *The Spirit also helpeth us*, while the band played famous test pieces. This continued connection with the St Hilda's band enabled Whittaker to avail himself of specialist cornet players for cantata performances that required clarino parts (extremely high by modern standards), which were only practical on modern larger instruments through the technical superiority of the local virtuoso brass band players.

Another St Hilda's band player who joined Whittaker's Bach Choir orchestra was the superb cornet player Jack Mackintosh (1891–1979). He had been hired professionally by the St Hilda's band in 1912, playing solos with Laycock in 1913 and replacing him when the latter was called up. In 1919 he joined the Sunderland Empire Theatre orchestra, also helping the Harton Band to win the Belle Vue open championship, by which time the brilliance of his execution caused a sensation. His rendition of 'The trumpet shall sound' from *Messiah* was in great demand. When Hemingway left, Mackintosh replaced him and 'proved a brilliant artist', allowing Whittaker to prove that Bach's cantata trumpet parts could be performed. Many of Bach's horn parts exceeded the compass of known horns, equalling the range of the trumpet; so Whittaker, in consultation with Hemingway, solved the problem by hanging a bowler hat over the end of each trumpet. Whittaker kept the three trumpets and their hats concealed and no one noticed.

A recital in St Nicholas's Cathedral on 6 May 1922 was simple in nature, with unaccompanied chorales and the five-part motet *Jesu, priceless treasure* (*Jesu, meine Freude*) in the programme, together with organ chorale preludes on 'Liebster Jesu' and 'Erbarme dich' and the giant fugue on the chorale *Wir glauben all an einen Gott*, all played by Ellis. By way of relaxation, on 10 June ninety Bach Choir members, friends and WEA class members travelled to Northumberland in three charabancs to give a concert in Whitfield parish church. The choir had picnicked before the concert, and there was tea afterwards in the grounds of Whitfield Hall provided by Mrs Blackett-Orde, from whom Whittaker was now renting a cottage.

Whittaker reported in the prospectus that for two months before the festival the season had been blighted by influenza, audience figures being the lowest ever, and that 'empty halls were the order of the day'. In London, by contrast, halls were not big enough for the potential audience. Although choristers had funded themselves, a loss of £10 had occurred. Whittaker reported an improvement in audiences since moving to the King's Hall. Rehearsals now took place in Jesmond parish church and the Jesmond Presbyterian Church.

Tudor Music, Bax, Vaughan Williams and a Change in Holst

ON 28 January 1922, at the forty-fifth concert of the Society, which featured Tudor and modern British music, Annie Eckford was solo pianist and Olive Tomlinson accompanist. Dowland's *Ayres for Four Voices* and three Thomas Ford songs opened the concert, which continued with Wilbye madrigals, three songs by Parry, including *I'm wearing sweet violets*, and Balfour Gardiner's *Cargoes* for solo quartet and chorus. Wall and Eckford performed Eugene Goossens's Violin Sonata No. 1, composed in 1918. Wall also performed his own unpublished violin sonata. On St Cecilia's Day, 22 November 1922, Herbert Howells gave, with the Bach Choir, a BMS recital of his compositions in a crowded St James's Congregational Church Hall, Northumberland Road. Through Whittaker's new friendship with the pianist Harriet Cohen, another renowned composer, Cohen's friend Arnold Bax, came to hear his motet *Mater ora Filium* sung by the Bach Choir at the end of their concert on Saturday 16 December. He refused to conduct, but he and Wall played Bax's Violin Sonata No. 1. Whittaker had intended to meet him at the station, but Bax had taken an earlier 'relief' train and was at Granville Road when Whittaker returned.

Whittaker thought the work magnificent, and it appealed to the choir enormously. The choral effects were superb, and despite its difficulties it was 'fine singing' and the rehearsals 'a wonderful thrill'. Other works given were Bax's Christmas Motet for double choir, Warlock's difficult *Corpus Christi Carol*, carols by Howells, Walford Davies's *Traditional Carol*, Cecil Sharp's Worcester carol *As I sat on a sunny bank*, and Vaughan Williams's *Hereford Traditional Carol* (to the tune 'Dives and Lazarus'). Bach's Violin Sonata in B minor was played by Wall and Arthur Floyd, and afterwards a BMS reception was held.

Bax would offer no criticism until he and Whittaker were walking home 'in the wee sma' oors' after supper at the Baintons'. Then Bax went through the work bar by bar, 'discussing point after point as though the score was in front of him'. He was, however, pleased with the performance. The *Newcastle Journal* critic disliked the violin sonata, but the choir was admired by the *Yorkshire Post*.

A changed Holst arrived in Newcastle on 11 November 1922 to conduct a second performance of his *Ode to Death* for chorus and orchestra at a choral concert otherwise consisting of cantatas. (The *Ode* had had a first performance in Leeds Town Hall the previous month, with the festival chorus conducted by Coates.) The Newcastle performance was the first time that Whittaker had inserted a modern British composition into a programme largely devoted to Bach cantatas.

The *Ode*, a setting of Whitman's poem 'When Lilacs last in the Dooryard Bloom'd' from *Leaves of Grass*, was dedicated, according to Imogen Holst, to Cecil Coles 'and the others'. Holst had written it soon after the signing of the Treaty of Versailles, motivated by the futility and waste of life of the First World War. The choir awaited Holst's visit with eager anticipation, though he was vague about arrangements. In July he admitted forgetting the concert date and having no record of it. Next he agreed to come, but only to listen, as he did not want to miss two or three days' work through having to rehearse. On 18 August, Holst, realizing that the concert was on a Saturday and that he could arrive on Friday, apologized for the confusion. He was very depressed, and was progressing towards the nervous breakdown that overtook him the following year.

At the concert three Bach cantatas opened the programme: No. 156, *Death comes apace* (*Ich steh mit einem Fuß im Grabe*), No. 153, *How many and how mighty, Lord* (*Schau, lieber Gott, wie meine Feind*), and No. 45, *Of old hast thou known* (*Es ist dir gesagt, Mensch, was gut ist*), scored for flutes, oboes and strings, which had two arias 'of outstanding merit'. The concert ended with Bach's Concerto for two violins, played by Elsie Pringle and Flo Gavin. The *Ode to Death* was played twice. A local reviewer thought the choir 'below par' on a couple of occasions, and though the orchestra played well in Whittaker's arrangement for small orchestra, it was suggested that perhaps this arrangement did not give 'an adequate representation' of the work. Holst received a great ovation at the conclusion. Afterwards seventy BMS members, including the young Arthur Milner, attended a reception and *conversazione* for the composer at Tilley's Assembly Rooms.

Four unknown cantatas were given in St Nicholas's Cathedral on 3 February 1923: No. 13, *Lord, my weeping tears* (*Meine Seufzer, meine Tränen*), No. 29, *We praise thee, O Lord* (*Wir danken dir, Gott, wir danken dir*), No. 191, *Glory to God on high* (*Gloria in excelsis Deo*), and No. 195, *For the righteous* (*Dem Gerechten muß das Licht*), a wedding cantata. Strings, oboes, trumpets and continuo were in the orchestra. Cantata No. 13 was 'a cantata of sorrow' according to Whittaker, while No. 29 was composed for the election of the town council and, according to Whittaker, was put together by Bach, 'with the fever of transcription upon him', by 'scissor-and-paste methods'. The *Gloria in excelsis* was the only cantata not in the vernacular, and had been written for Christmas Day. The acoustics of the building were said to have marred the opening 'Gloria in excelsis', a borrowing from the B Minor Mass, with its 'florid and brilliant writings'. Extra sopranos were used in this work to achieve a better balance. A second performance of the B Minor Mass was given in the King's Hall on 17 March 1923 with the same soloists.

In 1923 celebrations for the tercentenary of Byrd's death were held throughout the country. Harriet Cohen played with the Bach Choir on 24 February, giving works by Byrd (including his *Earl of Salisbury's Pavan*), Weelkes, Vivaldi and Scarlatti, arrangements of Bach chorale preludes by Hummel and Busoni, with pieces by Ireland, Bax and Goossens. The Bach Choir sang secular songs by Byrd (ten members also singing the Sanctus, Benedictus and Agnus Dei from the five-part Mass), and also performed Weelkes madrigals and ayres and a part-song composed by Edgar Crowe, *Ah! county guy* (a prize-winning song at the North of England Musical Tournament (NEMT) with words by Sir Walter Scott). Bax's *Mater ora Filium* concluded the programme.

On 5 May 1923 another distinguished guest, Ralph Vaughan Williams, conducted his Mass in G minor for solo quartet and double choir in the cathedral. The *Newcastle Journal* reported that 'Dr Williams . . . brilliant pioneer and cultured leader of the modern British School' had given a short but expressive tribute to the choir after the performance: '"Beautifully sung"'. Also sung were Byrd motets and movements from the five-part Mass. Dr A. C. Tysoe of Leeds parish church performed Vaughan Williams's chorale prelude on the hymn tune *Rhosymedre* and Bairstow's *Vexilla Regis*.

Vaughan Williams's letter if thanks to Whittaker, written on 21 May, is reproduced opposite.

The Bach Choir prospectus for the ninth season revealed that, athough 'Beethoven week' had incurred a considerable financial loss, 'generous extra subscriptions' and choral concert profits (now reaching a 'high water mark' with the B Minor Mass) had made up the deficit, sustaining the momentum of the choir since 1918.

Financial Problems and Byrd's Great Service

WHILE Whittaker was in Australia for his Associated Board examining tour in the second half of 1923, his friends undertook his commitments. Bainton conducted the Bach Choir in a concert of Tudor music in November, with works by Gibbons, Wilbye, Morley and Byrd. John Goss was a visiting guest performer (singing Schubert's *The Erl King* and a group of lieder from *Die Schöne Mullerin* and modern English songs by Warlock, Bainton and Norman Peterkin). Annie Eckford played Dale's impromptu *Night Fancies*, Frank Bridge's *The Dew Fairy* and two Scriabin preludes. But Dale did not arrive to conduct his cantata *Before the Paling of the Stars* or perform his large-scale Violin Sonata Op. 11 with Wall on 15 December; his place was taken by Max Pirani, whose 'masterly efforts are worthy of the warmest praise'. Dale's piece was unappreciated by most critics: 'Judging by the number of closed eyes in the audience, much of it had an unusually soporific influence', although another critic observed: 'One could not fail to be impressed by the sensitiveness and sincerity of his musical thinking, his feeling for beauty, and his power of expression.' One critic preferred the title 'Afternoon of Strange Noises' to that of 'Christmas Concert'. No Bach cantatas were given in Whittaker's absence.

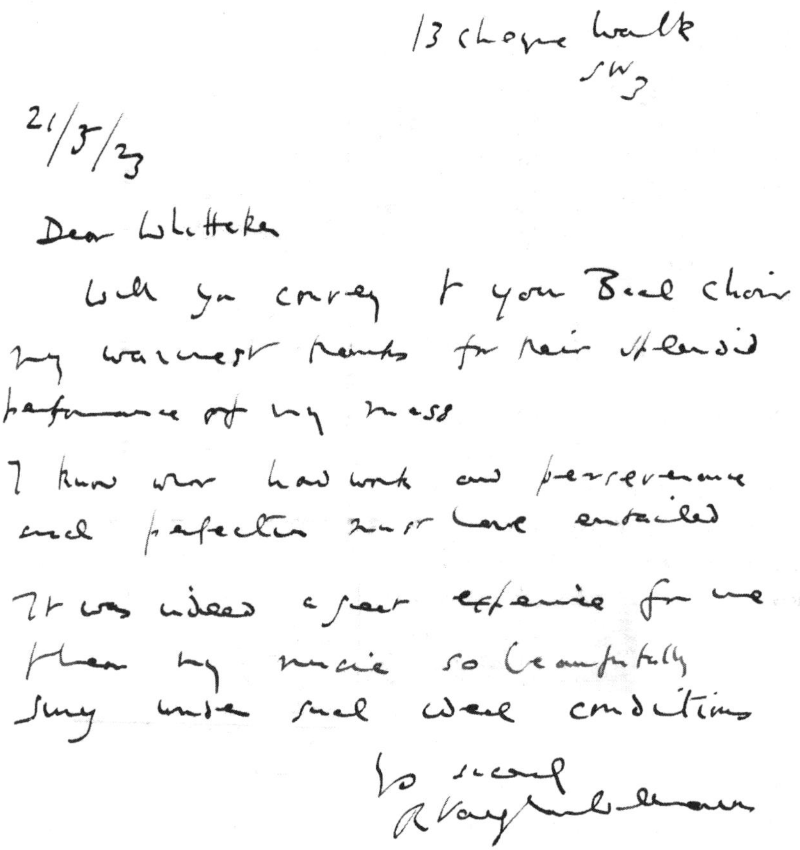

13 Cheyne Walk
SW3

21/5/23

Dear Whittaker

Will you convey to your Bach Choir
my warmest thanks for their splendid
performance of my Mass
I know what hard work and perseverance
and perfection must have entailed
It was indeed a great experience for me
to hear my music so beautifully
sung under such ideal conditions

Yrs sincerely
R Vaughan Williams

Fig. 16 Letter from Ralph Vaughan Williams to W. G. Whittaker, 21 May 1923, after the performance of his Mass in G Minor. *Newcastle Bach Choir archive*.

Whittaker returned to a quickly deteriorating national financial situation that threatened many institutions and organizations, including the Bach Choir; but he was probably more concerned that Holst, who had planned to conduct his new *Fugal Concerto* with the Bach Choir on 1 March 1924, with *The Cloud Messenger* (its fourth Newcastle performance), was still suffering from depression after a head injury sustained in 1923.

Holst's friends Vally Lasker and Nora Day travelled north without him. At a two-piano recital to the local BMS on 29 February they performed Holst's suite *The Planets* and *The Perfect Fool*. Next day, before the concert, Whittaker explained his absence to the very large audience, telling of Holst's sadness that he could not hear his *Cloud Messenger*, as he had longed to hear it sung well since its poor first performance. A local critic commented that the *Fugal Concerto* was 'splendid', the orchestra playing 'on a very high plane'. Bach's secular cantatas No. 208*a*, *Was mir behagt, ist nur die muntre Jagd*, and No. 206, *Glide, playful waves, and murmur gently!* (*Schleicht, spielende Wellen*), were given what were probably their first performances in England, using texts translated by C. S. Terry for the occasion. The *Journal* critic thought Norah Allison 'marred some otherwise beautiful and effective singing by an acute and irritating attack of vibrato', while the *Chronicle* commended Whittaker's pupil, Marjorie Amati, for taking on the tenor part.

A memorable guest was Harold Samuel, the well-known Bach pianist, who played with the choir on 5 March 1924. The increase in the popularity of Bach's keyboard music encouraged him to give 'all-Bach' weeks, never repeating a work and playing from memory. At the Bach Choir concert Samuel performed three preludes and fugues from *The Well-tempered Clavier*, the Toccata in C minor and the Partita No. 1 in B flat. He also performed Bach's Chromatic Fantasia and Fugue and the Clavier Concerto in E major. The Bach Choir sang Bach's motet *Jesu, priceless treasure* as a welcome interlude.

Through his new editing role at OUP, Whittaker became a close colleague of Hubert Foss, head of the new educational music department. The Carnegie Trust issued Byrd's Great Service at Christmas 1922. The following year Edmund Fellowes's *William Byrd: A Short Account of his Life and Work* was published by OUP. As Fellowes, editor of the Trust's Church Music series, had recently rediscovered Byrd's Great Service in a Durham Cathedral manuscript, OUP had published the service in a 'complete and accessible form'. This smaller-sized performing edition would be sold at 6*s*. each as opposed to 30*s*. a volume. With 'a high reputation as a scholar and choral conductor', Whittaker's interpretation of early music was already approved of by Fellowes; this, with his recent Carnegie Award and the publicity surrounding his London Bach performances with the Bach Choir, made him the natural choice to perform the Byrd Great Service with the choir. Foss invited Whittaker to give the performance, and he seized the opportunity, deciding to give the performance at the cathedral recital usually reserved for

Bach cantata performances. Since eleven months had elapsed since the last cantata performance by the Bach Choir in February 1923, however, Whittaker knew he must fit in an extra concert. He succeeded in arranging a cantata concert in his sister Lily's home town of Dumfries, on Saturday, 15 March 1924 in the Lyceum Theatre, as part of the Dumfries orchestral subscription concerts series. The event signalled a brief improvement in relations with Lily, who was a proficient local cellist in the Dumfries area, and now had three children.

The Bach Choir programme at Dumfries included four cantatas: No. 4, *Christ lay in Death's dark prison* (*Christ lag in Todes Banden*), No. 6, *Stay with us; the evening approaches* (*Bleib bei uns, denn es will Abend werden*), No. 53, *Strike, then, longed-for hour* (*Schlage doch, gewünschte Stunde*) and the solo cantata for bass, No. 56, *I will my cross with gladness carry* (*Ich will den Kreuzstab gerne tragen*). The choir also sang the motet *Jesu, priceless treasure*. The audience was small and Annie Lawton was not admired; the *Dumfries and Galloway Standard & Advertiser* critic wrote: 'To be quite candid the solo performances were not on a par with those of the choir.'

In Newcastle, a Bach concert took place on 12 April 1924 at the King's Hall: a second performance of the St John Passion. On 30 May 1924 Fellowes lectured to the Newcastle BMS on the Byrd Great Service, with illustrations by the Bach Choir conducted by Whittaker. Hadow was present. Fellowes had travelled north with James and Louise Dyer. The latter founded the music publishing company Éditions de l'Oiseau-Lyre in Paris. Fellowes visited Durham Cathedral *en route*, where he wondered what ancient choristers would have thought of the fact that the work was about to be 'carried by broadcasting to remote corners of the country'.

The complete Great Service was given, for the first time in three hundred years, by the Bach Choir in St Nicholas's Cathedral next day. *The Times* correspondent recorded: 'Dr W. G. Whittaker and his very intelligent singers of the Newcastle Bach Choir gave a memorable performance . . . only a few miles from Durham City'. An interesting feature of the performance was that the proceedings began with *Hymns Ancient & Modern* No. 165, and numbers were interspersed by two groups of organ solos given by Ellis. *Hymns A.&M.* No. 634 and a silver collection preceded the Kyrie and the Credo, and there were more solos before the Magnificat and Nunc Dimittis. Fellowes praised Whittaker's performance, in which the complex rhythms were 'handled with remarkable clarity'. At the close, Dr Fellowes remarked that 'everything had been done just as he would have wanted it.' Through Foss's ministrations, the Bach Choir was now invited by the Carnegie Trust to sing the Byrd Great Service twice more in London, on 25 and 26 November, at St Margaret's, Westminster, through the kindness of the rector and the organist, Mr Stanley Roper, organist of the Chapel Royal. Another Newcastle performance was scheduled for Saturday, 29 November.

In summer 1924, Whittaker's *Fugitive Notes on Some Cantatas and the Motets of Bach* had been published by OUP, dedicated 'To the Past and Present Members of the Newcastle-upon-Tyne Bach Choir as a slight appreciation of their splendid enthusiasm and devotion'. In that year Whittaker and C. S. Terry began their collaboration on a cantata series for OUP, Terry contributing the translations. In the same month Whittaker presented Terry for an honorary doctorate at Durham University. In December 1924 Whittaker sent his first cantata publication to Holst, who pronounced his editing to be 'admirable'. In February 1925, Terry lectured, with Bach Choir illustrations, to NLPS on 'Bach's Original Hymn Tunes'.

The yearly visit to Whitfield by the Bach Choir to the home of Mrs Blackett-Orde (that year 'ticket secretary' for the event), on 7 July 1924 became something of a publicity opportunity for both the choir and Whittaker. The choir performed on the lawns after a garden fête, Whittaker conducting in plus-fours, and a dance followed at 8 p.m. Whittaker now introduced new blood to his performances with solo vocalists such as Lillian Liniker and Archie Armstrong. Beryl Cresswell was the oboist. Rosina Wall was among the players, and Olive Tomlinson was the pianist. In reality, during the season there had been a 'falling-off of support' for the Bach Choir, a loss of £28 being made on the choral concerts, no doubt largely caused by the financial depression but damaging still further Whittaker's hope of continuing the cantata concerts.

Another visit by Harriet Cohen on, 1 November 1924, brought Bach's Chromatic Fantasia and Fugue, Bax's Sonata in G minor and solos by Byrd, Morley and Gibbons to the concert platform. The choir also sang Whittaker's *Song of the Virgin Mother*, Stanford's *The Blue Bird*, Delius's *Midsummer Song*, Foss's *The Three Cherry Trees* and two Howells settings dedicated to the Bach Choir, *The Shadows* and *Creep afore ye gang*. The *Newcastle Journal* reported 'incomparably beautiful unaccompanied singing' at the concert, a musical standard that concealed an underlying anxiety among the choir's organizers.

Percy Corder chaired a special meeting at which Deans Forster appealed for 'systematic support'. Corder's nephew, William Corder, a local schoolmaster, was elected chairman of the Bach Choir with Francis Culley as vice-chairman, and they pulled the choir back from the brink of disaster.

Another London Visit and a BBC Broadcast from Newcastle

Two weeks later, invited by Foss, the Bach Choir travelled to London (see fig. 17) to give two performances of the Byrd Great Service at St Margaret's, Westminster on 25 and 26 November 1924. The Great Service had previously been performed only in Newcastle, at St Michael's College, Tenbury, and in Cambridge. Part of the choir also went to record some of Whittaker's folk song arrangements for the HMV Company, though it does not appear that the recording was ever released. Foss wrote a publicity article in the *Musical News and Herald* of 1 November, describing the Newcastle performance of the Byrd, which was 'I can assure you, from personal knowledge, a very thrilling experience for the listener.' Free tickets, available from OUP (with donations welcome), had all been taken a month before. Holst wanted to attend Wednesday's performance, but asked whether he might eat alone with Whittaker, since 'parties and crowds take it out of me horribly'. Predictably, however, he withdrew: 'My head has been bad for the last four days and I'm only fit for solitary walking, reading by the fire or bed.' The performance was again interspersed by organ solos – sixteenth- and seventeenth-century pieces played by Stanley Roper.

Intense interest was shown in the Bach Choir visit, the *Morning Post* printing a lively description of the scene on Wednesday at the second concert:

> The ancient church was again crowded, there not being standing room, and large numbers of people failed to get into the church. The Newcastle Bach Choir sang the music with wonderful feeling and perfection, not a note was missed in any part of the church, although the voices were sometimes reduced to a whisper.

Outside the church a crowd had gathered. The *Daily Express* reported: 'The setting for the singing was perfect in the warm lights, the grey arches, [and] the gleam of colour over the altar. The women singers in white were grouped at the choir steps.' Canon Carnegie (unrelated to the philanthropist) likened the choir's singing to 'far-off strains coming from another world, and the music of angels and archangels'. Contemporary press reports complimented the choir's 'purity of tone' and their ability to sustain pitch and overcome rhythmic difficulties. Holst wrote to Whittaker on 8 December: 'I was very sorry to miss your triumph in London. I gather that you and your singers scored more heavily than Byrd and I am still wondering whether that Service is the Man at his best.'

On Friday Whittaker wrote to Herbert Foss, thanking him for arranging the visit to London. The *Musical Mirror* thought it 'an artistic feather in

Fig. 17 The choir at Newcastle Central Station *en route* to London, November 1924. *From the Illustrated Chronicle, courtesy Eric Hebron.*

2. John Storey Hebron, tenor
3. Ernest James Potts, bass
5. Nathaniel Keys, bass
6. Ethel Jane Browne, contralto
7. Eric Rimer, bass
10. Ernest Rimer, bass

12. William Robert James, bass
13. Stewart Edington Hattle, tenor
14. Isaac Winter, bass
15. William Wilson Large, tenor
16. William Bean, tenor
Annotation by Philip Owen

Dr Whittaker's well-plumaged cap to have directed two memorable perform-ances of Byrd's fine work within such a comparatively brief space of time'. On returning, the choir gave the Byrd again in St Nicholas's Cathedral, singing with 'increased intimacy, freedom and elasticity', according to the *Newcastle Journal*, and with 'impeccable attack and precision, and beautiful and artistic mixing of tone colours'. But some found the difficult acoustics more 'hampering' than ever.

At the first concert held under Bach Choir Society auspices since the choir was constituted along business lines, Percival Driver, Whittaker's fellow examiner from his Australian tour, was the guest vocalist in a Bach Choir programme of Christ-mas music on 20 December. The programme accentuated the fact that Whittaker's imagination and appetite for British music was in no way flagging. Parry's *Ode on the Nativity*, Armstrong Gibbs's *Before Dawn*, Whittaker's *Morning, Noon and Evening Quatrains* for female voices and Bax's *Of a rose I sing a song* were enjoyed. There were madrigals: Weelkes's ayre *The Ape, the Monkey, and Baboon*, Morley's madrigal *Lady, why grieve you still me?* and Bennett's *Lure, falconers, lure*. Driver sang two groups of songs, which included Stanford's *To the Soul* and *Why so pale and wan?* and songs by Wolstenholme, Bullock and Parry, while the choir sang part-songs by Malcolm Davidson, Stanford (*The Blue Bird*), carols by Whittaker and three Peter Warlock settings, the last being *The Sycamore Tree*. Plant and Dodds played two Bach sonatas for pedal claviers transcribed for two modern pianos. Three songs by Whittaker, including *Love's Coming*, given first at Kinnoull in Melbourne, were sung by Driver.

The tercentenary of the death of Gibbons, on 8 November 1925, provided another pretext for a special concert, marked by the return of Adila Fachiri to play Bach's Violin Concertos in A minor and E, as well as two pieces by Rebecca Clarke, *Midsummer Moon* and *Chinese Puzzle*. Four Gibbons madrigals were performed and *The Cryes of London* for voices and strings was repeated, as was Whittaker's *Newcastle Quayside Cries*.

Despite Whittaker's continued enthusiasm for the English choral repertory, its magic seemed to be wearing thin with local audiences. The *North Mail* reported a 'disappointingly small' audience, commenting too on the 'worn tone' produced occasionally by the sopranos and the 'tired, forced effect among the tenors'. But Whittaker was not to be discouraged; on 6 February 1926 he conducted the Bach Choir in Peter Warlock's immensely demanding *The Full Heart*, the work having been twice abandoned by the choir when it was clear that more rehearsals were needed. Whittaker thought the work 'the most difficult piece written by an Englishman', and after demands for an encore replied, 'Ladies and gentlemen, better leave well alone!' Dowland ayres and Arnold Bax's challenging motet *This Worlde's Joie* were finely sung. The soprano Joan Elwes (suggested by Holst as an excellent singer of Bach) was the guest vocalist, and Whittaker performed in John Ireland's *Phantasie Trio*.

At the cathedral recital of 7 February 1925, the choir sang four cantatas. The running order of the programme was: Cantata No. 104, *Thou guide of Israel* (*Du hirte Israel*), No. 172, *Sing praises* (*Erschallet ihr Lieder*), No. 54, *Watch and pray* (*Widerstehe doch der Sünde*), and No. 11, *Praise Jehovah* (*Lobet Gott in seinen Reichen*). The alto aria of the last-named became the Agnus Dei of the B Minor Mass. The soloists were Ida Cowey and Annie Lawton, with Stewart Hattle, H. Frater and W. H. Hobkirk and Arthur Lewis from the cathedral choir.

In July 1925 the Bach Choir gave a mixed programme at Alnwick parish church (see fig. 18) that included excerpts from Bach's St Matthew Passion and Byrd's Great Service.

Two memorable events followed. The first was an historic early BBC outside broadcast on Newcastle Radio 5NO of a Bach Choir concert from Brunswick Methodist Church (the church attended by Whittaker's family), occasioned by the return of Edward Clark (son of J. B. Clark) in 1924 to his native city as musical director of the BBC local station. The broadcast took place on the evening of Sunday, 15 February 1925 and began at 8.30 p.m. Five chorales enveloped an address by the Dean of Durham Cathedral, after which, at 9 p.m., Whittaker conducted the Byrd Great Service, interspersed with lessons.

The second important event for the choir was another complete performance of the St Matthew Passion, on Saturday, 4 April. Girls from the ACCS and Rutherford College Girl's School formed the ripieno soprano chorus of between forty and fifty. The 'thunder and lightning' and mocking choruses were given with 'graphic force and power', and Tom Danskin sang so well that 'his performance could hardly have been bettered'. Muriel Plant played the continuo part on a modern spinet made by Arnold Dolmetsch. 'The agreeable "plucking" tone of the little instrument helped materially to create appropriate atmosphere.' In 1925 Whittaker was in close touch with Dolmetsch, who was preparing to hold the first of his annual early music festivals in August that year. The decision to obtain a spinet for the Bach Choir's use would have undoubtedly been Whittaker's. (The instrument was probably donated by J. B. Clark, who had supplied the wind instruments for Bainton's Newcastle Philharmonic Orchestra.) Not all of Whittaker's musical contemporaries shared his opinion on the matter of appropriate Bach accompaniments. Vaughan Williams certainly preferred to make his own 'improvements' to Bach's orchestrations, by such methods as using both trombones and trumpets in the same piece. He also criticized 'those nasty detached twangs on the harpsichord which we hear nowadays' in continuo realizations. But Whittaker's close collaborator C. S. Terry remained steadfast in his resolution to discover the way to perform Bach's works with integrity.

In May, Whittaker combined a second performance of Bach's motet *Be not afraid* with John Taverner's Mass, *The Western Wynde*, at a recital in the cathedral. Also included in the programme were some chorale preludes played by Arthur Milner, organist of the Jesmond Presbyterian Church. Whittaker placed the choir in the chancel, facing the south-west part of the building, endeavouring thus to counter the acoustic problems, and probably obtained the best possible results. Attendance was poor. Nevertheless, the loyal band of Bach Choir supporters had turned round the financial situation, and when the Bach Choir Society's annual

Fig. 18 The choir at Alnwick parish church, July 1925. *Newcastle Bach Choir archive.*

2. Matthew Bambrough, bass
4. Ernest George Robinson, bass
6. Eric Rimer, bass
7. William Robert James, bass
10. Florence Railton, soprano
12. Elizabeth Byers, contralto
13. Edward Thomas Stewart, bass
15. John Bell Cartner, tenor
19. Ernest James Potts, bass soloist

20. W. G. Whittaker, conductor
26. Ethel Jane Browne, contralto
27. William Wilson Large, tenor
28. Isaac Winter, bass
29. James Osborne Richardson, bass
30. Lancelot Swindale Hughes, tenor
31. Stewart Edington Hattle, tenor

Annotation by Philip Owen

general meeting was held in Armstrong College, Walter Corder announced a reduction in the overdraft from £258 to £34. This more optimistic financial position was supported by a season's profit of £71 0s. 2d., reported by the choir's bank manager, Deans Forster, and the new earnestness with which the choir now monitored its pecuniary affairs was marked by the assistance of a new honorary financial secretary, the accountant Isaac Winter.

Dolmetsch Instruments and a Visit to Frankfurt

CHAMBER music concerts came to an end in the eleventh season, through lack of money. However, four choral concerts, two cathedral recitals and a celebration of Gibbons's tercentenary were planned, with rehearsals at the High School and the King Edward VII School of Art. It was decided to appeal for more subscribers, but a great advantage for future performances of Bach, the gift to the society of the spinet and of oboes d'amore, was reported by the *Musical Standard*:

> The Society received from a kind anonymous friend a specially constructed spinet to take the place of the pianoforte in playing continuo, and to the orchestral resources two oboe[s] d'amore have been added, one a generous gift from Mr Arnold Dolmetsch. It is thus hoped to reproduce the music of Bach more exactly and it is hoped other gifts of old instruments, such as viola d'amore, viola da gamba and violone, will be forthcoming for this laudable purpose.

The concert of 19 December 1925, featuring these new acquisitions, began with the choir's second performance of Holst's *Ode to Death*. The orchestra then played Bach's Brandenburg Concerto No. 5 in D (with flautist R. Thornton). The concert concluded with three of Bach's Epiphany and Christmas church cantatas with English texts by C. S. Terry. In order of performance they were Cantata No. 64, *See now, what great affection* (*Sehet, welch eine Liebe hat uns der Vater erzeiget*), No. 154, *My Master now hath left me* (*Mein liebster Jesus ist verloren*), and No. 122, *Sing we the birth* (*Das neugeborne Kindelein*). The audience was 'gratifyingly large'.

A third performance of Bach's B Minor Mass was given on 27 March 1926. Whittaker felt it was a great achievement that all the performers were from Newcastle. They included the soloists, all of whom were prizewinners from the NEMT: Norah Allison, Gladys Thompson, Ruby Longhurst, Tom Danskin, William Hendry and H. Shuttleworth. Apart from 'a little temporary fogginess in the orchestra' during the 'Quoniam tu solus Sanctus', all went well.

The Bach Choir made a fifteenth visit to the cathedral on Saturday afternoon, 30 January 1926, for the first cantata concert for almost a year. With an orchestra of flutes, oboes d'amore, cor anglais, trumpets, strings and continuo, the choir performed Bach's church cantatas Nos. 1, 16, 81 and 88. The first of these, *How brightly shines yon star of morn* (*Wie schön leuchtet der Morgenstern*), was the first issued in the new Bach-Gesellschaft edition in 1851, representing the caravan of the magi. However, the next performance in the cathedral, on 1 May, offered a mixed programme, and featured Byrd's five-part Mass and Bax's *This Worldes*

Joie. It was a repertory with which the choir was familiar and now closely associated both locally and nationally. The organist designate of Hexham Abbey, C. S. Richards, played Bach's Toccata and Fugue in D minor, fugues and chorale preludes by Bach including *Christ, unser Herr*, and Vaughan Williams's prelude *Rhosymedre*.

The choir had planned to sing at St Hilda's Church, South Shields, on 12 May, but the performance was postponed, owing to the General Strike, until 3 November. At the concert (with organist Mr F. Younger Robson), Byrd's five-part Mass was sung by only twenty-five voices and *This Worldes Joie* by the full choir. Whittaker justified his recent work with the choir in the season's report as a 'normal year's work', though it was also fair to say that the singing of Byrd's Great Service had given the choir a higher profile nationally. Donations had further reduced the Society's debt, and it was decided to start to hold evening concerts to attract larger audiences. From now on, all rehearsals would be at Armstrong College, where the music lecture room was available. On the whole, the scheme of English music and guest artists was the most successful line for the choir to follow, even though some modern compositions were not appreciated by the audience. Arthur Benjamin, newly appointed professor at the Royal College of Music, and Harriet Cohen played in Bach's Concerto in C major for two claviers and strings at the first concert of the twelfth season, on 6 November 1926. The choir sang unaccompanied works, ayres by Dowland, Moeran's new *Robin Hood borne on his Bier*, Walmisley's *Sweete Flowers* and Benjamin's *I see His Blood upon the Rose*. James Mark led a small orchestra in two Byrd fantasias for strings and a Gibbons pavane and galliard. Cohen played Bach's Clavier Concerto in D minor, pieces by Byrd and three pieces by Bax. The choir then sang part-songs by Parry and Stanford with 'perfect intonation, and immaculate phrasing'.

Hubert Foss's interests in the International Society for Contemporary Music also involved Whittaker, when Whittaker's setting of Psalm 139 (Robert Bridges's version from his anthology *The Spirit of Man*) was selected for their festival in June 1927. In December, the local press published the news that the Bach Choir was to perform the work in Frankfurt. Deans Forster launched an appeal to finance the trip. To send the sixty choristers £900 would be needed, and £620 was soon promised. The festival would last a week and would perform modern music of an international character, the works having been selected by an international jury with representatives from France, Germany, Denmark, Bohemia and the United States. Edwin Evans chaired the British committee, which called for the submission of works for selection, submitting its choice to the international jury. In February 1927 Deans Forster managed to obtain a gift of £250 from Jane

Cowen (niece of Joseph Cowen, former owner of the *Newcastle Chronicle*) for the Frankfurt fund, but more money was still needed. The choir was determined to make the journey with Whittaker, knowing that only they could do justice to his setting. Professor Edward Dent of Cambridge University had suggested that the choir should visit several other German towns to give concerts of British music.

Plans for a Newcastle Beethoven festival, from 10 to 27 February 1927, marking the centenary of Beethoven's death, progressed well, encouraged by the musical mayor, Arthur Lambert, a local organist who was to chair a local BMS festival lecture in the King's Hall by Walford Davies. As the Chamber Music Society had decided against joining in, no Beethoven quartets would be played during the festival, but the Bach Choir Society would contribute at least some chamber music. On 19 February, Whittaker's Psalm 139 (first performed by Vaughan Williams with the London Bach Choir in November 1925) was performed at a choral concert, with canzonets by Giles Farnaby. Soprano Bertha Steventon sang Butterworth's *Bredon Hill* and Martin Shaw's *The Rivulet*, and the Newcastle Wind Quintet played Beethoven's Trio, Op. 87, arranged for flute, clarinet and cor anglais, and the Serenade in D, Op. 25, for flute, violin and viola. An unidentified critic reports that the Psalm was sung 'with great sensitiveness', surmounting 'sometimes trying technical difficulties', but that it ran into problems of pitch when repeated. This was an indication of just how demanding Whittaker's new work was.

A recital in the cathedral on 21 May included a second performance of Psalm 139, sung with Byrd's three-part Mass, fantasias for strings by John Dowland and Henry Purcell, and sixteenth-century songs with strings, recently printed by OUP and edited by Warlock. Soon afterwards it was announced officially that the choir was to sing at the summer festival at Frankfurt. Apart from a quartet by Bernard Van Dieren, Whittaker's Psalm 139 was to be the only British work performed. The *Daily Telegraph* announced the programme for the festival, to be held between 30 June and 5 July.

Continuing to demonstrate extraordinary imagination in his Bach programmes, Whittaker devised a varied combination of soloists for the next recital in the cathedral on 22 January 1927. This again offered an all-cantata programme, a year after the previous one: No. 65, *Sie werden aus Saba alle kommen* (*They will all come from Sheba*), No. 161, *Komm, du süße Todesstunde* (*Come, sweet hour of death*), and No. 51, *Jauchzet Gott in allen Landen* (*Shout for joy to God in every land*). No. 171, *God, as your name* (*Gott, wie dein Name, so ist auch dein Ruhm*), was for chorus and SATB. No. 65, another Epiphany cantata, begins with a depiction of camels. The

Bach Choir was 'in top form', and Jack Mackintosh of the St Hilda's Colliery Band played admirably in the solo cantata No. 51. But despite this success, cantata concerts remained few, partly because the Bach Choir now regularly gave performances of the larger Bach works, a local tradition having been created. At the hundredth performance by the Bach Choir, on 9 April, the St John Passion was given for the third time.

Francis Culley chaired the AGM of the twelfth season, when the choir heard that finances were still a problem, exacerbated by the effect of the coal strike and reduced income from subscriptions. A balance of £10 13s. 2d. was carried forward, however, and receipts from the Beethoven week chamber concert given to the festival committee came to £8 10s. When Renwick (who had supplied the German words for OUP's German edition of Psalm 139) proposed that Whittaker be reappointed conductor, Whittaker was reticent, for his mind was fixed at this time on leaving Newcastle, though those around him were as yet unaware. Walter Corder, who was no longer in robust health, had written to the meeting to say that a fresh chairman with more strength and vigour should be elected. It was decided to re-elect him as a compliment, but to allow Francis Culley, the vice-chairman, to take over his duties.

On the evening of 12 June, a 'public service of worship, dedication and God-speed' for the journey abroad was held at St James's Congregational Church, Northumberland Road. Mayor Lambert gave an official farewell to the Bach Choir, and the party left Newcastle by the 12.56 train on Saturday, 2 July. Some photographs of the German tour form figs. 19–23.

Critical reception from Frankfurt was mixed. Professor Dent, chairman of the festival, immediately came over to say to the choir: 'You have had a great success; you have amply justified the enormous trouble you have been to in coming over here.' The *Daily Mail* critic, however, thought an opportunity had been missed, criticizing Whittaker's 'itch to be odd' and finding 'much of the festival music so painfully curious'. This response, grudgingly negative and not a little personal, led Whittaker never to trust the views of music critics again.

On Wednesday, 6 July, the choir went on a tour of university cities organized by Professor Dent, first travelling by train to the medieval town of Marburg, where the choir was met by Dr Wolfgang Schmidt and students. After listening to the German university choir, the Bach Choir sang to their hosts, Potts's unaccompanied north country folk songs bringing 'a furore of applause'. The choir gave an evening concert, singing Byrd and movements from Vaughan Williams's Mass in the crowded thirteenth-century Lutherkirche. Next day, the choir travelled to

Fig. 19 The choir in Germany, June 1927. *Family photograph.*

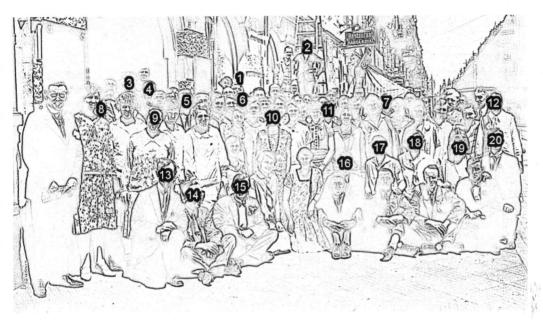

1. Ernest James Potts, bass soloist
2. William Robert James, bass
3. William Gillies Whittaker, conductor
4. Edward Thomas Stewart, bass
5. William Bean, tenor
6. Matthew Bambrough, bass
7. Ernest George Robinson, bass
8. Jane Walton Fleming, soprano
9. Mrs George Danskin, soprano
10. Alice Beryl Cresswell, soprano
11. John Bell Cartner, tenor
Annotation by Philip Owen

Göttingen, where they were cared for by Dr Weber, Pallister Barker (an English lecturer at the university) and students. With no time to view the town, the concert was given in a concert hall in the town park. Professor Hecht, head of the English seminar, had brought a good audience. Whittaker first lectured on how England was *not* 'a land without music'. The concert then 'went with an enormous swing', being the best of the tour, and Whittaker noticed that the Germans especially enjoyed Potts's 'renderings in dialect', which 'soon placed him on intimate terms with his audience'. Afterwards they dined at an open-air restaurant, and the next morning students gathered to say farewell, singing 'Auld Lang Syne' 'in excellent Scottish!'

After a tedious journey to Münster, with little rest, Dr Herman Erpf, a well-known musician and supervisor of the English-speaking students, met the party. The Bach Choir, as 'official guests of the Municipality', was accompanied by the Oberburgermeister and the Stadtrat, and visited beautiful gardens outside the city. After speeches, an official municipal dinner was provided. The host was the

Fig. 20 The Newcastle Bach Choir sopranos in Germany, June 1927. *Back row and behind*: 1. Jane Walton Fleming; 6. W. G. Whittaker, conductor. *Middle row*: 1. Mrs George Danskin; 2. Alice Beryl Cresswell; 4. May Ireland; 5. Clara Mary Ireland. *Newcastle Bach Choir archive, annotation by Philip Owen.*

professor of English, who discussed the Venerable Bede with Whittaker, and the meaning of local northern words, before Potts again 'warmed them up'. A Bach Choir member, Edward Stewart, sketched cartoons during the visit, sixteen of them published by William Large on the choir's return. (See pp. 193–4.)

Reaction to the choir's performance at Frankfurt was conflicting, often heated. Whittaker's letter to Deans Forster, used for press releases, told of 'a most tremendous success'. Whittaker reported 'many recalls' and quoted Furtwängler's remark that Whittaker had come to Germany 'to teach the Germans how to sing'. But Dorothy Darlington wrote in the *Daily News*: 'The Béla Bartók Piano Concerto was a disappointment, but not so great a one as that of Dr Whittaker's 139th Psalm.' She accused the Bach Choir of singing out of tune and of being 'scarcely equal to its task'. On 7 July the *New York Musical Courier* led its musical column with the heading 'A British Radical' and, discussing the British entry with particular reference to the performance of Psalm 139, said:

The biting dissonances and the absolute independence and often polytonal facture of the piece made the conservatives gasp. In retrospect the work offers little

Fig. 21 The Newcastle Bach Choir contraltos in Germany, June 1927.
Back row: 1. Elizabeth Byers; 2. W. G. Whittaker, conductor. *Newcastle Bach Choir archive, annotation by Philip Owen.*

real originality of content, however, and its manner is certainly more remarkable than its matter. The shaggy-haired Northumbrian was gleefully received into the ranks of the left-wingers and greeted with enthusiasm before the audience recovered from its surprise.

The party left Münster at 4.30 a.m. and reached their London hotel at 9.15 p.m. Next day they had a recording session at the Parlophone Company, between 11 a.m. and 4 p.m. 'After having recorded Holst's "Song of the Blacksmith", Dr Whittaker's arrangement of "Bobby Shaftoe", and Stanford's "The Blue Bird" for the Parlophone Company, the tired but cheerful party left King's Cross by the 5 p.m. train for home.' Three of the recordings were to be published in the autumn, but they seem not to have been released.

Afterwards Whittaker was 'disinclined' to reply to adverse press criticism about his composition and the choir's performance, saying only, 'There is nothing more notoriously erratic than musical criticism.' One choir member collected all comments, whatever their view, and reprinted them in a pamphlet, where they were 'startling in their disagreement', while Whittaker wrote an account for August's *The Sackbut*. Dent wrote to the *Musical Times* in December 1927 in defence of the

Fig. 22 The Newcastle Bach Choir tenors in Germany, June 1927. *Extreme rear*: W. G. Whittaker, conductor. *Back row*: 1. Lancelot Swindale Hughes. *Middle row*: 1. William Bean; 3. James Webster; 4. William Wilson Large; 5. John Storey Hebron. *Front row*: 1. John Bell Cartner. *Newcastle Bach Choir archive, annotation by Philip Owen.*

Bach Choir's performance. 'I may add that many German musicians have spoken to me with the greatest admiration for the Newcastle Choir, and of the revelation that it was to hear English music sung by them.'

Swan Songs

WHITTAKER realized that high attendance at Bach Choir concerts depended on the appeal of the programmes. The first concert of the season, on 12 November 1927, largely consisted of music prepared for the German tour but included a work by the young Australian composer Arthur Benjamin, who played his Suite for piano and three harpsichords and pieces by Richard Jones, and also performed his Sonatina for violin and piano, with Alfred Wall. Two Giles Farnaby canzonets were sung, and more British fare consisting of songs by Morley, Weelkes, Parry, Stanford, Holst, Vaughan Williams and Balfour Gardiner, as well as Whittaker's own 'Bobby Shaftoe', completed the programme. Edmund Rubbra's *La Belle Dame Sans Merci*, a manuscript arrangement for semi-chorus and two pianos replacing

Fig. 23 The Newcastle Bach Choir basses in Germany, June 1927. *Back row*: 1. W. G. Whittaker, conductor; 3. Ernest James Potts, bass soloist; 5. James Osborne Richardson. *Middle row*: 2. Ernest George Robinson; 3. Matthew Bambrough; 5. Edward Thomas Stewart; 6. Isaac Winter. *Front row*: 2. William Robert James; 4. Ernest Rimer. *Newcastle Bach Choir archive, annotation by Philip Owen.*

the original scoring for small choir and chamber orchestra, was sung. Cantatas had not been sung for some time, and although two recitals in the cathedral were planned, only one took place; this was on Saturday afternoon, 26 November, when cantatas Nos. 22, 80, 169 and 185 were performed. The *Newcastle Chronicle* reported 'a polished recital' of the four cantatas.

Vaughan Williams's *Sancta Civitas*, a challenging work composed in 1925, was performed twice by the choir on 4 February 1928. The young bass-baritone Keith Falkner of New College, Oxford, was the soloist. The composer had allowed a considerably reduced score to be used, an arrangement for strings, flutes, trumpet, timpani and piano for the distant chorus, 'excellently sung by the Cathedral boys' and conducted by Ellis. 'The entries of this distant chorus, preceded every time by a trumpet call, were among the most impressive of many impressive things during the performance.' The concert was followed by another performance of the St Matthew Passion, this time given on two successive nights (2 and 3 April). *The Yorkshire Post* of 3 April reported that the choir had given 'a brilliant performance', a response that threw into relief the choir's efforts to perform contemporary music.

Whittaker's interest in the choir waned as he sought a university post elsewhere, and an intended performance of the B Minor Mass was postponed. Another indication of Whittaker's decision was the naming on programmes of his official deputy, Joseph Robinson. In gratitude to old friends, Whittaker organized a concert of music by Holst and Vaughan Williams on Saturday 8 December. It included two of Vaughan Williams's works of 1925 – *Flos Campi*, in which James Mark played the taxing viola solo well, and the *Concerto Accademico* – and Holst's *The Golden Goose* in a stage arrangement. On 2 February 1929 Whittaker gave a 'Northumbrian concert' with Ernest Potts, Ena Mitchell of Cumberland, and Jeffrey Mark (who accompanied his own songs and arrangements). Annie Eckford played piano settings of Northumbrian folk tunes by Holst, Ernest Farrar's *North-Country Sketches* and 'A Cumbrian Suite' (in manuscript) by Jeffrey Mark. The B Minor Mass was given for a fourth time by Whittaker on 23 March 1929, with the choir augmented by ACCS singers. Whittaker made a surprisingly unorthodox alteration, placing the Sanctus at the end of the work: 'an arrangement which certainly averts any sense of anti-climax', according to the *Newcastle Journal*.

The Mass by this time was familiar territory, but there was time for one last 'adventure' with the choir, described in Whittaker's *Collected Essays*: 'It is the custom of the Newcastle-upon-Tyne Bach Choir . . . to embark each year upon some new adventure.' When the Carnegie Tallis volume was published by OUP in 1928, Whittaker developed 'an absolutely irresistible desire to tackle Tallis's forty-part motet, "Spem in alium"'. He shrank from asking his choristers to pay 30s. each for a copy, even had they been physically strong enough to hold them during rehearsals. W. R. ('Willie') James, a schoolmaster from Gateshead and also a choir bass, offered to make two copies of every part. OUP agreed to this, and plans went ahead. James penned eleven thousand bars (assisted by his 'no less energetic sister'), inventing his own admirable scheme of cues (given in red ink) to enable every singer to trace some easily heard line throughout every rest. In addition, this noble pair of enthusiasts bound every copy in strong covers. Although the work was originally composed for eight five-part choirs, each SATBB, Whittaker's group was forty-eight strong. The choir performed the 9½-minute work three times at the concert, together with Byrd's four-part Mass.

At the annual general meeting of 1929, Walter Corder finally resigned the chairmanship, on grounds of ill health. Francis Culley became chairman and Mowbray Thompson vice-chairman. The news of Whittaker's impending departure for

Glasgow was now well known. Unusually, Whittaker conducted his first cantata concert of the fifteenth season in the King's Hall rather than in St Nicholas's Cathedral, on Saturday afternoon, 2 November 1929. He gave three Bach cantatas: No. 130, *Lord God, we all praise you* (*Herr Gott, dich loben alle wir*), written for the feast of St Michael and All Angels, which was relevant to the season, with three trumpets and drums; then followed No. 170, *Contented peace* (*Vergnügte Ruh, beliebte Seelenlust*), from some derived material, and the substantial No. 30, *Rejoice, redeemed host* (*Freue dich, erlöste Schar*), in the same category but with an opening chorus considered by Whittaker to be 'one of the finest that Bach ever wrote'.

The next concert was unmistakably one of thanks and tribute to Holst, when the Bach Choir performed the composer's *The Hymn of Jesus* and Cantatas Nos. 130, 170 and 30. The soloists were Grace Scott, Helen Anderton, Tom Danskin, Jack Chicken and Ernest Potts, with Jack Mackintosh's 'brilliantly played florid trumpet passages'. The *Yorkshire Post* critic praised the small Bach orchestra and the magnificent singing of the last chorus in Cantata No. 30: 'Saturday afternoon's performance must rank with the finest ever given by the choir.'

The Christmas Concert, on the afternoon of Saturday, 7 December, was tinged with nostalgia as Dale's *Before the Paling of the Stars*, first sung by the ACCS in 1915 and by the Bach Choir in 1917, was sung again. But the choir also sang 'new and traditional carols', inspired by the publication of *The Oxford Book of Carols* by OUP in 1928. Looking forward to Whittaker's new appointment, the guest soloist was Bessie Spence, a violin teacher from the Scottish National Academy of Music, where Whittaker was shortly to take up his position as principal. She played in Cecil Armstrong Gibbs's *Lyric Sonata*, given for the first time in the north. Other soloists were G. Varming and Whittaker's colleague the excellent amateur flautist, Professor C. M. Girdlestone of Armstrong College. As well as the *Boar's Head Carol*, *The Holly and the Ivy* and many others, three old carols arranged by Holst's former pupil Jane Joseph were played in her memory. (It was she who made the vocal score of *The Hymn of Jesus*.)

Lambert Large, who sang in the choir for many years, remembered Whittaker's departure for Glasgow; he had thought Whittaker a rather old-looking man for his fifty-four years of age. He also remembered the sadness of the occasion. The deputy conductor took over rehearsals until Patrick Hadley arrived as temporary lecturer (soon to be replaced by Sidney Newman). The Armstrong College authorities had allowed Whittaker to leave immediately for Glasgow.

Whittaker returned to Newcastle on Saturday, 1 February 1930, to give the first performance of Herbert Howells's *Sir Patrick Spens*. It had been written for chorus and orchestra, but the composer had given his permission for the accompaniment to be reduced on this occasion to two pianos and timpani. Edgar Bainton and Muriel Plant played the pianos and Rene Houison the timpani. William Hendry and Lance Hughes were the vocal soloists. The work was repeated at the end of the concert, but it was received rather 'guardedly' by the audience, many of whom left before the repeat.

Sadly, Ellis (who had recently been awarded an honorary Lambeth doctorate in music by the Archbishop of Canterbury) was not able to play for Whittaker's last concert in the cathedral; he was replaced at short notice on 16 February 1929 by Reginald Tustin Baker of Hexham. After Bach's Cantata No. 17, *Wer Dank opfert, der preiset mich* (*Who gives thanks praises me*), No. 35, *Geist und Seele wird verwirret* (*Soul and spirit are thrown into confusion*), written as a solo cantata for alto soloist without chorus, was sung by the whole section. The concert ended with Cantata No. 168, *Give an account of yourself! word of thunder* (*Tue Rechnung! Donnerwort*), with its splendid opening bass aria, and No. 31, *The heavens laugh* (*Der Himmel lacht! Die Erde jubilieret*), for Easter Day. The soloists were Ethel Durrant, Rosa Burn, Tom Danskin and Arthur Lewis.

It was hoped that Whittaker would continue to conduct Bach Choir concerts, but the *Evening World* of 10 April gave the news: 'Bach Choir woes increase. Dr Whittaker gives up conductorship.' A real doubt hung over the future of the choir. Public support was lukewarm and its membership was falling. The secretary, Isaac Winter, looked forward to 'calmer weather', but hinted that if indifference continued, the Bach Choir, 'though crowned with honours', would die.

At the fourth performance of Bach's St John Passion, given by the choir on Saturday, 12 April, Whittaker was now described on the programme as the 'honorary conductor'. There was one last triumph. On 14 April, the St John Passion was broadcast for Holy Week, the choir and same soloists singing at the Northern Regional Station in Manchester. Urgent newspaper publicity sought help to continue the choir, as in the *Newcastle Journal*, which said: 'Somebody must be found to carry on and keep alive the organization which incidentally is as fine a monument as any musician could desire to his work and worth.'

Whittaker chose a programme of unaccompanied sixteenth-century music for his last concert with the Bach Choir, which was also his last concert in the cathedral, on 30 April 1930, reflecting his deepening interest in older music. Thomas Christy, sub-organist of the cathedral, played in Dr Ellis's absence; and in the memorable performance Whittaker turned his gaze towards Scotland as he conducted a work he loved, Robert Carver's nineteen-part motet *O Bone Jesu*, one of the oldest pieces performed by the choir, from a manuscript in the National

Library of Scotland. The *Journal* reported: 'For the last time . . . Professor Whittaker gave an inspiring lead to his forces.'

Despite the worries about a suitable successor to 'carry on and keep alive the organization', these concerns about the choir's future were happily to prove unfounded; as we shall read in later chapters, the next eighty-five years were to see many of Whittaker's founding principles maintained into the next century.

PART TWO

Whittaker's People

Chapter 3
Mining the Archives
Philip Owen

CHOIRS are usually remembered for their conductors and musical directors. It is said, however, that the whole is only as good as the sum of its parts. The account that follows in the following eight chapters is a celebration of the lives of many of the choristers, soloists and orchestral performers who sang and played in the concerts under the conductorship of W. G. Whittaker from 1915 until 1930, when he left Newcastle to become Gardiner Professor of Music and director of the Scottish Academy of Music in Glasgow. Also remembered are those who gave of their time to the choir in administrative roles.

Inevitably it has not been possible to undertake genealogical research on all those named in the concert programmes. Uncommon surnames were the easiest to study, and the more common name and surname combinations sometimes presented insuperable challenges. Those who are omitted, however, are not forgotten. Some of the problems encountered are now reviewed.

The illustration shown below is from the programme for the choir's second concert in February 1916:

The Choir:—Mrs. Bainton, Misses F. Brown, J. W. Fleming, N. Freeling, E. Pickering, G. Strachan—Misses C. Forster, A. M. Havelock, Mrs. Lamb, Misses L. Liniker, G. Rodgers, H. Scott—Messrs. E. W. Carmichael, G. F. Carmichael, J. Harding, L. S. Hughes, R. Peel, G. Prest—N. Bambrough E. Crowe, H. L. Featherstone, J. O. Richardson, E. G. Robinson, I. Winter.

This demonstrates three of the problems encountered. The first is posed by common forename initials and surname combinations. You will note a contralto listed as Miss H. Scott. Scott is an extremely common surname. Did the forename initial stand for Helen, Henrietta or some other name? There are vast numbers of people called H. Scott in contemporary census records. This contralto's identity has not been discovered and remains an enigma. The second problem encountered is that choristers and orchestral players are entered by surname and forename initials only. For example, was Miss E. Pickering's first name Elizabeth, Eleanor or Elaine? In fact she was called Elsie. The third problem is that of typographical errors in forename initials. Note a soprano listed as 'N. Freeling' and a bass listed as 'N. Bambrough'. In fact Miss Freeling's first name was Maud and Mr Bambrough's was Matthew.

Another problem area encountered was incorrect or inconsistent spelling of surnames. In the picture below, from the concert programme for April 1919, you will see one of the sopranos listed as 'Miss F. Railston':

The Choir.—Mrs. Dodds, Misses F. Brown, J. W. Fleming, A. Plews, F. Railston, L. Rowell, G. Strachan, E. Temple, H. Wilkinson; E. J. Browne, C. Foster, A. M. Havelock, L. Liniker, M. F. Richardson, G. Rodgers,

A variant of her surname recorded in subsequent programmes was 'Railstone'. The first concert programme in which she was correctly entered as 'F. Railton' (Florence) was some two years later, in November 1921, as shown below:

The Choir—Misses A. Blair, A. B. Cresswell, J. W. Fleming, I. Holmes, Misses D. and R. Ireland, E. Pickering, M. Pratt, F. Railton, G. Strachan, H. Wilkinson. Misses

Another difficulty issue arose with the use of diminutive (familiar) forms of forenames. This is illustrated in the picture below, from the concert programme for November 1924. In it you will note a contralto listed as 'Miss B. Byers'.

Contraltos.
Mrs. Bainbridge, Misses E. G. Browne, B. Byers, K. Forster, A. Havelock, Mrs. Lamb, Misses L. Liniker, M. Richardson, G. Rodgers, H. Scott, G. F. Thompson, Mrs. Mowbray Thompson.

I searched in vain for a 'Miss B. Byers', and eventually discovered that the initial 'B.' stood for 'Bessie', the name by which she was commonly known to friends and family. In fact her first name was Elizabeth.

Married women presented unique identification challenges. The first of these is illustrated in the picture below, taken from the concert programme for March 1924. In this you will find a violinist listed as Mrs W. E. Alderson.

The Orchestra— Violins : Mr. Alfred M. Wall, Mrs. W. E. Alderson, Mr. James Mark. Mrs. Wilson. Violas : Miss Ethel Page, Miss Rosina Wall. 'Cello : Miss Hetty Page, Miss V. Atkinson. Contra Bass : Mr. S. Beers.

The initials W. E. are in fact those of her husband, Wilfred Ernest Alderson. Her actual forenames were Ida May.

Occasionally, marriages solved some identification conundrums. In the picture below, from the concert programme for May 1922, you will note a contralto listed as Miss E. Rochester.

G. Strachan, H. Wilkinson. Misses E. J. Browne, W. Elliott, A. M. Havelock, Mrs. Lamb, Misses L. Liniker, M. Newton, E. Rochester, G. Rodgers, H. Scott, G. Thompson. Messrs. W.

This lady had caused me some considerable identification problems, until I began studying a contralto called Mrs Gustard, who first appeared in the choir in May 1923, about the time that Miss E. Rochester disappeared from the choir list, as shown below:

son.—Miss E. J. Browne, Mrs. Carter, Mrs. Gustard, Miss A. M. Havelock, Mrs. Lamb, Misses L. Liniker, M. Newton, G. Rodgers, Mrs. Thompson, Miss G. Thompson. Messrs. W. Bean, J. Benson,

Gustard is not a very common surname, and I soon found a marriage of a Robert Sydney Gustard to a Miss Isabella Rochester in April 1923. It then became clear that Isabella was known to friends and family as 'Ella', a familiar form of her name, and that she was the 'Miss E. Rochester' I had been seeking.

For each person studied it was necessary to assemble a detailed family history. This was done using standard genealogical methods, entailing searches of census, parish, birth, marriage, death, probate, telephone and immigration and emigration records. In some cases it was necessary to look overseas for information. The final stage of investigation was undoubtedly the most difficult and yet the most reward-ing; it involved tracing direct descendants or close living relatives, using a variety of resources, such as electoral registers, telephone records and online forums, and then contacting them. In some cases, when the person sought had moved house, the present occupier passed on the letter to the intended recipient. Occasionally the trail went cold.

I have acquired a number of photographs of the choir taken between 1922 and 1927; but they were not annotated, and family contacts were requested to identify their relatives in them. These photographs of the choir, which have been sub-sequently annotated by me, may be seen in Chapter 2.

I acknowledge the help and forbearance of relatives and descendants of past choral and orchestral members who have responded generously to many requests for information and have provided family photographs and other memorabilia. Some of the relatives I have had the pleasure of meeting in person, and others grown to know through prolonged correspondence. I am also grateful for the generous co-operation of many professional institutions, which are acknowledged in the relevant biographies.

I am particularly indebted to my wife Elaine for her selfless support and for carefully reading many drafts of the manuscript.

Chapter 4
Sopranos

Philip Owen

Elsie Atkinson (1896–1918)
Soprano 1916–17

In Memoriam.

ELSIE ATKINSON,
February 27th, 1918

THE CHOIR:

Miss E. Atkinson, Mrs. Bainton, Misses F. Brown, E. Charlton, J. W. Fleming, N. Freeling, ~~E. Pickering~~, G. Strachan—Misses E. J. Browne, ~~C. Forster~~, A. M. Havelock, ~~Mrs. Lamb~~, Misses A. Lawton, L. Liniker, G. Rodgers, H. Scott—Messrs. G. F. Carmichael, W. Carmichael, J. Scott Dickson, J. Harding. J. T. Hebron, R. Peel, ~~G. Prest~~, *Left* W. E. Robinson, Messrs. C. Beetham, ~~J. Charlton~~, E. Crowe, J. O. Richardson, J. Robinson, T. Thompson, C. Wood.

Fig. 24 From the March 1918 concert programme.

ELSIE ATKINSON, the third and youngest child of Matthew Atkinson and Margaret Sisterson, was born in Heworth, County Durham, as were her parents. Her father, who was a grocer and provision merchant, died in 1902, aged forty-four, when Elsie was six. The Sisterson family were herbalists, and Elsie's mother had worked in the family business in Heworth before her marriage. Elsie and her parents lived at 4 Coldwell Street, Heworth. In 1911 Elsie, her siblings and their widowed mother were living at Richmond House, Felling.

Elsie's sister Annie (Nance) became a schoolteacher and in 1911 her brother was a Cambridge undergraduate.

In May 1916, Annie married John Percy Ison, an official for the Government Railway in Sierra Léone who had previously worked for the North Eastern Railway Company. Elsie was a bridesmaid at the wedding, and the groomsman was Hugh Latimer Featherstone.

Elsie joined the Bach Choir for the May concert of 1916. During her time with the choir she sang in two programmes wholly or partly devoted to Bach cantatas, in one performance of the St John Passion and in several concerts of British music. She was scheduled to sing in the March concert of 1918, but tragic events prevented this, as shown above from a copy of the concert programme.

Ethel Frances Bainton, ARCM (1885–1954)
Soprano 1915–18 and in the 1922 London Bach festival concerts
Pianist in the February and November concerts of 1916

ETHEL FRANCES EALES, third child of the Rev. Francis Henry Eales and Elizabeth Dickinson, was born in Woolsingham, Weardale. Her father was an Anglican clergyman who had been curate at Holy Trinity in Washington, County Durham, before moving to Woolsingham, where he taught at the Woolsingham Grammar School. He died in 1904 at Ancroft Vicarage, Northumberland. Ethel's only brother, Francis, was killed in action in France in 1917, serving as a second lieutenant in the Leicestershire Regiment. She had an elder sister, Constance.

Fig. 25 From the 1922 choir photograph.

In 1901 an aspiring young musician, Edgar Leslie Bainton (b.1880), moved to Newcastle to take up the post of professor of pianoforte and composition at the Newcastle Conservatoire of Music. Edgar, whose father was a Methodist minister, had obtained an open scholarship in pianoforte to the Royal College of Music, where he studied under Sir Charles Villiers Stanford and others.

Ethel studied pianoforte under Edgar, becoming an ARCM. Edgar and Ethel's relationship blossomed, and they were married on 31 July 1905. Their first home was 'The Chalet' in Stocksfield-on-Tyne, a village situated between Hexham and Newcastle. They had two daughters: Guendolen (known as Guenda), who was born in 1906 and studied at the Royal College of Art, and Helen, who was born in 1909 and studied at the Royal College of Music.

In 1912 Edgar became principal of the Newcastle Conservatoire. Commuting regularly from their home in the Tyne valley to Newcastle became less convenient, and the family moved to 40 Moorside, Newcastle.

Fig. 26 Edgar and Ethel in the English Lake District, 1919. *Courtesy the Edgar Bainton (UK) Society.*

Details of Edgar Bainton's many compositions and attainments have been published elsewhere and will not be covered here. Bainton was a great friend of William Gillies Whittaker, and even deputized for him, conducting the Newcastle Bach Choir for one season. Ethel made a great contribution to his career. In August 1914 Ethel and Edgar were on a Wagner pilgrimage to the Bayreuth Festival, when war was declared and they were arrested. Ethel was released after about three months, and returned home to find the family home deserted, the children having been taken into temporary care by a relative. Edgar was less fortunate, and spent the entire war in an internment camp at Ruhleben near Berlin. An article in the *Newcastle Daily Journal* of 1916 describes him as 'an unwilling guest of the Huns', reflecting public attitudes of the time. In addition to her domestic duties Ethel took on the administration of the Conservatoire in his absence.

Ethel first sang soprano with the Bach Choir at its inaugural concert in November 1915. In the February 1916 concert of Bach cantatas she also played the Clavier Concerto in D minor, and in the December 1916 concert the Clavier Concerto in F minor, in addition to singing in the choir. A contemporary press report recorded that she played the concerto 'with beauty and fluency'. She sang consistently in the choir until February 1918. She was recruited to sing in the concerts for the London Bach Festival of 1922, however, and her last appearance with the choir was on 25 February that year. During her time with the choir she sang in nine concerts wholly or partly devoted to Bach cantatas, in one performance of the St John Passion and in several concerts of British music.

The Baintons' daughter Helen was a violinist in orchestras accompanying the choir on three occasions. An account of her life will be found in Chapter 10.

In June 1933 Edgar Bainton was appointed director of the Sydney Conservatorium of Music, and he and Ethel travelled to Australia in May 1934. They were joined by Helen and Guenda in August that year. Edgar conducted choral and orchestral classes at the Sydney Conservatorium and founded an Opera School.

In 1935 Ethel and Edgar Bainton were part of a small group of enthusiasts who campaigned for the establishment of a full-time professional orchestra in Sydney. This was brought to fruition in 1936 with the formation of the Sydney Symphony Orchestra, under the auspices of the Australian Broadcasting Commission.

In 1946, having reached the mandatory retirement age, Edgar reluctantly relinquished his post at the Sydney Conservatorium, but did not return permanently to England.

Ethel died on 8 April 1954, aged sixty-eight, and Edgar on 8 September 1956, aged seventy-six.

The author acknowledges the collaboration of Michael Jones of the Edgar Bainton (UK) Society with this biography.

Ailsa Blair (1897–1964)
Soprano: as A. Blair 1919–30; as Mrs Ballantyne 1930–35

AILSA BLAIR, second of four children of Robert Scott S. Blair and Frances Mary Eltringham, was born in Newcastle. Her father, a ships merchant's clerk, was born in Enfield, Middlesex, and her mother in Newcastle. Robert Blair died in 1905 at the age of forty-one, and his wife then supported the family by running their home at 74 Rothbury Terrace, Heaton, as a boarding-house.

It is believed that Ailsa attended Chillingham Road School, Newcastle. She then trained as a schoolteacher and taught at the Jubilee School, City Road, Newcastle.

Ailsa joined the Bach Choir as a soprano for the November concert of 1919. Between then and May 1930 she performed in every concert, under her maiden name. During that period, which was entirely under the conductorship of W. G. Whittaker, she sang in twenty-one programmes wholly or partly devoted to Bach cantatas and three performances each of the St John and St Matthew Passions and the B Minor Mass. She sang in concerts with music by Holst (*The Hymn of Jesus*, the *Ode to Death*, *The Cloud Messenger* and *The Golden Goose*), Vaughan Williams (the Mass in G minor, *Sancta Civitas* and *Flos Campi*) and Bax (*Mater ora Filium* and *This Worldes Joie*). Notably she was in the semi-chorus for the performance of *Sancta Civitas*. She sang in the 1922 London Bach Festival and in the 1924 London and Newcastle performances of Byrd's Great Service (in which she sang in the semi-chorus) and was on the 1927 tour of Germany. She was in the semi-chorus for the November 1927 performance of Rubbra's *La Belle Dame sans Merci* and sang in the May 1929 performance of the Tallis forty-part motet *Spem in alium*.

Fig. 27 From the 1922 choir photograph.

Fig. 28 Family photograph, 1930.

In 1930 Ailsa married Ray Mortimer Ballantyne, an accountant. From December 1930 she sang in the Bach Choir under her married surname of Ballantyne. She sang with them from that date, under the conductorship of Sidney Newman, until April 1935. During this period she sang in one performance of Bach's St Matthew Passion, in several concerts of madrigals and in works by Byrd and Purcell.

Their only child, Shirley, was born in June 1934. For many years the Ballantyne family lived at 8 Thistley Close in the Walkerville area of Newcastle, but they also had a family holiday cottage in the Hexham area. Like Ailsa, their daughter and granddaughter became schoolteachers.

Relatives recall that at one time Ailsa conducted choirs for the Townswomen's Guild and also learned Esperanto, at which she excelled.

Ray died in 1962, aged sixty-one, and Ailsa on 6 July 1964, aged sixty-six.

The author acknowledges the collaboration of Penny Little with this biography.

Mrs C. H. Brackenbury (1901–1985)
Soprano 1926–9

FLORENCE ELIZABETH (ELISE) CUMING, the eldest child of Francis Edward Cuming and Dorothy Celia Knox, was born in Dublin. Her parents were both born in Ireland, her father in Belfast and her mother in County Antrim. Her father attended the Oratory School in Edgbaston, Birmingham, where Cardinal John Henry Newman was principal. He read classics at University College, Oxford, graduating as a BA in 1885. He then trained as a barrister and was admitted to the Inner Temple in 1893. In 1911 the family lived at 'Summercourt', Romford, Essex.

Elise met Charles Hereward Brackenbury, an Oxford undergraduate, and they married in London in 1924. They can be seen together in fig. 96 on p. 174. They moved to Charles's home town of Newcastle and set up home at 12 Manor House Road. Their first child, Rosamund, was born in Newcastle in 1925.

Elise first sang with the Bach Choir as an additional soprano in the March concert of 1926. Charles also joined the choir for that concert, singing as a bass. Elise formally joined the soprano line of the choir for the May concert of 1927, and sang in two more concerts that year, which included the tour of Germany. Her second child, Miles, was born in the summer of 1928 but died that autumn. Elise returned to the choir in December 1928.

Under Whittaker's conductorship, Elise sang in two concerts wholly or partly devoted to Bach cantatas, in two performance of the B Minor Mass and in one performance of the St John Passion. She sang in performances of Holst's *The Golden Goose* and *The Hymn of Jesus*, and took part in the May 1929 performance of Tallis's forty-part motet, *Spem in alium*. Her last concert with the choir was in May 1930.

Their third child, Mark, was born in 1931, and at about this time the family moved to Dublin, where Charles had been appointed to a new post. Soon afterwards, problems arose within their marriage, and they separated. Elise moved with the children to live in London.

In 1937 Elise married a solicitor, Michael Hugh Barrie Gilmour, and they lived

Fig. 29 Family photograph, undated.

Fig. 30 From a 1927 choir photograph.

at 42 Ladbroke Road, London W.11. Their only child, Harriet, was born in 1939. During the Second World War the children were evacuated to the north-east of England and lived with Charles and his new wife.

Michael Gilmour served as a pilot officer in the RAF during the war. He is the subject of a portrait by the artist Robert Lutyens that hangs in the National Portrait Gallery in London. About 1944, he and Elise moved to 55 Strand-on-the-Green, Chiswick, where they lived for the rest of their lives. Michael died in 1982, aged seventy-eight, and Elise in 1985, aged eighty-three.

The author acknowledges the collaboration of Mark Brackenbury with this biography.

Alice Beryl Cresswell (1901–1984)
Soprano 1921–2 and 1927   Soprano soloist 1926 and 1927   Oboe 1927–9

ALICE BERYL CRESSWELL, fifth of six surviving children of John Cresswell and Louisa Dredge, was born in Faversham, Kent. Her father was born in Grant-chester, Cambridgeshire; he was a piano tuner who worked for the Newcastle firm of J. G. Windows before going freelance. Her mother was born in St Pancras, London. The family moved to Newcastle at some time between 1901 and the birth of the final child, Clifford, in 1908.

Beryl, as she was known by friends and colleagues, was known within her family as 'Bet', because her initials were A.B.C. (alpha*bet*). Beryl attended Canning Street School, Newcastle, until the age of fourteen. In addition to singing she played the oboe, the cello and the lute. She studied the oboe under the famous Léon Goossens (who played with the Newcastle Bach Choir on many occasions), subsequently passing on her skills to Roger Lord, who became principal oboist in the London Symphony Orchestra. She and her sister Esther (who was known as 'Et') played the piano in cinemas for silent movies and also broadcast on BBC local radio Newcastle 5NO.

Fig. 31 From the 1922 choir photograph.

Beryl joined the Bach Choir as a soprano in 1921, and sang fairly regularly until 1924. During this time she sang in ten concerts wholly or partly devoted to Bach cantatas and in one performance of the B Minor Mass. She sang in concerts with music by Holst's (the *Ode to Death* and *The Cloud Messenger*) and Vaughan Williams (the Mass in G minor). She sang in the 1922 London Bach Festival and in the 1924 London and Newcastle performances of Byrd's Great Service, in which she sang in the semi-chorus. After this concert she was not involved with the choir again until January 1926, when she was the soprano soloist in a concert of Bach cantatas with co-soloists Annie Lawton and Newcastle Cathedral choristers Stewart Hattle, Ernest Hudspith, W. H. Hobkirk and Arthur Lewis. In March 1926 she played the oboe in a performance of the B Minor Mass. She was the soprano soloist in another concert of Bach cantatas in January 1927, this time with Rosa Burn, Tom Danskin and Arthur Lewis. A report of the concert in the *Yorkshire Post* commented that 'Miss Beryl Cresswell's clear but small soprano voice was somewhat overpowered [where] voice and trumpets vie with one another.' She returned to the soprano choral line for the German tour in the summer of 1927 and for the November concert of that year. She played the oboe in the Bach cantata concert of November 1927, in the April 1928 performance of the St Matthew Passion, and again in the cantata concert of February 1929. Beryl was undoubtedly one of the most

Fig. 32 Family photograph, 1951.

versatile musicians associated with the Bach Choir under Whittaker.

Music featured prominently in the lives of the Cresswell children. Esther was a cellist and Margaret (Meg) a bassoonist. Patti graduated from Armstrong College in mathematics and also obtained an Intermediate Bachelor of Music qualification. She taught music at Newcastle Dame Allen's School and Tynemouth High School. All the sisters were ardent fans of Richard Wagner, and formed a 'secret society for the study of the *Ring*'. Their brother Clifford (known as Max) was also musically gifted, and played the clarinet, saxophone, trombone and trumpet. He performed professionally in 'tea bands' at dance halls throughout the North of England. He was given a signed and dedicated photograph of the jazz legend Louis Armstrong in 1933 for making an emergency repair to the star's trumpet.

In 1940 Beryl married John Mark Maddison, a negative engraver working in wood and horn, but they had no children. Sadly they did not stay together. In later life Beryl developed severe rheumatoid arthritis, which adversely affected her quality of life at a time when treatment options were limited. Despite her problems she maintained a resolute and cheerful disposition and a keen interest in music, literature and the arts. Her motto for life was 'The best is only just good enough.'

Beryl died on 26 April 1984 in Shotley Bridge Hospital, County Durham, aged eighty-three.

The author acknowledges the collaboration of Richard Bird and Susan Barkes with this biography.

Mrs George Danskin (1892–1965)
Soprano 1925–31

ETHEL RYDER, elder of two daughters of
Robert Garthwaite Ryder and Sarah Jane
Bowman, was born in Newcastle upon Tyne.
Her parents were born in Middlesbrough.
Ethel's father was an engine fitter, and family
records indicate that he worked at some stage
for both Armstrong Whitworth and Dorman
Long in that town. In 1901 the family were
living at 52 Pelham Street, Middlesbrough.

In 1911 Ethel was an assistant schoolteacher, boarding with Thomas Wilkinson,
an accountant, and his family in the village
of Trimdon in County Durham. Her parents
remained in Middlesbrough at 52 Pelham
Street.

Fig. 33 From the 1927 choir photograph.

Ethel Ryder married George William Dans-
kin in Newcastle in 1917. Their first son, Erik, was born in 1918, and their second,
Alan, in 1924. Their third child, Margaret, was born in 1934. For many years the
family lived at 24 Lyndhurst Avenue in Jesmond, Newcastle.

Ethel first sang with the Bach Choir as an extra soprano in the March concert of
1924. Her first concert as a full member of the soprano line was the April 1924
performance of Bach's St John Passion. During her years in the choir she sang
in two more performances the St John Passion, in two performances of the St
Matthew Passion (singing the First Maid's part in both) and in two performances
of the B Minor Mass. She sang in eight concerts wholly or partly devoted to Bach
cantatas and in concerts with music by Holst (the *Ode to Death*, *The Golden Goose*
and *The Hymn of Jesus*), Vaughan Williams (*Sancta Civitas* and *Flos Campi*) and
Bax (*Mater ora Filium*). Notably she was in the semi-chorus for the performance
of *Sancta Civitas*. She was in the 1924 London and Newcastle performances of
Byrd's Great Service (in which she sang in the semi-chorus), and was on the 1927
tour of Germany. She sang in the semi-chorus in the November 1927 performance
of Rubbra's *La Belle Dame sans Merci*, and was in the May 1929 performance of
Tallis's forty-part motet, *Spem in alium*.

Fig. 34 Ethel and George Danskin. Family photograph, 1917.

After Whittaker left Newcastle, Ethel sang under Sidney Newman until her final concert with the choir in 1931.

George died suddenly on 17 July 1945 at the Newcastle General Hospital, aged fifty-six. Ethel died on 18 December in 1965 at the family home, 24 Lyndhurst Avenue, Jesmond, aged seventy-three.

The author acknowledges the collaboration of Judith Steen and Gill Clancy with this biography.

Jane Walton Fleming, ATCL (1885–1969)
Soprano 1915–31 and frequent soloist

JANE WALTON FLEMING was born in Hexham, Northumberland, the only surviving child of William George Peter Fleming and Mary Riddell. William Fleming was a saddler whose business was at Hallstile Bank, Hexham.

Jane was a second cousin of William Gillies Whitaker, by descent from children of Henry Walton and Jane Taylor. Henry Walton was the schoolmaster at the Hexham Subscription School and also actuary for the Tindale Ward Savings Bank.

Jane's mother died in childbirth in 1886; the child did not survive. Her father remarried in 1906, but there were no children from this marriage. In 1891 Jane and her father were living at 124 Gilesgate Road, Hexham; by 1911 they were at 3 Croft Terrace with William's new wife.

Jane studied the violin, receiving her first lesson from her father at the age of three, and later studied under Thomas Walton Hardy. In 1915 she obtained the ATCL for solo singing.

She first sang with the Bach Choir at its in-augural concert in 1915 and in every other concert under W. G. Whittaker until 1930, and then in two seasons under Sidney Newman. In 1916 she sang in a quintet in a programme of British music. During her years with the choir, under the conductorship of Whittaker, she sang in twenty-nine concerts wholly or partly devoted to

Fig. 35 From the 1922 choir photograph.

Bach cantatas, singing solos in four of them. In the December concert of 1920, which featured Parts 1 to 3 of Bach's Christmas Oratorio, she not only sang in the chorus but showed her musical versatility by singing the tenor recitatives, owing to the sudden indisposition of the tenor soloist, Tom Purvis. In the January concert of 1921, which featured Parts 4 to 6 of the Christmas Oratorio, she sang the echo part in the soprano aria 'Ah, my saviour', in which Mrs George Dodds was the solo lead. Jane sang in the chorus and took minor solo roles in four performances of the St John Passion and in three performances each of the St Matthew Passion and the B Minor Mass.

She sang in concerts with works by Holst (*The Hymn of Jesus*, the *Ode to Death*, *The Cloud Messenger* and *The Golden Goose*), Vaughan Williams (the Mass in G minor, *Sancta Civitas* and *Flos Campi*) and Bax (*Mater ora Filium* and *This Worldes Joie*). Notably she sang in a quartet for the Vaughan Williams Mass in G minor and in the semi-chorus for *Sancta Civitas*. She was in the 1922 London Bach Festival and the 1924 London and Newcastle performances of Byrd's Great Service (in which she sang in the semi-chorus), and was on the 1927 tour of Germany. She was in a semi-chorus in the November 1927 performance of Rubbra's *La Belle Dame sans Merci* and sang in the May 1929 performance of Tallis forty-part motet, *Spem in alium*. Her last concert with the choir was in February 1931. She was a loyal servant of the Bach Choir, performing in nearly ninety concerts over a period of sixteen years.

Jane became engaged to a young man who sadly perished in the First World War. She vowed thereafter that she would never marry.

Fig. 36 Jane in her Hexham garden. Family photograph, undated.

She taught many generations of children in the Hexham district to play the violin, played in various orchestras and gave recitals. She trained choirs at Wall, Lowgate and Branch End and also the Newcastle YMCA choir. She was associated with the Tynedale Musical Festival for more than fifty years as a competitor, teacher and administrator. The Jane Fleming Cup and Certificate are presented annually at the festival in her memory.

After the death of her father in 1940, Jane ran the family saddlery business until 1954, in addition to her many musical commitments. For much of her life she lived at the former family home, 3 Croft Terrace, Hexham. She died at Hexham General Hospital on 13 July 1969, aged eighty-four. She was unmarried. She is fondly remembered by a god-daughter, Jane Pegram, who was named after her.

The author acknowledges the collaboration of Jane Pegram with this biography.

Maud Eleanor Freeling (1888–1973)
Soprano 1915–18

MAUD ELEANOR FREELING, sixth child of Henry Vrielinck and Jane Ann Hetherington, was born in Newcastle upon Tyne. Her father was born in Brussels, and her mother, the daughter of a gunsmith, in Sunderland, County Durham. The couple seem to have assumed an Anglicized version of Henry's surname after their marriage in Newcastle in 1875. Their first child was born there in 1876 but died in infancy. The second and third children were born in London and the fourth and fifth in Essex. In the late 1880s the family moved back to Newcastle, where Henry worked as a foreman engine fitter at Armstrong's ordnance factory on the banks of the river Tyne in the suburb of Elswick. After living in Elswick for some years the family moved to 24 Grosvenor Drive, Whitley Bay, and finally settled at 23 Roseworth Avenue, Gosforth.

Maud joined the Bach Choir as a soprano for the choir's inaugural concert in November 1915. During her years in the choir she sang in six concerts wholly or partly devoted to Bach cantatas and in one performance of the St John Passion. She was also in three concerts of British music. In all of the concert programmes she was incorrectly entered as 'N. Freeling'.

Maud trained as a nurse. In 1922 she was living at 18 Bouverie Square, Folkestone, and on 19 August that year sailed from London to Yokohama on the *Fushima Maru*, bound for Shanghai.

Her brother William Charles Freeling (b. 1883) was a schoolmaster. He served with the Durham Light Infantry from 1914 but was captured by the enemy in April 1915 and interned until the cessation of hostilities in 1918. William married in 1920, had one daughter and eventually moved to the coastal town of Allonby, in Cumberland, where he spent most of his professional life. He and his family lived at De Grey House, where they were later joined by his parents, Henry and Jane Freeling. Henry died there in 1936 and his wife in 1947. Eventually Maud also moved to De Grey House, some time before 1957.

Maud continued to live in Allonby for many years, but eventually moved into retirement accommodation at The Towers in the nearby coastal resort of Silloth, where she died on 28 April 1973, aged eighty-five. She was unmarried.

Amy Gent (1904–1993)
Soprano 1924–8

AMY GENT, youngest of four children of Charles Frederick Gent and Margaret Forster Rochester, was born in Newcastle upon Tyne. Both her parents had been born there: her father in Walker and her mother in Jesmond. Amy's father was a newsagent and tobacconist operating from the family home at 72 Addison Road, Heaton. Her mother was the daughter of a solicitor's clerk.

Amy attended North View School, Heaton, and won a Newcastle Education Committee junior scholarship for secondary school admission in 1916. She became a schoolteacher.

Amy's elder brother, Charles, attended Armstrong College of Durham University in Newcastle, and graduated as a bachelor of science in chemistry. He served in the Durham Light Infantry in the First World War, attaining the rank of captain. He later taught at the Queen Elizabeth Grammar School in Hexham.

Amy joined the soprano line of the Bach Choir in April 1924. During her years in the choir she sang in six concerts wholly or partly devoted to Bach cantatas, in two performances each of the St John and St Matthew Passions and in one performance of the B Minor Mass. She sang in the 1924 London and Newcastle performances of Byrd's Great Service and was on the 1927 tour of Germany. In addition she sang in performances of Holst's *Ode to Death*, Vaughan Williams's *Sancta Civitas* and Bax's *This Worldes Joie*. Her last concert with the choir was in April 1928.

Amy lived for many years at 37 Longridge Avenue in Heaton.

She died on 15 December 1993 at the Freeman Hospital, Newcastle, aged eighty-nine. She was unmarried.

Ivy Holmes (1895–1972)
Soprano 1921–3

IVY HOLMES, youngest of five children of William Wilkie Holmes and Martha Parkin, was born in Barton St Mary, near Gloucester. Her father was born in North Shields, Northumberland, and her mother near Victoria Bridge (a railway viaduct crossing the River Wear), close to the town of Washington, County Durham. Her parents married in 1879, and by 1881 they were living at 3 Leopold Street, Gateshead. William was recorded as a 'picture frame maker'. Their first two children were born in Gateshead in 1882 and 1883. By 1891 they had moved to Bury, Lancashire, and were living at 8 Hanson Street. At this time William's occupation was 'manager of an evening newspaper'. Their third child was born in that year. By 1892 the family had moved to Gloucester, and it was there that their fourth child, Lilian, was born. Ivy was born in 1895, when they were living at 4 Providence Villas, Hanman Road, Barton St Mary, a suburb of Gloucester. William was then recorded as a 'superintendent journalist'. In September and October of 1900 the *Gloucester Journal* reported that Mr William Wilkie Holmes, of 52 Conduit Street, Gloucester, was a supporter of the successful local Liberal candidate in the general election. According to the 1901 census the family was still living at 52 Conduit Street and William's occupation was recorded as 'supt. publish books'. In 1911 the Holmes family had returned to the North East and were living at 65 Bewick Road, Gateshead. William was now an 'auctioneer and valuer'.

Ivy and her mother (who was listed in concert programmes as 'Mrs W. W. Holmes') were members of the soprano line in the Newcastle and Gateshead Choral Union in the 1915/16 season. Her mother continued to sing soprano with the Choral Union (there listed as 'Mrs M. Holmes'), together with her daughter Margaret Florence Holmes (a schoolteacher), until about 1939.

Ivy's elder brother, George Wilkie Holmes, a millwright, served in the Royal Navy from November 1916 until the end of hostilities in 1918. He was assigned to land operations and at one stage during 1917 served with the Royal Flying Corps. Ivy's other brother, William Wilfrid Holmes, served in the Merchant Navy during the first World War, but his service record has not survived.

Ivy joined the soprano line of the Bach Choir in February 1921. During her years in the choir she sang in five concerts wholly or partly devoted to Bach cantatas and in one performance of Holst's *The Hymn of Jesus*. She sang in the December 1921 Christmas concert (which mostly featured carols by British composers), in the January 1922 concert of Tudor and British music, and in the 1922 London Bach Festival. Her final concert with the choir was in February 1923.

On 1 April 1924 she married John Todd (then a milkman) at the Wesleyan Methodist Chapel, High West Street, Gateshead. At the time of their marriage Ivy was living at 21 Patterdale Terrace, Gateshead, and John at Chester House, Kenmir Street, Gateshead. Their only child, Peter William, was born, some five months later, on 25 August. John Todd eventually became a catering manager, and they lived for many years at 3 Ashtrees Gardens, Gateshead.

Ivy died at Ashtrees Gardens on 1 November 1972, aged seventy-seven. John predeceased her but the date of his death has not been ascertained.

The author acknowledges the collaboration of David Holmes with this biography.

The Ireland Sisters

HENRY CLARKE THOMAS IRELAND and Clara Farminer were both born on Portsea Island, Hampshire, where they married in 1889. Henry was a marine surveyor employed by Lloyds of London, whose work necessitated the family's moving around the United Kingdom. They had six daughters and a son, who were born between 1889 and 1907. Two girls were born in Hampshire, one in London, one in Glasgow and two in Middlesbrough; finally a son was born in Barry, Glamorganshire. The family settled in Newcastle between 1907 and 1911 and for many years lived at 32 Wingrove Road in the Fenham district. Five of their daughters sang with the Newcastle Bach Choir; all of them are seen in this family photograph.

Fig. 37 The Ireland family. *Standing*: Daisy, Ruby, Winnie, May. *Seated*: Clara, Clara Jun., Henry. *On ground*: Lily, Thomas. Family photograph, *c*. 1913.

The author acknowledges the collaboration of Ann Hartley, William Ireland, Jennifer Large and Judith Parkin with these biographies.

Daisy Elizabeth Ireland (1889–1974)
Soprano: as D. Ireland 1919–22; as Mrs D. Southern 1922–31

Fig. 38 From the 1922 choir photograph.

Fig. 39 From a family photograph, 1930s.

DAISY ELIZABETH IRELAND, eldest of the seven children of Henry Clarke Thomas Ireland and Clara Farminer, was born on Portsea Island, Hampshire.

Daisy, who worked as a secretary, first sang with the Bach Choir in December 1919 and then in every concert until May 1922. During this phase in the choir she was entered in concert programmes as 'D. Ireland'.

On 20 April 1922 Daisy married William Southern at Bath Lane Congregational Church, Newcastle. William worked as a clerk for the Newcastle and Gateshead Gas Company and later became district lighting engineer.

Daisy missed the concerts between November 1922 and March 1923, and then returned as 'Mrs Southern', singing until March 1924. On 9 November 1924 their only child, Mary, was born in Newcastle. In November 1927, having just missed the tour of Germany, Daisy rejoined the choir, now appearing on concert programmes as 'D. Southern'.

During her years in the choir she sang, solely under the conductorship of W. G. Whittaker, in eleven concerts wholly or partly devoted to Bach cantatas, in two performances of the St Matthew Passion, and in one performance of the B Minor

Mass. She sang in concerts with music by Holst (*The Hymn of Jesus*, *The Cloud Messenger* and *The Golden Goose*), Vaughan Williams (the Mass in G minor, *Sancta Civitas* and *Flos Campi*) and Bax (*Mater ora Filium*). She took part in the 1922 London Bach Festival was in the May 1929 performance of the Tallis forty-part motet *Spem in alium*. Her membership of the choir overlapped that of her sister Ruby between December 1919 and November 1922 and again between November 1923 and February 1924. She sang with her sister Clara in the November 1927 concert. Her last concert with the choir was in December 1929.

For many years Daisy and William lived at 36 Redewater Road in the Fenham district of Newcastle and attended St Paul's Congregational Church on Two Ball Lonnen.

Daisy died in Newcastle in 1974, aged eighty-five. William then went to live with his daughter in Heddon-on-the-Wall, where he died in 1975, aged eighty-two.

May Ireland (1895–1996)
Soprano 1925–7

Fig. 40 From the 1927 choir photo-graph.

Fig. 41 From a family photograph, 1930s.

MAY IRELAND, second of the seven children of Henry Clarke Thomas Ireland and Clara Farminer, was born on Portsea Island, Hampshire. She trained as a schoolteacher and became headmistress of Cowgate Junior School in the West End of Newcastle.

She married Robert Marshall Ireland, a marine engineer and no relation, in

Newcastle in 1922. Their first child, William, was born in Newcastle in 1925. At first they lived at her family home at 32 Wingrove Road in Fenham, Newcastle, but eventually they moved to 39 Kingsway, Fenham.

May joined the soprano line of the Bach Choir for the December concert of 1925. During her years with the choir she sang in three concerts wholly or partly devoted to Bach cantatas, in one performance each of the B Minor Mass and the St John Passion, and in one performance of Holst's *Ode to Death*. She was on the 1927 tour of Germany. Her membership of the choir overlapped that of her sister Clara between December 1925 and June 1927. The German tour was her last appearance with the choir.

Her second child, Patricia, was born in Newcastle in 1929. Sadly her marriage was cut short by the untimely death of Robert on 21 February 1931 in Walton, Liverpool, at the age of thirty-four.

After her husband's death May returned to teaching and taught for many years at Atkinson Road School in the Elswick area of Newcastle. In later years her sister Lily came to live with her. May did not remarry, and in her final years she moved to Hampshire to be near her son. She died in 1996, aged 100.

Ruby Ireland (1898–1989)
Soprano 1919–25

RUBY IRELAND, third of seven children of Henry Clarke Thomas Ireland and Clara Farminer, was born in Wandsworth, London.

Ruby, who was a clerical worker, joined the soprano line of the Bach Choir in November 1919. During her years in the choir she sang in thirteen programmes wholly or partly devoted to Bach cantatas, in one performance of the St John Passion, in two performances of the St Matthew Passion (singing a minor role in one and in the semi-chorus for the other), and in one performance of the B Minor Mass. She sang in concerts with music by Holst (*The Hymn of Jesus*, the *Ode to Death* and *The Cloud Messenger*) and Vaughan Williams (the Mass in G minor). She was in the 1922 London Bach Festival and in the 1924 London and Newcastle performances of Byrd's Great Service (in which she sang in the semi-chorus). Her membership of the choir overlapped that of her sister Daisy from December 1919 to May 1922 and again between May 1923 and February 1924. Her membership also overlapped that of her sister Clara between April 1924 and May 1925. Ruby's last appearance with the choir was in May 1925, in a programme of music by Bach and Taverner, in which she sang in the semi-chorus.

Fig. 42 From the 1922 choir photograph.

Fig. 43 From a family photograph, 1930s.

On 13 August 1927 Ruby married John Abdale Broumley, a commercial clerk from Redcar, at the Bath Lane Congregational Church, Newcastle. They adopted a daughter and lived for many years at 181 Redcar Lane, Redcar.

Eventually John became labour manager of the engineering firm Dorman Long (which built the Sydney Harbour Bridge) at their South Bank Works in Middles-brough.

John died in Redcar in 1978, aged eighty-one. Ruby also died in Redcar, in 1989, aged ninety-one.

Clara Mary Ireland (1903–1992)
Ripieno soprano 1920 and Soprano 1924–7

CLARA MARY IRELAND, fifth of seven children of Henry Clarke Thomas Ireland and Clara Farminer, was born in Middlesbrough. She attended Rutherford College, Newcastle, and trained as a schoolteacher.

Clara she first sang with the Newcastle Bach Choir in February 1920 as part of the ripieno soprano chorus in a performance of the St Matthew Passion. Her elder sisters Daisy and Ruby also sang in that concert.

She was not formally enrolled into the soprano line of the Bach Choir until May 1924. During her years in the choir she sang in four concerts wholly or partly

Fig. 44 From the 1927 choir photograph. Fig. 45 Family wedding photograph, 1928.

devoted to Bach cantatas, in two performances of the St John Passion, and in one performance each of the St Matthew Passion (in 1920) and the B Minor Mass. She also appeared in one performance of Holst's *Ode to Death*. She sang in the 1924 London and Newcastle performances of Byrd's Great Service and was on the 1927 tour of Germany. Her last concert with the choir was in November 1927. Her membership of the choir overlapped that of her sister Ruby from April 1924 to May 1925, that of her sister May from December 1925 to November 1927, and that of her sister Daisy (by then Mrs Southern) in the concert of 26 November 1927.

Clara married Henry Hepple Thubrun (known as Harry) in Newcastle in 1928. Harry was working for the Employers' Liability Insurance Corporation in Newcastle. In 1929 Harry transferred to London and became a tutor in insurance at the Metropolitan College. He also joined the staff of the *Post Magazine* (the principal magazine of the UK insurance industry). Their first daughter, Sheila, was born in St Albans in 1930, in which year Harry became editor of the *Post Magazine*. Later, the family moved to the Mill Hill area of outer London and in 1936 were living at 13 Glendor Gardens. Their daughter Jennifer was born that year.

Fig. 46 Family photograph, 1980s.

Harry was the longest-serving editor of the *Post Magazine*, steering it through a traumatic period in the Second World War when its central London premises and printing equipment were destroyed by enemy action on two separate occasions in 1941. Under his stewardship the magazine flourished.

After the war the family moved to 6 Lawrence Court, Newcombe Park, Mill Hill, where they lived until Harry's death. In 1963 Clara was Mayor of Hendon.

Harry retired in 1971 and died in 1979, aged seventy-three. Clara died in Bury St Edmunds in 1992, aged eighty-eight.

Lily Elsie Ireland (1905–1993)
Soprano 1920

Fig. 47 From a family photograph, 1930s.　Fig. 48 Family photograph, 1928.

LILY ELSIE IRELAND, sixth of seven children of Henry Clarke Thomas Ireland and Clara Farminer, was born in Newcastle. She became a schoolteacher. Her main hobby was as a leader in the Girl Guide movement.

Lily sang soprano in the Bach Choir in only two concerts, in 1920, with her sisters Ruby and Daisy. The concert on 11 November consisted of Bach cantatas and that on 20 November of works by Balfour Gardiner and others. It is not known why she did not sing with the choir again.

For some year Lily lived with her sister May. She was single for most of her life but married William R. Parkin, the widower of her late sister Winnie, in 1963 at the age of fifty-eight.

She died in Bromsgrove, Worcestershire in 1993, aged eighty-seven.

Fig. 48 Family photograph, 1930s: Lily in the back row, second left.

Isobel Mary Fullarton James (1900–1992)
Soprano 1927–39

ISOBEL MARY FULLARTON JAMES, one of the twin daughters of Captain Sir Fullarton James, Bt (sixth Baronet James of Dublin) and Helen Mary Hichens, was born in Rhayader, Radnorshire.

Her father had a distinguished background and professional career. He was born in Dublin, eighth of ten children of Francis Edward James, a wealthy East India merchant who was one of the sons of John Kingston James (High Sheriff and first Baronet James of Dublin). He was educated privately and admitted to Magdalene

Fig. 49 From a 1938 choir photograph: Isobel (right) with Greta Large (née Capel).

College, Cambridge, in 1883. He became a BA in 1886 and an MA in 1919. He was called to the Bar at Gray's Inn in 1891. He served with the 3rd Battalion the Royal Scots Fusiliers and attained the rank of captain. He then entered the police force, and from 1897 to 1900 was chief constable of Radnorshire.

Isobel's mother, who was born in the civil parish of St George, Hanover Square, London, was the eldest of three children of John Knill Jope Hichens, a wealthy stockbroker who was a partner in the firm of Hichens, Harrison & Co. of 21 Threadneedle Street, London. Helen Hichens and Fullarton James married near her parents' home in Sunninghill, Windsor, in 1899.

In 1900, Fullarton was appointed chief constable of Northumberland, and the family moved to the Northumberland market town of Morpeth, where they lived at The Farm House, Stobhill, a suburb of Morpeth. They integrated well into the local community. Fullarton was a keen amateur archaeologist and a member and later president of the Berwickshire Naturalists' Club. He was also a keen golfer and donated the Captain Fullarton James Cup to the Morpeth Golf Club for an annual competition.

Helen James was a talented soprano soloist. In 1902 she sang in a charity concert at the Morpeth Mechanics' Institute, a concert in which the Page sisters both played. In 1903 she sang at a concert for the Northern Police Orphanage in Blyth. In 1906 she was the soprano soloist in a performance of Mendelssohn's *St Paul* at St James's Church, Morpeth, the first of many concerts in which she sang there. Helen and Fullarton were strong supporters of the Wansbeck Musical Festival, and donated the Fullarton James Challenge Cup, awarded annually for choral singing.

Helen James was also actively involved with the Morpeth Voluntary Aid Detachment (VAD) of the British Red Cross, becoming commandant in 1911. Isobel and her sister Penelope also served with the detachment.

Isobel and Penelope were educated at home by a governess and appear to have inherited their mother's musical interests. In 1917 they 'performed brilliantly on the piano' at a concert for the Red Cross held at Mitford Hall, in which their mother also sang. Helen James and her daughter Penelope also played the violin in the Newcastle Symphony Orchestra, Helen from 1923 to 1936 and Penelope from 1923 to 1930.

In the late 1920s Isobel broadcast on Newcastle Radio 5NO concerts as a solo pianist and accompanist. These broadcasts were relayed to the London and Daventry transmitters. In these performances she appeared under the name Isobel Fullerton-James.

Isobel first sang with the Bach Choir as a soprano in the April 1925 performance of Bach's St Matthew Passion; it was not until April 1927, however, that she began to sing as a regular member of the soprano line. She then sang with the choir until 1939. She is entered in programmes as either I. James or I. M. James. Her membership of the choir spanned the conductorships of W. G. Whittaker and his successor, Sidney Newman.

Under Whittaker's conductorship, Isobel sang in three concerts wholly or partly devoted to Bach cantatas, in two performances of the St John Passion, in one performance of the St Matthew Passion and in one performance of the B Minor Mass. In addition she sang in concerts with music by Holst (*The Golden Goose* and *The Hymn of Jesus*), Vaughan Williams (*Sancta Civitas* and *Flos Campi*) and Bax (*Mater ora Filium*). She was not on the 1927 tour of Germany or in the Newcastle concert in preparation for that tour. She was in the May 1929 performance of the Tallis forty-part motet *Spem in alium*.

Isobel's sister, Penelope, died suddenly on 26 August 1931 at Beech Grove, Sunninghill, Windsor (the home of her mother's parents) of endocarditis. She is buried near by at St Michael and All Angels' Church, Sunninghill.

From December 1930 Isobel sang in the choir under Sidney Newman. During his years as conductor she sang in several performances of the St Matthew Passion (which had become almost an annual event), in performances of Bach's Christmas Oratorio, Bach cantatas and Brahms's *A German Requiem*; and in several concerts of madrigals. Choir membership lists were suspended from April 1939 until after the war, but Isobel did not appear in later programmes.

In 1935 her father, Fullarton James, announced his retirement. In July that year the executive committee of the Wansbeck Musical Festival presented Fullarton and his wife with a watercolour painting of the river Wansbeck by the artist Eyre Walker and Isobel with a valuable book. In August that year the Morpeth VAD presented Helen and Isobel with gifts to mark their contributions to its work, and both responded with gracious speeches.

In 1942, after the death his brother Edward, the fifth Baronet, Fullarton inherited the title, becoming sixth Baronet James of Dublin. Helen James died in 1954 and Fullarton James in 1955; both are buried with their daughter Penelope at Sunninghill.

In later years Isobel adopted the surname Fullarton-James, and was entered as such in telephone directories. She moved to the village of Shaldon, which is not far from Teignmouth, Devon. From 1956 she lived at Brookvale Close, Shaldon, with her mother's unmarried sister Edith Annie Hichens, who was a retired college matron. Edith died in 1966, and from that date until about 1980 Isobel lived at The Chantry, Fore Street, Shaldon.

Isobel died in Newton Abbott in 1992, aged ninety-two. She was unmarried.

Mrs A. L. Lewis (1891–1980)
Additional soprano 1922, 1923, 1924, 1926 and 1929

GLADYS AMELIA SALTER, eldest of five children of Edward Henry Langford Salter and Sarah Jane Rogers, was born in Neath, Glamorganshire. Her father was born in Llanidloes, Montgomeryshire. Her paternal grandparents, Edward and Hannah Salter, were both schoolteachers, but Edward abandoned teaching and became a celebrated landscape painter and illustrator. Many of his paintings are held in the National Collection. Her father (greatly influenced by his father, Edward, who was the organist at St Idloe's Church) trained as a piano and organ tuner and became a musical instrument dealer and organ manufacturer. He was also organist at the parish church of St Catwg in the nearby village of Cadoxton. Her mother was born in Knighton, Radnorshire.

The Salter family lived at a variety of addresses, but at the time of Gladys's marriage were at 123 Windsor Road, Neath. Gladys was brought up in an English-speaking household.

Gladys Amelia Salter and Arthur Llewellyn Lewis were married on 13 June 1909 at the parish church in Neath. Amelia and Arthur set up home at 1 Osborne Street, Neath, where their first child, Enid, was born in 1910. Their second child, Henry John, was born on 30 September 1912 in Hammersmith, London.

Gladys and her family moved to the North East of England about 1920 and for many years lived at 19 Onslow Gardens, Low Fell, Gateshead. Arthur eventually became a housing manager.

Not much is known about their musical careers before they settled in Gateshead, but it would appear that they were established soloists. Arthur became a chorister at St Nicholas's Cathedral, Newcastle.

Although Gladys never formally joined the Bach Choir, she was co-opted to sing as an additional soprano in nine concerts between 1922 and 1929. In the concert programmes she appears as 'Mrs Lewis' or 'Mrs A. Ll. Lewis'. In May 1922 she sang in the Bach motet *Jesu, Priceless Treasure*; in February 1923 in Cantata No. 191 (the original versions of the Gloria and Cum Sancto Spiritu of the B Minor Mass); in February 1929 in Cantata No. 31, *The heavens laugh* (*Der Himmel lacht! Die Erde jubilieret*); in May 1929 in Tallis's forty-part motet *Spem in alium*; and in November 1929 in the semi-chorus for Holst's *The Hymn of Jesus*. She sang in performances of the B Minor Mass in 1923, 1926 and 1929. Gladys and Arthur also performed solos and duets together on local radio Newcastle 5NO in the 1920s.

Their daughter Enid died in tragic circumstances in North Ormsby Hospital Middlesbrough on 24 July 1945, aged thirty-four. Their son Henry John became an insurance manager and lived in Rottingdean, Sussex.

Arthur died on 3 August 1969 at Bensham Hospital, Gateshead, aged eighty-two, and Gladys on 23 December 1980 at the Queen Elizabeth Hospital, Gateshead, aged eighty-nine.

The author acknowledges the collaboration of Michael Salter with this biography.

Elsie Kathleen Pickering, LRAM, ARCM (1894–1978)
Soprano 1915–27

ELSIE KATHLEEN PICKERING, third child of Henry Pickering and Harriet Ann Cook, was born in Newcastle upon Tyne, as were her parents. Henry Pickering, who had worked for some years as a mercantile clerk, eventually became a coal fitter – a person who acted as an intermediate agent between coal owners and shipowners to ensure that a ship had a cargo of coal to carry. Henry's father, Thomas, was a cheesemonger who worked in Newcastle, and his brother William became a steamship owner. Elsie's brother Thomas was an accountant.

A local newspaper report from July 1914 records Elsie passing the ISM (Incorporated Society of Musicians) examination for pianoforte, playing at Grade 5, with honours. She continued to study music, and obtained the LRAM in 1916 and the ARCM in 1920, both for piano teaching. She attended the Conservatoire of Music in Newcastle, studying under Edgar Bainton, from 1919 to 1921. She also obtained a Cambridge Senior Local Certificate for teaching.

Elsie was a soprano in the Newcastle and Gateshead Choral Union in the 1915/16 season. She joined the soprano line of the Bach Choir at its inaugural concert in November 1915. She was absent from the choir from April 1924 until November 1925, thus missing the 1924 London and Newcastle performances of Byrd's Great Service. During her years in the choir she sang in twenty-six concerts wholly or partly devoted to Bach cantatas, in one performance each of the St John and St Matthew Passions, and in two performances of the B Minor Mass. She sang in concerts with music by Holst (*The Hymn of Jesus*, the *Ode to Death* and *The Cloud Messenger*), Vaughan Williams (the Mass in G minor) and Bax (*Mater ora Filium* and *This Worldes Joie*). She sang in the 1922 London Bach Festival and was on the 1927 tour of Germany. Her final concert with the choir was in June 1927.

She made a broadcast on local radio Newcastle 5NO in January 1925, accompanying the soprano Grace Angus.

Elsie worked throughout her professional life as a pianoforte teacher and lived with her sister Laura at 11 Queens Road, Monkseaton.

Neither Elsie nor her siblings married. Her brother Thomas died in 1956 and her sister Laura in 1963. Elsie died on 16 December 1978, at a rest home in Whitley Bay, aged eighty-four.

The author acknowledges the collaboration of John Smithson with this biography.

Anne Purvis Shiell Plews (1894–1974)
Soprano 1917–21

ANNE PURVIS SHIELL PLEWS, the only daughter of George Walton Plews and his second wife, Jane Steuart Shiell, was born in Newcastle. Her father, who was a foreman engineering draughtsman at an ordnance factory, was born in Gateshead and her mother in County Kildare, Ireland. Her father was widowed in 1890 and had three children from that marriage. He remarried in 1893, at Old Jedward Parish Church, Roxburghshire, near where his new wife's father ran a farm. For many years the family lived at 99 Clumber Street in the Elswick suburb of Newcastle.

Anne joined the soprano line of the Bach Choir in February 1917. She next sang in May 1918. During her years in the choir she sang in nine concerts wholly or partly devoted to Bach cantatas and in one performance of the St Matthew Passion. She sang in one performance of Holst's *The Hymn of Jesus* and in a concert of British music. Her last appearance with the choir was in May 1921.

In the summer of 1921 she married Lowther Lee Hamilton, a bank manager and son of a police constable from Egremont in Cumberland. They moved to Devon and in 1923 were living at The Cottage, Cullompton, near Tiverton. While living there they had three children, Joan (b.1923), James (b.1924) and George (b.1928). From 1933 to about 1945 they lived at 10 Shepherd's Hill, Haslemere, Surrey. They returned to Devon and lived for many years in Rowdens Ipplepen, near Newton Abbott. There is a record of Anne and Lowther sailing as tourists to Montreal on 15 July 1959.

Lowther died in 1971, aged seventy-seven, and Anne in 1974, aged seventy-nine.

Margery Isabel Pratt (1902–1991)
Soprano 1921–6

MARGERY ISABEL PRATT, second of three children of George Pratt and Isabella Keen Kennedy, was born in Newcastle upon Tyne. Her father was born in Tweedmouth, Northumberland and her mother in Newcastle. Her father was a schoolmaster at a Newcastle council school, and her mother had also been a pupil teacher before her marriage. Their first child, Hilda, was born in 1898, and their son, Thomas Forster, in 1906. At first the family lived at 9 Croydon Road in the Arthur's Hill area of Newcastle, but by 1911 they were living at 21 Warkworth Avenue, Whitley Bay. Eventually the family moved to 77 Queens Road, Monkseaton.

Margery first joined the soprano line of the Bach Choir in November 1920. During her years in the choir she sang in fourteen concerts wholly or partly devoted to Bach cantatas, in one performance each of the St John and St Matthew Passions, and in two performances of the B Minor Mass. She sang in concerts with music by Holst (*The Hymn of Jesus*, the *Ode to Death* and *The Cloud Messenger*), Vaughan Williams (the Mass in G minor) and Bax (*Mater ora Filium*). She sang in the May 1924 Newcastle performance of Byrd's Great Service, but did not sing in the London and second Newcastle performances of the work. Her final concert with the choir was in February 1926.

Margery married Arnold Gladstone Porter, a clerk, in Tynemouth in 1930, and they lived first at 2 Seacombe Avenue, Cullercoates. They had two daughters, Jean (b.1935) and Ann (b.1938). At some stage Arnold became a surveyor.

Margery's brother, Thomas, was an industrial chemist who worked for Imperial Chemical Industries (ICI). He married, had two sons and spent many years living and working in Argentina.

Isabella Keen Pratt died on 12 November 1942. After her death Margery and Arnold moved into the family home in Queen's Road, Monkseaton, where they lived until about 1949. They then moved to 85 Holywell Avenue, Whitley Bay, where they lived for some years. In about 1963 they acquired the West Flat in Foxton Hall in the Northumberland coastal village of Alnmouth. The hall had originally belonged to the Duke of Northumberland, but was bequeathed as a clubhouse for the local golf club (of which the Duke was president) in 1929.

Arnold died in 1973, aged seventy-one. The flat in Foxton Hall was still in use by the family until about 1980, when Margery moved to a flat in nearby Manor House, Northumberland Road, Alnmouth. In the final years of her life, Margery moved into sheltered accommodation at Ravenslaw House, Alnwick, not far from her daughter Ann. She died on 26 June 1991 at Grovewood House, South Charlton (near Alnwick), aged eighty-nine.

Florence Railton (1896–1975)
Soprano 1918–39

FLORENCE RAILTON, sixth of eight children of Richard Railton and Mary Elizabeth Watson, was born in Newcastle upon Tyne. Her father was born in Newcastle and her mother in Bermondsey, London. Her father, who started his working life as a boiler smith, worked for a number of years as a railway clerk, but returned to engineering, as a machinist in electrical engineering. The family lived in Newcastle, first in Elswick and finally at 88 Wharton Street, Heaton. Florence's brother James became an electrical engineer.

She attended Rutherford College Girls Secondary School from 1910 to 1914 and Armstrong (later King's) College Newcastle from 1916 to 1918. She obtained the Durham matriculation (in six subjects) and in 1918 a teacher's certificate with distinction in advanced education and also a music teacher's certificate. She taught at a number of schools in Newcastle. From 1918 to 1926 she was an assistant mistress at St Peter's School. From 1927 to 1930 she was a second mistress, first at Welbeck Road School and later at the Victoria Jubilee School.

From 1930 to 1934 Florence was at Shieldfield School, first as acting headmistress and then as headmistress. From 1934 to 1941 she was headmistress at Whickham View Junior and Infants School, where she founded the first parent–

teacher Association in Newcastle. From 1941 to 1948 she was headmistress at Cowgate Infants School, where she introduced education through the media of music and art. She was at one time vice-president of the Newcastle Head Teachers' Association.

Fig. 50 From the 1922 choir photograph.

Fig. 51 From the 1927 choir photograph.

Florence joined the soprano line of the Bach Choir in April 1919. In the first few years of her choir membership the concert programme editors seem to have experienced difficulties spelling her surname, for she appears in some programmes as 'F. Railston' and in others as 'F. Railstone'. During her time in the choir under the conductorship of W. G. Whittaker she sang in twenty-two concerts wholly or partly devoted to Bach cantatas and in three performances each of the St John and St Matthew Passions and the B Minor Mass. She sang in concerts with music by Holst (*The Hymn of Jesus*, the *Ode to Death*, *The Cloud Messenger* and *The Golden Goose*), Vaughan Williams (the Mass in G minor, *Sancta Civitas* and *Flos campi*) and Bax (*Mater ora Filium* and *This Worldes Joie*). Notably she sang in the semi-chorus for *Sancta Civitas*. She was in the 1922 London Bach Festival and the 1924 London and Newcastle performances of Byrd's Great Service (in which she sang in the semi-chorus), and was on the 1927 tour of Germany. She sang in the semi-chorus in the November 1927 performance of Rubbra's *La Belle Dame sans Merci* and was in the May 1929 performance of the Tallis forty-part motet *Spem in alium*.

After the departure of Whittaker, Florence sang under Sidney Newman. The last concert programme record of her singing is in 1939. It is possible that she sang beyond this time, but choir lists were suspended during the Second World War and she is not listed in post-war programmes.

In 1948 she became senior lecturer in education at the Kenton Lodge Teacher Training College, Newcastle. She lectured widely, specializing in religious education, and she published many articles, courses of lessons and (jointly) a book entitled *Nil Desperandum*: *Sixteen ten-minute talks to girls and boys*.

Although she left the Bach Choir in 1939, Florence continued her support as a patron.

Florence retired from Kenton Lodge Teacher Training College in 1960. In a tribute to her, the college principal, Miss M. A. Robson, noted that her main weakness had been 'overwork'.

She died at the Royal Victoria Infirmary Newcastle on 17 January 1975, aged seventy-eight. She was unmarried.

Marjorie Florence Sherborne, LRAM, ARCM (1904–1994)
Soprano 1920 and 1924–30

MARJORIE FLORENCE SHERBORNE, second of two children of George Herbert Sherborne and Rose Ada Lee, was born in Newcastle upon Tyne. Her father was born in Sunderland and her mother in York. The Lee family had moved from York to Newcastle, where her father worked as a printer and compositor, and they lived at 151 Dilston Road in the Arthur's Hill area. The Sherborne family were very musical. Marjorie's paternal grandfather was a music seller and her paternal grandmother and aunt were music teachers. Her father ran Sherborne's Music and Piano Tuners from the family home at 245 Westgate Road, Newcastle.

In 1914 Marjorie was awarded the Lower Grade examination for Piano of the Associated Board of the Royal Schools of Music.

Marjorie went to Rutherford College for Girls, Newcastle, and first sang soprano with the Bach Choir in the 1920 performance of Bach's St Matthew Passion as part of the ripieno chorus, which was provided by the school.

She attended Armstrong College of the University of Durham in Newcastle and in 1920 obtained the University of Durham matriculation certificate by passing six relevant subjects in pure science. However, she had inherited the family's musical talents, and instead of reading for a degree transferred to the Newcastle Conservatoire of Music, where she studied from 1921 to 1923, obtaining the LRAM for pianoforte teaching. In 1921 she entered the Newcastle Musical

Tournament and won second prize for advanced elocution. She became a private teacher of music from 1922.

Marjorie first sang with the Bach Choir as an additional soprano in the February concert of 1923. She was also an additional soprano in March 1923 and March 1924. She formally joined the soprano line in April 1924 for a performance of Bach's St John Passion. During her time in the choir she performed in eight concerts wholly or partly devoted to Bach cantatas, in three performances of the St John Passion and in two performance each of the St Matthew Passion and the B Minor Mass. In addition she sang in concerts of music by Holst (the *Ode to Death* and *The Golden Goose*), Vaughan Williams (*Sancta Civitas* and *Flos Campi*) and Bax (*This Worldes Joie*). She was in the 1924 London and second Newcastle performances of Byrd's Great Service and was on the 1927 tour of Germany. She sang in the May 1929 performance of the Tallis forty-part motet *Spem in alium*. After the departure of Whittaker she sang for two seasons under Sidney Newman. Her last concert with the choir was in February 1931.

In 1929 she played piano accompaniment for the baritone William Talbot in a broadcast on Newcastle radio station 5NO. In 1933 she broadcast on the radio in a satirical sketch with the Newcastle Radio Players, and in 1937 took part in a charity concert in Rothbury in aid of the local Coquetdale Cottage Hospital.

Her father died in 1931, but the family music business continued from Westgate Road until the 1950s. By about 1958 Marjorie was living at 17 Hawthorne Gardens in the Kenton area of Newcastle and running the Sherborne School of Music and Drama from 4 High Swinburne Place in Gosforth.

She died in Newcastle in 1994, aged ninety. She was unmarried.

Gladys Strachan, ARCM (1892–1974)
Soprano 1915–24

GLADYS STRACHAN, the elder of two daughters of John Henry Strachan and Louisa Burnip, was born in Brentford, Middlesex. Her father, the son of a river pilot who was born in Howdon-on-Tyne near Newcastle, became a civil engineer and surveyor. Her mother, also born in Newcastle, was the daughter of a master draper. John Henry Strachan went to London in 1883, initially to join his brother George R. Strachan (also an engineer and surveyor). He eventually rose to become borough surveyor, first in Brentford and finally in Heston and Isleworth. In 1887 he was a co-founder of the Brentford Rowing Club, chairman of the Brentford Football Club in 1892, and a member of the Boston Park Cricket Club. At the time of Gladys's birth in September 1892, the family lived in Windmill Road, Brentford. Gladys was four and her mother was pregnant with their second child when her father died suddenly of pneumonia at the age of thirty-one. Louisa moved her daughters north to Newcastle to be close to her family, and supported them by running a lodging-house at 15 Otterburn Terrace, Jesmond.

Fig. 52 From the 1922 choir photograph.

Gladys studied at the Newcastle Conservatoire of Music and obtained an external ARCM in piano teaching in 1913. She played in a performance of Schumann's Piano Quartet in E flat at the Pupils' Concert of the Conservatoire in 1914. Later that year she performed in a concert for the Free Church League for Women's Suffrage in Newcastle. She was a member of the soprano line of the Newcastle and Gateshead Choral Union in the 1913/14 and 1915/16 seasons.

She first sang soprano with the Bach Choir at its inaugural concert in November 1915. During her years with the choir she sang in twenty-one concerts wholly or partly devoted to Bach cantatas, and in one performance each of the St John and St Matthew Passions and the B Minor Mass. It is interesting to note that her sister, Hope, also sang soprano in the February 1917 concert, the only time that she sang with the choir. Gladys also sang in concerts of music by Holst (*The Hymn of Jesus* and *Ode to Death*) and Bax (*Mater ora Filium*). She sang in the 1922 London Bach Festival. She missed the performance of the Vaughan Williams Mass in G minor in May 1923 and most of the 1924 season, including a performance of Bach's St John Passion, and all the London and Newcastle performances of Byrd's Great Service. Although she had effectively left the choir in December 1923 she returned for one final concert in December 1924.

Gladys married Gordon Page Evans in Hampstead, London, in 1928. She was then thirty-six and Gordon twenty-four. For many years they lived at 7 Gerald Road, SW1, in a basement flat, and she ran a charity shop near by. Her mother came to live with them and died at their home in 1952.

Gordon had a long association with the United Nations Association (UNA). He was a founder member of the Westminster branch of UNA, eventually becoming its chairman. He worked with his friend and colleague Leslie Aldous for the journal *New World* and helped to found the UN Parliamentary Group. He became president of the Eastern Regional Council of UNA and was made an OBE in 1969.

Fig. 53 Gladys and Gordon at his investiture as an OBE. Family photograph, 1969.

Gladys died on 28 June 1973 at the Westminster Hospital, London, aged eighty-two. After her death Gordon moved to 138*b* Ebury Street, which ran parallel to Gerald Road and was only a short walk from their old home. Gerald died in 1991, aged eighty-seven. They had no children.

The author acknowledges the collaboration of Roger and Alan Turner-Smith with this biography.

Chapter 5
Contraltos

Philip Owen

Mary Winifred Bainbridge (1897–1965)
Contralto 1923–31

MARY WINIFRED ELLIOTT, only child of Thomas Elliott and Elizabeth Jane Harrison (formerly Rowell), was born in Gateshead, County Durham. Her parents were also born in County Durham, her father in Hunstanworth and her mother in Darlington. Thomas Elliott worked as a railway guard. Her mother had two sons from an earlier marriage which was ended by her first husband's death. The Elliott family lived in Northbourne Street, Gateshead, first at No. 67 and later at No. 79. Thomas Elliott died on 10 February 1923.

On 6 September 1923 Mary married Harold Pearson Bainbridge at Durham Road Primitive Methodist Church, Gateshead. Harold was employed as a silica moulder in a foundry; his job was to bond silica gel with ceramic powder to make moulds for hot metal castings. At the time of her marriage Mary was living in Brislee Avenue, Tynemouth and Harold in Station Road, Wallsend. Mary was a friend of fellow Bach Choir contralto Margaret Fitzpatrick Richardson, who was living with her at Brislee Avenue her at the time of her marriage in 1926.

Mary joined the contralto line of the Bach Choir in November 1923. She was usually entered in the concert programmes as 'Mrs Bainbridge', which would have made identifying her almost impossible, as the surname is very common in the North East of England. However it was fortunate that she was entered in the 1927 and 1928 programmes with her initials 'M. W.' appended. During her years in the choir under the conductorship of W. G. Whittaker, she sang in eleven concerts wholly or partly devoted to Bach cantatas, in two performances each of the St John Passion and the B Minor Mass, and in three performances of the St Matthew Passion. She sang in concerts with music by Holst (*The Cloud Messenger*, the *Ode to Death*, *The Golden Goose* and *The Hymn of Jesus*), Vaughan Williams (the Mass in G minor, *Sancta Civitas* and *Flos Campi*) and Bax (*This Worldes Joie* and *Mater ora Filium*). She sang in the 1924 London and Newcastle performances of Byrd's Great Service (in which she sang in the semi-chorus), was on the 1927 tour of Germany, and sang in the May 1929 performance of the Tallis forty-part motet

Spem in alium. She sang under Sidney Newman in the 1930 and 1931 seasons. Her final concert with the choir was in February 1931.

Mary and Harold lived for some years at 4 Brislee Avenue, Tynemouth. During a brief period in 1923 Robert and Mary Peel were neighbours at No. 5. Harold eventually became a foreman. Mary died on 25 April 1965 at her home in Tynemouth, aged sixty-eight. Harold died in 1973 in Tynemouth, aged eighty-two. They had no children.

Ethel Jane Browne (1873–1963)
Contralto: as E. J. Browne, 1917–25; as Mrs Jas. White, 1926

Fig. 54 From the 1922 choir photo-graph.

Fig. 55 From the 1925 choir photo-graph.

ETHEL JANE BROWNE, third of five children of Charles Redhead Browne and Mary Jane Thompson (or Thomson) was born in Newcastle upon Tyne. Her father was an elementary school teacher. The family lived for many years in the Elswick area of Newcastle. In 1911 they were living at 15 Alnwick Avenue, Whitley Bay.

In 1891 Ethel was a pupil teacher, and by 1914 was teaching at the Whitley and Monkseaton South council elementary school.

Ethel first sang soprano with the Bach Choir in the March concert of 1917. Between 1917 and November 1926 she sang in seventeen concerts wholly or partly dedicated to Bach cantatas, in two performances each of the St John and St Matthew Passions and in one performance of the B Minor Mass. She sang in concerts of music by Balfour Gardiner, Holst (*The Hymn of Jesus*, the *Ode to Death* and *The Cloud Messenger*), Vaughan Williams (the Mass in G minor) and Bax (*Mater ora Filium*). She sang in the 1922 London Bach Festival and in the 1924 London and Newcastle performances of Byrd's Great Service.

In 1925, at the age of fifty-two, she married James White, who was a 72-year-old widower and a retired railway clerk.

After their marriage she continued in the choir under her married name ('Mrs Jas. White'). She sang in three concerts between February and May 1926, which included one further performance of the B Minor Mass and a concert including Bax's *This Worldes Joie*. She did not sing with the choir again.

Ethel and James lived at Groote Schuur, 32 The Gardens, Monkseaton, until James's death in 1939, aged eighty-five. Ethel did not remarry, and after James's death moved to 22 Whitley Road, Whitley Bay.

Surviving relatives recall spending holidays with their aunt Ethel at her chalet in Ovington/Ovingham (a small village situated between Newcastle and Hexham), where they played in the woods near the River Tyne. They remember the chalet's green corrugated roof and outside lavatory, and their aunt's culinary eccentricities.

Ethel died on 6 April 1963 at the Thomas Taylor Homes, Stannington, near Morpeth, aged ninety. She had no children.

The author acknowledges the collaboration of Christopher Browne and Margaret Giovanni with this biography.

Elizabeth Agnes Byers (1900–1976)
Contralto: as B. Byers, 1922–30; as Mrs Pendlington, 1930–32

ELIZABETH AGNES (BESSIE) BYERS, second of three children of John Young Byers and Anna Kate Robinson, was born in Newcastle, as were her parents. Her grandfathers were both grocers in the Elswick area of Newcastle.

In the early 1890s John Byers worked as a clerk in a Newcastle insurance office. John and Anna were married in 1893. They emigrated from England to Canada on 10 April 1896, sailing on the *Scotsman* from Liverpool to Halifax, Nova Scotia. The passenger list described John as a farmer and gave their final destination as Wetaskiwin, Alberta, a small town some forty miles south of Edmonton. Their first child, Bernard Robinson Byers, was born in Wetaskiwin in 1899. In 1900, Anna visited the United Kingdom, where Bessie was born, and then returned to Canada with her new baby. The 1901 Canadian census for Wetaskiwin village listed John, Anna, Bernard and Elizabeth (as 'Bessie'), recording that they were all

Canadian nationals. John was described in the census as a bookkeeper. Their third child, Lillian Vinycomb Byers, was born in Wetaskiwin in 1903.

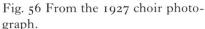

Fig. 56 From the 1927 choir photo-graph.

Fig. 57 Family photograph, undated.

Problems seem to have arisen in their marriage. The UK census of 1911 recorded Anna, Bernard, Elizabeth (Bessie) and Lillian living with Anna's father, Joseph Robinson, at 84 Brighton Grove, Newcastle. Anna was described as a housekeeper. For 27 September 1911 there is a record of John Young Byers obtaining naturalization in the USA.

Bernard Robinson Byers became a bank clerk. He was called up for military service in September 1916, at which time he was still living with his mother and sisters at 84 Brighton Grove. On 15 March 1917 he was mobilized and transferred to the 7th Battalion the East Yorkshire Regiment. On 23 October he was posted to Étaples, France, where he served as a private. While in action he received gunshot wounds to his arms and chest, and died of these injuries at the military hospital in Rouen on 21 January 1918. He was eighteen years old. Contemporary War Office records show that his father was living in a flat at 195 Broadway, New York City.

The first reference to Bessie's singing activities is on 15 and 16 March 1922, as a contralto soloist in concerts for the Armstrong College Choral Society, conducted by W. G. Whittaker. She sang alongside Norah Allison, Robert Peel and Arthur Llewellyn Lewis in a mixed programme that included Bach's Magificat in D.

Bessie joined the Bach Choir as a contralto for the November concert of 1922, and sang thereafter in every performance until December 1930, appearing in concert programmes as 'B. Byers'. During this period she sang in twelve concerts wholly or partly dedicated to Bach cantatas, in three performances of the St John Passion, and in two performances each of the St Matthew Passion (in one of which she took a minor solo role) and the B Minor Mass. In addition she was in concerts of music by Holst (the *Ode to Death*, *The Cloud Messenger* and *The Golden Goose*), Vaughan Williams (*Sancta Civitas* and *Flos Campi*), and Bax (*Mater ora Filium* and *This Worldes Joie*). Notably she sang in the semi-chorus for *Sancta Civitas*. She was in the 1924 London and Newcastle performances of Byrd's Great Service, in which she sang in the semi-chorus, and was on the 1927 tour of Germany. She sang in the semi-chorus in the November 1927 performance of Rubbra's *La Belle Dame sans Merci*. She was a member of a quartet in the May 1928 performance of a mass by Sir George Henschel, and was in the May 1929 performance of the Tallis forty-part motet *Spem in alium*.

During the mid to late 1920s she broadcast under the name Bessie Byers on local Newcastle Radio 5NO as a soloist and in duets with the singer Mollie Seaton.

In 1930 Bessie married Cyril Atkinson Pendlington, youngest of four children of John Atkinson Pendlington, an engineer who founded the the Tyneside Electrical Supply Company, later the British Electrical and Manufacturing Company (BEMCO). He also invented the modern way in which cricket test matches are scored. Bessie and Cyril set up home at 34 Otterburn Avenue, Gosforth. The 1939 *Ward's Directory* listed Cyril as an electrical engineer.

Bessie continued to sing with the Bach Choir in the 1930 and 1931 seasons under Sidney Newman, and was entered in the programmes as Mrs Pendlington. She did not sing with the choir after this date.

Bessie and Cyril lived at 34 Otterburn Avenue until 1959, when they moved to 29 Belle Vue Avenue, Gosforth, where they lived until Cyril's death in 1971 at the age of seventy-six. Bessie then moved to 7 St Just Place, Newcastle, where she lived until her death in 1976, aged seventy-five. They had no children.

The author acknowledges the collaboration of Robert Pendlington with this biography.

Mary Ann Carter (1889–1947)
Contralto: as Mrs Carter, 1915, 1923, 1924–June 1927;
as Mrs Robson Alder, December 1928 to February 1933

MARY ANN SIVEWRIGHT, fourth of five children of Robert Sivewright and Isabella Doig Fairweather, was born in Newcastle upon Tyne. Both her parents were born in Scotland, her father in Dundee and her mother in Arbroath. Her father was a riveter at a shipyard. Their first two children were born in Dundee in

1876 and 1884, and while in Dundee they lived at 8 Graham Place. In about 1885 the family moved to Newcastle and lived at first at 53 Park Road, Elswick, Robert having been promoted to foreman riveter at a Tyneside shipyard. Mary was born in 1886 and her younger sister in 1890. By 1891 they were living at 6 Ashfield Terrace East, Elswick, where they were still living in 1911.

Mary became a schoolteacher. In March 1915 she married Ralph Herbert Carter in Newcastle. Ralph initially worked for his father, Charles Carter, who was a bootmaker and dealer of 94 Brighton Grove in the Newcastle suburb of Fenham. Ralph eventually became an engineer. Mary and Ralph went to live at School House in the small hamlet of Dalton, near Ponteland to the north-west of Newcastle.

She first sang as a contralto with the Bach Choir at its inaugural concert in November 1915. Personal circumstances were to prevent from her singing again with the choir for some years. Dalton was a community with poor transport links at a time when few people had cars, and Mary was still teaching at the local school. Her marriage to Ralph was brief: he died on 2 April 1918, aged thirty-two. The marriage was childless.

Mary's next appearance with the choir was in the May 1923 concert, singing in Vaughan Williams's Mass in G minor and some Byrd motets. From May 1924 she performed more regularly with the choir until June 1927. During this period she sang in five concerts wholly or partly devoted to Bach cantatas and in one performance each of the St John and St Matthew Passions and the B Minor Mass. In addition she sang in concerts with music by Holst (the *Ode to Death*) and Bax (*This Worldes Joie*). She sang in the 1924 London and Newcastle performances of Byrd's Great Service (in which she sang in the semi-chorus), and was on the 1927 tour of Germany.

On 19 July 1927 Mary married Robson Alder, a farmer from the nearby village of Milbourne, in the John Knox Presbyterian Church, Westmorland Road, Newcastle. Robson had a child from a previous marriage that had ended in divorce. Mary went to live with him at East Farm, Milbourne.

She missed the remainder of the 1927 series of concerts, but returned to the choir for the concert in December 1928, from which date she was entered in concert programmes as 'Mrs Robson Alder'. During this final phase in the choir she sang in two concerts wholly or partly devoted to Bach cantatas and in one performance each of the B Minor Mass and the St John Passion. She sang in concerts of music by Holst (*The Golden Goose* and *The Hymn of Jesus*), Vaughan Williams (*Flos Campi*), Tallis (the forty-part motet *Spem in alium*) and Bax (*Mater ora Filium*), and in several concerts of madrigals. After the departure of

W. G. Whittaker she sang under Sidney Newman. Her final concert with the choir was in February 1933.

Mary and Robson lived at East Farm until Mary's death at the Royal Victoria Infirmary, Newcastle, on 24 September 1957, aged seventy-one. Robson moved to 22 Northumberland Avenue, Gosforth, and died in a nursing home at 72 Marine Avenue, Whitley Bay on 3 June 1962, aged eighty-three. They had no children.

Catherine Isabella Forster (1895–1958)
Contralto 1924–8 and 1934–c.1939

CATHERINE ISABELLA (KATE) FORSTER, eldest of the four surviving children of Alfred Llewellyn Forster and Isabella Lishman, was born in Newcastle upon Tyne. Her father was born in Llanelly, Carmarthenshire, and her mother in Horsley-on-Tyne, Northumberland. Both parents had Northumbrian roots. Alfred's father, John Reay Forster, was born in Wallsend, Northumberland, and had briefly moved the family to Carmarthenshire in the early 1860s in the course of his work as a civil engineer. By 1871 the family had returned to Tyneside and were living at 5 Alexander Terrace, Newcastle.

Alfred Llewellyn Forster had previously been married to Jemima Elliott, the daughter of George Elliott, a farm bailiff. They had four children between 1883 and 1891, but Jemima died in 1893, aged thirty-three. Alfred then married Isabella Lishman in 1894. Like his father, John Reay Forster, Alfred was a civil engineer.

At the time of the 1901 census, Kate and her father, Alfred, were boarding at 3 Hall Bank, Buxton, Derbyshire, and the rest of the family were living at 5 Haldane Terrace in the Newcastle suburb of Jesmond. It is reasonable to assume that in 1901 Alfred was working on a civil engineering project in the Buxton area and had temporarily taken Catherine with him.

In 1911 the Forster family were united under one roof and living at 'Tynewood' in the village of Wylam-upon-Tyne. Alfred was working as a civil engineer for the Newcastle and Gateshead Water Company. In about 1923 the Forsters moved to 23 Brandling Park, Jesmond, Newcastle. Alfred died suddenly on 14 June 1924, aged sixty-two.

Kate first sang as a contralto with the Bach Choir in May 1924. Under the conductorship of W. G. Whittaker she sang in five concerts wholly or partly devoted to Bach cantatas, in one performance each of the St John Passion and the B Minor Mass, and in two performances of the St Matthew Passion. She sang in concerts with music by Holst (the *Ode to Death* and *The Golden Goose*), Vaughan Williams (the Mass in G minor, *Sancta Civitas* and *Flos Campi*) and Bax (*This Worldes Joie* and *Mater ora Filium*). She sang in the May 1924 Newcastle performance of Byrd's Great Service, but did not sing in the London and second Newcastle performances of that work that were given in November. She was on the 1927 tour of Germany. Her last concert under Whittaker was in December 1928. Kate was missing from the choir from that date until about 1934, when she rejoined under the conductorship of Sidney Newman. From then on she was the choir's honorary subscription secretary in addition to singing in the contralto line. Under Newman her most notable concerts were performances of Bach's Christmas Oratorio and St Matthew Passion and Brahms's *A German Requiem*. The final programme reference to her was in February 1939 in a concert of Bach cantatas.

For many Kate lived with her mother and younger siblings Dorothy and Lawrence in the family home at 23 Brandling Park. Close neighbours were the orchestral musicians Ethel and Hetty Page at No. 20 and Constance Leathart at No. 21.

Kate's mother died at the family home on 16 April 1953, aged eighty-three. Kate was still living at Brandling Park in 1955, but at some time after this date she moved to Four Walls, Lead Lane in the village of Horsley, the village where her mother had been born.

Kate died on 12 October 1958 at the Hexham General Hospital, aged sixty-three. She was unmarried.

Charlotte Evelyn Foster (1896–1952)
Contralto 1915–22

CHARLOTTE EVELYN FOSTER, only child of Thomas Dukesel Foster and Emma Armstrong, was born in Small Heath, Birmingham. Her father was born in Darlington, County Durham, and her mother in Penrith, Cumberland. In 1891 Thomas Foster, who was a schoolmaster was living at 26 Brougham Street, Penrith, a boarding-house run by Mrs Elizabeth Armstrong. Also living at the address was the landlady's daughter Emma, whom Thomas married in 1894. Charlotte was born in Birmingham in 1896, but by 1891 Charlotte and her parents were living at 27 High Street, Brough, a small town between Penrith and Barnard Castle. By 1911 the family had moved to the Northumberland mining community of Killingworth, near Newcastle, where Thomas was headmaster at the local council school. They lived at 'Greencroft', Killingworth Station.

Charlotte joined the contralto line of the Bach Choir for the inaugural concert in November 1915 and sang in every concert until November 1920. During this period in the choir she sang in thirteen concerts wholly or partly dedicated to Bach cantatas, in one performance each of the St John and St Matthew Passions, and in several programmes of British music.

On 18 September 1921 Charlotte, who was living at 4 Oakhurst Terrace, Benton, married a farmer, Thomas Henry Ainsley, at the Gateshead Register Office. At the time of their marriage Henry was living at 283 Whitehall Road, Gateshead. Henry's father, Robert Ainsley, farmed at Hill Head Farm, Burradon, Northumberland, not very far from Charlotte's parents' home in Killingworth.

Charlotte returned to the Bach choir for the January concert of 1922 and was also in the concerts for the London Bach Festival of 22–25 February that year. These were the last concerts in which she sang with the choir.

She and Thomas eventually moved to live at Wet Furrows Farm, North Skelton, near Saltburn. Their first child, Henry Dukesel, was born on 5 February 1925 and their daughter Elizabeth in 1929.

Charlotte, who had been in poor health for some years, died of a stroke in Hemlington Hospital, Stokesley, on 24 July 1952, aged fifty-six. Thomas died at the family home on 13 May 1963, aged seventy-four.

Alice Michaelina Havelock (1882–1968)
Contralto 1915–30

Fig. 58 From the 1922 choir photograph.

ALICE MICHAELINA HAVELOCK, youngest of the four children of Michael Havelock and Elizabeth Burn Bell, was born in Newcastle upon Tyne, as were her parents. Her father was a consulting marine engineer. At first the family lived in the Newcastle suburb of Elswick, but by 1891 they had moved to Jesmond.

Alice had one sister and two brothers. Her sister, Mary Elizabeth, married William Marchbank, a wealthy coal exporter. Her brother William John went into the shipping business and eventually became a director of the Moor Line. Her brother, Sir Thomas Henry Havelock, FRS, was a brilliant scientist who became professor of mathematics at

King's College, Newcastle, of Durham University (now the University of New-castle). The University's Havelock Hall of Residence is named after him.

Fig. 59 Alice extreme right. Family photograph, undated.

Alice sang contralto with the Newcastle and Gateshead Choral Union between 1911 and 1916. She joined the contralto line of the Bach Choir for the inaugural concert of November 1915. During her years in the choir she sang in thirty concerts wholly or partly devoted to Bach cantatas, in three performances each of the St John and St Matthew Passions, and in three performance of the B Minor Mass. She sang in concerts with works by Holst (*The Hymn of Jesus*, the *Ode to Death*, *The Cloud Messenger* and *The Golden Goose*), Vaughan Williams (the Mass in G minor and *Sancta Civitas*) and Bax (*Mater ora Filium*). Notably she sang in the semi-chorus for *Sancta Civitas*. She was in the London Bach Festival of 1922 and in the London and Newcastle performances of Byrd's Great Service, in which she sang in the semi-chorus, and was on the 1927 tour of Germany. She sang in the semi-chorus for the November 1927 performance of Rubbra's *La Belle Dame sans Merci*. She did not sing in the May 1929 performance of the Tallis forty-part motet *Spem in alium*. Her final performance with the choir, in May 1930, was also the last concert conducted by Whittaker. Her singing career with the choir had comprised eighty-four concerts.

Fig. 60 Sir Thomas Henry Havelock, FRS. *Courtesy the Royal Society.*

Alice lived with her brothers William and Thomas at 8 Westfield Drive, Gosforth. In a biographical memoir of Sir Thomas Henry Havelock published by the Royal Society in 1971, it is recorded that he owed much to the 'housekeeping and car driving' of his younger sister, Alice Michaelina.

Her brother William died in 1956, aged eighty-two. Thomas died on 1 August 1968, aged ninety-one; and Alice died only a few weeks later on 22 September at their home in Westfield Drive, aged eighty-five. She was unmarried.

The author acknowledges the collaboration of Judith Barter and Michael Marchbank with this biography.

Maud Lamb (1883–1969)
Contralto 1915–24

MAUD SIMPSON NICHOLSON, the natural daughter of Jane Elizabeth Nicholson, was born at 4 Beaconsfield Street in the Arthur's Hill area of Newcastle upon Tyne on 21 June 1883. Jane Nicholson was the daughter of John Nicholson, a licensed victualler who ran a public house in Gallowgate, Newcastle. Maud was taken into care by Thomas and Mary Jane Easten, formerly Wilson. In 1891 Maud was living with the Eastens at 29 Callerton Place in the Elswick area of Newcastle. Thomas Easten, who was born in Newcastle, worked as a mechanical engineer. His wife was born in the Northumberland fishing village of North Sunderland, near Seahouses. Thomas and Jane Easten had six children of their own. Maud was informally adopted by the Easten family, for in the 1901 census she is recorded as 'Maud Easten'. Formal adoption was not introduced in England and Wales until the passing of the Adoption of Children Act in 1926.

Not much is known about Maud's early life. On 3 June 1907 she married George Lamb, the son of James Lamb, a wine merchant's cashier, at the Arthur's Hill Presbyterian Church, Newcastle. She was married under the name of Maud Easten. Her adoptive parents were still living at 29 Callerton Place at the time of the marriage. George Easten died suddenly in 1908, aged sixty.

In 1911 Maud and George Lamb were living at 50 Salisbury Gardens in the Jesmond area of Newcastle, close to Jesmond Dene. George was working as a ship-owner's clerk.

Maud joined the contralto line of the Bach Choir for its inaugural concert in November 1915. During her years in the choir she sang in twenty-one concerts wholly or partly dedicated to Bach cantatas, in two performances of the St John Passion and in one performance each of the St Matthew Passion and the B Minor Mass. She sang in concerts with music by Holst (*The Hymn of Jesus*, the *Ode to Death* and *The Cloud Messenger*), Vaughan Williams (the Mass in G minor) and Bax (*Mater ora Filium*). She sang in the 1922 London Bach Festival and the 1924 London and Newcastle performances of Byrd's Great Service. Her last concert with the choir was in December 1924.

In the 1930s Maud and George moved to 28 Jesmond Dene Road, not far from their original home. George died there on 24 August 1941, aged sixty. At the time of his death he was described as a shipowner. Maud died on 1 January 1969 at the Preston Hospital, North Shields, aged eighty-five. They had no children.

Lillian Liniker (1895–1958)
Contralto: as Lillian Liniker 1915–25; as Mrs Pougher 1926–58

LILLIAN LINIKER, the elder of two children of John Edwin Liniker and Eliza-beth Smith, was born in Newcastle upon Tyne. Her father was born in Kingston upon Hull and her mother in Greatham, County Durham. Her father was clerk and cashier to the county court judge in Newcastle. The family lived at 93 Croydon Road in the Arthur's Hill district of Newcastle.

Lilian joined the contralto line of the Bach Choir at its inaugural concert in November 1915, singing until 1925 under her maiden name.

In 1925 she married George Alexander Pougher, the son of George Henry Pougher, who ran a confectionary business in Westgate, Haltwhistle. Her husband was a schoolmaster who at one time taught at the Monkseaton West county primary school. He was called up for military duties on 19 June 1917, serving with the Royal Naval Air Service at its shore-based accounting department (HMS

President II) in Chatham, London, with the rank of AC2. He was admitted to Chatham Hospital on 20 February 1918 and invalided out of the service on 10 September the same year.

From the date of her marriage Lillian was entered in Bach Choir concert programmes as Mrs Pougher. During her years in the choir under the conductorship of W. G. Whittaker, she sang in twenty-seven concerts wholly or partly devoted to Bach cantatas, in four performances of the St John Passion and in three performances each of the St Matthew Passion and the B Minor Mass. She sang in concerts with music by Holst (*The Hymn of Jesus*, the *Ode to Death*, *The Cloud Messenger* and *The Golden Goose*), Vaughan Williams (the Mass in G minor, *Sancta Civitas* and *Flos Campi*), and Bax (*Mater ora Filium*). She sang in the London Bach Festival of 1922 and the 1924 Newcastle and London performances of Byrd's Great Service (in which she sang in the semi-chorus), and was on the 1927 tour of Germany. She took part in the May 1929 performance of the Tallis forty-part motet *Spem in alium*. Under Whittaker she sang in eighty-eight concerts.

For many years Lillian and George lived at 32 Studley Gardens, Whitley Bay. George was a patron of the Newcastle Bach Choir.

After the departure of Whittaker in 1930 Lillian continued to sing in the choir under three subsequent conductors, singing for the last time in March 1958, shortly before her death. Her association with the choir spanned forty-three years. She died of breast cancer at the Victoria Jubilee Infirmary, North Shields, on 10 August 1958, aged sixty-three. George died in a Newcastle nursing home on 8 January 1980, aged eighty-six. They had no children.

Margaret Fitzpatrick Richardson (1897–1992)
Contralto: as Miss M. F. Richardson from 1924–January 1927;
as Mrs M. F. Flintoff from February 1927–1930

MARGARET FITZPATRICK RICHARDSON, fifth of six children of Edward Joseph Richardson and Margaret Shea, was born in Gateshead, County Durham. Her father, who worked as a railway clerk, was born in Sunderland and her mother in the Walker area of Newcastle. For the brief eight-year period of their marriage they lived at 50 Sidney Grove in the Bensham area of Gateshead.

Margaret Richardson (Shea) died, at the age of forty-four, early in 1903, shortly after the birth of their daughter Annie. Edward remarried in 1906, this time to Isabella Dickman, who was born in Newcastle. They had one child, a boy, born in 1907. In 1911 the family were living at 45 Fern Dene Road, Gateshead. Edward Richardson died in 1918, aged fifty-seven.

Margaret became a schoolteacher. She first joined the contralto line of the Bach Choir in May 1924 but was incorrectly entered in the programme notes as 'F. M. Richardson'. This was the first of a series of performances of Byrd's Great Service given that year in Newcastle and London. In all these concerts she sang in the semi-chorus.

On 29 December 1926 she married Francis Robert Flintoff, a schoolmaster from Gateshead who had served in France with the 16th Northumberland Fusiliers during the First World War and been wounded in action in 1916. The marriage took place at the Chapel of Our Lady and St Oswin, Front Street, Tynemouth. One of the bridesmaids was Gladys May Rodgers, a fellow member of the contralto line in the Bach Choir. At the time of her marriage Margaret was living at 4 Brislee Avenue, Tynemouth, which was the home of Mary Winifred Bainbridge, a fellow member of the contralto line of the Bach Choir.

Margaret continued singing with the Bach Choir after her marriage. In the concert programme for 22 January 1927, the first concert after her marriage, she was entered under her maiden name, presumably because the programme had gone to press before the wedding. Thereafter in concert programmes she was entered either as 'Mrs Flintoff' or 'Mrs M. F. Flintoff'.

During her years in the choir under Whittaker's conductorship she sang in seven concerts wholly or partly dedicated to Bach cantatas, in two performances of the St John Passion, in one performance of the St Matthew Passion (missing the April 1925 performance of that work) and in two performances of the B Minor Mass. She sang in concerts with music by Holst (the *Ode to Death*, *The Golden Goose* and *The Hymn of Jesus*), Vaughan Williams (*Sancta Civitas* and *Flos Campi*) and Bax (*Mater ora Filium*). She was on the 1927 tour of Germany and in the May 1929 performance of the Tallis forty-part motet *Spem in alium*. She survived one concert under the conductorship of Sidney Newman in December 1930 and then left the choir.

Margaret and Francis lived at 16 Salkeld Gardens, Gateshead, from about 1948 until Francis's death in 1968 at the age of 75. Margaret remained at this address until 1983. She died on 26 January 1992 at Edith House, Coatsworth Road, Gateshead, aged ninety-five. They had no children.

Isabella Rochester (1898–1972)
Contralto: as Miss E. Rochester, 1919–February 1923;
as Mrs Gustard, May 1923–May 1924

Fig. 61 From the 1922 choir photograph.

Fig. 62 Family photograph, 1920s.

ISABELLA (ELLA) ROCHESTER, fourth of five children of John Rochester and
Mary Jane Charlton was born in Ryton, County Durham. Her father, who was
a colliery overman, was also born in Ryton and her mother in Allenheads, a remote
lead-mining village in Weardale. Isabella spent all her childhood in Ryton, initially
at 6 Hargate, then at 5 Simpson Street and finally at Granville House in the
Greenside area.

She developed an interest in music, obtaining primary and elementary certificates of the London College of Music for pianoforte playing in 1914 and 1915
respectively. She joined the Bach Choir as a contralto at the November concert
of 1919 and then sang in every concert under her maiden name until March 1923.

On 14 April 1923 Ella married Robert Sydney Gustard (known as Sydney),
a musician and son of a schoolmaster from Tynemouth, at the parish church,
Greenside. Sydney trained in music at the Newcastle Conservatoire under Edgar

Bainton and specialized in organ playing. In 1914 he was accompanist in a lecture recital on 'Bach's Church Cantatas' at the Newcastle YMCA, at which Herbert Yeaman Dodds presided and explanatory remarks were given by W. G. Whittaker. Sydney was called up for military service and served with the Sherwood Foresters. He was promoted as a temporary second lieutenant on 11 March 1917 but was wounded in action the following August.

Ella continued to sing with the Bach Choir after their marriage, under her married surname. Her final concert with the choir was in the April 1924 performance of Byrd's Great Service in Newcastle, so she missed the London performances of this work. By the late autumn of 1924 she was in the early stages of pregnancy, and her only child, Patricia, was born in Newcastle in the summer of 1925. During her years in the Bach Choir, Ella sang in twelve concerts wholly or partly devoted to Bach cantatas and in one performance each of the St John and St Matthew Passions and the B Minor Mass. She sang in concerts with music by Holst (*The Hymn of Jesus*, the *Ode to Death* and *The Cloud Messenger*), Vaughan Williams (the Mass in G minor) and Bax (*Mater ora Filium*). She was a soloist in the December 1921 concert performance of traditional English carols collected and arranged by Vaughan Williams. Her final concert with the choir was in May 1925.

Fig. 63 Sydney Gustard, 1930s.

After their marriage Sydney Gustard embarked on a highly successful career as a cinema organist. He made many radio broadcasts and gramophone recordings in the 1930s, 1940s and 1950s, from a variety of venues including the Gaumont Palace Cinema in Chester and the Apollo Theatre, Manchester. His recordings are still widely available in traditional and modern digital formats.

Ella died in Suffolk in 1972, aged seventy-three, and Sydney in Norwich in 1977, aged eighty-four.

The author acknowledges the collaboration of Ella's granddaughter, Gillian Grigg, with this biography.

Gladys May Rodgers (1897–1981)
Contralto 1916–19 and 1921–8

GLADYS MAY RODGERS, the elder of two children of Frederick Somers Rodgers and Margaret Ann Macdonald, was born in Gateshead, County Durham. Her father, who had risen from a clerical post to become company secretary of an engineering works, was born in Heworth. Her mother, who before her marriage was a pupil teacher, was born in Gateshead. Frederick Rodgers's family originated in Derbyshire, and Margaret Macdonald's family came from Scotland.

The Rodgers family started their married life at 23 Ross Terrace, Gateshead. By 1911 they had moved to 227 Saltwell Road before finally settling at 'Hazelmere', Low Fell.

Gladys became a schoolteacher. She joined the Bach Choir as a contralto in February 1916, and then sang in every concert until May 1919. There were breaks in her membership from November 1919 to March 1921 and from November 1925 to March 1926, and she was absent from the May and November concerts of 1926.

In 1926 she was a bridesmaid at the wedding of her fellow Bach Choir contralto Margaret Flintoff (formerly Richardson).

During her years in the Bach Choir, Gladys sang in twenty-three concerts wholly or partly dedicated to Bach cantatas, in three performances each of the St John and St Matthew Passions, and in two performances of the B Minor Mass. She sang in concerts with music by Holst (*The Hymn of Jesus*, the *Ode to Death* and *The Cloud Messenger*), Vaughan Williams (the Mass in G minor and *Sancta Civitas*), and Bax (*Mater ora Filium*). She sang in the 1922 London Bach Festival and the 1924 London and Newcastle performances of Byrd's Great Service (singing in the semi-chorus), and was on the 1927 tour of Germany. Her final concert with the choir was the April 1928 performance of Bach's St Matthew Passion.

On 20 September 1928 Gladys married Ernest Frederick Willis, 'an agent' (nature unspecified) and son of a rope works clerk, in St Chad's Church, Gateshead. At the time Ernest was living in Yorker, Glasgow, and Gladys joined him there after the wedding. Audrey Margaret, their only child, was born in Glasgow on 17 April 1930. Gladys later became a state registered nurse.

By the mid to late 1930s the Willis family was living at 22 Manor Road, Glasgow. Ernest had made steady progress in his career and became a clerical manager at a salt works.

Ernest died of lung cancer at the family home on 8 November 1961, aged sixty-four. Gladys continued to live at 22 Manor Road for the next twenty years, but in the final month of her life moved to join her daughter in Harrogate, Yorkshire. She died on 17 July 1981 at the Scotton Banks Hospital, Knaresborough, aged eighty-four.

Mrs Mowbray Thompson (1877–1950)
Contralto 1924–31

HENRIETTA CLULEY ALDERSON (known as Cluley), the eldest of five children of Thomas Alderson and Elizabeth Reay, was born in South Shields, County Durham. Her father, who was born in Sedgefield, County Durham, was a water rate collector for the Sunderland and South Shields Water Company. Her mother was born in South Shields. For many years the family lived at 8 Lane Cottages, South Shields.

A newspaper article dated May 1900 records that Miss Alderson sang a solo at a meeting of the South Shields YMCA. The guest speaker was a young man called Mowbray Thompson. Cluley married him in 1908 in South Shields. He and Cluley set up home at The Briery in the Newcastle suburb of Fenham.

Their first child, Helen, was born in Newcastle in 1909. They still maintained contact with their roots south of the River Tyne, for in 1911 they were involved in the anniversary celebrations for the Queen Street church, South Shields, at which Mowbray lectured and Cluley sang solos.

Their second daughter, Alison, was born in 1913. In May 1915 Cluley sang solos at a meeting of the Newcastle Mother and Babies Welcome Society. Their third daughter, Grace, was born in 1916. By 1921 the family had moved to 30 Eslington Terrace in the affluent Newcastle suburb of Jesmond.

Cluley joined the contralto line of the Bach Choir in April 1924. During her time in the choir under the conductorship of W. G. Whittaker she sang in eight concerts wholly or partly dedicated to Bach cantatas, in three performances of the

St John Passion, and in two performance each of the St Matthew Passion and the B Minor Mass. In addition she sang in concerts with music by Holst (the *Ode to death*, *The Golden Goose* and *The Hymn of Jesus*), Vaughan Williams (*Sancta Civitas* and *Flos Campi*) and Bax (*Mater ora Filium*). She sang in the 1924 London and Newcastle performances of Byrd's Great Service (in which she sang in the semi-chorus), and was on the 1927 tour of Germany. She took part in the May 1929 performance of the Tallis forty-part motet *Spem in alium*. Her last concert under Whittaker was in May 1930.

After Whittaker's departure from Newcastle, Cluley sang under Sidney Newman until February 1931 and then left the choir. In addition to her Bach Choir activities she occasionally sang solos in concert parties.

In 1933 the Thompson family was living at 7 Lindisfarne Road in Jesmond. In October 1935 Cluley sailed alone to Sydney, Australia, returning in March 1936, but the reason for her journey is not known.

Her second daughter, Alison, married in 1938, and their youngest, Grace, in 1944. During the Second World War their daughter Helen served with the Women's Royal Naval Service (WRNS); she attained the rank of third officer in 1942 and was listed as a first officer in 1948. She married in 1953, aged forty-four.

Mowbray died at the family home at Lindisfarne Road, Newcastle, on 30 November 1945, aged seventy-one. After his death Cluley went to live with her daughter Alison at Alpenrose, Kennylands Road, Sonning Common, Reading, where she died on 27 April 1950, aged seventy-two.

Chapter 6
Tenors

Philip Owen

Kenneth Grisedale Armstrong (1903–1983)
Tenor 1925–31

KENNETH GRISEDALE ARMSTRONG, the elder of two sons of Thomas Armstrong and Isabel Emma Carruthers, was born in Gateshead, County Durham. His father was born in Howden-on-Tyne, Northumberland, and his mother in Carlisle, Cumberland. Thomas Armstrong's parents both hailed from Cumberland; his father (also Thomas) was a foreman railway car inspector. The Armstrongs moved to Tyneside in about 1870. Kenneth's father followed in his father's footsteps and worked for the railways as a clerk in a locomotive depot. Kenneth and his parents lived at 5 Affleck Street, Gateshead.

He joined the tenor line of the Bach Choir in November 1925. During his years in the choir under the conductorship of W. G. Whittaker he sang in seven concerts wholly or partly devoted to Bach cantatas, in two performances each of the St John Passion and the B Minor Mass, and in one performance of the St Matthew Passion. He sang in concerts with music by Holst (the *Ode to Death* and *The Golden Goose*), Vaughan Williams (*Sancta Civitas* and *Flos Campi*) and Bax (*This Worldes Joie* and *Mater ora Filium*). He was on the 1927 tour of Germany and sang in the 1929 performance of the Tallis forty-part motet *Spem in alium*. After the departure of Whittaker he sang in the 1930 and 1931 seasons under Sidney Newman. His final concert with the choir was in February 1931.

In addition to singing with the Bach Choir, Kenneth was also a member of the Newcastle and Gateshead Choral Union from about 1928 until around 1938.

On 27 August 1935 Kenneth married Doris Mary Barton at the Methodist Chapel, High West Street, Gateshead. At the time of their marriage he was still living at his childhood home in Affleck Street and was employed as a commercial clerk. In 1936 he was appointed 'assistance clerk' to the Unemployment Assistance Board.

From about 1947 Kenneth and Doris lived at 14 Norwood Gardens, Gateshead. He was eventually promoted to the grade of executive officer in the Civil Service.

Kenneth died on 12 March 1983 at Bensham General Hospital, Gateshead, aged seventy-nine. Doris died in 1998, aged ninety-four. They had no children.

William Bean, MA (DUNELM) (1900–1933)
Tenor 1920–33

Fig. 64 Family photograph, 1918.   Fig. 65 From the 1922 choir photograph.

WILLIAM BEAN, the elder of two children of William Bean and Elizabeth Ann Davison, was born in North Shields, Northumberland, as were his parents. His father trained as a plumber and worked for many years for the Longbenton Urban District Council, initially in the combined post of inspector of nuisances, highway surveyor and fire brigade superintendent but latterly as sanitary inspector. In 1911 the family lived at 3 South View, Forest Hall, but by 1921 they had moved to 7 Ashleigh Grove, Benton.

William attended Rutherford College Boys' School from 1912 to 1917. He was called up for military service in 1918. From to 1919 to 1922 he studied English, French, history, and education at Armstrong College of Durham University in Newcastle, becoming a bachelor of arts. He showed an interest in singing as an undergraduate, coming to the attention of W. G. Whittaker when he joined the Armstrong College Choral Society. He later became its secretary. He joined the tenor line of the Bach Choir for the March concert of 1920.

William did further training and gained an MA degree in education in 1924 and a Board of Education certificate. He was a student teacher at Forest Hall School and then served as an assistant master at Chillingham Road School and Welbeck Road Upper Standard School from 1924 to 1925. From 1925 to 1928 he taught

English, French, history and mathematics at his alma mater, Rutherford College Boys' School, where he was also a form master. In 1928 some three hundred boys and nine members of staff, including William Bean, were transferred to the newly-opened Heaton Secondary Boys' School, Newcastle where he taught until his death.

Fig. 66 Family photograph, 1927.

Fig. 67 From a 1927 choir photograph.

He married Mary Ellen Batie in 1928 in Tynemouth. They lived at 4 St Margaret's Avenue, Benton, near Newcastle.

During his years in the Bach Choir under Whittaker's conductorship, William sang in twenty concerts wholly or partly devoted to Bach cantatas, in three performances each of the St John and St Matthew Passions and the B Minor Mass. He sang in concerts with music by Holst (*The Hymn of Jesus*, the *Ode to Death*, *The Cloud Messenger* and *The Golden Goose*), Vaughan Williams (the Mass in G minor, *Sancta Civitas* and *Flos campi*) and Bax (*Mater ora Filium* and *This Worldes Joie*). Notably he sang the tenor solo in the performance of *Sancta Civitas*. He was in the 1922 London Bach Festival and the 1924 London and Newcastle performances of Byrd's Great Service (in which he sang in the semi-chorus), and he was on the 1927 tour of Germany. He sang in the semi-chorus for the

November 1927 performance of Rubbra's *La Belle Dame sans Merci* and was in the May 1929 performance of the Tallis forty-part motet *Spem in alium*. After Whittaker's departure he continued in the choir under Sidney Newman. His final concert with the choir was in February 1933.

William died on 23 December 1933 of septicaemia after surgery for a neck abscess at the Leazes Hospital (part of the Royal Victoria Infirmary, Newcastle), aged thirty-three. Mary did not remarry and died at the Royal Victoria Infirmary in 1949, aged forty-nine. They had no children.

The author acknowledges the collaboration of Mrs Moira Foreman with this biography.

James Alexander Benson (1897–1951)
Tenor 1921–7

JAMES ALEXANDER BENSON, the younger of two sons of James Benson and Mary Elizabeth Lisgo, was born in Carlisle. His father, who was a draper and mill-

Fig. 68 From the 1922 choir photograph.

iner, was born in Spennymoor, County Durham and his mother in Potterspury, Northamptonshire. In 1901 the Benson family were living in Newcastle at 30 Wandsworth Road, Heaton, but by 1911 they were at 89 Cardigan Terrace. James Benson ran his millinery business from 170 Heaton Road.

James Alexander Benson was a motor engineer. He joined the tenor line of the Bach Choir in February 1921. He married Evelyn Armstrong in Newcastle in 1925. They had two daughters, born in 1925 and 1926, but both died shortly after birth. Their only surviving child, Frank, was born in 1927.

During his years in the Bach Choir, James sang in fourteen concerts wholly or partly devoted to Bach cantatas and in two performances each of the St John Passion and the B Minor Mass. He sang in concerts with music by Holst (*The Hymn of Jesus*, the *Ode to Death* and *The Cloud Messenger*), Vaughan Williams (the Mass in G minor) and Bax (*Mater ora Filium* and *This Worldes Joie*). He sang in the 1924 London and Newcastle performances of Byrd's

Great Service and was on the 1927 tour of Germany. His final concert with the choir was in November 1927.

James and Evelyn lived for many years at 12 Shaftsbury Grove, Newcastle. James was an adherent of a Protestant Christian denomination known the United Brethren (sometimes referred to as the Holmes Brethren after their founder, the Moravian bishop John Beck Holmes).

James died suddenly of a stroke on 17 November 1951 at the Royal Victoria Infirmary, Newcastle, aged fifty-four. Evelyn died in 1982, aged eighty-one.

The Carmichael Brothers

WILLIAM MAGEE CARMICHAEL married Emily Worlock in Newcastle upon Tyne in 1863. William, who was born in Gateshead, County Durham, was a watch- and clockmaker as was his father Robert before him. Emily was born in Islington, London. They had seven children, two girls and five boys. The family lived in Cullercoats, Northumberland, latterly at 5 Station Road, from where they ran the family business. William died in 1910. Two of the Carmichael sons sang in the Newcastle Bach Choir, as described below.

Edward Wilson Carmichael, BA (CANTAB) (1882–1959)
Tenor 1916–18

EDWARD WILSON CARMICHAEL, youngest of seven children of William Magee Carmichael and Emily Worlock, was born in Newcastle upon Tyne. From 1886 to 1890 he studied at Bentinck Infants' School and from 1891 to 1894 at Cullercoats Elementary School. From 1894 to 1897 he studied at the Newcastle Royal Grammar School and from 1897 to 1902 at the Newcastle PT Centre. From 1902 to 1905 he was a non-collegiate student at the University of Cambridge Day Training College and graduated with a BA degree in the Historical Tripos and a Board of Education teaching certificate.

Edward worked as an assistant master at a number of schools in Newcastle. From 1905 to 1908 has was at Heaton Park Road council school; from 1908 to 1910 at Royal Jubilee council school; and from 1910 to 1916 at Westgate Hill council school.

He joined his brother George in the tenor line of the Bach Choir in February 1916.

Fig. 69 Rutherford School photograph, undated. *Courtesy Tyne & Wear Archives and Museums.*

In 1916 Edward was appointed a form master at Rutherford College, Newcastle, where he taught history (specializing in modern and medieval European history), English and French and gave speech training. In 1923 he helped to found the school's chess club, becoming its chairman. A history of Rutherford school described him as an 'excellent exponent of the game' who encouraged the club's members with 'his simultaneous and blindfold displays'. He continued his association with school chess until his retirement. In 1930 he was one of four masters who began to teach swimming to boys in the second and third forms at one of the city baths. Under their tuition the school won several local swimming championships in the 1930s.

During his time in the Bach Choir, Edward sang in four concerts wholly or partly devoted to Bach cantatas, in one performance of the St John Passion and in several concerts of British music. His final concert with the choir was in May 1918.

He married Maud Violet Bulmer in Tynemouth in 1920 and they had two daughters. For many years they lived at 32 Primrose Hill, Low Fell, Gateshead.

Edward died on 17 January 1959 at Bensham Hospital, Gateshead, aged seventy-six. Maud died in 1967, aged seventy-three.

George Frederick Carmichael (1874–1941)
Tenor 1915–20

GEORGE FREDERICK CARMICHAEL, fifth child of William Magee Carmichael and Emily Worlock, was born in Newcastle upon Tyne. George trained as a watch- and clockmaker and took on the family business after his father's death in 1910, operating from 22 Station Road, Cullercoates.

George was a tenor in the Newcastle and Gateshead Choral Union for the 1913/14 season. He joined the tenor line of the Bach Choir for its inaugural concert in November 1915. During his years in the choir he sang in twelve concerts wholly or partly devoted to Bach cantatas, in one performance each of the St John and St Matthew Passions, and in several concerts of British music. His membership of the choir overlapped that of his brother Edward from February 1916 to May 1918. His final concert with the choir concert was in May 1920.

He died on 6 June 1941 at his home in Station Road, Cullercoates, aged sixty-six. He was unmarried.

John Bell Cartner (1885–1973)
Tenor 1919–28

Fig. 70 From the 1922 choir photograph.

Fig. 71 From a 1927 choir photograph.

JOHN BELL CARTNER, the first of two children of William Henry Cartner and Sarah Emma Bell, was born in Newcastle upon Tyne, as were his parents. In 1891 the family were living at 35 Rosedale in the Heaton district of Newcastle, and William Cartner was employed as a bookkeeper. By 1901 the family had moved to 85 Dinsdale Road in the Jesmond area of Newcastle and William was working as a clerk in the offices of the *Newcastle Evening Chronicle*. By 1911 the Cartner family had moved to the village of Stocksfield on Tyne, near Hexham, and were living at Lesbury, Meadowfield Road.

John attended the Bath Lane Schools in Newcastle, where he was described in 1899 as having 'abilities above average' and being 'diligent and obedient, honest and truthful and most willing to oblige'. He trained as a schoolteacher.

He was a member of the tenor line of the Newcastle and Gateshead Choral Union in the 1907/08 and 1908/09 seasons.

In November 1915 he was called up for military service and served with the Royal Fusiliers Army Pay Corps in France, attaining the rank of corporal.

John was an all-round musician and taught the piano and organ. He joined the tenor line of the Bach Choir for the April concert of 1919.

He married Annie Rose Taylor in Newcastle in 1921. They lived at 11 Kingsley Place in the Newcastle suburb of Heaton and worshipped at the nearby St Teresa's Roman Catholic church, where John was organist.

Fig. 72 John Cartner extreme right. Family photograph, undated.

During his years in the Bach Choir, John sang in eighteen concerts wholly or partly devoted to Bach cantatas, and in two performances each of the St John and St Matthew Passions and the B Minor Mass. He sang in concerts with music by Holst (*The Hymn of Jesus*, the *Ode to Death* and *The Cloud Messenger*), Vaughan

Williams (the Mass in G minor and *Sancta Civitas*) and Bax (*Mater ora Filium*). He was in the 1922 London Bach Festival and the 1924 London and Newcastle performances of Byrd's Great Service, and was on the 1927 tour of Germany. He missed a number of concerts in 1926, and his final concert with the choir was in February 1928.

Annie died in 1970, aged eighty-three. John died on 11 August 1973 at the Royal Victoria Infirmary, Newcastle, aged eighty-eight. He and Annie are buried in Heaton cemetery. They had no children.

The author acknowledges the collaboration of Trevor Cartner with this biography.

Herbert Stanley Crace, MA (CANTAB) (1886–1968)
Tenor 1922–37

HERBERT STANLEY CRACE, youngest of five children of John Dibblee Crace and Caroline Elizabeth Foster, was born in Marylebone, London. His father, who was also born in Marylebone, was a famous architectural decorator from a distinguished family of English interior designers and decorators. Ancestors included John C. Crace and his son Frederick Crace, who worked for King George IV (then Prince of Wales) in 1788, providing chinoiserie for the Brighton Pavilion. Frederick Crace and his son John Gregory Crace ran a family business, Frederick Crace & Son, which designed the interiors of many London theatres, including the St James's Theatre. John Gregory Crace worked extensively for the sixth Duke of Devonshire at Devonshire House and Chatsworth. He also worked with A. W. N. Pugin on the decoration of the new Palace of Westminster. The Crace family worked for British monarchs from George III to Queen Victoria. Frederick Crace and John Gregory Crace were appointed freemen of the City of London. Original interior design prints by the Crace family are highly prized and feature in museums and private collections. John Dibblee Crace and family lived at 15 Gloucester Place, London.

Herbert Stanley Crace attended Rugby School. He enrolled at the University of Cambridge in October 1904 and was initially admitted to King's College. Within the first term he migrated to Clare College, where he studied for an ordinary BA (without honours), specializing in mechanical sciences. He graduated as a BA in 1907 and became an MA in 1911. As an undergraduate he appeared in the 1904/5 Footlights Dramatic Club performance of the revue *Paying the Piper: A Tale of Old Cambridge*. He became a marine engineer and worked for R. and W. Hawthorne, Leslie and Company on Tyneside.

Herbert was a tenor in the Newcastle and Gateshead Choral Union between 1911 and 1916. He joined the tenor line of the Bach Choir in December 1922, thus just missing the London Bach Festival concerts. Under Whittaker's conductorship he sang in twelve concerts wholly or partly devoted to Bach cantatas, in three performances each of the St John Passion and the B Minor Mass, and in two performances of the St Matthew Passion. He sang in concerts with music by Holst (*The Cloud Messenger*, the *Ode to Death* and *The Golden Goose*), Vaughan Williams (the Mass in G minor, *Sancta Civitas* and *Flos Campi*) and Bax (*Mater ora Filium*). He sang in the 1924 London and Newcastle performances of Byrd's Great Service (in which he sang in the semi-chorus) and was on the 1927 tour of Germany. He sang in the semi-chorus for the November 1927 performance of Rubbra's *La Belle Dame sans Merci* and was in the May 1929 performance of the Tallis forty-part motet *Spem in alium*. After Whittaker's departure for Glasgow he sang under Sidney Newman. His final concert with the choir was in February 1937.

In 1935 Herbert was elected a serving brother in the Venerable Order of St John of Jerusalem.

He married Sarah Bartlett Clarke in 1938 at the age of fifty-two, and they lived at 36 Beach Road, Tynemouth.

Herbert died on 9 August 1968 at the Preston Hospital, North Shields, aged eighty-two and Sarah in 1984, aged eighty-three. They had no children.

John Scott Dickson (1871–1939)
Tenor 1916–21

JOHN SCOTT DICKSON, eldest of six children of John Russell Dickson and Ann Merchant Bolton, was born in Newcastle upon Tyne. His father was born in the Scottish border town of Melrose and his mother in Layston, Hertfordshire. His father was a tea and coffee merchant whose business premises were in St Martin's Court, Newgate Street, in the centre of Newcastle. The family first lived at a variety of addresses in the Elswick area of Newcastle: first at 111 Gloucester Road, then at 1 St Paul's Terrace and finally at 36 Normanton Terrace.

It is likely that John attended the nearby Rutherford College in Bath Lane. By 1891 he was a chemist's apprentice and eventually became a dispensing pharmacist.

In 1915, at the age of forty-three, he married Helen Grieve, a cookery teacher, in Newcastle. She was the daughter of Walter Grieve, a veterinary surgeon who practised in Blaydon on the south bank of the River Tyne. Walter was born in the Scottish border town of Selkirk and died in 1901. Before her marriage Helen, her mother, Elizabeth, and sister, Marguerite, had moved to live at 48 Osborne Avenue in the Newcastle suburb of Jesmond. It appears that the newly married couple first lived at this address.

John Scott Dickson was a tenor in the Newcastle and Gateshead Choral Union from 1907 to 1921. He joined the tenor line of the Bach Choir for the February concert of 1916. During his years in the choir he sang in eleven concerts wholly or partly devoted to Bach cantatas and in one performance each of the St John and St Matthew Passions. He sang in the first performance of Holst's *The Hymn of Jesus* in February 1921 and in several concerts of British music. His final concert with the choir was in May 1921.

On 22 July 1921, John, his wife Helen and his mother-in law Elizabeth Grieve set sail on SS *Demosthenes* of the Aberdeen Line, from London to Brisbane, Australia. They settled in Doncaster, a suburb of the city of Melbourne, and lived there for many years in Springvale Road. John continued to work as a pharmacist until his death in 1939, aged sixty-eight. Elizabeth Grieve died in 1941, aged eighty-four. Helen was still living at Springvale Road in 1954, but the date of her death has not been ascertained. She and John had no children.

John Harding, B.SC. (1887–1964)
Tenor 1915–32 and 1935   Assistant Secretary 1917   Librarian 1919–32

JOHN HARDING, only child of Charles James Harding and Isabella Chisholm, was born in Newcastle upon Tyne. His father came from Biddick, County Durham, and worked as a joiner and carpenter in house-building. His mother came from the Haddington area of East Lothian, Scotland. The family lived for many years at 118 Glenthorn Road in the Newcastle suburb of Jesmond.

John obtained the degree of bachelor of science and became an elementary teacher at a Newcastle council school. He married Henrietta Anderson in 1911. Their first child, Charles James, was born in 1912. In 1915 Henrietta gave birth to twins, a boy and a girl. Their daughter, Isabella, survived, but their son, John, died in infancy.

John was a tenor in the Newcastle and Gateshead Choral Union from about 1911 until at least 1936. He joined the tenor line of the Bach Choir for its inaugural concert in November 1915 and was its first assistant secretary and librarian. Under the conductorship of Whittaker he sang in thirty concerts wholly or partly devoted to Bach cantatas, in four performances of the St John Passion, and in three performances each of the St Matthew Passion and the B Minor Mass. He sang in concerts with music by Holst (*The Hymn of Jesus*, the *Ode to Death*, *The Cloud Messenger* and *The Golden Goose*), Vaughan Williams (the Mass in

G minor, *Santa Civitas* and *Flos Campi*) and Bax (*Mater ora Filium*). He was in the 1922 London Bach Festival and the 1924 London and Newcastle performances of Byrd's Great Service (in which he sang in the semi-chorus), and was on the 1927 tour of Germany. He sang in the semi-chorus for the November 1927 performance of Rubbra's *La Belle Dame sans Merci* and was in the May 1929 performance of the Tallis forty-part motet *Spem in alium*. Under Whittaker's conductorship he sang in about eighty-four concerts.

After the departure of Whittaker in 1930, John sang under Sidney Newman in the 1931 and 1932 seasons, and returned for the Bach Festival series in April 1935, which included a performance of the St Matthew Passion. This was his final concert with the choir.

Fig. 73 John Harding (rear and partially obscured by W. G. Whittaker). From the 1922 choir photograph.

For many years the Harding family lived at 26 Huntcliffe Gardens in the Newcastle suburb of Heaton, next door to his parents. They also had a holiday cottage at Nine Banks, a small community between Allendale and Alston in Cumbria, where their grandchildren spent many memorable holidays. W. G. Whittaker and his family stayed there on a number of occasions.

John was a car enthusiast, and in 1924 became the proud owner of a short-chassis 'J' type Lea-Francis manufactured in Coventry.

Henrietta died in 1959, aged seventy-one, and John on 8 February 1964 in Carlisle, aged seventy-seven.

The author acknowledges the collaboration of the Rev. Jim Canning and Mrs Ruth Nygren with this biography.

Stewart Edington Hattle (1896–1975)
Tenor 1921–6

Fig. 74 From the 1922 choir photograph.

Fig. 75 Family photograph, 1949.

STEWART EDINGTON HATTLE, only child of George Stewart Hattle and Sarah Smith, was born in Gateshead, County Durham. His father, who was born in Glasgow, worked as a railway signalman. His mother died in 1902 when he was only six years old. His father remarried but had no more children.

Stewart showed an early talent for singing. He was a Newcastle Cathedral chorister for most of his life, first as a treble and finally as lead tenor.

In November 1915 he was called up for military service and served with the 16th Northumberland Fusiliers in France, attaining the rank of lance corporal. He fought in the Battle of the Somme, and was fortunate to survive when a sniper's bullet ricocheted off a silver matchbox that was in the breast pocket of his tunic.

Like his father Stewart joined the railway, serving as a clerical officer in the superintendents' department of the London and North Eastern Railway Company, working mostly in the Sunderland and Dunston (Gateshead) offices. He became a freemason of the Shipcote Lodge.

Stewart joined the tenor line of the Bach Choir for the November concert of 1920 and sang in every concert until December 1922. In early 1923 he married Jane Short in Gateshead. He returned to the Bach Choir for the December concert of that year, and thereafter sang in every concert until May 1926.

During his years in the Bach Choir, Stewart sang in thirteen concerts wholly or partly devoted to Bach cantatas. He was tenor soloist in the cantata concerts of February 1925 (Cantatas Nos. 11 and 172) and January 1926 (Cantatas Nos. 1, 16 and 88). He sang in one performance each of the St John and St Matthew Passions and the B Minor Mass. He sang in concerts with music by Holst (*The Hymn of Jesus*, the *Ode to Death* and *The Cloud Messenger*) and Bax (*This Worldes Joie*). He was in the 1922 London Bach Festival and took part in the 1924 London and Newcastle performances of Byrd's Great Service. His final concert with the choir was in May 1926.

Jane and Stewart had two daughters, Joyce, born in 1930 and Gwenda, born in 1935. Joyce contracted meningitis in infancy and lost her hearing. The family lived for many years at Millbrook, 22 Sunderland Road Villas, in Heworth. In their youth Stewart and Jane enjoyed playing tennis and in later years golf.

Jane died on 4 May 1948 at the Royal Victoria Infirmary, Newcastle, aged forty-nine, leaving Stuart to bring up his two daughters, then aged thirteen and eighteen. His daughter Joyce had been taught at the Thornfield Open Air School, Sunderland, which specialized in pupils with hearing difficulties. Stuart devoted much time at home to teaching her to speak, boycotting the use of sign language so that she could concentrate on the spoken word. A report in the *Yorkshire Post* of July 1949 records that Joyce gave the vote of thanks at the school open day.

Stuart retired in 1961 and continued to live at the family home in Heworth. He died on 10 July 1975 at Dunston Hill Hospital, Gateshead, aged seventy-nine.

The author acknowledges the collaboration of Gwenda Graham with this biography.

John Storey Hebron (1877–1953)
Tenor 1918–27 and 1929

JOHN STOREY HEBRON, eldest of six children of Ralph Hebron and Hannah Storey, was born in Newcastle upon Tyne. His father, who worked as an hydraulic engine fitter, was born in Manchester and his mother in Newcastle. In 1881 the family were living at 9 Kyle Place in the Newcastle suburb of Elswick; later they moved to 12 Clara Street, Benwell. In 1911 John's parents were living at 111 Gerald Street, Benwell.

John became an accountant, and at one time worked as a cashier and bookkeeper for a livery stable. He married Kate Doughty Broughton in Newcastle in 1902. They had three children: Leslie, born in 1903, Ella, in 1904, and Eric, in 1907.

In 1911 John and Kate were living at 14 Atkinson Terrace, Benwell, in the

West End of Newcastle. They eventually moved to the Gosforth Area, first to 60 Windsor Terrace, before settling at 25 Balmoral Terrace, where they were living in 1921.

Fig. 76 John and Kate Hebron. Family photograph, *c*.1904.

John sang in the tenor line of the Newcastle and Gateshead Choral Union from about 1911 and was its registrar in the 1920s. He first sang with the Bach Choir in February 1918 and then in the May concert of that year. He missed most of the 1919 season, returning to the choir for the December 1919 concert. He then sang in most concerts until June 1927, returning in May 1929 to sing in one final concert. He was incorrectly entered in several concert programmes as 'J. T. Hebron'.

During his time in the choir John sang in eighteen concerts wholly or partly devoted to Bach cantatas and in two performances each of the St John and St Matthew Passions and the B Minor Mass. He sang in concerts with music by Holst (the *Ode to Death* and *The Cloud Messenger*), Vaughan Williams (the Mass in G minor) and Bax (*Mater ora Filium*). He was in the 1922 London Bach Festival and took part in the 1924 London and Newcastle performances of Byrd's Great Service, and was on the 1927 tour of Germany. He was recruited to sing as an additional tenor in the May 1929 performance of the Tallis forty-part motet *Spem in alium*. His final concert with the choir was in May 1929.

Fig. 77 From the 1922 choir photograph.

Fig. 78 From a 1927 choir photograph.

On 3 August 1926 John and Kate's two sons emigrated to Australia, sailing on SS *Hobson's Bay*. They both married and brought up families in their adoptive country. Many Australian descendants survive, one of whom is an eminent architect. Their daughter did not marry, and lived in Northumberland working as a matron at St Cuthbert's Girls' School, Langley Castle, near Haydon Bridge.

John was honorary treasurer of the Newcastle Postal Telegraph Choral Society. The society's president was W. Deans Forster, and the honorary conductor of the choir was the composer Edgar Bainton.

John was also the honorary secretary and treasurer of Newcastle's Benwell Hill Cricket Club, for which he played for many years. He started playing competitive tennis for the Newcastle YMCA club, at the age of fifty-four.

John died on 17 February 1953 at Elswick Dene, Georges Road, Newcastle, aged seventy-five. Kate died in 1962, aged eighty-eight.

The author acknowledges the collaboration of John and Eric Hebron, both living in Australia, with this biography.

Fig. 79 Benwell Hill Cricket Club. John Hebron in front row with bat. Family photograph, 1930s.

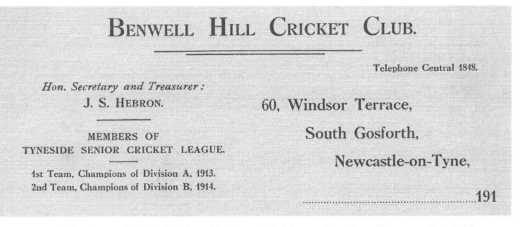

Fig. 80 The Benwell Hill Cricket Club's official letter-heading. *Courtesy Eric Hebron.*

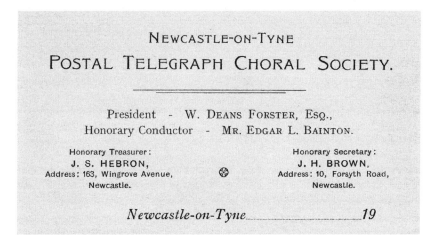

Fig. 81 The Newcastle upon Tyne Postal Telegraph Choral Society's official letter-heading. *Courtesy Eric Hebron.*

Lancelot Swindale Hughes, B.SC. (1888–1963)
Tenor 1915–c.1947   Honorary Assistant Secretary 1916–17
Honorary Secretary and Treasurer 1917–21   Choir Secretary 1925–30
Assistant Conductor 1931–5

LANCELOT SWINDALE (LANCE) HUGHES, the eldest of nine children of Thomas George Hughes and Anne Swindale, was born in Newcastle upon Tyne. His father, who was born in Cramlington, Northumberland, was the headmaster of an elementary school in Newcastle. His mother was born in Newcastle. In 1891 the family were living at 2 Gainsbro Grove in the Newcastle suburb of Elswick. By 1901 they had moved to the Heaton area of Newcastle, first to 9 Holmside Place and finally to 19 Wandsworth Road.

Lance attended Armstrong College of Durham University in Newcastle and graduated as a bachelor of science. He became a schoolteacher and worked as an assistant master in a secondary school in Gateshead, teaching English.

He married Lilian Davison on 4 August 1923 in Gateshead; they had a son, Roger, born in 1924, and a daughter, Pamela Mary, born in 1927. The family lived for many years at Treen, Shibden Bank, Blaydon, near Gateshead.

He was a tenor in the Newcastle and Gateshead Choral Union in the 1915/16 season. He joined the tenor line of the Bach Choir for its inaugural concert in November 1915, and sang in all but one concert until March 1917, when he was called up for military service. Although his detailed service records have not survived, it is known that he served as a private in the Royal Army Medical Corps and was awarded the Victory and British Medals. He rejoined the choir for the April concert of 1919.

Fig. 82 From the 1922 choir photograph.

Fig. 83 From the 1927 choir photograph.

Under the conductorship of W. G. Whittaker, Lance sang in twenty-six concerts wholly or partly devoted to Bach cantatas and in three performances each of the St John and St Matthew Passions and the B Minor Mass. In all the performances of the Passions he sang minor solo parts. He sang in concerts with music by Holst (*The Hymn of Jesus*, the *Ode to Death*, *The Cloud Messenger* and *The Golden Goose*), Vaughan Williams (the Mass in G minor, *Sancta Civitas* and *Flos Campi*), and Bax (*Mater ora Filium*). Notably he was in the semi-chorus for *Sancta Civitas*. He was in the 1922 London Bach Festival and the 1924 London and Newcastle performances of Byrd's Great Service (in which he sang in the semi-chorus), and was on the 1927 tour of Germany. He was in the semi-chorus for the November 1927 performance of Rubbra's *La Belle Dame sans Merci*, and sang in the May 1929 performance of the Tallis forty-part motet *Spem in alium*.

Lance continued to sing in the choir after the departure of Whittaker in 1930, taking on the role of assistant conductor from 1930 to 1935. He sang under three subsequent conductors, Sidney Newman, J. A. Westrup and Chalmers Burns. His final concert with the choir was in March 1954; he had sung with the choir for thirty-nine years. Lance and his wife were on the list of Bach Choir patrons until about 1958. Their daughter Pamela was a contralto in the Newcastle Bach Choir for many years, her membership overlapping that of her father in the 1950s.

Lance died on 27 December 1963 at the Bensham General Hospital, Gateshead, aged seventy-five, and Lilian in 1975, aged seventy-seven.

The author acknowledges the collaboration of Daphne Hughes with this biography.

William Wilson Large (1889–1949)
Tenor from 1919–mid 1940s   Assistant Secretary 1920–21
Financial Secretary and Treasurer 1921–5

Fig. 84 From the 1922 choir photograph.

Fig. 85 From a 1927 choir photograph.

WILLIAM WILSON LARGE (known as Wilson), sixth child of William Lambert Large and Sarah Jane Houseman, was born in Newcastle upon Tyne. His father, who was born in Necton, Norfolk, was a printer and compositor. His mother was born in Hull. In 1871 the family were living at 43 Diana Street in the Westgate area of Newcastle. By 1881 they had moved to the Byker area, first at 5 Norfolk Road, but by 1901 they were living at 1 Stratford Grove Terrace. William Lambert

Fig. 86 Alice and Wilson camping. Family photograph, undated.

Large founded W. L. Large & Sons Ltd (Letter Press Printers), which operated from 54 Shields Road, Newcastle. In 1911 the family were living at 37 Appletree Gardens, Walkerville.

Wilson attended the Great Ayton Friends' (Quaker) School (founded in 1841 and closed in 1997). He developed an early interest in singing, and was a chorister in St Barnabas's (Anglican) church in Sandyford, Newcastle. Wilson became a master printer and (along with three of his surviving brothers) joined the family business, which later printed some of the early Bach Choir programmes and posters. He also became a freemason.

On 27 May 1912 William married Alice Stainton, the daughter of William Stainton, a foreman at an electric power supply company. They had a son, William Lambert, who was born in 1913. For many years they lived at 19 Falmouth Road in Heaton, Newcastle. Wilson was called up for military service in June 1916, joining the Army Service Corps before being transferred to the Machine Gun Corps (Heavy Branch). In 1917 he was transferred to the Tank Corps, serving as a Lewis gunner with the rank of private. He was captured by the enemy on

24 March 1918 and held as a prisoner of war in Münster until the conclusion of hostilities later that year. For some years he remained in touch with many of his fellow internees.

Wilson joined the tenor line of the Bach Choir in December 1919. During his years in the choir under the conductorship of W. G. Whittaker, he sang in nineteen concerts of music wholly or partly devoted to Bach cantatas and in three performances each of the St John and St Matthew Passions and the B Minor Mass. He sang in concerts with music by Holst (*The Hymn of Jesus*, the *Ode to Death*, *The Cloud Messenger* and *The Golden Goose*), Vaughan Williams (the Mass in G minor, *Sancta Civitas* and *Flos Campi*) and Bax (*Mater ora Filium*). He was in the 1922 London Bach Festival and the 1924 London and Newcastle performances of Byrd's Great Service, and was on the 1927 tour of Germany. He was in the May 1929 performance of the Tallis forty-part motet *Spem in alium*. After the departure of Whittaker in 1930 he sang under Sidney Newman, J. A. Westrup and Chalmers Burns. The last concert programme record of him is in February 1939 (after which time choir lists were suspended for some time), but he is known to have sung until the middle of the 1940s.

Wilson died suddenly at his home on 2 May 1949, aged fifty-nine. Alice died in 1977, aged eighty-nine.

The author acknowledges the collaboration of Roy and Maurice Large with this biography.

James Fairley Pedelty (1901–1925)
Tenor 1921–3

JAMES FAIRLEY PEDELTY, fifth of six children of Joseph Pedelty and Jane Isabella Fairley, was born in Wallsend, Northumberland. His father, who was born in Grahamsley, County Durham, was a printer's traveller. Joseph Pedelty was a very religious man, who in the 1890s attended Highbury Theological College in Islington, London. James's mother was born in Ryhope, County Durham. Her father, James Fairley, was a mining engineer; the family lived at Shafto House, Craghead near Lanchester, County Durham. Joseph Pedelty died in 1904, aged thirty-nine, when James was only three. Jane Pedelty then supported the family by running a boarding-house at 52 Fern Avenue in the Newcastle suburb of Jesmond.

In 1911, at the age of forty-seven, his mother Jane married Utrick Alexander Ritson, who was eleven years her junior. Utrick was the son of Utrick Alexander Ritson senior, a wealthy coal owner who was chairman of U. A. Ritson & Sons Ltd of Milburn House, Newcastle. The Ritson family owned Calf Hall near Muggleswick, County Durham. Utrick senior was a prominent person in Newcastle, serving as a justice of the peace. He funded the John Wesley centenary memorial and fountain (erected in 1891), which stands in Newcastle to this day. Sadly Jane's marriage to Utrick Jun. did not last.

Fig. 87 Family photograph, undated.   Fig. 88 From the 1922 choir photograph.

James Pedelty trained as a mining engineer and was elected to membership of the North of England Institute of Mining and Mechanical Engineers.

James had a younger brother, Joseph Cecil Donovan Pedelty (known as Donovan), who was a famous journalist and theatre and film director. After a career in England he moved to the USA, where he worked as the Hollywood correspondent for journals and as a writer and broadcaster until his death in 1989.

James joined the tenor line of the Bach Choir in March 1921. There was some initial uncertainty about the correct spelling of his surname, as he was entered in his first concert as 'Pendelby' and in his second concert as 'Pendelty'. During his years in the choir he sang in seven concerts of music wholly or partly devoted to Bach cantatas and in one performance of the B Minor Mass. He sang in concerts with music by Holst (*The Hymn of Jesus* and the *Ode to Death*), Vaughan Williams (the Mass in G minor) and Bax (*Mater ora Filium*). He sang in the 1922 London Bach Festival. His final concert with the choir was in December 1923.

James' life was tragically cut short. On 28 August 1925, while working in the Holder Yard seam at the Horton Colliery, South Shields, County Durham, he was crushed between two coal tubs and died of severe pelvic injuries. He was twenty-three years old and unmarried.

Fig. 89 Joseph Pedelty as 'John Barleycorn' in *Phoney Dick*. Family photograph, undated.

The author acknowledges the collaboration of Donovan Pedelty Jun. and Aileen Waldron-Kelly with this biography.

Robert Peel (1871–1945)
Tenor 1915–20   Tenor soloist 1916–20

ROBERT PEEL, the third of seven children
of George Peel and Elizabeth Eltringham,
was born in Eighton Banks, near Gateshead,
County Durham. Both his parents were born
in Gosforth, near Newcastle. His father
worked as a master wasteman at Langley Park
Colliery. This role, according to the Durham
Mining Museum archive, consisted in 'building pillars for the support of the roof in the
waste and in keeping the airways open and
in good order'. A wasteman worked under a
viewer or under-viewer and had 'the charge of
the waste, and should be a steady and careful
man'. In 1881 the family were living at 128
North Street, Langley Park, but by 1891 they
had moved to No. 10. In 1901 they were living
at 27 Langley Street, where they continued to reside for many years.

Fig. 90 At the Newcastle Festival, 1909. Family photograph.

Robert was educated in a local school and in 1881 obtained a first class certificate in art and geometry as an external student of the Department of Science and
Art at South Kensington, London.

From 1891 to 1892 Robert attended Bede Teacher Training College, Durham.
He was a member of the college cricket team and one of the winning rowing crew.
He obtained a first class teaching certificate. There was the possibility of his
attending a course at Oxford University, but he preferred to start work. In 1893 he
began teaching at North Brancepeth Colliery School, County Durham, where he
was a keen and popular teacher, frequently taking classes of eighty to ninety pupils
and earning recommendations from HM Inspectors.

He continued his love of cricket, playing with the Langley Park Cricket Club,
and was their captain in the 1899 season when they won the Durham Challenge
Cup.

In 1902 Robert married Mary Stubbs, the daughter of Matthew Stubbs, an
engineman at Bearpark Colliery, in Sedgefield, County Durham. Their first child,
Neville, was born in 1904.

In 1905 Robert took up a post at Heaton Park Road School in Newcastle, and he and Mary moved to live at 48 Hulne Avenue, Tynemouth. School inspection reports described him as 'an excellent and thoughtful teacher of music'. He broadened his qualifications, obtaining certificates in organic and inorganic chemistry at Rutherford College, Newcastle. It is likely that he first met W. G. Whittaker at this time.

Robert had a fine tenor voice, and had also been an organist in Wesleyan Methodist Church circles. In 1909 he was involved with a Newcastle Festival to raise funds for the city's Royal Victoria Infirmary. The event, stretching over three days, brought together a chorus of 370 voices and various international celebrities such as Sir Edward Elgar. Robert sang with distinction in quartets during a performance of Mendelssohn's *Elijah*.

Robert and Mary's second child, Douglas, was born in 1910. In that year Robert became leader of the Tynemouth Priory Orchestral Society. He eventually became its honorary conductor, a post he was to hold for nineteen years. In about 1911 he joined the tenor line of the Newcastle and Gateshead Choral Union, with which he sang for many years; he also served on its committee.

Their son Douglas died in 1912. In 1915 Robert and Mary moved from Hulne Avenue to 5 Brislee Avenue, Tynemouth.

Robert joined the tenor line of the Bach Choir in 1915. He was scheduled to sing in the inaugural concert in November 1915, but a note in Whittaker's handwriting on the Bach Choir archive copy of the programme records that he missed the event owing to illness. But he sang with the tenor line for the remainder of the 1916 season, in which the November concert was a performance of three Bach cantatas. In that year he sang a minor solo part in a performance of the St Matthew Passion with the Newcastle and Gateshead Choral Union.

In 1916 he became president of the Newcastle Certificated Teachers' Association.

Robert continued to sing with the Bach Choir as a member of the tenor line throughout the 1917, 1918 and 1919 seasons. In March 1917 he took a small solo role in a performance of the St John Passion. In the December 1917 concert of British music, his performance in Walford Davies's *O little town of Bethlehem* was sung 'with a purity of style and absence of affectation'. In February 1918, December 1918 and February 1922 he was a soloist in further concerts devoted to music by early and modern British composers. In December 1918 he was a soloist in a programme of Christmas music by Bach and British composers. Between 1916 and 1920 he was a soloist in seven concerts. His final appearance with the choir was as a soloist in May 1920 in a performance of three Bach cantatas.

In 1918 Robert was appointed organizer of music for the Newcastle schools. He was an enthusiastic supporter of music teaching and appreciation in schools, and inaugurated popular children's classes for the North of England Musical Tournament. He was appointed lecturer in music at Kenton Teachers' Training College, Newcastle, in 1922.

In 1923 he organized and conducted a concert involving forty thousand children to welcome the Prince of Wales at the local football ground, St James's Park. That year, Robert and Mary moved from Brislee Avenue to live at 15 Hotspur Street, Tynemouth. For a brief period in 1923 they were neighbours of Mary and Harold Bainbridge, who just moved into No. 4 Brislee Avenue.

In 1925 Robert produced a syllabus of vocal instruction for elementary schools. He retired in 1929, leaving behind a record of exceptional industry and a legacy of goodwill recognized by numerous tributes. At one ceremony to mark his retirement, held at the Connaught Hall, Newcastle, Robert and Mary were presented with many gifts including a silver tea service engraved 'From the Teachers of Newcastle upon Tyne'. After his retirement Robert continued be musically active, and in 1930 produced an illustrated study guide to Mendelssohn's *Elijah*, published by the Newcastle Education Authority, for the benefit of schoolchildren who were attending a performance of the work given by the Newcastle and Gateshead Choral Union.

Robert died on 17 October 1945 at the Victoria Jubilee Infirmary, Tynemouth, aged seventy-three, and Mary in 1972, aged 102.

The author acknowledges the collaboration of Alwin Peel, grandson of Robert Peel, with this biography.

George Prest (1872–1945)
Tenor 1915–17

GEORGE PREST, the second of two children of Joseph Prest and Jane Graham, was born in Knayton, near Northallerton, Yorkshire. His father began his working life labouring on farms and later on the railway. From about 1871 Joseph and Jane Prest lived at the home of Thomas Ward, a grocer, and his wife, Mary, in Main Street, Northallerton. Jane Prest (née Graham) was Mary Ward's niece. Eventually Joseph and Jane took on and ran the grocery business.

In 1891 George was apprenticed to James Porter, a draper in Town Street, Northallerton. By 1901 he had moved to Middlesbrough, where he worked as a draper's assistant in Sussex Street.

Shortly before 1905 he moved to Newcastle and set himself up as a draper, and in that year married Margaret Ann Waterston, the daughter of another Newcastle draper. They lived at 69 Jesmond Dene Road, Newcastle. They had two sons, of whom the first, George Arthur, was born in 1906. Margaret died in 1911, aged thirty-seven, at the time of the birth of their second child, Reginald, who died shortly afterwards.

George joined the tenor line of the Newcastle and Gateshead Choral Union in 1911 and was a member until about 1936. He joined the tenor line of the Bach Choir at its inaugural concert in November 1915. During his years with the choir he sang in five concerts wholly or partly devoted to Bach cantatas and in several concerts of British music. He missed the March concert of 1917, when he married Louisa Ellen Stephenson in Newcastle. His final concert with the choir was in May 1918.

George and Louisa lived for many years at 8 Harley Terrace, Gosforth, but had no children.

George's surviving son, George Arthur, joined the Merchant Navy and qualified as a second mate in 1926. He became master of SS *Dalemoor* and died at sea on 13 June 1941, aged thirty-five. The *Dalemoor* was mined and sunk on 15 January 1945 during a voyage from Antwerp.

George died in Newcastle in 1945, aged seventy-two. Louisa died on 1 December 1954 at the Ponteland Hospital, Northumberland, aged seventy-four.

James Webster (1884–1943)
Tenor 1919–27

JAMES WEBSTER, second of seven children of James Webster and Jane Julia Donina MacKenzie, was born in Gearwen, Anglesey. Both his parents were born in Scotland, his father in Edinburgh and his mother in Duror, a small village in Appin not far from Fort William. James Webster senior was the son of an Edinburgh tea merchant of the same name. Jane was the only daughter of the Rev. Donald MacKenzie, an Episcopalian minister, who was born in Kilmalie, Inverness-shire. Julia's mother, who was born in Wooler, Northumberland, met her husband while he was a curate in Wooler. She died of tuberculosis in 1858 a few months after Julia was born. Donald remarried in 1862 and had one son from that marriage.

James Webster senior and Jane MacKenzie were married on 20 April 1881 in Edinburgh. During the first few years of their married life James held teaching posts in a number of widespread places. Their first child, Frances, was born in 1882 in Newent, Gloucestershire, and their second, James, in 1884 in Gaerwen on Anglesey. By 1887, when their third child, Thomas Herbert, was born, they had moved to Northumberland, where James senior had been appointed schoolmaster in the hamlet of Dalton, a few miles north-west of Newcastle. For many years James and Jane lived at the School House in Dalton, which also served as the local post office. Jane Webster was the postmistress and operated the telegraph service. It was from his mother that James Jun. acquired his interest and skills as a telegraph operator. Their next four children were born in Dalton between 1889 and 1902. By 1911 James senior had been appointed headmaster of the school in the village of Whitley near Hexham.

Fig. 91 From the 1922 choir photograph.

Fig. 92 From the 1927 choir photograph.

By 1911 James was a qualified telegraphist working for the Post Office, and that year he joined the tenor line of the Newcastle and Gateshead Choral Union.

The Webster family continued to live at the schoolhouse in Whitley until the death of James senior on 4 January 1914 at the age of fifty-eight. In 1915 James Jun. and his mother moved to live at the home of James's brother Thomas, a civil engineer, at 172 Ladykirk Road, Newcastle.

In December 1915 James was attested for military service, posted to the Corps of Royal Engineers and placed on the Army reserve list. He continued to work for the Post Office telegraphy service.

James was finally summoned for mobilization in December 1917, but a recruitment medical examination revealed that he had marked hearing impairment in his right ear, and he was placed on the Class W Army reserve for signal service. He was discharged in December 1918.

James had left the Choral Union in 1916. He joined the tenor line of the Bach Choir in April 1919. During his years with the choir he sang in nineteen concerts wholly or partly devoted to Bach cantatas, in two performances each of the St John Passion (taking minor solo parts in both concerts), and in two performances each of the St Matthew Passion and the B Minor Mass. He sang in concerts with music by Holst (*The Hymn of Jesus*, the *Ode to Death* and *The Cloud Messenger*), Vaughan Williams (the Mass in G minor) and Bax (*Mater ora Filium* and *This Worldes Joie*). He was in the semi-chorus for the performance of a Taverner Mass in May 1925. He sang in the 1922 London Bach Festival and the 1924 London and Newcastle performances of Byrd's Great Service (in which he sang in a semi-chorus), and was on the 1927 tour of Germany. James's final concert as a regular member of the Bach Choir was in November 1927, but he was recruited as an additional tenor for the May 1929 performance the Tallis forty-part motet *Spem in alium*.

At some stage in the 1930s James and his mother moved to Corbridge, a small town along the Tyne valley between Newcastle and Hexham, where they lived at 1 Corchester Avenue. James's career progressed, and he was eventually promoted to chief superintendent telegraphist.

James died of a rare malignant melanoma of his right eye at his Corbridge home on 21 October 1943, aged fifty-nine. He was unmarried. His mother survived him and died in Corbridge on 23 June 1946, aged eighty-eight.

Chapter 7
Basses

Philip Owen

Matthew Bambrough (1890–1949)
Bass 1915–47

Fig. 93 From the 1922 choir photograph.

Fig. 94 From a 1927 choir photograph.

MATTHEW BAMBROUGH, third of five children of Henry Bambrough and Mary Ann Wood, was born in Newcastle upon Tyne, where his parents had also been born. His father was a gas fitter and plumber. The Bambrough family lived in the Sandyford area of Newcastle, first at 10 Sarah Street and finally at No. 17. By 1911 they had moved to 44 Grosvenor Gardens in the Ouseburn area of Newcastle.

Matthew trained as an elementary school teacher, obtained a Board of Education certificate, and worked all his life in Newcastle. He was an assistant master from 1910 to 1917 at the Royal Jubilee School.

He married Alice Jane Pallister, the daughter of a provision merchant from Gateshead, on 28 July 1915. His wife, also an elementary school teacher, was some fifteen years older. Jane's sister Frances was also a schoolteacher, as was Matthew's brother Henry.

Matthew joined the bass line of the Bach Choir in November 1915, but on

7 December he was called up for military service. When a medical examination revealed that he was extremely short-sighted, he was declared unfit for general service and placed on the reserve list.

Matthew continued to sing in the choir until February 1917, and was finally mobilized for military service in April that year. He enlisted in the Royal Army Medical Corps and served in Salonika, Greece, until the end of the war.

He rejoined the choir in April 1919. From 1919 to 1920 he was an assistant master at the Bentinck School. He then became a second master, working first at St Thomas's Church of England School from 1920 to 1924, and then at Christ Church School from 1924 until his retirement.

During his years in the choir under the conductorship of W. G. Whittaker he sang in twenty-seven concerts wholly or partly dedicated to Bach cantatas, in four performances of the St John Passion (with a minor solo role in the 1917 performance), and in three performances each of the St Matthew Passion and the B Minor Mass. He sang in concerts with music by Holst (*The Hymn of Jesus*, the *Ode to Death*, *The Cloud Messenger* and *The Golden Goose*), Vaughan Williams (the Mass in G minor, *Sancta Civitas* and *Flos Campi*) and Bax (*Mater ora Filium* and *This Worldes Joie*). He was in the 1922 London Bach Festival and the 1924 London and Newcastle performances of Byrd's Great Service (in which he sang in the semi-chorus), and was on the 1927 tour of Germany. He was in a semi-chorus for the 1927 performance of Rubbra's *La Belle Dame sans Merci* and was in the May 1929 performance of the Tallis forty-part motet *Spem in alium*.

After Whittaker's departure in 1930 Matthew sang under Sidney Newman, Jack Westrup and Chalmers Burns. The last record of him singing in the choir is in February 1947, after an association of thirty-two years.

Matthew and Alice lived for many years at 6 St Gabriel's Avenue, Newcastle. Matthew died at home on 8 January 1949, aged fifty-eight. Alice died on 6 April 1958, aged eighty-two. They had no children.

George Alfred Bocock (1882–1951)
Bass 1921–4

GEORGE ALFRED BOCOCK, only child of John William Bocock and Catherine Anne Hutchinson, was born in Newcastle upon Tyne. His father was born in Birmingham and his mother in Newcastle. His parents married on 10 November 1880; they are not recorded in the 1881 census, so it is not known where they were living at that time. George was born in 1882. His mother died in 1889, aged thirty-one, when he was seven years old. In 1891 George was living with his father, paternal grandmother and his father's sister Annie at 4 Charles Street, Heaton. On 22 June 1897 his father married Elizabeth Margaret Keenan, and there were four children from that marriage. In 1901 the Bocock family were living at 57 Church Street in the Walker area of Newcastle. His father held a variety of clerical posts but eventually worked as a weighman for a Tyneside antimony manufacturer.

Fig. 95 From the 1922 choir photograph.

George spent part of his childhood living in the Heaton area of Newcastle, where there was a large railway maintenance works. This may have influenced his choice of career, for he joined the London and North Eastern Railway Company as a clerk. The LNER had its own musical society, with a choir and orchestra drawn entirely from railway staff.

In 1907 George was a bass in the Newcastle and Gateshead Choral Union. Also singing in the contralto section of the choir was a Miss S. Falcus. George married Selina Falcus in Gateshead in 1908. Their first child, George Edwin, was born in 1910. By 1911 they were living at 12 Windsor Terrace, Corbridge, a small town on the River Tyne between Hexham and Newcastle. Their second child, Dorothy, was born in 1914, and their third, Winifred, in 1917.

George ceased to sing with the Choral Union in about 1912. He joined the bass line of the Bach Choir in November 1921. During his years in the choir he sang in nine concerts wholly or partly devoted to Bach cantatas and in one performance each of Bach's St John Passion and the B Minor Mass. He sang in concerts with music by Holst (the *Ode to Death* and *The Cloud Messenger*), Vaughan Williams (the Mass in G minor) and Bax (*Mater ora Filium*). He sang in the 1922 London Bach Festival. His last concert with the choir was the May 1924 Newcastle performance of Byrd's Great Service, so he missed the London concerts in November that also featured that work.

Selina was co-opted to sing in the contralto line of the Bach Choir in the February 1923 performance of Bach's B minor Mass and in the choir's first performance of Byrd's Great Service at St Nicholas's Cathedral, Newcastle, in May 1924.

George's career progressed, and he eventually became works manager of the LNER stores department in Newcastle. His son became a company director. George retired on 6 April 1942, aged sixty.

Selina died on 2 November 1949 in Low Fell, Gateshead, aged sixty-four. George died of a stroke on 26 September 1951 at St Camillus Hospital, Hexham, aged sixty-nine.

The author acknowledges the collaboration of Ken Bocock and David O'Farrell with this biography.

Charles Hereward Brackenbury, BA (OXON) (1901–1979)
Bass 1926–39

Fig. 96 Elise and Charles on their honeymoon in Algiers. Family photograph, 1924.

CHARLES HEREWARD BRACKENBURY, the elder of two children of Hereward Irenius Brackenbury, CBE, JP, and Winifred Isabel Browne, was born in Newcastle upon Tyne. His father was born in Kent, the son of Maj.-Gen. Charles Booth Brackenbury, Royal Artillery, later director of artillery at Woolwich. Maj.-Gen. Brackenbury married Hilda Elizabeth Campbell, who achieved notoriety in her eightieth year as a member of the Women's Suffrage movement, when she was arrested and imprisoned for eight days for breaking two windows in the United

Services Institute in London. Charles Brackenbury's mother, Winifred, born in Newcastle, was the daughter of Sir Benjamin Charles Browne, DCL, JP, chairman of R. and W. Hawthorne, Leslie & Co., the Tyneside shipbuilders.

Hereward Irenius Brackenbury, who was educated at Dover College from 1883 to 1886, was the youngest of seven brothers. He moved to Tyneside in 1886, to take up an engineering apprenticeship at the Elswick Works of Sir W. G. Armstrong, Whitworth & Co. Ltd. He married Winifred Browne on 14 February 1900. In 1901, at the time of Charles Hereward Brackenbury's birth, he was promoted to departmental manager. In 1901 the Brackenbury family were living at 1 Clifton Road, Elswick. Their second child, Barbara, was born in 1906. In that year Hereward was elected a member of the Institution of Mechanical Engineers. One of his proposers was his father-in-law, Sir Benjamin Charles Browne. By 1911 the family were living at Benwell Lodge, Benwell. Hereward Brackenbury established a business as H. I. Brackenbury, Engineer, which operated between 1922 and 1926 from Seaton Burn House in the south-east Northumberland mining community of Dudley.

In additional to his professional life Hereward Brackenbury was a keen musician, who played the clarinet; there is a report of him playing that instrument at a concert by the Newcastle Symphony Orchestra in 1931. He was an avid collector of old musical instruments, and possessed several dating from the late seventeenth and early eighteenth centuries. He was also a patron of the Newcastle and Gateshead Choral Union in the 1930s.

Charles Hereward Brackenbury was educated at New College, Oxford, graduating as a BA in 1922. In 1924 he was married in London to Florence Elisabeth Cuming (known as Elise), whom he had met at Oxford. She was the Dublin-born daughter of Francis Edward Cuming, a barrister. They set up home at 12 Manor House Road, Newcastle. At about this time Charles was registered as a student member of the Institution of Electrical Engineers. It is likely that he went into business with his father. Their first child, Rosamund, was born in 1925. A second child was born in the summer of 1928 but died shortly afterwards.

Charles joined the bass line of the Bach Choir in March 1926. His wife, Elise, also sang in that concert, as an additional member of the soprano line. Under Whittaker's conductorship Charles sang in four concerts wholly or partly dedicated to Bach cantatas, in two performances each of the St John Passion and the B Minor Mass, and in one performance of the St Matthew Passion. He sang in concerts with music by Holst (*The Golden Goose*), Vaughan Williams (*Sancta Civitas* and *Flos Campi*) and Bax (*This Worldes Joie* and *Mater ora Filium*). He was in the May 1929 performance of the Tallis forty-part motet *Spem in alium*.

His last concert under Whittaker was in May 1930. He then sang under Sidney Newman in the 1930 and 1931 seasons.

Their third child, Mark, was born in April 1931. At about this time the family moved to Dublin, where Charles had taken up a new post. Shortly after the move their marriage began to deteriorate, and they separated and eventually divorced.

Charles then married Ethne Mary Radcliffe, whom he had met in Dublin. They first settled in London, living for a few years at 6 Doughty Street, St Pancras. Charles and Ethne moved to Newcastle towards the end of 1935, where they set up home at 74 Jesmond Road. Meanwhile Elise and the children moved to London.

Charles rejoined the Bach Choir for the January concert of 1936, in which he sang a minor solo part. The last concert for which he is recorded took place in March 1940, at about the time that Jack Westrup became conductor. Choir lists in concert programmes were not produced during the war years.

In 1937 Charles's former wife, Elise, married Michael Hugh Barrie Gilmour, a solicitor, with whom she had a further child, Harriet, who was born in 1939.

His second wife, Ethne, was a talented viola player and was a member and later secretary of the Newcastle Symphony Orchestra.

Hereward Brackenbury died on 17 September 1938. He had been living for some years at Tweedhill, a large ten-bedroomed house on the Scottish border near Berwick-upon-Tweed. His widow continued to live there until her death in 1943.

From about 1939 Charles ran C. H. Brackenbury (Engineers) from the Forth Bank Works in Newcastle. After the war he founded C. H. Brackenbury and Partner, engineers' agents, initially operating from 2 Saville Place, Newcastle, before moving in 1952 to offices at 76 Jesmond Road, next door to his home. In the following years he began to spend more time at Tweedhill. By about 1964 Charles and Ethne had sold 74 Jesmond Road and were living wholly at Tweedhill.

Although Charles no longer sang with the Bach Choir, he occasionally sang solos in other concerts. In 1945 he was one of a group of enthusiasts who proposed the formation of a professional orchestra to serve the needs of the north of England. This led to the foundation of the Northern Sinfonia orchestra in 1958, which subsequently became the Royal Northern Sinfonia in 2013.

Charles died in 1979, aged seventy-eight. He had inherited his father's collection of ancient musical instruments, and on his death the greater part of the collection was donated by his son Mark to the University of Edinburgh and became the C. H. Brackenbury Memorial Collection.

His first wife, Elise, died in 1985 aged eighty-two, and his second wife, Ethne, in 1990, aged eighty-seven.

The author acknowledges the collaboration of Mark Brackenbury with this biography.

Edgar Crowe (1891–1967)
Bass 1915–24

EDGAR CROWE, the elder of two children of William Crowe and Josephine Crowe, was born at 12 Bishop's Avenue, Newcastle upon Tyne. His parents were not related by birth, but were both born in the Mickley/Ovingham area of Northumberland. Edgar's paternal grandfather was a coal miner, and his maternal grandfather a provision merchant in the village of Prudhoe. At the time of Edgar's birth his father was working as a clerk for the River Tyne Commissioners, but he eventually became its assistant secretary. In 1916 the family lived at 16 Queen's Road, Monkseaton.

Edgar studied music and became a music teacher. He was a bass in the Newcastle and Gateshead Choral Union from 1913 to 1916. Edgar was also a founder member of the Newcastle Bach Choir, and sang in the inaugural concert in November 1915. During his years in the choir he sang in twenty-two concerts wholly or partly devoted to Bach cantatas and in one performance each of the St John and St Matthew Passions (taking minor solo parts in the latter concert) and the B minor Mass. He sang in concerts with music by Holst (*The Hymn of Jesus*, the *Ode to Death* and *The Cloud Messenger*), Vaughan Williams (the Mass in G minor) and Bax (*Mater ora Filium*). At the concert in November 1920, Edgar gave the first performance of his own part-song *Aye she kaimed her yellow hair*. This work had won an award at the North of England Musical Tournament in 1921. Edgar sang in the 1922 London Bach Festival. His final concert with the choir was in February 1924; he therefore missed the London and Newcastle performances of Byrd's Great Service that were given later that year.

In 1930 Edgar married Linda Lawson Wright, the daughter of Robert Wright, a pharmaceutical chemist whose business was in Shields Road, Newcastle. Edgar was then thirty-nine and Linda thirty-seven. For many years they lived at 3 Wentworth Terrace in the Northumberland village of Allendale.

In 1933 he was a co-author (with fellow Bach Choir member Annie Lawton and its conductor W. G. Whittaker) of the 'Folk Song Sight Singing' series. (See fig. 97.)

Edgar died on 26 July 1967 at Hexham General Hospital, aged seventy-six. After his death Linda moved to Whitley Bay, where she died on 27 October 1974 at the Star Cross Rest Home, aged eighty-one. They had no children.

Fig. 97 Book I of the 'Folk Song Sight Singing' series, pub. 1933.

The author acknowledges the collaboration of John Rutherford with this biography.

Hugh Latimer Featherstone, MA (DUNELM) (1893–1976)
Bass 1915–16

HUGH LATIMER FEATHERSTONE, fourth of five children of John George Featherstone and Eleanor Gills, was born in Newcastle upon Tyne. His father, who was a building society cashier, came from Newcastle and his mother from Sunderland, County Durham. For many years the family lived at 15 Larkspur Terrace in the Newcastle suburb of Jesmond.

Hugh obtained a first class honours MA degree at Durham University in English and modern history. While at Durham he joined the Officers' Training Corps, in which he served for three years, attaining the rank of second lieutenant. He undertook a two-year research studentship at Armstrong College of Durham University in Newcastle, where he also received teacher training and obtained a Board of Education certificate. While in training he became a lecturer for the

Workers' Educational Association, in which he maintained an interest throughout his life.

Hugh first met W. G. Whittaker while he was at Armstrong College, and joined the bass line of the Bach Choir for its inaugural concert in November 1915. During his time in the choir he sang in three concerts devoted to Bach cantatas and in one concert of British music. His last concert with the choir was in May 1916.

In 1916 Hugh was appointed to a teaching post at Oswestry Grammar School, but in January that year he was called up for war service and placed on the Army reserve list. From 1917 to 1920 he taught at Lancaster Royal Grammar School. In July 1918 he was finally mobilized for military service, and qualified as a driver of heavy military vehicles, serving in the

Fig. 98 From the *Nottingham Evening Post*, 1941. *Courtesy Local World Limited and the British Library.*

Royal Army Service Corps (Motor Transport Division) at Woolwich dockyard. He attained the rank of corporal and was demobilized in February 1919. In 1920 he was appointed assistant lecturer in history at the City of Leeds Training College.

In 1924 Hugh married Mabel Gertrude Holmes in Driffield, Yorkshire. Mabel was born in Canada on 24 May 1885.

In 1927 he was appointed organizing lecturer for the Miners' Welfare Adult Education Joint Committee of University College, Nottingham, where he taught modern history until his retirement. For many years he and Mabel lived at 13 Huntingdon Drive, Nottingham.

In 1939 Hugh published his seminal work *A Century of Nationalism* (Thomas Nelson & Sons). Throughout his professional life he was a popular local public speaker, and during the Second World War gave several speeches in which he analysed and condemned Nazi ideology.

Hugh died on 13 March 1976 at his home 13 Huntingdon Drive, aged eighty-three. Mabel survived him by only fifteen days, and died on 28 March at the home of her niece in Charlbury, Oxfordshire. She was ninety.

Archibald Scott Gillies (1886–1950)
Bass 1916

ARCHIBALD SCOTT GILLIES, only child of Henry Walton Gillies and Anne (Annie) Scott, was born in Hexham, Northumberland. His father was also born in Hexham and his mother in Alston, Cumberland. His father was an ironmonger, who had inherited the family business from his father William and operated it from 28 Market Place, Hexham. Archibald in turn inherited and ran the ironmongery business. Ann Scott's father, Thomas, was a Hexham boot- and shoemaker who was born in Wark, near Bellingham. Henry Gillies and family lived at a variety of addresses in Hexham, but by 1911 they were at 4 Crescent Avenue.

Archibald was a first cousin of W. G. Whittaker by descent from their grandparents William Gillies and Susanna Walton. He was also a second cousin of Jane Walton Fleming.

Archibald joined the bass line of the Bach Choir in the March 1916 concert, which featured Bach cantatas. His final concert with the choir was its next performance, in May 1916, in a programme of British music. One possible reason for his brief association with his cousin's choir is given on p. 33.

Archibald married Hannah Meggie Hewitson in Hexham in 1917, and they had one daughter, Edna Ritson, who was born on 14 June 1921. They lived at Glenariffe, Elvaston Drive, Hexham.

Edna became an elementary school teacher and taught in Stocksfield, Prudhoe and Hexham. She did not marry, and died on 4 November 2007.

Archibald died on 19 October 1950 in Hexham, aged sixty-four. Hannah died in 1983, aged ninety.

William Robert James, M.SC. (1902–1985)
Bass 1924–81   Choir Secretary 1936–47
Assistant Conductor and Secretary 1947–81

WILLIAM ROBERT (WILLIE) JAMES, eldest of three children of William Edward James and Mary Ellen Batey, was born in Gateshead, County Durham. His father, who was born in Gateshead, worked as a labourer for the Newcastle and Gateshead Gas Company; his mother was born in Newcastle. The family lived at 56 Hyde Park Street, Gateshead.

William attended Armstrong College of Durham University in Newcastle, where he studied chemistry and graduated as a master of science. He later taught chemistry at Gateshead Grammar School, where his friend and fellow Bach Choir bass Eric Rimer also taught. William played an active part in the musical life of the school, conducting and training the school choir. He eventually became deputy headmaster. In his final professional years he was headmaster of Heathfield Grammar School, Gateshead.

Fig. 99 From the 1925 choir photo-graph.

Fig. 100 From a 1927 choir photograph.

William joined the bass line of the Bach Choir in April 1924. During his years in the choir under the conductorship of W. G. Whittaker he sang in six concerts wholly or partly devoted to Bach cantatas, in three performances of the St John Passion, and in two performances each of the St Matthew Passion and the B minor Mass. William sang in concerts with music by Holst (the *Ode to Death* and *The Golden Goose*), Vaughan Williams (*Sancta Civitas* and *Flos Campi*) and Bax (*This Worldes Joie* and *Mater ora Filium*). He sang in the 1924 London and Newcastle performances of Byrd's Great Service and was on the 1927 tour of Germany. He was in the May 1929 performance of the Tallis forty-part motet *Spem in alium*.

He married Annie Wright on 25 December 1931 at the Whitehall Road Primitive Methodist Church, Gateshead. For many years they lived at 21 Glenbrooke Terrace, Low Fell, Gateshead.

After the departure of Whittaker in 1930 William maintained his membership of the choir, singing under Sidney Newman, J. A. Westrup, Chalmers Burns and Percy Lovell. His last concert with the choir was on 7 March 1981, in a performance of Bach's St John Passion. His membership of the choir had spanned fifty-seven years. His contributions to the life of the choir were immense. Between about 1947 and 1965 he held the positions of assistant conductor and choir secretary. From 1964, after the amalgamation of the two secretarial posts, he was assistant conductor and secretary.

William and Annie were also patrons of the Bach Choir. Among his other musical activities William also conducted the Blyth Oriana Choir, which combined with the Bach Choir in several concerts.

In about 1969 William and Annie moved to Whitley Bay, where they lived at Lerwick, 24 South Parade. Annie died in Newcastle in 1972, aged seventy-four. They had no children.

William died on 7 May 1985 at his home in Whitley Bay, aged eighty-two. To commemorate his life, the Bach Choir performed the final chorale from the St John Passion at its concert on 22 June that year.

Fig. 101 At Gateshead Grammar School, 1951.

Nathaniel Keys (1869–1929)
Bass 1921–7

NATHANIEL KEYS, only child of James Keys Robins and Emma Murfin, was born in Derby. At birth he was registered as Nathaniel Keys Robins. His father, who was also born in Derby, was a cordwainer (shoemaker), as his father, William Robins, had been before him. Nathaniel's mother, who was born in Brailsford, Derbyshire, was the daughter of a blacksmith. In the 1871 census the family had adopted the surname Keys. Nathaniel's father died in 1873. The next record

we have of Nathaniel is in the 1881 census, when he was a pupil at the Chester
Certified Industrial School and was registered under the name 'Nathaniel Robin
Key'. He followed in his father's and grandfather's footsteps and became a shoe-
maker.

Nathaniel married a local girl, Eliza Chadwick, in Christ Church, Chester, in
1890. They had seven children and settled in the Cheshire town of Farndon. On
1 April 1900 Nathaniel signed up with the Cheshire Yeomanry and remained with
them until 1917. He served with the regiment in the Boer campaign in South
Africa.

Fig. 102 Family photograph,   Fig. 103 From the 1922 choir
c. 1900.   photograph.

The Keys family were still living in Farndon in August 1918, when their son
George joined the Royal Welsh Fusiliers for war service. By the time George was
demobilized in October 1919 the family had moved to Newcastle, where they were
living at 11 Queen's Gardens in the Newcastle suburb of Longbenton. Nathaniel
had returned to shoemaking.

Nathaniel joined the bass line of the Bach Choir in November 1921. During his
years in the choir he sang in fourteen concerts wholly or partly devoted to Bach
cantatas and in one performance each of the St John and St Matthew Passions and
the B Minor Mass. He sang in concerts with music by Holst (the *Ode to Death* and
The Cloud Messenger), Vaughan Williams (the Mass in G minor) and Bax (*Mater
ora Filium* and *This Worldes Joie*). He was in the 1922 London Bach Festival and
the 1924 London and Newcastle performances of Byrd's Great Service. His last
concert with the choir was in January 1927, so he missed the choir's tour of
Germany later that year.

Fig. 104 Family photograph, undated.

Nathaniel died suddenly of a stroke on 30 August 1929, aged sixty, while on holiday with his wife at the home of their son John Henry Keys in Worthing. He is buried in Benton churchyard in Newcastle.

Eliza died at 3 William Street Gosforth, Newcastle, on 4 March 1944, aged seventy-four, and is buried with her husband.

The author acknowledges the collaboration of John Keys with this biography.

James Osborne Richardson (1887–1965)
Bass 1915–28

JAMES OSBORNE RICHARDSON, third of five children of George Richardson and Mary Ann Davison, was born in South Shields, County Durham, where his parents had been born. His father was a civil servant who worked in the Mercantile Marine Office of the Board of Trade in South Shields, where he progressed from clerk to cashier and finally became deputy superintendent. In 1911 the family lived at 22 Mowbray Road, South Shields.

James was a pupil at the Mortimer Road Schools in South Shields. He followed his father into the Mercantile Marine Office, where he was enrolled as a boy clerk in June 1902. From 1907 to 1915 he was a member of the bass line of the Newcastle and Gateshead Choral Union.

Surviving War Office records show that he voluntarily enlisted in the Durham University Officers' Training Corps as a cadet on 10 May 1915, and on 14 October was appointed to a temporary commission as second lieutenant with the 20th Battalion the Durham Light Infantry. He then served in France with the 123rd Infantry Brigade of the British Expeditionary Force from 11 February until 9 September 1916. His experiences of army life were not good, and it became clear to his superiors that he did not possess 'the character or temperament required of a leader of men'. He then resigned his commission and returned to England. He was admitted to an army hospital, where he was treated for a number of health problems including trench foot. He was placed on the Army reserve list for the duration of the hostilities.

Fig. 105 From the 1922 choir photograph.

Fig. 106 From a 1927 choir photograph.

James joined the bass line of the Bach Choir for its inaugural concert in November 1915. During his years in the choir he sang in twenty-eight concerts wholly or partly devoted to Bach cantatas, in three performances each of the St John and St Matthew Passions, and in two performances of the B Minor Mass. He sang in concerts with music by Holst (*The Hymn of Jesus*, the *Ode to Death* and *The Cloud Messenger*), Vaughan Williams (the Mass in G minor and *Sancta Civitas*) and Bax (*Mater ora Filium* and *This Worldes Joie*). He sang in the 1922 London Bach Festival and in the 1924 London and Newcastle performances of Byrd's Great Service, and was on the 1927 tour of Germany. His last concert with the choir was in April 1928.

In 1933 he was promoted to 'clerk special class' and spent the remainder of his working life as a clerical officer for the Board of Trade.

His elder brother, George Ernest, became a bank manager and lived for many years at Osborne House, Hexham.

James eventually settled in Corbridge, a small town situated between Newcastle and Hexham, where he is known to have lived at Ingleneuk, Princes Street, from about 1954 until his death.

He died on 13 December 1965 at the Hexham General Hospital, aged seventy-eight. He was unmarried.

The Rimer Brothers

WILLIAM THIRKELD RIMER, who was born in Howdon-on-Tyne, was a railway engineering inspector. He married Elizabeth Polhill (who was born in Dover, Kent) in Birmingham in 1866. They went to live at Rowan Tree Cottage in the village of Ratho, near Edinburgh, where their first four children were born between 1868 and 1875. The third of these children, Alfred Henry Rimer, was born on 23 November 1871. About 1876 the Rimer family moved to Tyneside, where they first lived at 70 Rosedale Terrace, Tynemouth. Their sixth child was born in 1877 and their seventh in 1883, by which time they were living at 39 Tenth Avenue, not far from the Heaton railway maintenance depot.

Alfred Henry Rimer followed in his father's footsteps and joined the London and North Eastern Railway Company in 1885, serving his apprenticeship at the Gateshead engine works. In 1896 he married Edith Lizzie Redshaw (Gateshead-born) in Gateshead. She and Alfred had seven children between 1897 and 1912. The first two were born in Blyth, Northumberland; the third and fourth in Middlesbrough; and the fifth and sixth in Berwick-upon-Tweed. During those years Alfred held supervisory posts at the Heaton, Middlesbrough and Tweed-mouth engine sheds, and at some stage was posted to Newport, South Wales. Their sixth child died in infancy in 1907. In 1911 the family were living at 98 Rothbury Terrace, Heaton, at which time Alfred was a foreman at the Heaton engine works. Their seventh child was born in 1912. In 1924 Alfred was appointed assistant to the divisional locomotive running superintendent at the Gateshead engine works, and the family moved to live at Glendale, Alverstone Avenue, Low Fell. In 1926 he was appointed technical assistant to the locomotive running superintendent at the Gateshead works. He held this post until his retirement, owing to ill health, in 1932. He died in 1934.

Of Alfred and Edith's many children two, Eric and Ernest, were associated with the Bach Choir. The author acknowledges the collaboration of Pauline Rimer, David Rimer, Jeremy Rimer and Hugh Hedley with the biographies that follow.

Eric Rimer, M.SC. (1903–1972)
Bass 1924–6 and 1931–late 1960s   Choir Secretary 1950s–1960s

Fig. 107 In Cheadle Hume, 1930.   Fig. 108 At Gateshead Gram-
Family photograph.   mar School, 1951.

ERIC RIMER, fourth of seven children of Alfred Henry Rimer and Edith Lizzie
Redshaw, was born in Middlesbrough.

Eric's primary education was at Kells Lane School, Gateshead. He attended
Gateshead Higher Grade Intermediate School, where he passed the Oxford Local
Examination in 1915 at the age of twelve. He progressed to the Gateshead
Co-educational Grammar School and went on to read physics at Armstrong College
of Durham University in Newcastle, graduating as a master of science.

It was at Armstrong College that Eric first met W. G. Whittaker. He joined the bass line of the Bach Choir with his brother Ernest for the May concert of 1924. Both brothers sang together in the next eight concerts. During that period in the choir Eric sang in two concerts wholly or partly devoted to Bach cantatas and in one performance of the St Matthew Passion. He sang in one performance of Holst's *Ode to Death*, in a performance of a Taverner mass and in the Gibbons tercentenary concert. He was in the 1924 Newcastle and London performances of Byrd's Great Service (in which he sang in the semi-chorus). His final concert in that phase of his membership of the choir was in December 1925.

In 1926 Eric was appointed to teach physics at Cheadle Hulme Boys' Grammar School. He remained there until 1931, when took up a similar position at his alma mater, Gateshead Grammar School.

Eric returned to the North East and married Kate Dawson in December 1931. Kate was an Armstrong College graduate teacher of French and Latin and a former pupil of Gateshead Co-educational Grammar School. At first they lived in Alderley Road, Low Fell, but after a couple of years they moved to 14 Lime-trees Gardens, Low Fell, where they lived for many years. They had two children: Jonathan, born in 1937 (who became a dentist) and David, born in 1945 (who became a veterinary surgeon).

Eric resumed his membership of the Bach Choir in 1931, and began a long and active phase in which he sang under three subsequent conductors, Sidney Newman, J. A. Westrup and Chalmers Burns. He occasionally sang solo parts, as for example in a concert at Alnwick parish church in 1951 and in the choir's 1954 performance of Bach's St Matthew Passion. The final programme record of his singing comes from February 1958.

At Gateshead Grammar School, Eric was a friend and professional colleague of that other Bach Choir stalwart and fellow bass, William Robert James. He was honorary secretary of the Bach Choir in the 1950s and early 1960s, and also secretary of the National Federation of Music Societies. Kate and Eric hosted many famous soloists to the Bach Choir, including Celia Arieli, Mona Benson, April Cantelo, Alfred Deller, Carl Dolmetsch, Léon Goossens, Margaret Moncrieff, Joseph Saxby, Peter Wallfisch and Denis Weatherley.

Eric's teaching career progressed, and he eventually became deputy headmaster of the school. He was a formidable teacher, remembered however with affection by many former pupils. Although he had had no formal musical education, his main hobby was music. At Gateshead Grammar School he taught musical appreci-ation, ran a recorder club and helped to direct the school choir, taking the lead in a 1937 production of *Dido and Aeneas*. He had other outside interests. He was a keen sportsman, playing hockey at county level, and was an active member of the Newcastle Lawn Tennis Association.

Eric retired in 1969 but taught mathematics part-time for a further two years at the newly-built Heathfield Comprehensive School.

Eric died on 11 January 1972, aged sixty-eight, and Kate in 2000, aged ninety-four.

Ernest Rimer, B.SC. (1905–1975)
Bass 1924–30

Fig. 109 From a 1927 choir photograph.

Fig. 110 Family photograph, *c.*1955.

ERNEST RIMER, fifth of seven children of Alfred Henry Rimer and Edith Lizzie Redshaw, was born in Berwick-upon-Tweed. He followed in his elder brother Eric's footsteps and studied physics at Armstrong College of Durham University in Newcastle from 1923 to 1926, graduating as a bachelor of science.

It was at Armstrong College that Ernest first met W. G. Whittaker. He joined the bass line of the Bach Choir with Eric in May 1924. The brothers sang together in the next eight concerts until Eric took up a teaching post at Cheadle Hulme. After his brother's departure, Ernest was entered in the programmes as 'E. Rimer'. During his time in the choir he sang in eight concerts wholly or partly dedicated to Bach cantatas and in two performances each of the St John and St Matthew Passions and the B Minor Mass. He sang in concerts with music by Holst (the *Ode to Death*, *The Golden Goose* and *The Hymn of Jesus*), Vaughan

Williams (*Sancta Civitas* and *Flos Campi*) and Bax (*Mater ora Filium*). He sang in the 1924 Newcastle and London performances of Byrd's Great Service and was on the 1927 tour of Germany. He was in the May 1929 performance of the Tallis forty-part motet *Spem in alium*. There is a May 1929 newspaper report of him obtaining second prize in the open bass song class at the North of England Musical Tournament in Newcastle. In December 1929 he was the bass soloist in the fifty-first concert of the Armstrong College Choral Society; this was the last concert with this society that Whittaker conducted. It is thought that Ernest's final performance with the Bach Choir was in Whittaker's last concert as its conductor, in May 1930. It is known that his brother Eric returned to the North East in 1931, and it is likely that Eric is the bass referred to thereafter in the programmes as 'E. Rimer'.

Ernest left the North East in about 1931 to take up a post teaching physics at Lowestoft Grammar School. In August 1936 he married Mary Kathleen Devereaux (known as Kathleen), the daughter of Ernest Devereaux, a local grocer, at South Cliff Congregational Church, Lowestoft. They had one son, Jeremy, who was born in 1939, and they adopted a daughter, Sally, in 1943.

During the Second World War, Lowestoft Grammar School was evacuated to Worksop in Nottinghamshire, returning to Lowestoft in 1944 after the cessation of hostilities.

From 1958 to 1968 Ernest and Kathleen lived at 18 Gunton Drive, Lowestoft, and from 1968 to 1975 at Hillcrest, Lound, Suffolk.

Ernest continued with his singing as a member of the Lowestoft Amateur Operatic and Dramatic Society, with the Suffolk Singers and in the Aldeburgh Festival chorus. He was a keen hockey player and latterly became a hockey umpire.

Ernest died suddenly on 2 January 1975 at Lowestoft Hospital, aged sixty-nine. Kathleen died on 16 September 1984 in Norwich, aged seventy-nine.

Ernest George Robinson (1890–1968)
Bass 1915–29   Honorary Auditor from 1925

ERNEST GEORGE ROBINSON, the eldest of four children of George Robinson and Ann Jane Mitford, was born in Newcastle upon Tyne. His father was born in Belsay, a small village about fifteen miles west of Newcastle, and his mother in Newcastle itself. George Robinson worked for most of his life as an engine fitter, but in 1911 was recorded as a retired restaurant proprietor. From about 1891 the family lived at a variety of addresses in Longley Street, Newcastle, but finally at No. 68.

Ernest started his working life as a clerk with the Westminster Insurance Company at their branch in Mosley Street, Newcastle. The firm was later taken over by the Guardian Assurance Company.

Fig. 111 From the 1922 choir photograph.

Fig. 112 From a 1927 choir photograph.

He was a member of the bass line of the Newcastle and Gateshead Choral Union from 1911 to 1914. He joined the bass line of the Bach choir for its inaugural concert in November 1915 and sang in all concerts until May 1916, when he was called up for military service in the Yorkshire and Lancashire Regiment.

On demobilization (with the rank of colonel) he rejoined the Bach Choir for its concert in November 1921. During his years in the choir he sang in seventeen concerts wholly or partly dedicated to Bach cantatas, in two performances each of the St John and St Matthew Passions (taking minor solo parts in each concert), and in three performances of the B Minor Mass. He sang in concerts with music by Holst (the *Ode to Death*, *The Cloud Messenger* and *The Golden Goose*), Vaughan Williams (the Mass in G minor, *Sancta Civitas* and *Flos Campi*) and Bax (*Mater ora Filium* and *This Worldes Joie*). Notably he sang in the semi-chorus for the performance of *Flos Campi*. He sang in the 1922 London Bach Festival and in the 1924 London and Newcastle performances of Byrd's Great Service (in which he sang in the semi-chorus), and was on the 1927 tour of Germany. He was in the semi-chorus for the November 1927 performance of Rubbra's *La Belle Dame sans*

Merci and sang in the May 1929 performance of the Tallis forty-part motet *Spem in alium*, but was incorrectly referred to as 'E. J. Robinson' in the concert programme. His final concert with the choir was in May 1929. Ernest was also honorary auditor for the choir for a number of years from about 1925.

Ernest married Gladys Josephine Weir, the daughter of William Stephen Weir, a chartered accountant from Whitley Bay, on 25 June 1929 at the parish church of St Hilda, Newcastle. At about his time Ernest was transferred by his firm to the company's branch in Leeds, and he and Gladys set up home at 5 Parklands Crescent, Stonegate Road. Their only child, George, was born in 1931 at the home of Gladys's mother in Newcastle.

While in Leeds Ernest sang in the bass line with the Leeds Philharmonic Choir, with the Leeds Triennial Festival Choir and with a small soirée group that he and a number of colleagues had formed to give recitals at private functions.

Ernest was eventually promoted to superintendent of the Leeds branch of the Guardian Assurance Company, and retired in 1955.

Gladys died in Leeds in 1964, aged sixty-five. Ernest then gave up singing and went to live with his son, who also lived in Leeds. He travelled frequently, however, to Newcastle to visit his sister. He died on 19 September 1968 at the Scotton Banks Hospital in Knaresborough, aged seventy-eight.

The author acknowledges the collaboration of George D. Robinson with this biography.

Edward Thomas Stewart (1883–1966)
Bass 1919–39

EDWARD THOMAS STEWART, sixth of nine children of Robert Stewart and Ellen Jane Kennedy, was born in Gateshead, County Durham. His father, who was an engineering machine worker, was born in Dundee, and his mother in Newcastle. The family lived at 126 St Cuthbert's Road, Gateshead.

Edward followed his father into engineering and by 1911 was working as a mill-wright. He married Elizabeth Mary Bamlett, the daughter of George Bamlett, a colliery engineer, in Gateshead in 1906. They had four daughters, born between 1907 and 1921, the last of whom died in infancy. Their first address was 31 Rectory Place, Gateshead.

Edward joined the bass line of the Bach Choir in November 1919. Under Whittaker's conductorship he sang in nineteen concerts wholly or partly dedicated to Bach cantatas, in three performances of the St John Passion (singing minor solo parts in each), in three performances of the St Matthew Passion (singing minor solo parts in two), and in three performances of the B Minor Mass. He sang in concerts with music by Holst (*The Hymn of Jesus*, the *Ode to Death*, *The Cloud Messenger* and *The Golden Goose*), Vaughan Williams (the Mass in G minor, *Sancta Civitas* and *Flos Campi*) and Bax (*Mater ora Filium* and *This Worldes Joie*). Notably he sang in the semi-chorus for the performance of *Sancta Civitas*. He sang in the 1922 London Bach Festival, the 1924 London and Newcastle performances of Byrd's Great Service (in which he sang in the semi-chorus) and was on the 1927 tour of Germany. He was in the semi-chorus for the November 1927 performance of Rubbra's *La Belle Dame sans Merci* and sang in the May 1929 performance of the Tallis forty-part motet *Spem in alium*.

Fig. 113 From the 1922 choir photograph.

Fig. 114 From a 1927 choir photograph.

Not only was Edward interested in singing but he was also an accomplished amateur artist. He produced a fine series of cartoon drawings of the 1927 tour of Germany and the associated recording in the Parlophone studio in London. They were published in booklet form by his fellow Bach Choir chorister Wilson Large. A typical example is fig. 115, showing Whittaker rehearsing the choir in the hot studio. (Note the label 'Parle voo'!)

After Whittaker's departure Edward sang under Sidney Newman. The last programme record of him singing in the choir was in February 1939. Choir lists were suspended during the Second World War, and it is possible that he sang under J. A. Westrup. There are no post-war records of him singing in the choir.

In 1939 Edward and Elizabeth moved to live at 96 Druridge Drive in the Fenham area of Newcastle.

Fig. 115 Stewart's cartoon of 1927.

In his final months Edward went to live with his daughter Lilian in York, and died at the City Hospital on 26 October 1966, aged eighty-three. Elizabeth died on 30 November 1971 at Laburnum Nursing Home, 4 Edwards Road, Whitley Bay, aged ninety-five.

The author acknowledges the collaboration of Douglas S. Blackett with this biography.

Henry Stanley Todd (1895–1931)
Bass 1920–24

HENRY STANLEY TODD (known as Stanley), youngest of six children of John Francis Todd and Elizabeth Campbell, was born in Newcastle upon Tyne. His father, who was born in Seaton Delaval, Northumberland, was a tailor and mercer whose business was at 40 Westmorland Road, Newcastle. His mother was born in the Cramlington area of Northumberland. In 1881 John and Elizabeth Todd were living at 1 Dobson Street in the Elswick area of Newcastle, and in 1891 they were living in the Arthur's Hill area at 96 Beaconsfield Street. By 1901 the family had moved a short distance within the same area to 60 Malvern Street, where they lived for many years.

Fig. 116 From the 1922 choir photograph.

Stanley became a schoolmaster. In the First World War he served with the 2nd Battalion the Royal Engineers as a sapper (the equivalent of a private in other regiments). It is not known when he enlisted, but he began serving in France on 16 July 1915. At some stage he was discharged from service for medical reasons. He was awarded the 1915 Star (awarded to those who entered service before 31 December 1915) and the Allied Victory Medal. The Royal Engineers were very much in the front line of combat, involved in the construction and maintenance of railways, roads, bridges, waterways, communications (signalling and wireless) and tunnelling. Stanley's war experiences were to have a lasting impact on him.

He joined the bass line of the Bach Choir in May 1920. During his time in the choir he sang in twelve concerts wholly or partly dedicated to Bach cantatas and one performance each of the St John Passion and the B Minor Mass. He sang in concerts with music by Holst (*The Hymn of Jesus*, the *Ode to Death* and *The Cloud Messenger*), Vaughan Williams (the Mass in G minor) and Bax (*Mater ora Filium*). He sang in the 1922 London Bach Festival. His last concert with the choir was in April 1924; he therefore missed the London and Newcastle performances of Byrd's Great Service later that year.

From the mid to the late 1920s he taught at Wingrove School, Newcastle.

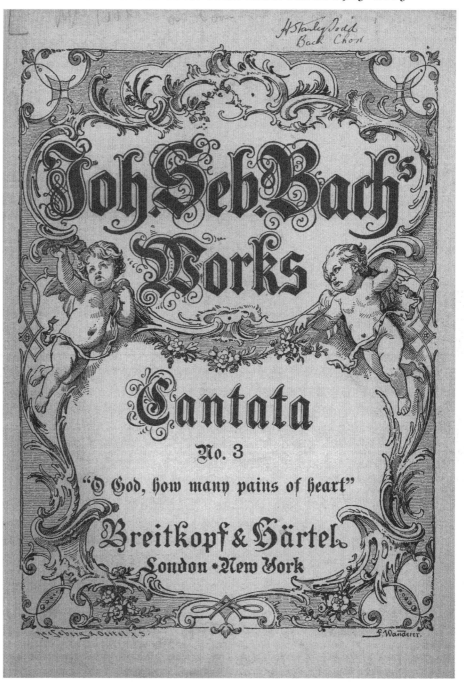

Fig. 117 Stanley's personal score from the London Bach Festival concert on 22 February 1922.

Fig. 118 With the Wingrove Amateur Football Club, late 1920s. Family photograph.

Stanley's war service had had a profound effect on his mental health, and he developed a problem with alcohol. He was found dead by his father at the family home in Malvern Street on 16 January 1931, aged thirty-five. He was unmarried.

Many of Stanley's autographed musical scores, from which he sang in the Bach Choir's early concerts, were presented to the author by his sister, Ethel, in the 1960s.

The author acknowledges the collaboration of the late Margaret Davies, the late Ethel Todd and Carol Cowley with this biography.

Isaac Winter (1890–1967)
Bass 1915–c.1939   Honorary General Secretary 1924–34

ISAAC WINTER, the second of two children of William Winter and Isabella Jane Walton, was born in North Shields, Northumberland. His father, who worked for an estate agent, was born in Newcastle and his mother in Haltwhistle, Northumberland. For many years the family lived in Croydon Road, Newcastle, first at No. 104 and later at No. 135.

Isaac worked for the Tyne Improvement Commission, first as a clerk but finally as assistant treasurer. On 6 September 1922 he married Mary Hetherington, a clerk at an electric works, at Jesmond parish church, Newcastle. Her father,

Fig. 119 From the 1922 choir photograph.

George Hetherington, had been a foreman at the Elswick Cemetery, Newcastle, but at the time of the marriage he was a superintendent registrar of births, marriages and deaths.

Isaac was a member of the bass line in the Newcastle and Gateshead Choral Union from 1915 until the late 1930s. He joined the bass line of the Bach Choir for its inaugural concert in November 1915. During his years in the choir under the conductorship of W. G. Whittaker he sang in twenty-four concerts wholly or partly dedicated to Bach cantatas, in four performances of the St John Passion, and in three performances each of the St Matthew Passion and the B Minor Mass. He sang in concerts with music by Holst (*The Hymn of Jesus*, the *Ode to Death*, *The Cloud Messenger* and *The Golden Goose*), Vaughan Williams (the Mass in G minor, *Sancta Civitas* and *Flos Campi*) and Bax (*Mater ora Filium* and *This Worldes Joie*). He sang in the 1922 London Bach Festival and in the 1924 London and Newcastle performances of Byrd's Great Service (in which he sang in the semi-chorus), and he was on the 1927 tour of Germany. He was in the May 1929 performance of the Tallis forty-part motet *Spem in alium*, but was incorrectly referred to in the concert programme as 'Mr S. Winter'. Isaac continued to sing in the choir under Sidney Newman, and the last concert programme record of him is in February 1939. It is possible that he sang with the choir after this date, but there were no choir lists published during the Second World War to verify this. He was not listed in 1947.

Initially Isaac and Mary lived in Stocksfield, a small village along the Tyne valley. At first they lived in New Ridley Road, but from about 1941 to 1955 were at Heather Wyn, East Ridley. Apart from his interest in music, Isaac was a keen golfer and a member of the Stocksfield Golf Club.

About 1955 they moved to Gosforth and lived at 15 Elmfield Grove. Isaac joined the City of Newcastle Golf Club. A relative remembers that he frequently wore plus fours, with long woollen stockings that his wife knitted for him.

Isaac died on 15 July 1967 at his home in Gosforth, aged seventy-seven. Mary died in 1978, aged eighty-two. They had no children.

The author acknowledges the collaboration of Edith Armstrong with this biography.

Fig. 120 From a 1927 choir photograph.

Chapter 8
Vocal Soloists

Philip Owen

Norah Lilian Allison (1898–1962)
Soprano soloist 1921, 1923, 1924 and 1926

Norah Lilian Allison, eldest of three children of Francis James Allison and Ellen Pickering, was born in Chester-le-Street, County Durham. Her father was born in Perkinsville, a small village near Chester-le-Street, and her mother in Sherburn, a village in the Ryedale district of North Yorkshire situated between Malton and Scarborough. Francis Allison began his working life as an iron-moulder but then entered the coal mining industry, where he became a colliery overman and finally a coal trade agent. Eventually he worked for his father, William Allison, who was a partner with Joseph English in the firm of Allison, English & Co., which owned the Union Brickworks in Birtley, near Chester-le-Street. William Allison was prominent in the local Primitive Methodist circuit and an alderman and member of the Durham County Council. Ellen Pickering was the daughter of Stephen Pickering, who was a railway signalman. The Pickering family moved from Sherburn to the Chester-le-Street area between 1878 and 1880. Norah and her parents lived in Birtley, first at 178 Wilfred Street, but later they moved to Morley House, where they were living in 1911.

Norah was a talented soprano. She first sang as a soloist with the Bach Choir in November 1921, in a concert featuring three Bach cantatas, of which she sang in two. Her co-soloists were Annie Lawton, Tom Purvis and Arthur Lewis.

In 1922 she sang in a concert with the Armstrong College Choral Society, Newcastle, under the conductorship of W. G. Whittaker, and in November 1923 was in a performance of Handel's *Belshazzar* with the Hetton-le-Hole church choir.

Norah's next Bach Choir concert was in March 1923, when she sang soprano arias in a performance of Bach's B Minor Mass, in which her co-soloists were Gladys Thompson, Hilda Rood, Tom Purvis, Arthur Lewis and Ernest Potts. In February 1924 she sang again with the Bach Choir, in a programme featuring Holst's choral work *The Cloud Messenger* and two of Bach's secular cantatas (in both of which she sang the soprano solos). In this concert her co-soloists were Marjorie Amati, Rosa Burn, Ernest Hudspith and Ernest Potts.

On 22 July 1925 Norah married Robert Wilson, a butcher who worked at a local Co-operative store, at the Primitive Methodist Church in Birtley. At the time of her marriage she was still living at the family home, Morley House in Birtley.

Norah's final concert with the Bach Choir was in March 1926, in another performance of the B Minor Mass. On this occasion her co-soloists were Gladys Thompson, Ruby Longhirst, Tom Danskin, William Hendry and Mr H. Shuttleworth. She was incorrectly entered in two Bach Choir concert programmes: as 'Lillian B. Allison' in one and as 'Lillian D. Allison' in the other.

Norah continued her singing career after her marriage, performing under her maiden name. There are numerous newspaper references to her as a soloist on Newcastle Radio 5NO between 1924 and 1931, often appearing with the local station's orchestra. She also broadcast from the Manchester studio with the Northern Wireless Orchestra. She was a soloist in December 1931 with the Newcastle and Gateshead Choral Union in a performance of Arthur Sullivan's *The Golden Legend*.

Her marriage to Robert Wilson, which was childless, did not last, and they eventually divorced. On 5 August 1939, at the age of thirty-nine, she married Daniel Pritchard, a bricklayer's labourer, at the register office of the Durham North Western registration district. They lived at 51 Douglas Gardens, Dunston. Daniel later became an overhead crane driver at an engineering works.

Norah died on 20 August 1962 at her home in Dunston, aged sixty-four, and Daniel on 3 February 1964 at the Newcastle General Hospital, aged fifty-eight. They had no children.

Rose Burn, ARCM (1889–1953)
Contralto soloist 1916–32

ROSE BURN (known as Rosa), second of three children of John Burn and Mary Ann Cowe was born in North Shields, Northumberland. Her father, who worked as a Tyne river pilot, was born in South Shields, County Durham, and her mother in the parish of Craig, Kincardineshire. At the time of her birth they were living at 4 East Percy Street, North Shields, but by 1901 they had moved to 5 Walker Place. In 1911 they were living at 2 King Edward Road, Tynemouth.

Rosa had a remarkable contralto voice, and received some of her training from William McConnell-Wood. The earliest newspaper reference to her is in February 1907, when she sang at an annual concert for the Shankhouse Children's Gala in the Shankhouse Co-operative Hall.

In 1909 Rosa obtained the ARCM diploma in singing as an external candidate of the Royal College of Music. That year she sang solos in three concerts. In March she sang at Seaton Burn under the auspices of the Cramlington and District Co-operative Society's educational scheme. In September she sang alongside Ernest Potts at a concert in the Co-operative Hall, Cramlington, and sang with him again later that month at the Co-operative Hall in Dinnington. In 1910 she was a soloist in a 'grand concert' given in Sunderland by the McConnell-Wood Northumbrian Select Choir. January 1911 saw her singing at the Prince Consort Road Primitive Methodist Church, Gateshead, at which George Danskin was the accompanist. In May that year she sang at a jubilee celebration in Cramlington Colliery for the Cramlington Co-operative Society. In December 1912 she sang at Newsham, near Blyth, for the New Delaval Co-operative Society.

In 1914 she married Christopher Brodie Thompson, the son of an accountant, who was a clerk in the coal trade. They set up home at 33 Albury Park Road, Tynemouth, close to her old home in King Edward Road and not too far from his parents' home in Preston Avenue. After her marriage she continued to perform in public as Rosa Burn.

W. G. Whittaker recruited Rosa to sing the contralto solos in the January 1914 performance of Mendelssohn's *Elijah* by the Tynemouth, Whitley and District Choral Union, of which he was the conductor. A contemporary newspaper reported that she had 'acquitted herself particularly well'. In February of that year she sang solos at one of Mr McConnell-Wood's 'popular concerts' as a member of his Northumbrian Select Choir. Edgar Bainton also conducted some orchestral pieces in the concert. In March that year she sang under Whittaker in a concert by the Armstrong College Choral Society that featured an early performance of Gustav Holst's *The Cloud Messenger* and a cantata and a motet by Bach. Her co-soloists included Ella Stelling and Ernest Potts. The next month she sang in Mendelssohn's *Elijah* with the Central Hall Choral Society in Newcastle alongside William Hendry.

In February 1915 she sang in a concert in the Heaton Electric Palace to raise funds for the St John Ambulance Brigade Field Force Hospital Fund. Later that month she performed with Edwin Kellett at the annual music service of the Tatham Street Primitive Methodist Church in Sunderland. She was described as 'possessing a voice of exceptional richness and sweetness'. In May 1916 she took part in a Richard Pearson Concert at Newcastle Town Hall.

She first sang with the Bach Choir in December 1916, in an all-Bach programme that contained two cantatas, a motet, the Clavier Concerto in F minor and the Violin Concerto in A minor. Her fellow soloists were Ella Stelling, John Vine and Ernest Potts. She sang 'with her usual steadiness and conviction'. Her next Bach Choir performance was in a concert of British music in May 1917 that featured Holst's *The Cloud Messenger*. A contemporary press report recorded that her solo work was 'artistic'. In May 1919 she was a soloist in a concert that included Bach cantatas and the Brandenburg Concerto No. 3.

January 1920 saw her in a fund-raising concert in aid of Comrades of the Great War at the Sunderland Empire Theatre. In December 1920 and January 1921 she sang in two concerts that featured Bach's Christmas Oratorio. A contemporary press report records that she 'was in beautiful voice and sang throughout with great taste'.

In April 1922 Rosa sang in the final concert of the season for the Hartlepool Harmonic Society, and in March 1923 she sang with the Northumbrian Select Choir under McConnell-Wood at the Newcastle Assembly Rooms. A contemporary press report recorded that she 'used her wonderful contralto voice with the most agreeable effect'.

Her next Bach Choir performance was March 1924, in a concert containing Holst's *The Cloud Messenger* and two of Bach's secular cantatas. Her co-soloists were Norah Allison, Marjorie Amati, Ernest Hudspith and Ernest Potts. A contemporary press report recorded that her singing in the solo 'Tarry not, O cloud' was undertaken 'with great expression'. In December 1925 she again sang with the Bach Choir, in a performance of Holst's *Ode to Death* in a programme that also included two Bach cantatas and the Brandenburg Concerto No. 5.

By 1925 her husband, Christopher, had been promoted to coal exporter's manager, but they were still living at Albury Park Road.

In 1926 Rosa was a soloist in several concerts broadcast from the local radio station, Newcastle 5NO, some of which were relayed to other stations.

Rosa's fifth appearance with the Bach Choir was in January 1927 in a programme of four Bach cantatas. Her co-soloists were Beryl Cresswell, Tom Danskin and Arthur Lewis. A contemporary press report recorded that her singing of the recitative in Cantata No. 161 was 'very advantageously heard'. In April 1928 she sang arias with the choir in a performance of the St Matthew Passion, in which her co-soloists were Ethel Durrant, Tom Danskin, Arthur Lewis and William Hendry. A contemporary press report recorded that 'Madame Burn was completely in her part emotionally, especially in "Have mercy, Lord" when the sobbing which was Bach's intention was most realistic.'

In February 1929 she appeared with the Bach Choir in a programme of four Bach cantatas with co-soloists Ethel Durrant, Tom Danskin and Arthur Lewis. Later that year she made several broadcasts on the local radio, and in November she sang in a concert with the Newcastle Philharmonic Orchestra conducted by Edgar Bainton.

Rosa's final concert with the Bach Choir under Whittaker's conductorship was the April 1930 performance of Bach's St John Passion, in which she sang the contralto arias. He co-soloists were Ena Mitchell, Tom Danskin and Arthur Lewis.

When Rosa's mother died on 8 October 1930, Rosa and Christopher moved in to the old family home at 2 King Edward Road, where her father was still living.

Rosa's penultimate Bach Choir appearance was in the March 1931 performance of the B Minor Mass, with co-soloists Norah Allison, Tom Danskin and William Hendry. Her final concert was in November 1932, in a programme that included a performance of Purcell's Ode for St Cecilia's Day. Her co-soloists were William Hendry, Thomas Newby and members of the choir.

In the early 1930s Rosa continued to perform on the radio, but there was a sharp decline in the number of her public appearances thereafter.

Christopher died on 14 November 1951 at 1 Hartside Gardens, Jesmond, aged sixty-three. Rosa died on 11 March 1953 at 87 Junction Road, Norton-on-Tees, also aged sixty-three. They had no children.

The Clapperton Family

WALTER AND ELLA CLAPPERTON were both soloists in the Bach Choir. Although Ella appears in the concert programmes under her maiden name of Stelling, it is appropriate to give their biographies together.

Walter Scott Clapperton (1892–1944)
Baritone soloist 1917, 1918, 1919 and 1920

WALTER SCOTT CLAPPERTON, youngest of four children of Walter Clapperton and Mary Ann Miller, was born in Wallsend, Northumberland. Both his parents were born in the Scottish border town of Galashiels. His father began his working life as an engine fitter. The family first lived with his maternal grandmother in Ladhope, Galashiels, where his parents were members of the parish church choir. Some time between 1881 and 1884 the family moved to Wallsend on Tyne when his father took up a post as a marine engineer in a local shipyard. He eventually became a foreman engineer. For many years the family lived at 15 The Avenue, Wallsend.

Fig. 121 Walter Clapperton and Ella Stelling. From the programme for the performance of Handel's oratorio *Samson* at the Wesleyan church in Consett on 21 April 1916.

The Clapperton family were very musical. Walter Clapperton senior was appointed leader of the Wallsend Presbyterian church choir in 1894. A newspaper
report from 1896 records a performance of Handel's *Judas Maccabaeus* given
by the church choir under the conductorship of Walter Clapperton senior, in
which the soloists included one of his daughters and the accompanist was his son
Gilbert.

Walter Scott Clapperton started his musical career as a boy chorister in
Newcastle Cathedral. He was a talented singer, and in adult life had a remarkable
baritone voice. He was auditioned by the Royal College of Music and offered
a scholarship, but his acceptance had to be deferred because he was called up for
military service in September 1914. He joined the Northumberland Division of
the Army Service Corps, serving as a driver, and was later promoted to lance
corporal. In November 1917 he was transferred to the Army Reserve on health
grounds.

Walter first sang as a soloist with the Bach Choir in the February 1917
performance of Bach's St John Passion, in which he sang the bass arias and in
the role of Jesus. He next sang with the choir in December 1917, in a programme

of British Christmas music by composers such as Byrd, Bainton, Holst, Parry and Whittaker. A contemporary press report recorded that he 'sang very artistically three traditional carols with string accompaniment'.

In 1918 he married Ella May Stelling; the remainder of his career and married life are summarized below.

Ella May Stelling (1890–1945)
Soprano soloist 1916

ELLA MAY STELLING, second of three daughters of Christopher Stelling and Mary Ann Ord, was born in Blackhill, Consett, County Durham. Both her parents were born in County Durham, her father in Consett and her mother in Greenside, then still a village. Her father worked as a wages clerk at the Consett Iron Works. The family first lived at 16 Siemens Street in Blackhill, near Consett, but finally moved to 58 Sherburn Terrace, Consett. Christopher Stelling died in 1909, aged fifty-nine.

Ella was an excellent soprano. She studied music and undertook some of her training at the Newcastle Conservatoire, where she was a pupil in 1914 and 1915. She performed at a concert by its pupils in February 1914. The following month she sang solos in a performance of works by Bach and Gustav Holst given by the Armstrong College Choral Society under W. G. Whittaker. She became a professional singer for the Newcastle and Provincial Concerts, performing at various venues in the North East.

Ella first sang as a soloist with the Bach Choir in February 1916, in a programme that included Bach's Cantatas Nos. 10, 38 and 104. On 21 April 1916 she was a soloist in a performance of Handel's *Samson* at the Wesleyan church in her native Consett. The professional bass soloist in the concert was the young Lance Corporal Walter Scott Clapperton, from Wallsend, who at the time was serving in the Army Service Corps. Ella's last concert with the Bach Choir was in December 1916 in a programme that included Cantatas Nos. 12 and 70.

Life after marriage

Walter Scott Clapperton and Ella May Stelling married in 1918; they had a son who was born in 1921 and a daughter born in 1923.

In April 1919 Walter took up his deferred scholarship at the Royal College of Music, studying singing as his principal subject and pianoforte as a subsidiary.

His teachers included Harry Plunket Greene, Arnold Smith, Charles Wood and Herbert Fryer. During his training he was a soloist with the Oxford University Choral Society and the London Bach Choir. He was awarded the Henry Blower Memorial Prize in 1921 during his final year of study. Royal College records make no mention of his being awarded any qualifications by it. Walter became a professional singer with the Newcastle and Provincial Concerts.

In May 1918 Walter sang with the Bach Choir in a concert that featured Bach's Cantatas Nos. 180 and 106 and the ode *Lord, rebuke me not*. In April 1919 he sang the baritone aria 'Amore traditore' from an unnamed Bach secular cantata and the aria 'My heart now is merry' from the cantata *Phoebus and Pan*. His final concert with the choir was in a performance of the St Matthew Passion in February 1920, in which he sang the role of the Saviour.

In 1921 Walter was appointed professor of singing and elocution at the McGill Conservatorium in Montreal, and the family emigrated to Canada. Among Walter's famous Canadian pupils were the bass Thomas Archer and the soprano Frances James. In addition to teaching, Walter conducted a number of local choirs, including the Montreal Operatic Society, the Royal Bank Men's Choir and the Masonic Choir of Montreal.

Walter and Ella sang for the King and Queen during their 1939 Royal Tour of Canada. Not much else is known about Ella's singing activities in Montreal, but it is believed that she continued to perform occasionally in public.

Their son remained in Canada and brought up a family, and their daughter returned to live in the United Kingdom. It is believed that Walter died in 1944 and Ella in 1945; their Canadian death notices are not available. Their ashes were brought to the United Kingdom by their daughter Ella Stelling Clapperton and were interred in the Stelling family grave in Blackhill Cemetery, Consett, on 14 January 1946.

The author acknowledges the collaboration of Caryn McLaughlin (née Clapperton) with Ella's biography and that of her husband.

Thomas Danskin (1894–1977)
Tenor soloist from 1925–late 1930s

THOMAS (TOM) DANSKIN, elder of two sons of Robert Danskin and Elizabeth Gatiss, was born in Blaydon, near Gateshead, County Durham. His father, who worked as a timekeeper at Spencer's Steel Works in Lemington on Tyne, was a first cousin to George William Danskin (1888–1945), a well-known local musician,

Fig. 122 Tom Danskin in the Royal Navy, *c.*1915. Family photograph.

whose biography, along with that of his wife, is to be found in Chapter 4. Robert Danskin was also very musical, and conducted the Lemington Choral Society. Tom's mother, Elizabeth, a schoolteacher, was born in Lanchester, County Durham, and lived with her parents in the Benwell and Elswick areas of Newcastle. In 1901 Tom and his parents were living at 20 West View, Newburn on Tyne, but by 1911 they had moved to 35 Sugley Road in nearby Lemington.

Tom went to elementary school in Lemington and then studied at Rutherford College in Newcastle from about 1907 until 1911. From 1912 to 1914 he undertook teacher training at St John's College, York.

In 1914 Tom volunteered for war service and enrolled in the Royal Navy, along with his brother William, and trained as a gunner at Chatham. He served initially on a destroyer but was later transferred to the armoured cruiser HMS *Kent*. At first the *Kent* undertook convoy escort duties, but in 1918 she returned to the China station, visiting Singapore and other ports. In 1919 the *Kent* was deployed in the Siberian intervention of the Russian civil war and visited Vladivostok. Tom attained the non-commissioned rank of warrant officer. While serving in the *Kent* he occasionally sang for the ship's company and found that his efforts were warmly appreciated. He was demobilized in late 1919.

Returning to civilian life, Tom began his teaching career at an elementary school in Westerhope, Newcastle. At this time he acquired a serious interest in singing and took lessons from Edwin Kellett, formerly of Durham Cathedral. While teaching in Westerhope he met another teacher, Jane Ritson, the daughter of a tenant farmer from Lanercost in Cumbria. They married in 1922 in the Northumberland town of Haltwhistle, and had a son who was born in 1927.

In 1923 Tom won four prizes for singing at the North of England Musical Tournament, which brought him to the attention of W. G. Whittaker, who recruited him as a soloist with the Bach Choir that year. This was the beginning of a long association with the choir.

Tom first sang with the Bach Choir in the April 1925 performance of Bach's St Matthew Passion, in which he sang the role of the Narrator (Evangelist) and in the tenor arias; his co-soloists were Mrs George Dodds, Annie Lawton, Ernest Potts and Arthur Lewis. His performance was described in a contemporary press report thus: 'Not only did he strike the right devotional feeling ... but his articulation was well-nigh faultless. This was a great personal success.' The December 1925 concert featured a performance of Holst's *Ode to Death* and three Bach cantatas. Tom sang the tenor recitatives and arias in the cantatas, and was referred to in a press report as 'one of the finest tenors and Bach interpreters the North has produced'. In April 1927 he sang the role of the Evangelist and in the tenor arias in the choir's performance of the St John Passion, in which his co-soloists were Reta Robinson, Gwladys Garside and Ernest Potts. One contemporary press report commented: 'He seems rarely gifted

Fig. 123 Tom with his prizes from the North of England Musical Tournament, 1923. Family photograph.

for this type of music,' and another that he 'sang in a very flexible style and his clear diction and the ease with which he obtained the numerous high notes made his performance memorable'.

In early April 1928 Tom appeared with the choir in a performance of the St Matthew Passion, again singing the role of the Narrator and in the tenor arias. On this occasion his co-soloists were Ethel Durrant, Rosa Burn, Arthur Lewis and William Hendry. A contemporary press report stated: 'Mr Thomas Danskin carried throughout the part of the Evangelist with fine sympathy, though obviously suffering from a cold'. Later that month he sang with the choir in a concert for the Workers' Educational Association in Ashington. In February 1929 he sang with the choir in a concert of four Bach cantatas with co-soloists Ethel Durrant, Rosa Burn and Arthur Lewis. In November that year he sang baritone arias in

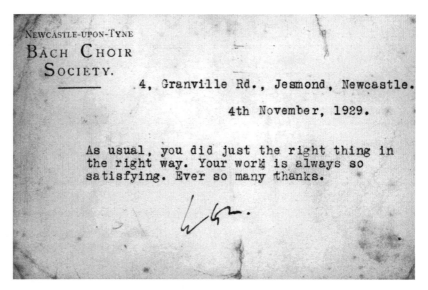

Fig. 124 Note from W .G. Whittaker after Tom's performance in
the concert on 2 November 1929. Family archive.

performances of Bach's Cantatas Nos. 30 and 130 in a concert that also featured
Holst's *The Hymn of Jesus*. Whittaker was delighted with his performances, as
illustrated in a note to Tom reproduced above.

Tom's final concert under W. G. Whittaker was in a performance of Bach's
St John Passion in April 1930, in which he sang the role of the Evangelist and
in the tenor arias. His co-soloists on that occasion were Ena Mitchell, Rosa Burn
and Arthur Lewis.

After the departure of Whittaker, Tom sang with the choir under Sidney Newman on many occasions, including performances of Bach's St Matthew Passion
and Heinrich Schutz's Christmas Oratorio.

In addition to his work with the Bach Choir, Tom broadcast regularly on local
radio and performed with many other choirs and music societies. He sang the part
of the Evangelist in a performance of Bach's St John Passion at the inaugural
concert of the Liverpool Bach Choir.

In about 1928 Tom was appointed headmaster of the school in the Northumberland village of Hartburn, near Morpeth, where he taught until 1942,
encouraging his pupils to enjoy music. He trained the school choir and achieved
success in the Wansbeck Musical Festival. The commemorative photograph is
reproduced opposite.

In 1943 Tom became headmaster of the elementary school in Holystone, a mining

Fig. 125 Hartburn School, 1935: Tom extreme left.

community in south-east Northumberland near Whitley Bay, where he remained until his retirement in 1954.

Apart from solo singing, which he continued well into the 1940s, Tom's leisure activities included boxing (while at school and in the Navy), football (which he played while at college), swimming and small-boat sailing.

Tom died on 21 September 1977, aged eighty-three, and Jane in 1986, aged ninety.

The author acknowledges the collaboration of Tom's son, Colin Danskin, with this biography.

Mrs George Dodds (1880–1945)
Soprano soloist 1915–25

AGNES JANE WINTER, youngest of six children of Stephen Robinson Winter and May Ann Blenkinsop, was born in South Shields, County Durham. Her father, who was a plumber, was born in Berwick-upon-Tweed and her mother in Newcastle. Their first two children were born in Newcastle. By 1871 the family had moved to Westoe, South Shields, where they lived first at 191 Eldon Street and then by 1881 at 116 Commercial Road. An article in the *Hartlepool Mail* of August 1883 reported that Stephen Robinson Winter, 'carrying on business at Corstorphine Town, South Shields, plumber, etc.' had gone into liquidation. By 1891 the family had returned to Newcastle and were living in the Arthur's Hill area, first at 144 Stanhope Street and by 1901 at 73 Dilston Road. Stephen Winter died in 1903, aged sixty-two.

In 1907 Agnes married George Robert Dodds, a professional musician from a distinguished local musical family.

Agnes had an excellent soprano voice. Little is known about her singing career before her marriage, from which time she is always referred to as 'Mrs George Dodds' in newspaper articles and in concert programmes. An early reference to her is at a concert by the Stannington Choral Society in 1912, in which she performed alongside her husband and brother-in-law.

She first sang as a soloist with the Bach Choir at its inaugural concert in November 1915, which featured three Bach cantatas. Her next appearance with the choir was in March 1917, in a performance of the St John Passion. In 1918 she sang in a concert of three Bach cantatas and in 1919 in a programme of music by British composers. In 1920 she appeared with the choir in two concerts: in March at a performance of the St Matthew Passion and in May in a concert featuring three Bach cantatas. That was her last appearance with the choir.

Fig. 126 Family photograph, early 1900s.

Between 1920 and 1928 there are newspaper reports of her singing as a soloist in many local concerts and also on radio Newcastle 5NO, performing folk songs accompanied at the piano by her husband. In the late 1920s she joined the soprano line of the Newcastle and Gateshead Choral Union.

For many years Agnes and George lived at 2 Queens Road, Newcastle. They had no children.

Agnes died on 9 July 1945 at her home in Queens Road, aged sixty-five. George died on 2 October 1946 at 13 Westbourne Avenue, Penarth, Glamorganshire (the home of his nephew Denis George Dodds), aged sixty-nine.

The author acknowledges the collaboration of Michael Dodds, Gareth Yeaman Dodds and Philippa John (née Dodds) with this biography.

Ethel Durrant (1897–1978)
Soprano soloist 1928 and 1929   Chorus soprano 1929–31

ETHEL DURRANT, eldest of four children of James Durrant and Elizabeth Weatherby, was born in Blyth, Northumberland, as were her parents. Her father worked as a coal trimmer, which was an arduous job that involved entering the coal bunkers in the hold of a ship and levelling the coal to 'trim' the ship ready for sea. In 1891 the Durrant family lived at 19 Wright Terrace in the Cowpen area of Blyth, but by 1911 they had moved to Crown Street.

In 1913 Ethel is recorded as having won a prize 'in the second stage of English' in the Northumberland County evening class examinations.

In 1916, at the age of nineteen, she was soprano soloist in a harvest thanks-giving service for the Primitive Methodist Church in Beaconsfield Street, Blyth. In 1920 she took part in an evening of entertainment at the Bebside Leisure Hall. In 1927 she sang in a musical programme on local radio Newcastle 5NO.

Ethel first sang as a soprano soloist with the Bach Choir in the performance of Bach's St Matthew Passion on 4 April 1928. Her co-soloists included Rosa Burn, Tom Danskin, Arthur Lewis and William Hendry. A contemporary press report recorded that 'Madame Durrant had a small share in the solo work of the evening, but her little was a thoroughly artistic performance.' She next sang with the choir on 22 April at a concert for the Ashington Branch of the Workers' Educational Association, performing selected scenes from the St Matthew Passion. On this occasion Tom Danskin and Ethel were joined by choir members in performing the solos. In February 1929 she and co-soloists Rosa Burn, Tom Danskin and Arthur Lewis sang in performances of four Bach cantatas. In the March 1929 perform-ance of the B Minor Mass she was recruited to sing in the chorus as an extra soprano. In November 1929 Ethel sang in the semi-chorus for the performance of Holst's *The Hymn of Jesus*. Her further activities with the Bach Choir were all as a member of the soprano line of the choir. Under the conductorship of W. G. Whittaker she sang in three more concerts, which included performances of Bach's St John Passion, Howells's *Sir Patrick Spens* and a programme of sixteenth-century music. She sang in two concerts under the conductorship of Sidney Newman. Her last concert with the choir was in February 1931.

On 4 April 1931 Ethel married John Arthur McKeown at the parish church of St Cuthbert, Blyth. John was a schoolmaster who hailed from County Tyrone. They had a daughter, Dorothy, who was born in 1932.

Ethel occasionally sang in public after her marriage, and there is a newspaper record of her winning (under her maiden name) a silver medal in the vocal duet open class, alongside the contralto Gladys Smith, in the 1939 Newcastle Musical Tournament.

For many years Ethel and John lived at 4 Broadway Gardens, Hexham. Ethel died on 16 April 1978 at the Hexham War Memorial Hospital (later called the General Hospital), aged eighty. John died in 1981, aged eighty-four.

Walter Haddon, AMIME (1882–1963)
Bass soloist 1916

WALTER HADDON, the elder of two children of George Haddon and Susannah Thompson, was born in North Shields, Northumberland as his parents had been. His father was an elementary school teacher and his mother an assistant teacher who both taught at the Hartley School near Seaton Sluice, where they were living in 1891. His father became relieving officer for the Board of Guardians of the Tynemouth Workhouse, and the family moved to live at 2 Hylton Terrace, North Shields.

From 1887 to 1898 Walter attended elementary and higher schools in New-castle. Between 1898 and 1905 he attended first Rutherford College and then Armstrong College, Newcastle, where he studied science and mechanical engineer-ing. From 1898 to 1903 he was an engineering apprentice at the works of C. A. Parsons & Co. in Heaton, Newcastle. Walter remained with this firm until 1920, serving in the drawing office, eventually becoming chief draughtsman. He later worked on design, estimating and experimental work. He became an Associate Member of the North East Coast Institution of Engineers and Shipbuilders.

Walter's sister, Annie, studied at the College of St Hild and St Bede, Durham, and became a schoolteacher. In 1908 he married Anna Maria Porter in Tyne-mouth; they had a son born in 1914 and a daughter born in 1918. They first lived at 2 Denwick Terrace, Tynemouth.

Walter joined the Newcastle and Gateshead Choral Union as a bass in about 1911, and sang with them until 1916 under the conductorship of W. G. Whittaker.

His only appearance with the Newcastle Bach Choir was as the bass soloist in the all-Bach concert in November 1916. The programme consisted of three Bach cantatas, the Brandenburg Concerto No. 5 and the Suite No. 2 in B minor. Walter's fellow soloists were Jane Fleming, Ruby Burns and Robert Peel.

In 1920 Walter became resident engineer and Midland district sales representative for the Crosby Valve and Engineering Company and moved to live at Tyneholme, 322 Boldmere Road, Erdington, near Birmingham. In 1923 he took up a similar post in the Midland District for British 'Arca' Regulators Ltd. By 1929 he was living at 316 Boldmere Road. In 1924 He was elected an associate member of the Institution of Mechanical Engineers.

Walter and Anna's marriage failed, and Anna seems to have returned to the North East with the children to live at 12 Birtley Avenue, Tynemouth. At some stage Walter went to live at 2 Woodlands Parkway, Timberley, near Altrincham, Cheshire.

Anna died on 7 May 1963 in Tynemouth and Walter on 27 September that year at the Withington Hospital, Manchester.

William Hendry (1890–1950)
Bass soloist 1919–39

WILLIAM (BILL) HENDRY, eldest of seven children of William Hendry and Janet Lochhead, was born in Newcastle upon Tyne. Both his parents were born in Scotland, his father in Bridge of Weir, Renfrewshire and his mother in Kilwinning, Ayrshire. His parents, who had married in Airdrie, Lanarkshire, in 1888, moved to live in Newcastle in about 1889. His father, who first trained as a joiner, later became an animal hide inspector. The family lived first at 346 Thomas Street, Wallsend. By 1901 they had moved to 123 Croydon Road, Fenham, and by 1911 to 36 Cherryburn Gardens, Fenham, where they lived for many years.

Bill Hendry became a commercial clerk and worked all his life for the local gas company. His main leisure interest was singing. He had an exceptionally fine baritone voice, and by his early twenties was forging a reputation as a soloist. In 1914 he performed in Mendelssohn's *Elijah* at a charity concert at the Jesmond United Methodist Church, and also at the annual conference of the Gas Association in Newcastle.

He was called up for military service at the end of 1914 and served with the Royal Marines Submarine Miners. Their role was to protect the eastern coastal waters of England and Scotland from attack by enemy submarines by placing

Fig. 128 With the Newcastle and Gateshead Choral Union, 1938. *Courtesy Newcastle City Libraries.*

defensive minefields in areas that could not be protected by booms or where additional protection was required. The unit was raised in Newcastle in 1915 under the command of Colonel F. G. Scott of the Tyne Electrical Engineers. In 1915 Bill was stationed in Broughty Ferry, Dundee. There is a contemporary newspaper report of a concert in Dundee in May 1915, praising Corporal William Hendry, 'a young Newcastle professional with a fine baritone voice'. In 1918 he was promoted to the rank of lieutenant.

On his discharge from military service Bill returned to Newcastle and continued with his singing and his job at the gas company.

Bill first performed with the Bach Choir in December 1919, in a concert of British music in which he sang the baritone solo in a performance of Vaughan Williams's Fantasia on Christmas Carols. His next appearance with the choir was in a performance of Bach's Christmas Oratorio, which was spread over two days in December 1920 (Parts 1–3) and January 1921 (Parts 4–6). A contemporary press report of these two concerts commented that 'Mr William Hendry was very fine throughout the bass solo work and especially so in the great aria "Mighty Lord and King all glorious"' and that 'he can always be relied upon for his artistic impression of any work he touches.'

In 1921 Bill married an Aberdonian schoolteacher, Isabella Walker, at the Station Hotel, Aberdeen. They set up home at 21 Simonburn Avenue, Fenham, a small street not far from his parents' home in Cherryburn Gardens, where they lived for the rest of their lives.

In 1922 he sang with the Newcastle and Gateshead Choral Union in a performance of Elgar's *The Dream of Gerontius*. A contemporary press report recorded that he 'maintained to the full the high place he has taken in his art and his resonant and ageeable voice served him well'.

Bill next sang with the Bach Choir in the March 1926 performance of the B Minor Mass. In December 1926 he sang with the choir in a concert that featured Purcell's Ode for St Cecilia's Day and three Bach cantatas. A contemporary press report recorded that 'the outstanding feature was the splendidly spacious bass

arias, sung excellently by William
Hendry'. In April 1928, in a performance of the St Matthew Passion, he
sang the bass arias and the roles of Judas
and Pilate. A contemporary press report
recorded that he 'had fine scope as
Judas, as Pilate and in some reflective
numbers of which he made the most'.
His final concert with the choir under
the conductorship of Whittaker was in
February 1930, when he sang the baritone solo in the first performance of
Sir Patrick Spens by Herbert Howells,
alongside tenor and choir member
Lance Hughes. He also sang a selection
of songs by various composers 'with
sincerity and good vocalism'.

After the departure of Whittaker, Bill
continued as a soloist with the Bach
Choir, appearing in concerts in March
1931 (the B Minor Mass), November
1932 (Purcell's Ode for St Cecilia's Day
and Bach's Cantata No. 34), January
1937 (the Christmas Oratorio), and
February 1939 (Bach cantatas).

Bill was a regular favourite of the
Newcastle and Gateshead Choral

Fig. 129 William with his sister Alice in
a performance of *Tom Jones*, 1902. Family
photograph.

Union in the 1920s and 1930s, performing in Handel's *Messiah* on many occasions.
He sang alongside famous soloists of the day, including Astra Desmond, Heddle
Nash and Isobel Baillie. In the 1930s he sang in many other concerts including
performances given by the Sunderland Philharmonic Society. There are many
references to his performing on local radio Newcastle 5NO and national radio
from 1925 onwards. In addition to his performing activities he also gave singing
lessons.

His niece recalls that her Uncle Bill 'was a lovely man and my favourite uncle.
He was married . . . but had no children [and] probably because of this he spent
a lot of time with my brother and me', and that he gave her away when she
married. (See fig. 130.)

William Hendry died on 19 February 1950 at 21 Simonburn Avenue, Newcastle, aged fifty-nine. Isabella died on 10 April 1956 at the Newcastle General Hospital, aged sixty-six.

The author acknowledges the collaboration of Sheila Emerson (née Hendry) with this biography.

Fig. 130 William at the wedding of his niece, 1949.
Family photograph.

Annie Lawton, LRAM, ARCM, ATCL (1885–1939)
Contralto soloist 1918–26   Contralto chorus 1917, 1918, 1927 and 1929

ANNIE LAWTON, youngest of six children of John Lawton and Annie Grassam, was born in Newcastle upon Tyne. Her father, a grocer and provision merchant, was born in Mossley, Lancashire, and her mother in Driffield, Yorkshire. The family lived in the Newcastle suburb of Elswick at several addresses but finally at 23 Malvern Street.

Annie attended Ackworth School in Ackworth, Yorkshire, which is run by the Society of Friends (Quakers).

Annie had a fine contralto voice, and in 1905, aged twenty, was a soloist at a Blyth Temperance Concert. She qualified as a singing teacher and became LRAM (in 1915), ARCM and ATCL, and was awarded the Royal Academy Honours Certificate for class teaching. She was a member of the contralto line of the Newcastle and Gateshead Choral Union from 1907 to 1914.

She was singing mistress at the Municipal High School for Girls in Hartlepool from 1915 to 1918, and then returned to Newcastle to take up a post at Atkinson Road Commercial School for Girls, which she held until 1928. In 1922 her school choir obtained first prize in the North of England Musical Tournament.

Annie first sang with the Bach Choir in December 1917, as a member of the contralto line, in a mixed programme of Bach Christmas music and British music. In February 1918 she was in a programme entirely dedicated to British music, in which she sang in the chorus and undertook the contralto solos. In May 1918 she was a chorus member in a concert of two Bach cantatas and his ode *Rebuke me not*. In 1919 she was a soloist in two concerts of British music in February and December, performing two carols by W. G. Whittaker in the latter. After the December 1919 concert a contemporary report recorded that she sang Whittaker's two carols 'charmingly'. She was in the March 1920 performance of Bach's St Matthew Passion, singing arias and in the role of the First False Witness. In May 1920 she was in a programme of three Bach cantatas, singing the contralto solo in Cantata No. 41, *Jesus, be now praised* (*Jesu, nun sei gepreiset*). In the November 1920 concert, in which works by Balfour Gardiner were given prominence, she was reported as having 'added some vocal solos tastefully'. In November 1921 she was in another programme of three Bach cantatas, singing the contralto aria in Cantata No. 34.

In March 1924 the choir travelled to Dumfries to perform a mixed concert of Bach cantatas, chorales and a five-part motet. Annie sang the aria in Cantata No. 6, *Stay with us, for evening approaches* (*Bleib bei uns, denn es will Abend werden*), and the entire Cantata No. 53, *Strike, then, longed-for hour* (*Schlage doch, gewünschte Stunde*), written for solo contralto, in which she was reported as giving 'her best work of the evening'. In April 1924 she sang the contralto arias in a performance of the St John Passion, of which a contemporary newspaper report recorded that she had sung 'very agreeably'. In 1925 she was soloist in two concerts: in February she was in a programme of four Bach cantatas, and in April she sang the contralto aria in a performance of the St Matthew Passion. Annie sang solos only once with the choir, in 1926, in the January performance of four Bach cantatas. She was co-opted to sing in the chorus for the choir's 1927 tour of Germany and in the preliminary concerts leading up to it. She also sang in the chorus in the November concert that year. Her final concert with the choir was as a choral member in the May 1929 performance of the Tallis forty-part motet *Spem in alium*.

Annie was lecturer in pianoforte teaching methods at the Newcastle Conservatoire of Music from 1920 to 1930, and was also singing mistress at the Central Newcastle High School from 1920 to 1925. Throughout her professional life she was a private teacher of pianoforte and singing, and was joint author of the *Folk Song Sight Singing* series with Edgar Crowe (a bass in the choir) and W. G. Whittaker.

In 1930 she joined W. G. Whittaker in Glasgow as an assistant mistress in the Scottish National Academy of Music, and lived at 60 Cleveland Drive, a university residence at which W. G. Whittaker was also living. There were hints of a personal relationship with Whittaker.*

Annie died of breast cancer on 17 January 1939 in a nursing home at 10 Fernwood Road, Newcastle, aged fifty-three.

Arthur Llewellyn Lewis (1887–1969)
Baritone soloist 1921–30

ARTHUR LLEWELLYN LEWIS, youngest of eight children of John Lewis, a tinplate worker, and Elizabeth Evans, was born in Neath, Glamorganshire, where his father had been born. His mother was born in Llangyfelach, Glamorganshire. The Lewis family lived at a variety of addresses, but in 1909 were at 29 Rope Walk,

* See p. 16n.

Neath. Arthur was brought up in a bilingual Welsh- and English-speaking household. He began his working life as a junior office clerk, but by the time of his marriage he had become a carpenter.

Arthur Llewellyn Lewis and Gladys Amelia Salter were married on 13 June 1909 at the parish church in Neath. They set up home at 1 Osborne Street, Neath, where their first child, Enid, was born in 1910. Their second child, Henry John, was born in London on 13 September 1912, at which time they were living at 29 Hetley Road, Fulham. Arthur was recorded as a journeyman carpenter.

Arthur and the family moved to the North East of England about 1920, and for many years lived at 19 Onslow Gardens, Low Fell, Gateshead. Arthur eventually became a housing superintendent.

Not much is known about Arthur and Gladys's musical careers before they settled in Gateshead, but it would appear that they were well-established soloists. Arthur became a chorister at St Nicholas's Cathedral, Newcastle.

Under Whittaker's conductorship Arthur was a soloist with the Bach Choir in around eleven concerts between 1921 and 1930; they comprised eight concerts dedicated to Bach cantatas (involving twenty-five separate cantatas) and two performances each of the St Matthew and St John Passions. In all the Passions Arthur sang the role of Jesus, and in the 1930 performance of the St John Passion he also sang the bass arias. In the April 1924 St John Passion, Ida Cowey, Annie Lawton and Tom Purvis sang the arias. A contemporary press report recorded that Arthur's singing was 'very fine in the music allotted to Jesus and other bass solos'. In the 1925 St Matthew Passion, Mrs George Dodds, Annie Lawton, Tom Danskin and Ernest Potts were co-soloists. At this concert Arthur's interpretation of the role of the Saviour was described as 'singularly attractive'. In the Bach cantata concert in January 1927 he was complimented for his singing of the bass recitatives in Cantata No. 171. In the November 1927 concert of Bach cantatas (in which his co-soloists were Margaret Magnay, Norah Wiggins and Mr R. Farrage), he was reported to have sung 'admirably' in Cantatas Nos. 22 and 185. In the April 1928 performance of the St Matthew Passion, Ethel Durrant, Rosa Burn, Tom Danskin and William Hendry were co-soloists; and in the April 1930 St John Passion, Arthur's co-soloists were Ena Mitchell, Rosa Burn and Tom Danskin. Arthur was also co-opted to sing in the chorus in the May 1929 performance of the Tallis forty-part motet *Spem in alium*.

In addition to his activities with the Bach Choir, Arthur was a soloist with the Newcastle Philharmonic Society. After a performance with this society in 1921 his voice was described in a local press report as 'smooth and pleasing'. He was also a soloist with the Newcastle and Gateshead Choral Union, performing Brahms's

A German Requiem with them in March 1930. Arthur and Gladys also performed solos and duets together on local radio Newcastle 5NO in the 1920s.

Their daughter, Enid, died in tragic circumstances at North Ormsby Hospital, Middlesbrough, on 24 July 1945, aged thirty-four. Their son, Henry John, became an insurance manager and lived in Rottingdean, Sussex.

Arthur died on 3 August 1969 at Bensham Hospital, Gateshead, aged eighty-two. Gladys died on 23 December 1980 at the Queen Elizabeth Hospital, Gateshead, aged eighty-nine.

Ernest James Potts, LRAM (1879–1936)
Bass soloist 1915–29

Fig. 130 From the 1925 choir photograph, Alnwick: Ernest Potts (standing) and W. G. Whittaker.

Fig. 131 From a 1927 choir photograph.

ERNEST JAMES (ERNIE) POTTS, first of four children of James George Potts and Emily Ann Thompson, was born in Sunderland, County Durham, as his parents had been. His father was a tailor's cutter. The family moved to Newcastle from Sunderland between 1884 and 1887, when the youngest child was born. The family lived in the Newcastle suburb of Heaton, first at 57 Chillingham Road, but by 1901 they had moved to 22 Stratford Grove.

Young Ernest entered the insurance profession as a junior cashier and progressed to become an insurance officer. He had a very fine bass voice, and studied music and singing in his own time, becoming an LRAM.

In 1907 he married Violet Isabella Surtees (formerly Robinson), who had been widowed in 1906; she had a son, Cecil Vivian De Laybourne Surtees, by her previous marriage. At the time of their marriage Ernest and Violet were both singing in the Newcastle and Gateshead Choral Union, Violet as a soprano and Ernest as a bass. Violet was still in the choir during 1915/16 season. Ernest and Violet lived in Jesmond, Newcastle, initially at 16 Lily Crescent, before moving to 35 Osborne Avenue. Ernest's stepson, Vivian, studied at Oxford University, becoming a BA in 1921 and an MA in 1925; he later became an Anglican clergyman.

Ernest began to develop a reputation as a concert soloist. In March 1909 he sang in the Morpeth Presbyterian Church Choir Festival under the conductorship of W. Deans Forster. In March 1912 he was in a concert given by the Armstrong College Choral Society under W. G. Whittaker, which included a performance of Bach's Ascension Cantata in which he 'sang very capably'. Later that year he was in a concert given at Newsham, Blyth, for the New Delaval Co-operative Society. In May 1914 he was a soloist in the Newcastle Amateur Operatic Society's performance of *The Mikado*. The local newspaper reported that 'Chief honours must be accorded to Mr Ernest J. Potts, whose Pooh-Bah was as fine a study as probably has ever been. His acting, his singing and his diction – particularly the latter – were highly praiseworthy and emphasised what a splendidly versatile artist and musician the society has.' Later that year he took part in a concert for the Belgian Refugees' Relief Fund at the Grand Theatre, Byker. In February 1915 he sang at a charity concert for the Blue Cross Fund to raise money for the care of military horses engaged in France. The following month he performed at another concert for the fund, and on 21 November sang in a concert for the Anglo-Russian Hospital Fund.

Ernest first sang as a soloist with the Newcastle Bach Choir at its inaugural concert on 27 November 1915, and then in three subsequent concerts in February, March and December 1916. The four concerts were largely devoted to performances of Bach cantatas, and included eleven separate cantatas in all.

He was called up for military service on 22 January 1917, and served as a driver in the Royal Army Service Corps until his discharge on 12 February 1919. His enrolment report described him as being 6 feet 1 inch tall and requiring spectacles for short-sightedness.

Ernest next appeared with the Bach Choir on 20 May 1919 at St Nicholas's Cathedral, in which his performance in the solo cantata *Ended now is my yoke* was described as 'admirable'. He then sang again with the choir on 31 May in a repeat of this concert at the Westgate Hall. He was reported as having sung the aria 'What doth it profit' with 'feeling'. He was in the February 1920 performance of Bach's St Matthew Passion, singing the bass arias and the roles of Pilate and Judas. The following month he was the bass soloist with the choir in a concert of three Bach cantatas. In the March 1921 concert, which featured Holst's *The Hymn of Jesus*, he was commended for his 'delightful interpretation of the Hebridean folk songs'. In February 1923 he was bass soloist in the choir's performance of Bach's B Minor Mass.

In 1924 Ernest was a soloist in a number of concerts with the choir. On 1 February he sang with them in a concert that featured Holst's *The Cloud Messenger* and two of Bach's secular cantatas. On 15 February he travelled with the choir to Dumfries for a concert of that included four Bach cantatas. A contemporary press report recorded that in the solo cantata No. 56 he 'proved himself once more a Bach singer of large calibre'. November 1924 was a busy month of Bach Choir engagements. Then, on 1 November, Ernest was co-opted into the bass line for a performance of the Magnificat from Byrd's Great Service. He then joined the choir in London for two performances of the entire Byrd Great Service on 24 and 25 November, and was present again on the 29th for a repeat performance in Newcastle.

In April 1925 he sang arias and the roles of Judas and Pilate in the Bach Choir's performance of Bach's St Matthew Passion. He had developed a heavy cold before the concert, and a local press report commented that 'E. J. Potts, although always capable, was scarcely in his best form.'

1927 was another busy year of concerts with the Bach Choir. On 3 April Ernest sang folk songs in a concert for the Workers' Educational Association in Ashington. On 9 April he sang the role of Jesus and the bass arias in a performance of the St John Passion. One of his co-soloists was the young Tom Danskin, to whom, after the concert, he wrote the letter that appears as fig. 132.

In May Ernest sang folk songs in a Northumbria–Cumbria concert. In July he was co-opted to sing with the choir on its tour of Germany. His main role on the tour was as a soloist for the concert on Friday, 8 May at the Stadthalle in Münster, at which he sang folk songs and part-songs by Whittaker, Stanford, Ireland, Vaughan Williams and Warlock. He also took a full part in the choirs' other performances as an uncomplaining member of the bass line.

In February 1928 he was the soloist in a Bach Choir concert broadcast on the

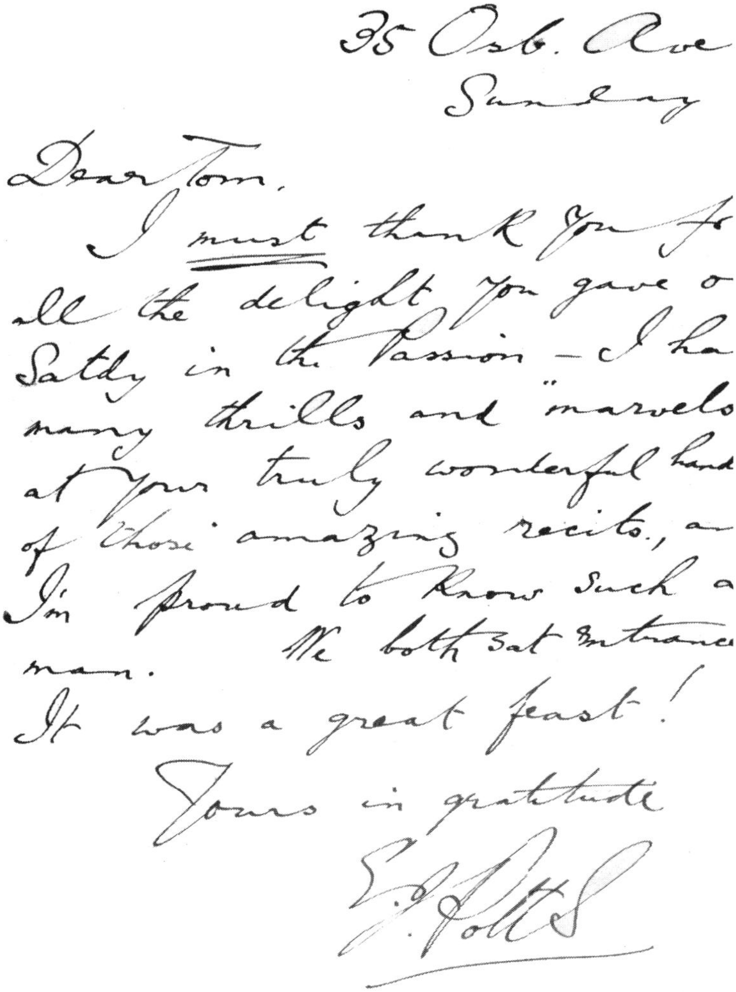
35 Osb. Ave
Sunday

Dear Tom,
I *must* thank you fo
all the delight you gave o
Satdy in the Passion – I ha
many thrills and "marvels
at your truly wonderful hand
of those amazing recits, a
I'm proud to know such a
man. We both sat entrance
It was a great feast!
Yours in gratitude
E. J. Potts

Fig. 132 Letter from Ernest Potts to Tom Danskin, April 1927.
Courtesy Colin Danskin.

radio. In February 1929 he was the soloist with the choir in another Northumbria–Cumbria concert of folk songs, this time by Whittaker and Jeffrey Mark. In May 1929 he was co-opted to augment the bass line in a performance of the Tallis forty-part motet *Spem in alium*. This seems to have been his final concert with the choir. Whittaker relinquished the conductorship of the choir the following year.

In addition to his Bach Choir activities, Ernest was a soloist with other societies, such as the Newcastle and Gateshead Choral Union, the Newcastle Wind Quintette, and the Buckie Oratorio and Operatic Society.

Ernest's reputation spread well beyond his native North East. In 1927 he recorded several of W. G. Whittaker's settings of Tyneside songs, and over the years made innumerable radio broadcasts both locally and nationally. He became established as a singing teacher, and trained many rising talents, including Owen Brannigan, the great North East bass.

Violet Potts was herself a capable individual, and made several radio broadcasts as an elocutionist in the 1920s.

In 1928 Whittaker tried to persuade Ernest Potts to join him in Glasgow, where he had recently been appointed principal of the Scottish National Academy of Music. Eventually Potts accepted, and became a part-time teacher of solo singing and voice production from 1934.

Ernest's career was tragically cut short when he died suddenly on 22 June 1936 at Green Cottage, Startforth, Yorkshire, aged fifty-seven, only a few weeks after the death of his father. Violet eventually went to live with her son from her first marriage at Shipham Rectory, Winscombe, near Bristol, where she died in 1963, aged eighty-six. She and Ernest had no children.

Thomas Stewart Purvis (1895–1984)
Tenor soloist 1920, 1921, 1923 and 1924

THOMAS STEWART (TOM) PURVIS, third of four surviving children of Jacob Short Purvis and Mary Ann Stewart, was born in Easington Lane, County Durham. His parents were also born in County Durham, his father in Jarrow and his mother in Easington Lane. Jacob Purvis was a joiner and wheelwright who worked at Hetton Colliery. Jacob was very musical, and played the cello in a local band. He was also a singer, as his father had been before him. The family attended the Wesleyan Methodist Church, Easington Lane, and from about 1901 lived at 88 Four Lane Ends, Hetton-le-Hole.

Tom followed in his father's profession, and by 1911 was a carpenter apprentice at Hetton Colliery. Tom also inherited his father's musical talents, and took an interest in singing. For some years he sang in the Houghton Church Choir. His vocal abilities were recognized and he became a chorister at St Nicholas's athedral, Newcastle.

He began to make a reputation as a tenor soloist. His first appearance with the Bach Choir was in the November concert of 1920, which included three Bach cantatas. In December of that year he sang in a performance of Mendelssohn's

Elijah with the Scarborough Musical Society. He sang with the Bach Choir in the performance of Bach's Christmas Oratorio that was spread over two concerts in December 1920 and January 1921. A contemporary press report recorded that in the recitatives 'he seemed [to] revel in the big range, singing the top notes with apparent ease'. He married Cissy Coates, the daughter of a miner from Hetton-le-Hole, in the late summer of 1921.

Tom's next appearance with the Bach Choir was in November 1921, in a performance of three Bach cantatas in which the other soloist was his Newcastle Cathedral colleague, the bass Arthur Llewellyn Lewis.

Tom and Cissy's first child, Ivan Coates Purvis, was born in Newcastle on 23 March 1922. In June that year Tom won first prize for solo singing in the tenor aria class at the North of England Musical Tournament.

In February 1923 he sang with the Bach Choir in another concert of Bach cantatas with his colleague, Arthur Lewis. At about this time Tom was appointed a chorister at Canterbury Cathedral, and his next public performance was at a concert with the Canterbury Male Voice Choir in Whitstable in May 1923. In December that year he sang in a performance of the Christmas Oratorio with the Leeds New Choral Society at Leeds Town Hall.

Tom and Cissy's sojourn in Canterbury was brief, for they moved to London in September 1923 when Tom was appointed a 'vicar choral', or chorister, at St Paul's Cathedral. Their second child, Sheila Miriam Purvis, was born in Lambeth on 1 March 1924.

Tom made a return visit to Newcastle in April 1924, to sing the part of the Evangelist in the choir's performance of Bach's St John Passion. A contemporary press report recorded that in his exacting role Tom's 'natural and melodious voice compass [was] no object', and that it had 'matured and improved since his removal to Canterbury Cathedral and thence to St Paul's'.

From the late 1920s Tom started to broadcast regularly on radio as a member of the Wireless Singers (the forerunner of the BBC Singers). In one such broadcast, from the Guildhall School of Music in September 1929, he performed Bach's Cantata No. 100 with Isobel Baillie, Ethel Barker and Keith Falkner. In March 1930 he performed Cantata No. 140 with Elsie Suddaby and Keith Falkner. These are only two examples of the many radio performances of Bach cantatas in which Tom sang with the Wireless Singers.

In 1930 Tom and Cissy were living at 23 Basildene Road, Hounslow, Middlesex. Throughout the 1930s, in addition to giving innumerable radio broadcasts, Tom was much in demand as a soloist. In March 1934 he sang at the Sussex and

West Kent Musical Festival in the Tunbridge Wells Pump Room under the baton of Adrian Boult, in a mixed concert that included Dvořák's *Stabat Mater*. In 1936 he sang for them again at the same venue in a fantasia on *Die Meistersinger*.

In February 1938, at the invitation of Reginald Redman, BBC Director of Music, Western Region, Tom joined the Avalon Quartet, which included Marjorie Avis (soprano), Gladys Jones (contralto) and the bass Glyn Eastman. They made many radio broadcasts together. In May 1938 Tom performed with the Reigate Oratorio Choir at the Central Hall, Redhill, in a programme featuring Elgar's *The Black Knight* and Purcell's *King Arthur*. In January 1943 he sang solos in a programme given in Barnstaple by the violinist Ella Herschmann.

Tom was a member of the Incorporated Society of Musicians and a Worshipful Brother in the Society's Freemasons' Lodge. He was forty-four at the outbreak of war in 1939, and the Lodge archives remember him among those 'who fought at home'. In 1948 he used his carpentry skills to make three gavels and a carrying-case out of timbers from the original choir roof of St Paul's Cathedral, which he presented to the Lodge.

In 1951 or 1952 Tom and Cissy moved to 28 Curtis Road, Hounslow, and then in 1954 or 1955 to 37 Curtis Road.

A St Paul's Cathedral Chapter minute of 6 December 1952 records that it was agreed that 'Purvis be re-appointed as a Vicar Choral from his retirement under the age rule until 30th June 1957'. On 8 August 1953 the Chapter minutes record that 'Purvis [be] allowed to take possession of two old harmoniums stored in the crypt that the organist deemed to be of no value to the Cathedral'. On 21 June 1958 Tom was granted a twelve-month renewal of his contract as a supernumerary vicar choral. In May 1959 discussions took place in the Chapter treasury concerning his pension, and he was granted an *ex gratia* payment of £100 a year for five years. The church authorities thought better of this parsimonious act, however, and on 17 September 1960 awarded Tom a pension of £100 a year for life.

Eventually Tom and Cissy moved to live at 3 Hilland Rise in the village of Headley, Hampshire. Tom died on 29 December 1984 at his home in Hilland Rise, aged eighty-eight. Cissy died in Chichester in 1989, aged ninety-four.

The author acknowledges the collaboration of Joseph Wisdom, Librarian to St Paul's Cathedral, with this biography.

John Vine, FRCO (1883–1953)
Tenor soloist 1915–22

JOHN VINE, the elder of two children of Richard Vine and Jane Ann Walker, was born in Bearpark, County Durham. His father, a coal miner, was born in

Fig. 133 At the organ of St Jude's Church Belfast, 1949. *Courtesy the National Library of Ireland (call number 1A 342).*

St Blazey, Cornwall, and his mother in Hetton-le-Hole, County Durham. In 1891 the family lived in Stanley in that county. John's mother died in the summer of 1893, aged thirty-one. Later that year Richard Vine married Mary Jane Seccombe, a widow, who had five children from her previous marriage. There were no further children. In 1895 the newly amalgamated family were living in Walbottle, New-castle, but by 1901 they had moved to the village of Eighton Banks, near Gates-head, County Durham.

Richard Vine had a profound influence on his son. He was a devout Christian with a strong social conscience, and played a prominent role in the local Labour movement. He had taught himself to read and write. He was in a local brass band, was able to play most brass instruments, and had also taught himself to play the harmonium.

John Vine joined the Stanley Mission Brass Band at the age of ten, and became a competent player of the euphonium. At the age of twelve, his parents having moved to Walbottle, he enrolled in the local Spencer Steelworks Brass Band. When the family moved to Eighton Banks he was working as a 'shaft lad' in a local coal mine. He was persuaded by his cousin, John Vine Trelease, to join the Hebburn Temperance Band, with which he was associated from 1902 to 1905, playing a variety of instruments. The band was successful in many competitions, winning the North of England Brass Band Championship. John was awarded the gold medal for best solo player on at least two occasions. Not only was he a talented instrumentalist but he had a fine tenor voice. Eventually he abandoned coal-mining to study singing and organ-playing full-time.

John became honorary organist to the Lord Nelson Street Methodist church, South Shields, where he formed a girls' choir. It was while he was conducting this choir, at a festival in Newcastle, that he came to the attention of W. G. Whittaker, who sent a note inviting him to meet him afterwards in his private room. At the meeting Whittaker invited him to his home. When John arrived there he was ushered into Whittaker's studio. In the conversation that followed, Whittaker asked him whether he could sing. John replied in the affirmative, but qualified his reply, saying that he 'did not go in for public engagements'. Whittaker sat at the piano and persuaded John to sight-read some difficult selections from Bach. He was overwhelmed by John's ability, and invited him to the next rehearsal of the embryo Newcastle Bach Choir. Whittaker later gave him lessons in voice production. While at South Shields John took lessons from the organist at the local parish church.

In 1907 John was appointed organist at Winlaton parish church, and in 1908 became organist at St John's Church, Seaton Hirst, Ashington, where he became first ARCO and later FRCO.

He married Margaret Urwin in South Shields in 1913 and they had three sons, one of whom died in childhood. In 1915 John was called up for war service, but was rejected for front-line service on health grounds and was sent to work in a nearby sawmill.

John first sang as a soloist with the Bach choir at its inaugural concert in November 1915. Between then and February 1917 he was a soloist in six concerts, four of which were devoted to Bach cantatas, comprising eleven separate cantatas.

His performance in Cantata No. 61, *Come, redeemer of our race*, at the concert in February 1916 was described as being 'very artistically sung'. His last concert in this series was in the February 1917 performance of the St John Passion, in which he took the role of the Evangelist and also sang the tenor arias.

John received another call-up in 1917, and was assigned to a labour corps and posted to a military camp near Ripon, where his musical abilities were recognized. He was later transferred to a convalescent camp in Newtonards, Northern Ireland, where once again his musical talents were noted and he was encouraged to start a string orchestra. While he was there he met Mr E. Godfrey Brown, the conductor of the Belfast Philharmonic Orchestra, who was greatly impressed by him. He was demobilized in 1918 and returned to Ashington. Around 1919 Mr Brown persuaded John to take up the post of organist at the parish church of St Malachy in Hillsborough, a few miles south of Belfast. While there Tom conducted a local brass band and was appointed an assistant music master at Campbell College.

There is a newspaper report of John singing in a performance of Bach's St Matthew Passion on 23 February 1920 with the Aberdeen Bach Society. The report stated that he was based at Hillsborough, County Down. His next concert with the Newcastle Bach Choir took place four days later, in Newcastle, on the 27th, in another performance of the St Matthew Passion, in which he sang the role of the Evangelist and also the tenor arias.

In 1921 John was appointed organist at the parish church of St Jude in Ballynafeigh, Belfast, where he was to remain until his death. The Vine family lived at Rossgaragh, 337 Ravenhill Road, Belfast.

John's final concert with the Bach Choir was in December 1922, in a mixed programme of music by modern British composers. John sang songs by Gerrard Williams, Whittaker and others 'entirely to the satisfaction of a large audience'.

For a number of years John was a soloist in a number of radio broadcasts from Belfast. He continued to conduct brass bands. Almost as soon as he arrived in Belfast he became conductor of the Queen's Island Choral Society, with which he achieved great success. He also established himself as a singing teacher; among his most famous pupils were James Johnston (tenor) and Nan Shaw (contralto).

In 1930, at the age of forty-seven, he began to develop a debilitating musculoskeletal disorder. Although increasingly immobile, he managed with great difficulty to travel with the Queen's Island choir to Glasgow, where he conducted them for the John Cullen Memorial Premier Challenge Trophy.

He later also became conductor of the Belfast Singers and, after the Second World War, the Ulster Singers, achieving considerable success with both societies. He made many radio broadcasts with the choirs.

Towards the end of his life, John found playing the organ increasingly difficult. He was a popular and much-loved person, greatly supported in adversity by his congregation, friends and family. He died on 31 August 1953, after a short illness, aged seventy.

The author acknowledges some material in this biography from 'John Vine FRCO: A memorial booklet' by James Quinn, BA, courtesy of the National Library of Ireland.

Chapter 9
Accompanists, Organists and other Performers
Philip Owen

The Dodds Family

No account of musical life in the North East of England in the late nineteenth and early twentieth centuries would be complete without mention of the Dodds family. Although their direct involvement in Bach Choir concerts was limited, they were teachers and trainers of many of the local singers and musicians from whom the choir drew its strength.

The author acknowledges the collaboration of Michael Dodds, Gareth Yeaman Dodds and Philippa John (née Dodds) with the biographies that follow.

George Dodds, L.MUS., LCM (1847–1901)

GEORGE DODDS was born in Gateshead on 30 November 1847, the sixth of seven children of George Dodds (1806–1870) and Thomasine Colverwell (1811–1902). His father worked for many years as a coal miner. From about 1851 they lived in Felling, east Gateshead, close to what is now the site of the Gateshead International Sports Stadium. In 1861 they were still living in that area at Old Fold Colliery, near the present Old Fold Road. In that year George was about fourteen years old and working as a grocer. George's father died in 1870. By 1871 his mother and the children were living at 1 Cumberland Court, which was in the centre of Gateshead between High Street

Fig. 134 Family photograph, c. 1890.

and High Street West, an area subsequently redeveloped. In that year George's occupation was recorded as 'grocer and tea dealer'.

On 23 December 1875 George Dodds married Sarah (Sally) Yeaman Laws at the Blenheim Street Methodist chapel, Newcastle. Sally was the daughter of Robert Laws, a butcher from the Elswick area of Newcastle who had previously run his business in the Northumberland village of Ponteland. Sally and her elder sister, Mary, were both schoolteachers. Sally had a fine soprano voice.

George and Sally set up home at 57 Grove Street, Elswick. Their first son, George Robert, was born on 30 September 1876, and their second son, Herbert Yeaman (known as Yeaman), on 10 June 1878. They had a third son, Sidney Colverwell, born on 13 October 1880, but he died the following year. In 1881 the family were still living at Grove Street, and George was recorded as a 'tea dealer'.

From 1881 George seems to have taken a serious interest in music. By about 1889 he had gained an L.Mus. from the London College of Music, an independent conservatoire of music founded in 1887 and now part of the University of West London. Around this time he published several musical articles in the local press.

In 1891 the family moved to 14 Bentinck Crescent, Elswick, not far from Westgate Road. George was entered in the census as 'professor of music', and his son George Robert as a 'student of music'. George was now organist at the Elswick Road Wesleyan Methodist church. He was also organizer and registrar of the Newcastle examination centre for the London College of Music, which was based at the family home in Bentinck Crescent under the title 'The Music Studio'. Over the next two years he gave a series of talks on the theory of music to schoolteachers at the Newcastle YMCA.

In 1896 George delivered a lecture on 'Mendelssohn and his Compositions' to the Low Fell Social Circle, at which his son Yeaman played piano solos.

He continued to run the local examinations for the London College of Music, which by 1899 had expanded its reach to include examining centres in Sunderland and Durham.

George died suddenly in June 1901, aged fifty-three. Sally outlived him by a considerable margin, and died in 1936, aged ninety.

George Robert Dodds, MUS.BAC. (DUNELM), LRAM, ARCM
(1876–1946)

GEORGE ROBERT DODDS, the eldest of three children of George Dodds and Sarah Yeaman Laws, was born in Newcastle upon Tyne. He inherited his parents' musical interests and began to study music at an early age. He was appointed organist and choirmaster of Corbridge parish church in 1892 at the age of sixteen. In 1894 he was appointed organist and choirmaster of St Paul's Church, Newcastle. From 1898 to 1899 he simultaneously held the post of choirmaster at Benwell parish church. The earliest reference to him in local newspapers is to a concert directed by his father in October 1893 at a Presbyterian church, where his organ solos were 'pleasingly applauded'.

In 1898 he was awarded the external Mus.Bac. degree by Durham University, for which he submitted an original composition entitled 'Rejoice in the Lord'. In 1899 he was awarded, as an external candidate, the ARCM in theory of music by the Royal College of Music, and also the LRAM in composition teaching by the Royal Academy of Music. He is known

Fig. 135 Family photograph, 1930s.

to have had lessons from Sir Charles Villiers Stanford, Sir Walter Parratt, Sir Hubert Parry, Sir Frederick Bridge, Albert Visetti and Dr William Stevenson Hoyte, but it is likely that these were in a private capacity.

After his father's death in 1901, George Jun. replaced his father as organist and choirmaster of the Elswick Road Wesleyan Methodist church. In November of that year he gave a report, as provincial registrar for the London College of Music, at an annual prize distribution and concert held at the Connaught Hall, Newcastle, at which his brother Yeaman was accompanist. In February 1902 he gave an organ recital at the United Methodist Free Church in Blyth, which included his own composition, 'Pedal Offertoire in C'.

From this time he began to develop a reputation as a teacher of singing, and many local choirs benefited from the skills of his pupils. His most creative period for musical composition was between 1902 and 1913.

On 14 August 1907 George married Agnes Jane Winter in Newcastle. Her biography will be found in Chapter 8. They set up home at 4 Warrington Road, Newcastle, where they lived with George's mother.

In 1908 he conducted his choir at the Elswick Road church in a performance of

Brahms's *A German Requiem*, in which his brother Yeaman was the organ accompanist. In April 1912 he took part alongside his wife and brother in a 'grand concert' by the Stannington Choral Society.

In 1914, with his private teaching commitments increasing, George decided to relinquish his post at the Elswick Road church. By 1915 he and his brother were joint provincial registrars for the London College of Music and were operating from Yeaman's home at 61 Fern Avenue. October 1915 saw him take part with his brother in the first of a series of piano and organ recitals at the Elswick Road church in which his wife, Agnes, was the vocal soloist. These recitals were continued in 1916 and raised funds for the local Red Cross.

George's teaching career was progressing, and in June 1916 it was announced that one of his pupils, Private Walter Clapperton, had been awarded one of three open scholarships to study singing at the Royal College of Music. In October he presided at a lecture on hymn tunes given by William Henry Hadow, principal of Armstrong College, at the Central Primitive Methodist Church, Newcastle. In an article on 'Pronunciation' in *The Choir* in 1917 he issued guidelines for vocalists.

Throughout 1922 George ran a course of four illustrated lectures on various technical aspects of singing at the YMCA in Newcastle, at which Agnes provided the musical illustrations. In 1924 they gave a concert entitled 'Folk Songs of Many Lands' on local radio Newcastle 5NO. Meanwhile George was becoming increasingly in demand as an adjudicator at musical festivals, presiding at the Border Music Festival at Hawick in 1925 and at the Hartlepool and District Musical Festival in 1926.

George succeeded W. G. Whittaker in 1927 as conductor of the Newcastle and Gateshead Choral Union, an appointment that was to prove a long and fruitful association. His brother became the honorary organist, and his wife and sister-in-law both sang in the chorus. In that year he published his *Practical Hints for Singers* (Epworth Press). During his conductorship of the Choral Union he gave many notable performances of works by classical composers from Bach to Verdi and works by English composers from Bantock to Vaughan Williams, and attracted famous soloists such as Dorothy Silk, Astra Desmond and Heddle Nash.

In August 1930 George lectured at the summer course in music-teaching at Oxford, making several forthright statements that were widely reported in the press. Headlines such as 'Those Awful Corsets', 'Wobbly Singing' and 'Lazy Singers' give a flavour of the comments.

The 1930s were busy years, particularly in relation to George's life as a competition adjudicator. His travels took him around the United Kingdom, from Inverness in the north to Bournemouth in the south, on several occasions making repeat visits. Newspaper headlines continued to follow him, such as 'Why Girls Sing Better Nowadays' (another reference to corsets) and 'Turning Out Musical Sausages' (a reference to the dangers of church choirs becoming static). He also visited Canada as an adjudicator in 1935, in the company of Gordon Slater, of Lincoln Cathedral, and the pianist Arthur Benjamin. In 1937, in one of his trips to Lincoln, he addressed a meeting at the cathedral chapter house, giving helpful practical advice on the organization of musical festivals. In the 1930s he was also assistant conductor and then conductor of the Newcastle Symphony Orchestra, which frequently accompanied the Choral Union in its concerts.

The Second World War had an adverse effect on the Choral Union, which suspended most of its activities. George next conducted the choir in the April concert of 1945.

For many years George and Agnes lived at 2 Queens Road, Newcastle. Agnes died on 9 July 1945 at their home in Queens Road, aged sixty-five. George died on 2 October 1946 at 13 Westbourne Avenue, Penarth, Glamorganshire (the home of his nephew Denis George Dodds), aged sixty-nine.

Herbert Yeaman Dodds, LRAM, ARCM (1878–1941)
Piano soloist 1916   Continuo 1923   Piano duet 1924

HERBERT YEAMAN DODDS (known as Yeaman), second child of George Dodds and Sarah Yeaman Laws, was born in Newcastle upon Tyne. Like his elder brother, George, he showed an early interest in and an aptitude for music. The earliest reference to him in local newspapers is to a concert directed by his father at the opening of the Elswick Road Library in September 1895, in which he was the pianist. The following February he was the pianist in a concert for the Low Fell Social Circle, again under his father's direction.

In 1899 he was awarded the ARCM in organ performing by the Royal College of Music. Also that year he was appointed organist and choirmaster at the Memorial Wesleyan Church, North Shields. He conducted his new choir in several concerts for the Tynemouth Jubilee Infirmary at the Howard Hall, North Shields. In December 1902 they gave Handel's *Samson*, in December 1903 Haydn's *The Creation*, and in December 1904 Mendelssohn's *Elijah*. In 1905 he was accompanist and solo pianist at a series of musically illustrated lectures for an educational scheme run by the Co-operative Movement. That same year he was awarded, as an external candidate, the LRAM for organ playing by the Royal Academy of Music.

Fig. 136 Family photograph, 1920s.

On 13 August 1908 Yeaman married Violet Katherine Bewick, the daughter of Spark Bewick, an ironmonger, who ran his business in Elswick Road. They set up home at 4 Akenside Terrace, Newcastle. In that year he was accompanist at a performance of Brahms's *A German Requiem* conducted by his brother, George, at the Elswick Road church. In December 1911 he was pianist at a performance of Handel's *Messiah* by the Stannington Choral Society. In April 1912 he was the organist in a performance of Arthur Sullivan's *Festival Te Deum* at St George's Presbyterian Church, Morpeth. Also that month the two brothers and George's wife took part in a 'grand concert' by the Stannington Choral Society.

George and Violet's only child, Denis George, was born in Newcastle on 25 May 1913.

By 1914 Yeaman was beginning to develop links with members of the Newcastle Conservatoire of Music, in particular with Edgar Bainton, who had become principal in 1912, and with W. G. Whittaker, who was one of its teachers. That year he was involved with both of them at a meeting held in Newcastle by the Incorporated Society of Musicians. In April he provided the organ accompaniment, 'with his customary ability', for the Newcastle Harmonic Society in a concert conducted by Bainton. In May 1915 he gave a lecture to the Newcastle Free Church Musicians' Union on the preparation of music for church services. In October that year he played the piano in the first of a series of recitals at the Elswick Road church, with his brother playing the organ and Mrs George Dodds singing solos.

His first concert with the Bach Choir was in March 1916, when he played, with Annie Eckford, Bach's Concerto in C minor for two claviers. In early 1919 he was involved with his brother George, Edgar Bainton, William Ellis, Alfred Wall, W. G. Whittaker and Deans Forster in the creation of the North of England Musical Tournament.

By 1921 Yeaman and Violet were living at 61 Fern Avenue in the Jesmond area of Newcastle.

In 1923 Yeaman presided at a club supper for the composer John Ireland, which was given in his honour by the Newcastle Pen and Palette Club. Alfred Wall and Edgar Bainton were also present. That year Yeaman played continuo in the Bach Choir's March concert performance of the B Minor Mass. In the December 1924 concert he assisted Muriel Plant in accompanying the choir, and also undertook a performance of Bach's Clavier Sonata No. 1 in E flat, arranged for two pianos (with W. G. Whittaker as his co-soloist). A contemporary press report recorded that they played the sonata 'in a masterly fashion'. This was Yeaman's last appearance with the choir.

Violet Dodds died in 1928, aged forty-three. The following year, at the age of fifty-one, Yeaman married 24-year-old Frances Mary Chapman (known as Mary), LRAM, LTCL, the daughter of a farmer, in her home village of Gawcott, near Brackley, Buckinghamshire. They set up home at 61 Fern Avenue.

After his brother's appointment as honorary conductor of the Newcastle and Gateshead Choral Union in 1927, Yeaman served as its honorary organist until the beginning of the Second World War. Mary joined the Choral Union, singing with her sister-in-law under her brother-in-law's direction.

During the 1930s Yeaman was musical instructor for the Tyneside Social Services Unemployed Welfare Centres and an adjudicator for several local musical festivals. In 1931 he conducted a choir of more than five hundred voices at a historical pageant held in Leazes Park. At the first rehearsal he chided the choristers, saying: 'Come along now! In these days of jazz, you are surely not going to be beaten by a little touch of syncopation.'

Yeaman died on 20 December 1941 at the Royal Victoria Infirmary, Newcastle, aged sixty-three. He and Mary had no children. Mary remarried in 1943 and died in 1996 aged ninety-one.

Annie Mary Eckford, LRAM, ARCM (1891–1960)
Contralto 1915 and 1919   Accompanist and frequent solo pianist 1916–29

ANNIE MARY ECKFORD, the youngest of five children of James Eckford and Alice Wait, was born in Newcastle upon Tyne. Her parents were both born in Northumberland, her father in the border village of Norham and her mother in the village of Eglingham, which is situated between Wooler and Alnwick. Her father was a house joiner. From about 1891 the family lived in Gloucester Terrace in the Newcastle suburb of Elswick, first at No. 7 and finally at No. 5.

Diedrichs, Helene Laura	1917
Dove, Annie M. ...	1918
Driver, Annie Florence May	1919
Dyer, Dora Edith	1914
Eckford, Annie Mary	1913
Edwards, Robert F. C....	1913
Elliott, Lottie	1912
Evans, Irene Grace	1913

Fig. 137 The 1913 LRAM list. *Courtesy the Royal Academy of Music.*

Annie was a talented musician, and obtained, as an external candidate, the ARCM in 1912 and the LRAM in 1913, both for pianoforte performing.

Annie's first appearance with the Bach Choir was as a member of the contralto line in the inaugural concert of November 1915. Walter Tait Roan, who was the first honorary accompanist of the choir, was involved with the rehearsals for the inaugural concert, but was called up for military service. Annie then took over his role.

In February 1916 Annie was involved in a performance of Bach's Brandenburg Concerto No. 5. In early March 1916 she was accompanist at a lecture by W. G. Whittaker on 'The Motets of Bach', in which the choir sang examples. In the late March concert of 1916 she and Herbert Yeaman Dodds played Bach's Concerto in C minor for two claviers, and she was the soloist in a performance of the *Italian Concerto*. In the May concert of 1916 she was the pianist for James Mark in performances of sonatas for violin and piano by Purcell and Babell. A contemporary press report recorded that they 'showed great sympathy and unity of artistic idea' in their treatment of the works. At that concert she also played in works by Percy Grainger, Benjamin Dale and Balfour Gardiner. In the November 1916 concert she and Edna Steele were the pianists in a performance of the Brandenburg Concerto No. 5. In the Bach Choir concert of 2 December 1916 she gave a performance of Bach's Clavier Concerto in F minor. Later that month, she and Whittaker gave musical illustrations at a lecture on French music by M. G. Jean-Aubry at the Newcastle Central Hall. (The lecturer was probably Georges Jean-Aubry, a French music critic and translator.)

In February 1917 she was the pianist in an all-Bach programme, playing in his Sonata No. 1 in B minor for flute and clavier, in two fugues for two claviers and in the Trio Sonata in G for clavier, flute and violin. In the May 1917 concert she performed in trios for piano, violin and viola by Arnold Bax and Thomas Dunhill. In the December 1917 concert she was the pianist in a performance of Percy

Grainger's *Room-Music Tit-Bits*, and also accompanied the choir in a performance of Benjamin Dale's *Christmas Hymn*, her playing in which was described as 'highly sympathetic'. In March 1918 she played violin and piano sonatas by John Ireland and Joseph Gibbs alongside Alfred Wall, and in November that year was piano soloist in a performance of Bach's Concerto in A minor for flute, clavier, violin and strings.

In December 1918 Annie was the piano soloist in the first performance of Alfred Wall's Piano Quintet in C minor. She was the piano soloist in the February 1919 concert of British music, playing works by Eugene Goossens and Gerald Tyrwhitt (Lord Berners). In the April concert of 1919 she was the pianist in performances of Bach's Sonata No. 4 in F minor for violin and his Partita No. 2 in C minor. In the latter work her playing was described as 'clean, artistic and undemonstrative'. In that concert Walter Clapperton sang two songs from the Anna Magdalena book, and Annie was credited with 'a most brilliant accompaniment, very nimbly played'. In May 1919 she returned to the contralto chorus line for the last time for a programme of Bach cantatas. In the December 1919 concert of British music she played in a performance of the *Six Pastorals* for voices, strings and piano by Walford Davies.

In late 1919 Annie married Frank Wallace Skinner, an electrical engineer, at St James's Congregational Church, Northumberland Road, Newcastle, and they set up home at 50 Bayswater Road, Newcastle. For professional reasons she continued to use her maiden name after her marriage.

In January 1922 Annie was the pianist in performances of the Violin Sonata No. 1, Op. 21, by Eugene Goossens and in Alfred Walls's Sonata in A. A contemporary press report had 'nothing but praise for Miss Eckford's extremely finished performances'. In November 1923 she played piano solos by Benjamin Dale, Frank Bridge and Scriabin, in which she 'displayed fine technique and skill'. In the Northumbria–Cumbria concert of February 1929, Annie was the solo pianist in Jeffrey Mark's *Cumbria Suite*, Holst's *Northumbrian Folk Songs* and Ernest Farrar's *North Country Sketches*. A contemporary press report acknowledged her as 'a pianist of fine technical and interpretive gifts'. This was her last concert with the Bach Choir.

Aside from her performances with the Bach Choir, Annie was much in demand elsewhere. She was a regular performer with Whittaker's Armstrong College Choral Society, the Northumbrian Chamber Music Society, the Newcastle Philharmonic Orchestra and the British Music Society. She also gave recitals on local radio Newcastle 5NO.

Annie's main singing activity was with the Newcastle and Gateshead Choral

Union, in which she sang in the soprano line (not the contralto line) between 1913 and the late 1930s.

Annie and Frank had no children. Frank died in 1930, aged forty-three. After his death Annie appeared less in public but was still giving some concert performances in the 1940s. She did not remarry, and continued to live at her home in Bayswater Road. She died on 27 March 1960 at the Northern Women's Hospital, Osborne Road, Newcastle, aged sixty-eight.

William Ellis, FRCO, B.MUS. (DUNELM), HON. MUS.DOC. (1868–1947)
Honorary Organist 1919–39

Fig. 138 William Ellis. *Courtesy Special Collections, University of Durham Library* (*Edis Photographic Negatives Collection No. EDIS Pi 86*).

WILLIAM ELLIS, the first of two children of Samuel Ellis and Eleanor Robson (formerly Fletcher), was born in Tow Law, a mining community in the southwest of County Durham. His father was born in Flintshire, and moved to Crook in County Durham with his younger brother, William, around 1850. Samuel began his working life as a coal miner; there followed a brief episode as a soda water manufacturer before he finally became a watchmaker and jeweller. Eleanor was born in Richmond, Yorkshire, where her father was a gardener and groom. Both Samuel and Eleanor had been married before and had children from their first marriages. In 1871 the Ellis family were living at 100 Wharton Street in the south Durham mining community of Coundon.

William was a talented musician with an early aptitude for playing the organ. By 1877, at the age of nine, he was organist at a chapel in Coundon. In 1881 the Ellis family were living at 26 High Row, Shincliffe, another Durham mining village. The family moved to the city of Durham later that year. By 1882, aged fourteen, William was organist at Old Elvet Methodist Church in the city. At about this time he began studying the organ under Philip Armes at Durham Cathedral, and in 1887 he was appointed organist at St Nicholas's Church in the city.

In 1891 the Ellis family were living at 36 Sutton Street in the Crossgate area, and the census describes William as a 'teacher of music and organist'. He became an FRCO that year, and in 1893 he graduated with a B.Mus. from the University of Durham.

On 26 February 1894 he married Jane Elizabeth Childs, a music teacher, at the parish church of St Luke in Chelsea, London. Jane's father was a butler, and her family lived at 13 Mackham Street, Chelsea. That year William was appointed organist of Richmond Parish Church in Yorkshire and organist to the Marquess of Zetland at Aske Hall. In 1901 he and Jane were living at 63 French Gate, Richmond.

In 1903 William returned to Durham to become cathedral sub-organist under his old teacher, Philip Armes. In December 1906 he was a guest organist at a performance of Handel's *Messiah* at Ripon Cathedral. By 1911 he and Jane were living at 12 Gilesgate, Durham.

In 1915 he was appointed organist at St Margaret's Church in Durham. In November 1916 he gave a lecture at the Newcastle Centre of the Free Church Musicians' Union on the music of Henry Purcell. He was appointed organist and master of choristers at St Nicholas's Cathedral in June 1918.

William's entry into the Newcastle music scene was to prove an important landmark in the early history of the Newcastle Bach Choir, and he was soon appointed honorary organist. From February 1919 the choir began to perform some of its concerts in the Cathedral and others in the King's Hall of Armstrong College. At that time the King's Hall did not have an organ, an omission that was not remedied until the 1960s; consequently the concerts at the Cathedral featured music that required the organ and William's musical skills. Between 1919 and 1929 he took part in twenty concerts. In the Cathedral concert in May 1919 his playing of the Prelude on the chorale *Schmucke dich* was said to be 'a truly artistic interpretation'. In the concert in May 1922 that was given at the Cathedral, the choir sang the five-part motet *Jesu, priceless treasure*, and William played a series of Bach organ preludes. A contemporary press report recorded that he 'used his magnificent instrument with loving care and tenderness'. In the programme for the concert on 1 May 1926, which featured a performance of William Byrd's five-part Mass, Whittaker wrote: 'The friendliness and co-operation of the officials . . . and of Mr William Ellis are such that our connection with the Cathedral is one of much happiness.' When he was not available to perform in person, William provided an assistant organist to take his place. In the concert at the King's Hall in February 1928, which featured a performance of Vaughan Williams's *Sancta Civitas*, he conducted a 'distant choir' of Cathedral choristers. Although his active contributions to the choir's concerts declined after Whittaker's departure from Newcastle, he was still acknowledged as the honorary organist in concert programmes as late as 1939.

His musical life in Newcastle was a busy one. In December 1919 he gave the organ accompaniment in a performance of Handel's *Messiah* in the Cathedral that was given by the Newcastle and Gateshead Choral Union. In December 1922 he conducted his own cathedral choir from the organ in a performance of Brahms's *A German Requiem*. He arranged a series of organ recitals by visiting organists in the 1923/4 season. He was one of the founders of the North of England Musical Tournament, and became an honorary teacher at the Newcastle Conservatoire of Music.

In 1929 an honorary doctorate of music was conferred upon him by the Archbishop of Canterbury. The award was commemorated by a ceremony in the Newcastle Cathedral Library, when he was presented with a cheque by 'clergy, churchwardens and worshippers at the Cathedral, in addition to musical friends and numerous others'.

William was involved, with a small group of other musicians, in the design specification of a new organ for the Newcastle City Hall, which was built by the Durham firm of Harrison & Harrison and was unveiled at a recital in September 1929. In September 1930 he gave a recital on a new organ at Christ Church, Hartlepool, and in September 1934 he was director of music for a service broadcast from St Nicholas's Cathedral on local radio.

William's eyesight, which had not been good for many years, began to fail, and in August 1938 he announced his retirement. In December that year he was presented with a cheque from the congregation and friends, and he retired on Christmas Day.

William lived quietly with his wife at Gyseburn, South Park, Hexham, where he died on 26 November 1947, aged seventy-nine. Jane died in Ebchester, County Durham, in 1959, aged ninety-two. They had no children.

The author acknowledges the collaboration of Richard D. Hird, MA, LTCL, with this biography.

Muriel Dorothy Lockey Plant, LRAM, ARCM (1895–1986)
Accompanist 1924–c. 1955

MURIEL DOROTHY LOCKEY PLANT, only child of Harry Plant and Isabella Jane Lockey, was born in Spennymoor, County Durham. Her father, who was born in the village of Parkgate, near Rotherham, Yorkshire, worked as a smelter in the steel manufacturing industry. Her mother, who was a schoolteacher, was born in Berwick-upon-Tweed, which at the time of her birth was in Northumberland. In 1901 the family were living at 30 Whitworth Terrace, Spennymoor. By 1911 they had moved to Lemington on Tyne, where they lived at Ellerslie, Union Hall Road, and remained there until the death of Muriel's father in 1949.

Muriel passed the Durham University intermediate examination in arts and studied at the Newcastle Conservatoire of Music, obtaining the LRAM and ARCM for pianoforte teaching. From 1920 onwards she was a private teacher of pianoforte theory and aural training. She was a visiting class singing mistress at several Newcastle schools, including Windsor Terrace School from 1922, Fenham High School from 1923 and the Central High School from 1926.

She became honorary accompanist to the Newcastle Bach Choir in December 1924, taking over the role from Olive Tomlinson. In that month's concert she and Herbert Yeaman Dodds played an arrangement for two pianos of Bach's Sonata No. 1 in E flat for clavier.

In 1925 Muriel was involved in three concert performances with the choir. In April she provided the continuo for the St Matthew Passion. This concert was the first performance to use the spinet that had been specially built for the choir by Arnold Dolmetsch and been presented by 'a kind friend of the Society'. (See p. 63.) In November she played in the Gibbons tercentenary concert, and in December she played the piano in a performance of Bach's Brandenburg Concerto No. 5. In February 1926 she provided the accompaniments for songs and part-songs by a number of composers. Whittaker, on this occasion, played a series of solos on the spinet. In December that year Muriel provided continuo on the spinet in a performance of the B Minor Mass.

In 1927 Muriel was actively involved in five concerts. In February she provided piano accompaniment for three rondels by Vaughan Williams, *Three Songs of Innocence* by Gordon Jacob and songs by Butterworth, Scott, Shaw and Whittaker. On 3 April she accompanied songs and folk songs by Whittaker, Stanford, Parry and Bainton in a concert for the Workers' Educational Association in Ashington.

On 9 April she provided the spinet continuo in a performance of Bach's St John Passion. In May, in a concert that provided another trial run of Whittaker's setting of Psalm 139, she played the spinet (in lieu of the lute) in a performance of three pieces from John Dowland's *Lachrimae, or Seaven Teares*. In November she provided accompaniments in a selection of songs and part-songs by Parry, Stanford, Vaughan Williams, Holst, Balfour Gardiner and Whittaker.

In April 1928 she accompanied a selection of songs and part-songs and provided the continuo in a performance of selected items from the St Matthew Passion in another concert for the Ashington WEA. In December 1928 she played the piano in a performance of Vaughan Williams's *Flos Campi*.

Muriel played in three concerts during 1929. In February she played piano accompaniments in folk songs and songs by Whittaker and Jeffrey Mark at a Northumbrian–Cumbrian concert. In March she provided the spinet continuo in another performance of the B Minor Mass. Her final concert under the conductorship of Whittaker was in November 1929, when she provided continuo for performances of three Bach cantatas.

After the departure of Whittaker she continued as accompanist to the choir under three subsequent conductors, Sidney Newman, J. A. Westrup and Chalmers Burns. The last Bach Choir concert programme record of her was in February 1955. She had served the choir uninterrupted for thirty-one years.

In addition to her Bach Choir activities Muriel was a regular performer in the 1920s on local radio Newcastle 5NO.

After the death of her father in 1949, she moved to 6 Hartburn Place in the Fenham district of Newcastle, close to Dame Allan's Girls' School. She died on 18 February 1986 at Eastfield Nursing Home, 15 Moor Road, Gosforth, aged ninety-one. She was unmarried.

Walter Tait Roan, B.SC. (DUNELM) (1893–1916)
Rehearsal accompanist 1915

WALTER TAIT ROAN, fifth of seven children of Walter Tait Roan and Jane White, was born in Newcastle upon Tyne, as his parents had been. His father, who trained as a brass-finisher, later became a beer-house keeper. He died in 1903, aged forty-four, when Walter Jun. was only eight. The family lived for many years at 125 Croydon Road in the Arthur's Hill area of Newcastle.

Walter attended Rutherford College, Newcastle, and then went to Armstrong College of Durham University in Newcastle, graduating as a bachelor of science.

He then trained as a teacher, and by 1915 was teaching at Walkergate County School in Newcastle.

He was the Bach Choir's first rehearsal accompanist, and took part in the inaugural concert on 27 November 1915, in which Bach's Cantatas Nos. 2, 68 and 140 were performed.

Walter was called up for military service and served with the 3rd/8th Battalion the Durham Light Infantry (DLI) attaining the rank of second lieutenant. From 1 July 1916 some fifteen thousand soldiers of the DLI fought in the Battle of the Somme, which raged for nearly five months. Sadly, Walter was missing or killed in action on 29 September 1916, and his body was never recovered. His name is inscribed, along with those of nearly 1,500 other DLI soldiers, on the Memorial to the Missing in Thiepval in France. Walter is also remembered, with other university colleagues who fell in the First World War, on a memorial in the entrance to the Armstrong Building of the University of Newcastle, close to the King's Hall, where the Newcastle Bach Choir has rehearsed and performed for many years.

At the time of his death Walter was aged twenty-three and unmarried.

The author acknowledges the collaboration of Hilary K. Roan and Ian Roan with this biography.

Olive Tomlinson, LRAM, ARCM, MUS.BAC. (DUNELM) (1902–1992)
Accompanist and pianist 1920, 1921, 1922 and 1924   Additional soprano 1924
Honorary Registrar 1919–20

OLIVE SANDERSON-TOMLINSON, eldest of five children of Thomas William Sanderson and Isabella Eleanor Brittain (or Brittan), was born in Newcastle upon Tyne. Her parents were born in Sunderland. When Thomas William's father died, his mother then married Thomas Tomlinson, and this marriage produced one child. For a while Thomas William Sanderson used the surname Sanderson-Tomlinson. He started his working life in Sunderland as a solicitor's clerk, but eventually moved into the building trade, first as a clerk and eventually as a building contractor. He was an accomplished cellist.

From about 1911 the family seem to have adopted Tomlinson as their surname, and were living at 64 Buston Terrace in the Jesmond district of Newcastle. In the early 1930s they moved the short distance to Queens Road, Jesmond.

Olive became an honorary accompanist to the Bach Choir in November 1920, joining Millie Twaddell (the incumbent honorary accompanist) for a Balfour

Fig. 139 From the 1922 choir photograph.

Gardiner concert. This was a mixed programme with songs by Balfour Gardiner, Granville Bantock, Edgar Crowe and others, and works for cello by Frank Bridge and J. S. Bach (featuring the cellist Carl Fuchs). In 1921 Olive appeared in the March concert, which was termed the Gustav T. Holst Concert. In it she provided the accompaniment for various folk songs and played the piano part in Holst's *The Hymn of Jesus*. In December 1921 she was the accompanist for carols, songs and folk songs and was the piano soloist in works by John Ireland, Percy Granger and Balfour Gardiner. A contemporary press report recorded that she 'played three pianoforte solos in an able manner'.

She obtained the LRAM for pianoforte playing, as an external candidate, in 1921, and the ARCM in pianoforte playing, again as an external candidate, in 1922. She was rehearsal accompanist for the choir's visit to the February 1922 London Bach Festival. In June 1922 she competed in the North of England Musical Tournament, winning the cello and pianoforte duet prize with cellist Doris Sear, and the trio of violin, cello and pianoforte prize with her sister Ella (violin) and Doris Sear (again on cello).

Olive studied at the Royal College of Music in London between September 1922 and December 1923. During her absence the Bach Choir's accompanists were Arthur Floyd and Ralph Elliott.

In November 1923 she appeared with the Newcastle Philharmonic Orchestra, performing Schumann's Piano Concerto, 'giving a remarkably fine account of the pianoforte solo', and she was 'worthily re-called'.

Olive's next Bach Choir concert was on 5 February 1924, when she sang as an additional choral soprano in a performance of Bach's motet *Jesu, priceless treasure*. On 15 February she was the pianist in a concert in the Lyceum Theatre, Dumfries in performances of Cantatas Nos. 4, 6, 53 and 56. On 1 March 1924 she was the pianist in a concert that featured Holst's *The Cloud Messenger* (arranged for small orchestra and piano) and two of Bach's secular cantatas. Gustav Holst was scheduled to conduct his work at the concert; but illness prevented him from attending, so Whittaker undertook the task. Olive's next concert with the choir was in April 1924, when she provided continuo for a performance of the St John Passion.

A contemporary press report recorded that she 'made the performance more than interesting'.

In April 1929 she made a radio broadcast as the pianist with the Bach Choir on Newcastle 5NO in a programme of music mostly written by Bach. This seems to have been her last performance with the choir.

For many years she taught music at Polam Hall School, Darlington (founded in the nineteenth century by the Society of Friends – Quakers). She obtained the Mus.Bac. from the University of Durham in the academic year 1936/7.

Olive's siblings were also very musical; Albert and Ella played the viola, Thomas played the violin, and Louise was a cellist and pianist. Louise taught music at Marlborough School, and published musical arrangements for cello and piano. Louise also played the cello in orchestras accompanying the Bach Choir in 1943 and 1944. Olive made many radio and concert performances with one or other of her sisters throughout the 1920s, 1930s and early 1940s. She also made broadcasts with other vocal and instrumental artistes.

In retirement Olive moved to Edgbaston, Birmingham, to live with her sister Louise and her husband, Robert Burrowes, who was also a professional musician. Olive died on 24 April 1992 at 161 Rotton Park Road, Edgbaston, aged ninety. She was unmarried.

The author acknowledges the collaboration of Gordon Tomlinson and Sheila Lewis (née Tomlinson) with this biography.

Amelia Twaddell (1899–1992)
Honorary Accompanist 1919 and 1920

AMELIA (MILLIE) TWADDELL, youngest of five children of James Lindsay Twaddell and Eliza Jane Webster, was born in Newcastle upon Tyne. Both parents were born in Scotland, her father in New Cathcart, Renfrewshire, and her mother in Burntisland, Fife. James Twaddell spent much of his early life in the Govan area of Glasgow, where his father was a clerk in a shipyard. He began his working life as an office boy but eventually trained as a draughtsman in the iron trade. At some stage between 1888 and 1891 he moved to Tyneside to become shipyard manager of Palmer's Shipbuilding and Iron Company of Jarrow, which was situated on the south bank of the River Tyne. He became a prominent figure in his local community. For many years the Twaddell family lived at Green Bank Villa, Ellison Street, in Jarrow. A daughter, Amanda, died in infancy in 1897, and a son, William, in 1902, aged sixteen. Eliza Twaddell died in 1904 in Davos, Switzerland, where she had been taken in an attempt to improve her health. Millie was only five years old at the time of her mother's death. In 1910 James Twaddell then married Mary Wilhelmina Marshall, the daughter of a draper from Whitley Bay, but had no more children.

Millie became a music teacher and was rehearsal accompanist to the Bach Choir from about December 1919 until about November 1920. She is named in only three concert programmes. In the December 1919 concert the piano was played by Annie Eckford. In the February 1920 performance of the St Matthew Passion, George Danskin played the continuo. In the November concert programme, Millie and Olive Tomlinson were joint honorary accompanists, but it is not known which of them played in the concert.

Millie moved to Walton-on-Thames, Surrey, near her sister Eliza and her family, and died there on 16 January 1992, aged ninety-two. She was unmarried.

Chapter 10
Orchestral Players

Philip Owen

Mrs W. E. Alderson (1877–1947)
Violin 1919–43

IDA MAY BREWIS, eldest of four children of Thomas Brewis and Ada Mary Davison, was born in Sunderland, County Durham, where her parents had been born. Her father qualified as a master mariner in 1876. In 1881 the family were living at 15 Suffolk Street in the Bishopwearmouth area of Sunderland, but in 1891 had moved to 16 Harold Street, and by 1901 to 30 Peel Street, the home of Ida's maternal grandmother, Sarah Davison.

In the summer of 1901 Ida married a medical practitioner, Wilfred Ernest Alderson, MB, BS, MD, MS, DPH, who graduated from Durham University (Newcastle) in 1894. Wilfred was the son of Thomas Albion Alderson, who was a composer and organist at St Andrew's Church in Newcastle. At the time of their marriage Wilfred was living at 5 Eldon Square in the centre of Newcastle. By 1911 He and Ida had moved to 28 Victoria Square in Jesmond, an area that is now close to the University of Northumbria and Newcastle University's Robinson Library.

Ida and Wilfred had three sons, the eldest of whom died at birth in 1902. Their second son, Ronald Eltringham, was born in 1906, and their third, Basil Roxby, in 1910.

Ida was an accomplished violinist, and first played with the Bach Choir in May 1919. Under the conductorship of W. G. Whittaker she played in twelve concerts wholly or partly devoted to Bach cantatas, in three performances of the St Matthew Passion, and in two performances of the B Minor Mass. She played in performances of choral music with string orchestra by Holst (*The Hymn of Jesus*, the *Ode to Death*, *The Cloud Messenger* and *The Golden Goose*) and Vaughan Williams (*Flos Campi*). In December 1919 she was in a programme of British music and played pieces by Walford Davies, Dowland, Boyce and Vaughan Williams (the Fantasia on Christmas Carols). In March 1924 she played in a performance of Bach's Violin Concerto in E major, and in December 1925 in the Brandenburg Concerto No. 5. In May 1927 she took part in performances of fantasias for strings by Dowland and Purcell and also some sixteenth-century songs with string accompaniment. In the December 1928 concert she played in Vaughan Williams's *Concerto Accademico* for violin and strings. Ida's last performance with the Bach Choir under Whittaker's conductorship was in March 1929. After his departure she continued to play for the Bach Choir under Sidney Newman and J. A. Westrup. The last programme record of her playing for the choir is from October 1943.

In addition to her activities with the Bach Choir, Ida was a violinist in the Newcastle Symphony Orchestra from 1919 to about 1931.

Both of her surviving sons became medical practitioners. Ronald Eltringham Alderson, MBBS, DMRE, graduated from Durham University (Newcastle) in 1927, obtained a Royal Aero Club aviator's certificate in 1928, joined the Royal Air Force and became a squadron leader. He was killed in Palestine in 1938 at the onset of the Second World War.

The youngest son, Basil Roxby Alderson, LRCP, LRCS, LRFPS, graduated from Edinburgh University in 1935 and was commissioned in the Royal Naval Volunteer Reserve (Tyne Division) as a surgeon sub-lieutenant. Later in 1935 he was commissioned into the Royal Navy and rose to the rank of surgeon captain. He served throughout the Second World War and had many subsequent postings (to the destroyer HMS *Kelly* and to shore bases in Portsmouth, Malta and Singapore). He ended his career at the Royal Naval Junior Training Establishment in Ipswich, and retired in 1965. In retirement he took an active interest in family history research, jointly publishing transcripts of parish registers for the Yorkshire Archaeological Society.

Ida and Wilfred moved to live at 56 Highbury in Jesmond, Newcastle, where they were residing at the time of Ida's death on 21 June 1947, aged seventy. Wilfred moved to live at 61 Osborne Road (not far from Highbury), but died in South Bailey in the city of Durham, on 3 September 1949, aged seventy-six.

Victoria Atkinson (1883–1974)
Violoncello 1915–27

VICTORIA ATKINSON, youngest of four children of Matthew Hutton Atkinson and Maria Adamson, was born in Newcastle upon Tyne. Her father, a mechanical engineer and director of the local gas company, was born in Newburn, Northumberland, and her mother in Gateshead, County Durham. Her father, Matthew, was the son of the Tyneside iron manufacturer George Clayton Atkinson of Wylam Hall, Wylam. Her grandfather was an amateur natural historian who undertook expeditions to the Hebrides and also to the Faroes, the Westerman Islands and Iceland in the early 1830s, publishing accounts of these trips. He also published a *Sketch of the Life of the late Thomas Bewick* in 1831, and had at one time owned copies of Bewick's *Quadrupeds*, *Birds* and *Vignettes*, including a dedicated autographed volume dated 1828.

Victoria spent her childhood and early adult life at the family home at 21 Windsor Terrace in the Newcastle suburb of Jesmond, not far from the city centre and close to the Hancock Museum of the Natural History Society of Northumbria. Nos. 21–24 Windsor Terrace are now the Law School of the University of Newcastle. The Atkinson family were comfortably off, and the children were taught by a Swiss governess called Swanhild Ettmüller. Both of her brothers became engineers. Victoria's elder brother, George Adamson Atkinson, attended Rossall College School, Fleetwood, Lancashire, in the 1890s. Her elder sister Sophia became an artist and permanently emigrated from England to Canada in the 1920s.

Victoria became a cellist. She first played for the Bach Choir at its inaugural concert in November 1915. During her years with the Bach Choir, which were all under the conductorship of W. G. Whittaker, she performed in nine concerts wholly or partly devoted to Bach cantatas, in two performances of the St John Passion and in one of the B Minor Mass. She played in performances of choral music by Holst that required string orchestras (*The Hymn of Jesus*, *The Cloud Messenger*, the *Fugal Concerto* and the *Ode to Death*). In the December 1917 concert she played the cello solo in Grainger's *Room-Music Tit-Bits* in addition to playing in Hubert Parry's *Lady Radnor's Suite* for strings and Frank Bridge's *Two Old English Songs* for string quartet. In the February 1921 concert, in addition to Holst's *The Hymn of Jesus*, she performed in some folk songs and in Bach's Concerto in D minor for two violins and string orchestra.

In the February 1923 concert she performed in Holst's *The Cloud Messenger* and the *Fugal Concerto*, and in two of Bach's secular cantatas. In the November 1925 concert she played in Bach's Concertos in A minor and E and in two works by Gibbons. In December 1925, in addition to Holst's *Ode to Death*, she played in performances of the Brandenburg Concerto No. 5 and three of the cantatas. In November 1926 she played in Bach's Clavier Concerto in D minor and his Concerto in C major for two claviers and strings. In February 1927, in a mixed programme that included the first performance of Whittaker's setting of Psalm 139, she played the cello obbligato in the aria from Cantata No. 151 and the accompaniment in songs by Vaughan Williams and Gordon Jacob. Her final concert with the choir was in November 1927.

In addition to accompanying the Bach Choir, Victoria was a member of the Newcastle Symphony Orchestra from 1917 to 1927.

Her father died in 1917, but she continued to live with her mother at Windsor Terrace until her mother's death in 1920.

Victoria moved to Edinburgh shortly after 1927. At first she lived at 20 Lennox Street, but later moved to 149 Liberton Brae in the late 1940s, where she remained for the rest of her life. Records show that she practised as a naturopath.

Victoria died on 22 June 1974 at the Royal Infirmary, Edinburgh, aged ninety-one. She was unmarried.

Helen Bainton, ARCM (1909–1996)
Viola and violin 1926–7

Fig. 140 Helen and Edgar Bainton outside the ABC studios, Sydney, 1942. *Courtesy the Edgar Bainton (UK) Society.*

HELEN BAINTON, younger of the two daughters of Edgar Leslie Bainton and Ethel Frances Eales, was born in Stocksfield, Northumberland. Both her parents were accomplished musicians, and a brief account of them and of Helen's early life will be found in her mother's biography in Chapter 4.

Helen inherited her parents' musical interests and abilities. She was taught to play the piano by both her parents, at first by her mother and later by her father, whom she described as 'a strict and sometimes forbidding teacher'. Helen also learned to play the viola.

Helen's performances with the Bach Choir were limited; she first played the viola with them at the age of seventeen in January 1926, in a programme featuring three Bach cantatas. In April 1927 she took part in a performance of the St John Passion. Her final concert with the choir was in May 1927, in a concert in which the choir sang William Byrd's three-part Mass and W. G. Whittaker's setting of Psalm 139; she also played works by Henry Purcell (various fantasias for strings) and anonymous sixteenth-century compositions for strings.

Helen studied at the Royal College of Music in London from September 1928 to July 1933, taking pianoforte as her first subject and violin as her second subject. She was awarded the ARCM for pianoforte solo in April 1931. She was also awarded the Ashton Janson Exhibition in 1929, 1930, 1931 and 1932.

Helen's sister Guenda studied at the Royal College of Art in London at about the same time as her sister was at the Royal College of Music. She became a successful commercial artist under her married name of Abbott.

In June 1933 Edgar Bainton was appointed director of the Sydney Conservatorium of Music, and he and Ethel travelled to Australia in May 1934. Their daughters joined them there in August that year.

Edgar conducted choral and orchestral classes at the Conservatorium and founded an Opera School (for which Guenda designed and painted many of the sets). Helen joined in her father's activities at the Conservatorium, and there is a record of her giving a violin and piano recital as early as 1935.

In 1935 Ethel and Edgar Bainton were part of a small group of enthusiasts who pressed for the establishment of a full-time professional orchestra in Sydney. This was brought to fruition in 1936 by the formation of the Sydney Symphony Orchestra under the auspices of the Australian Broadcasting Commission. Helen was an early member of the orchestra and eventually became its principal violist. She and her father gave the first performance of her father's Sonata for Viola and Piano on 12 October 1942. (See fig. 140.)

Ethel Bainton died in 1954 and Edgar in 1956. Helen continued to play with the Sydney Symphony Orchestra until her retirement. In 1960 she published a biography of her father entitled *Remembered on Waking*,* and in 1967 she published a history of the Sydney Symphony Orchestra entitled *Facing the Music*:

---

* Helen Bainton, *Remembered on Waking*: *A Memoir of Edgar Bainton*. 2nd edn (Hersham: Line Clear Editions, 2013).

An Orchestral Player's Notebook. She died in Sydney on 13 February 1996, aged eighty-six. She was unmarried.

The author acknowledges the collaboration of Michael Jones of the Edgar Bainton (UK) Society with this biography.

The Beers Family

THIS remarkable family of Dutch Catholic immigrants made significant contributions to the musical life of Newcastle and also further afield. Two family members, Simon Hubertus Beers and his son Leo Luke Beers, played in orchestras accompanying the Bach Choir.

Adrian (Adrianus) Beers and his wife Meine Johanna Hubertina Beers (also known as Mimi) were born in Holland in 1816 and 1815 respectively. Adrian was a professional musician. They had eight children, the first seven of whom were born in Rotterdam and their youngest in London in 1863. In London they lived first at 32 Gloucester Buildings in Tower Hamlets. By 1871 the family had moved to the North East of England and were living at 10 Bedford Street in the Bishopwearmouth district of Sunderland. Adrian died in 1879. In 1881 Meine and three of her children were living at 4 Day Street in the Sandyford district of Newcastle. Meine died in 1900.

Simon Hubertus Beers (1845–1931)
Double bass 1920, 1921 and 1924

SIMON HUBERTUS BEERS, third of the eight children of Adrian and Meine Beers, was born in Rotterdam. He was a music teacher and specialized in the double bass.

Simon married Elizabeth Hughes in Newcastle in 1882. Elizabeth was born in Liverpool but in 1881 was living in Bishopwearmouth and working as a domestic servant for a rope manufacturer named Craven. Simon and Elizabeth moved to Newcastle and in 1883 were living at 6 Lefroy Street, Elswick. Their six boys were born in Newcastle between 1884 and 1893. By 1891 the family were living at 30 Kingsley Place, Heaton. They continued to live in the Newcastle suburb of Heaton for many years. In 1901 they were living at 64 Meldon Terrace, and in 1911 at 18 Tenth Avenue.

Simon Beers first played the double bass with the Bach Choir in the March

1920 performance of the St Matthew Passion. In March 1921 he played in performances of Holst's *The Hymn of Jesus* and Bach's Concerto in D minor for two violins and string orchestra. His final season with the choir was in 1924. On 1 March 1924 he took part in a concert that featured two pieces by Holst (*The Cloud Messenger* and the *Fugal Concerto*) and two of Bach's secular cantatas. On 5 March he played in a programme of music by Bach starring the concert pianist Harold Samuel. The works performed included pieces from the *Well Tempered Clavier*, the Partita No. 1 in B flat major, the Chromatic Fantasia and Fugue and the Concerto in E major. The choir sang an unaccompanied motet. Simon's final concert with the choir was in the April 1924 performance of Bach's St John Passion.

Simon played in the Newcastle Philharmonic Orchestra in the 1924 season. He was principal double bass in the Newcastle Symphony Orchestra from 1920 to 1930.

It is also worth recording that Simon had a younger brother, Joseph Henry Beers, also living in Newcastle, who was a brilliant violinist and conducted the city's Theatre Royal Orchestra. Joseph's daughter, who was known as Mimi, was a contralto soloist.

Not much is known about Simon and Elizabeth's first child, Adrian Henry, except that in 1901 he was working as a wool merchant's clerk.

In 1911 their second son, Hubertus Charles, was living in Fulham, London, married with one child and working as a painter's labourer. He served in the First World War as a private with the Northamptonshire Regiment. He went on to make a reputation for himself as a music hall singer and comedian, appearing under the stage name of 'Jock Macpherson'. There is a record of him sailing to and from Cape Town in 1921 as a music hall artiste. He died in 1925, aged thirty-nine, and is buried in Streatham Park Cemetery.

The biography of Simon and Elizabeth's third son, Leo, appears later in this chapter.

Their fourth child, Joseph John Septimus, was a violinist and played from 1910 to 1912 with the Newcastle Philharmonic Orchestra. He served as a private with the 2nd Battalion the King's Own Yorkshire Light Infantry in the First World War, and was killed in action in Belgium on 10 July 1917, aged twenty-six.

Their fifth son, Aloysius Anthony (known as 'Wishy'), was a double bass player who moved to Glasgow, where he married and where two of his children, Adrian Simon and Leo Joseph John were born. He worked in the city's music halls and dance bands. The family moved to London and lived at a variety of addresses in the Kensington area before moving to Wimbledon. Aloysius played with the

BBC Palm Court Orchestra for many years. His son Adrian Simon attended the Glasgow Bellahouston Academy and won a scholarship to the Royal College of Music in London, where he later taught. He was a principal in the London Philharmonia Orchestra and the English Chamber Orchestra, and founded the Melos Ensemble. He was a friend of Benjamin Britten and was awarded the MBE in 1990.

Bernard, the youngest son of Simon and Elizabeth Beers, played the cello and was in the Newcastle Philharmonic Orchestra in the 1911 and 1912 seasons. He moved to Edinburgh, had a distinguished career with the Edinburgh String Quartet, and was much in demand as a soloist. He also served as musical director at the Princes Cinema, Princes Street, Edinburgh, in the mid 1920s.

Elizabeth Beers died in 1898, aged thirty-seven. Simon did not remarry, and died on 6 February 1931 at the family home at 18 Tenth Avenue, Heaton, aged eighty-six.

Leo Luke Beers (1888–1975)
Viola 1922, 1923 and 1927   Violin 1928 and 1930

Fig. 141 Leo in later life. Family photograph, undated.

LEO LUKE BEERS was the third of the six children of Simon Hubertus Beers and Elizabeth Hughes. He was a violinist and violist and played the violin with the Newcastle Philharmonic Orchestra in the 1910 season. According to contemporary newspaper reports, in August 1914, at a time of heightened international tension and public sensitivity, Leo and his brother Aloysius ('young men of foreign extraction') were observed by a local Sea Scout photographing a military installation associated with Tynemouth Castle and Priory. They were arrested and charged under the Official Secrets Act. They appeared before the Tynemouth Borough Police Court, where the Chief Constable read over the charge and they were asked if they understood English. 'We *are* English,' replied Leo Beers. 'We were born in Newcastle.' They were remanded in custody for eight days. Enquiries were then made and at a subsequent hearing 'the Chief Constable had satisfied himself that there had been nothing wrong'. They were discharged, but were cautioned by the Mayor that they had 'brought their troubles upon themselves by their own foolishness'.

In 1915 and early 1916 Leo played in classical concerts with the resident orchestra of the Pump Room in Bath. He was called up for military service in December 1915, but in February 1916 applied for an exemption from service on personal and domestic grounds. He appeared before a military tribunal, was granted an exemption of two months, and subsequently served as a private in the Duke of Cornwall's Light Infantry until August 1918.

After his demobilization Leo continued his musical career and joined the Newcastle Symphony Orchestra, in which he played the viola and occasionally the violin from 1919 until about 1936.

Leo was a versatile performer of both the viola and the violin, and first played with the Bach Choir in November 1922. During his years with the choir, all under the conductorship of W. G. Whittaker, he played in three concerts wholly or partly devoted to Bach cantatas and in one performance each of the St John Passion and the B Minor Mass. In the November 1922 concert Leo played in a performance of Holst's *Ode to Death*. In December 1928 he played in performances of Holst's *The Golden Goose* and in two works by Vaughan Williams, the *Concerto Accademico* and *Flos Campi*. His final concert with the choir was in April 1930.

In the 1920s he performed on radio Newcastle 5NO with his 'Leo Beers' Symphony Orchestra'. In 1920 he visited Montreal with a group of nine other musicians, and in 1929 visited New York.

At the end of the Second World War Leo moved to London, and from about 1945 until 1964 lived at 23 Stanley Gardens in the Kensington area, near his brother Aloysius and his family. He died in Kensington in 1975, aged eighty-seven. He was unmarried.

George William Danskin, LRAM (1888–1945)
Continuo 1920   Piano 1928   Orchestral timpani 1923, 1924 and 1926

GEORGE WILLIAM DANSKIN, first of two children of Isaac Danskin and Margaret Eleanor Storey, was born in Benwell, Newcastle upon Tyne. His father, who was born in Newburn-on-Tyne, worked first as a glass maker at the Lemington Glass Works. He then became a steamboat fireman before following in his father's footsteps to become a waterman or wherryman. This work involved using a small boat called a wherry or skiff to ferry passengers on the River Tyne. He was an active trade unionist, and was secretary to the Tyne Watermen's Association, which was based at 15 Broad Chare in the quayside area of Newcastle. George's mother died in 1893. His father married Sarah Hannah Palfreman the following year, but had no more children.

Fig. 142 Family photograph, undated.

At the age of eleven George showed early evidence of musical ability by playing at a concert for the Blaydon Co-operative Society, of which his father was chairman of the education committee. In 1900 he was awarded a Northumberland County Council scholarship to enable him to proceed from elementary school to Rutherford College in Bath Lane, Newcastle.

He trained as a teacher at Armstrong College of Durham University in Newcastle. He became an assistant master at Thornley council school, County Durham, in 1909, and was at Newburn Hall council school, near Newcastle, in the same capacity from 1909 to 1913. In 1914 he met Gustav Holst, who presented him with a dedicated copy of his choral work *The Cloud Messenger*. (See fig. 143.)

George's career was interrupted by war service from 1914 to 1919, but no official record of this has survived. He married Ethel Ryder in Newcastle in 1917. Her biography will be found in Chapter 4. They had a daughter and two sons, one of whom died in infancy. For many years they lived at 24 Lyndhurst Avenue in Jesmond, Newcastle.

From 1920 George began teaching music at his old school, Rutherford College, and also at Heaton Secondary Boys' School. A history of Rutherford College records that he was a very capable music teacher and that the school 'gained many successes under his guiding hand'. He also taught music privately and was organist and choirmaster at Jesmond Presbyterian Church. He obtained the LRAM for pianoforte teaching in 1922.

George's first concert with the Bach Choir was the March 1920 performance of Bach's St Matthew Passion, in which he provided the continuo. In February and March 1923, March 1924 and February 1926 he played the timpani for the Bach Choir. In the April 1925 performance of the St Matthew Passion he trained the ripieno chorus from Rutherford College Girls' School. In February 1928 he provided the piano accompaniment for a 'distant chorus' (in which his wife sang) in

Vaughan Williams's *Sancta Civitas*. His last recorded activities for the choir were training pupils from the Rutherford College Girls' School to sing in Bach's Christmas Oratorio in January 1936 and in the St Matthew Passion in April 1936.

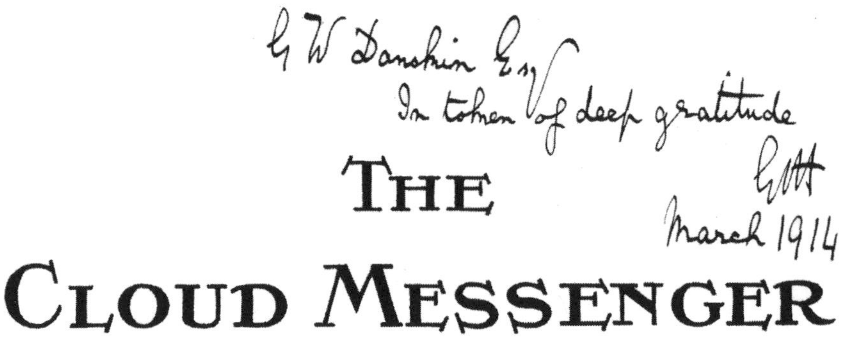

THE
CLOUD MESSENGER

G W Danskin Esq
In token of deep gratitude
GvH
March 1914

Fig. 143 Score dedicated to G. W. Danskin by the composer, Gustav Holst.

In the years leading up to the Second World War George conducted a number of choirs, including the Blaydon Choral Society, the Felling Operatic Society and the Fenham Operatic Society. He had an aptitude for training and handling massed choirs. The photograph overleaf shows him conducting a choir at the St James's Park football ground in Newcastle.

Fig. 144 George Danskin *c*. 1920. Family photograph.

George was director of the North of England Musical Tournament and an adjudicator at many other local festivals. In 1944 he was the piano accompanist at a series of celebrity concerts at the Ashington Methodist Central Hall, in which famous artists such as the soprano Isobel Baillie, the local bass Owen Brannigan, the Australian bass Clement Hardman and the contralto Kathleen Ferrier performed.

George died suddenly on 17 July 1945 at Newcastle General Hospital, aged fifty-six. Ethel died on 18 December 1965 at her home in Lyndhurst Avenue, aged seventy-three.

The author acknowledges the collaboration of Judith Steen, Gill Clancy and Colin Danskin with this biography.

Fig. 145 George conducting at St James's Park, Newcastle, undated.

Florence Gavin (1896–1955)
Violin: as F. Gavin 1919–23; as Mrs F. Wilson 1923–30

FLORENCE (FLO) GAVIN, second of two children of John Gavin and Alice Duncan, was born in Newcastle. Her father, the son of a blacksmith, was born in Fraserburgh, near Aberdeen. He was in the Merchant Navy and qualified as a master mariner in December 1880. Her mother, a music teacher, was born in Aberdeen, the daughter of an engineering draughtsman. John Gavin had been married before, but his first wife, Annie, died during pregnancy of renal disease in 1891 and they had no surviving children. John Gavin and Alice Duncan married in 1892 in Blythswood, Glasgow.

Florence's elder brother, Walter, was born in 1893 in Aberdeen. The Gavin family then moved to Newcastle, where John Gavin was appointed master of the cargo ship *Laurestina*. She was an iron-built, steam-powered, single-screw vessel displacing 2,051 gross tons and was owned by the Stag Line Ltd (J. Robinson & Sons) of North Shields. The family went to live at 13 Lansdown Terrace, Gosforth. Tragedy struck on 7 December 1895, when the *Laurestina*, on a voyage from Balimore to Sligo with a cargo of maize, was reported missing having passed Cape Henry at the mouth of Chesapeake Bay on the Atlantic coast of Virginia. John Gavin and his crew were presumed drowned. John left an estate valued at about £2,280.

Florence was born at the beginning of 1896. By 1901 Alice and the children had moved to 35 Rothwell Road, Gosforth, where they remained for many years. Alice supported the family from private means, probably a combination of her husband's pension and music teaching. By 1911 Walter was a pharmaceutical student, but he died the following year, aged eighteen.

Florence inherited her mother's musical talents and became an accomplished violinist. She first played with the Bach Choir at the inaugural concert in November 1919. She then played in every subsequent season until 1930. From 1919 to 1923 she played under her maiden name, and after her marriage as either Mrs Wilson or Mrs F. Wilson. During her years with the Bach Choir, all under the conductorship of W. G. Whittaker, she played in fourteen concerts with music wholly or partly devoted to Bach cantatas and in three performances each of Bach's St John and St Matthew Passions and the B Minor Mass. In the February 1921 concert Florence and Elsie Pringle were soloists in Bach's Concerto in D minor for two violins and string orchestra. One contemporary press report recorded that they were 'warmly applauded' for their performances; another that they had received 'well-deserved applause for their excellent work'. The programme also included performances of Hebridean folk songs and Holst's *The Hymn of Jesus*. The November 1922 concert, mostly devoted to Bach cantatas, also included a performance of Holst's *Ode to Death*. The February 1923 concert included performances of two works by Holst (*The Cloud Messenger* and the *Fugal Concerto*) and two of Bach's secular cantatas.

On 27 October 1923 Florence married Thomas Wilson at the Castle Ward

Register Office. Thomas had been her next-door neighbour at 33 Rothwell Road, and worked for his father, Thomas Michael Wilson, who was a building contractor and estate agent.

Florence next played with the choir in the November 1925 Orlando Gibbons tercentenary concert, performing in two Bach's Concertos in A minor and E major and in some of Gibbons's fantasias for strings and his *The Cryes of London*. At the concert in December 1925 she played in performances of Holst's *Ode to Death*, Bach's Brandenburg Concerto No. 5 and three of the cantatas.

In the concert of November 1926, in which Harriet Cohen was the guest pianist, Florence played in performances of Bach's Clavier Concerto in D minor and the Concerto in C major for two claviers. In May 1927 she played in some of Purcell's fantasias for strings and in various songs with string accompaniment by William Byrd and anonymous composers. This concert also featured an early performance of Whittaker's setting of Psalm 139.

In the February 1928 concert she played in performances of Vaughan Williams's *Sancta Civitas* and in Bach's *Ouverture* or Suite No. 2 in B minor. In December 1928 she played in Holst's *The Golden Goose* and in two works by Vaughan Williams, the *Concerto Accademico* and *Flos Campi*. Her final concert with the choir was in April 1930.

In addition to her activities with the Bach Choir, Florence was a violinist with the Newcastle Symphony Orchestra from 1921 to 1934.

Florence and Thomas had no children. After Thomas's death Florence continued to live at 35 Rothwell Road. She died at St George's Hospital, Morpeth, on 21 June 1955, aged fifty-nine.

Prof. Cuthbert Morton Girdlestone, MA (CANTAB) (1895–1975)
Flute 1928–47

CUTHBERT MORTON GIRDLESTONE, elder child of the Rev. James Hammond Le Breton Girdlestone and Edith Margaret Coles, was born in Bovey Tracey, Devon. His father was born in Hawkstone, Shropshire and his mother in Eltham, Kent.

The Girdlestones are an old Norfolk family long associated with the village of Kelling and Old Kelling Hall, which was replaced in 1913 by a newer building. J. H. Le Breton Girdlestone was the son of the Rev. Francis Paddon Girdlestone, who married Louisa Ann Charlotte Hammond in 1864. Louisa was the daughter of John Hammond (1801–1880), a lawyer who held several senior posts in the

States of Jersey, including those of bailiff and advocate general. John Hammond was famed for his exuberant sideburns. At the time of James Hammond's birth in 1865 his father was chaplain to Viscount Hill of Hawkstone Park in Shropshire. In 1866 his father became rector of Berrington and Sutton in Shropshire. Their second child was born in Jersey in 1869. In 1871 his father became clerk rector at St Mary's, Bungay, in Suffolk. He died suddenly in Lowestoft in 1874 at the age of forty-one.

James Hammond Le Breton Girdlestone studied at Haileybury College, Clerkenwell before going to St Edmund Hall, Oxford, where he graduated as a BA in 1891. He was appointed curate of Brighton later that year. By 1901 he was the incumbent at Holy Trinity Church, Worthing. In the summer of 1894 he married Edith Margaret Coles, the daughter of Charles A. Coles, a captain in the militia.

Cuthbert Morton Girdlestone was born in 1895, when his father was chaplain to the Devon House of Mercy in Bovey Tracey, an institution for 'reclaiming fallen women'.

Cuthbert was educated at the Sorbonne (Licence ès-lettres 1915) and the Schola Cantorum in Paris. During the First World War he served as a private in the Young Men's Christian Association (YMCA) Corps of the Norfolk Regiment. In 1915 the YMCA had received permission to establish 'recreational facilities within the area of army operation', and many members of the Corps were close to the firing-line.

After the war Cuthbert studied at Trinity College, Cambridge, where he became a lecturer in 1922. On 20 June 1923 he married Anne Marie Micheletti, the daughter of Jerome Micheletti, a chemist then deceased. The ceremony took place in Paris, in the presence of the British vice-consul, Mr Cyril F. W. Andrews, at the *mairie* (the mayor's office) at 31 rue Peclet. Both parties were resident in Paris at the time of the marriage. A marginal note in the register dated 14 August 1924 amended the bride's forenames to 'Anne Marie Eugénie' after receipt of a letter to the British consul general from Cuthbert Girdlestone.

In 1926 Cuthbert was appointed to the chair of French at Armstrong College (later King's College), Newcastle. Their first child, Magdalen Winifred, was born on 1 June 1926 at 95 Boulevard Arago, Paris. The birth was registered by the British vice-consul. Cuthbert, who was the informant, was registered as living at 30 Petty Cury, Cambridge. Their second child, Edith Ann, was born on 16 December 1928 in Marseilles. This time the birth was registered by the British consul general. Cuthbert, who was again the informant, was registered as living at 41 Sanderson Road, Newcastle. Newcastle electoral registers reveal that the Girdlestones lived at that address in Jesmond until at least 1933, although the

Fig. 146 Cuthbert Girdlestone (second right) at his retirement presentation by Dr Charles Bosanquet (Rector of King's College, Newcastle), 1960. *Courtesy the Robinson Library, University of Newcastle upon Tyne.*

register for 1933 showed only Cuthbert at the address.

Cuthbert and his wife Anne Marie played with the Bach Choir in February 1928; Cuthbert played the flute and his wife the violin. Cuthbert played consistently thereafter until about 1947. His wife played only once more with the choir. During his time under the conductorship of W. G. Whittaker, Cuthbert played in one performance each of the St John and St Matthew Passions and the B Minor Mass. In the February 1928 concert they both played in Vaughan Williams's *Sancta Civitas* and Bach's *Ouverture* or Suite No. 2 in B minor for flute and strings. In December 1928 Cuthbert played in two works by Vaughan Williams (the *Concerto Accademico* and *Flos Campi*) and in Holst's *The Golden Goose*. In November 1929 Cuthbert played in performances of Holst's *The Hymn of Jesus* and three Bach cantatas. Cuthbert and Anne Marie both played in the April 1930 performance of the St John Passion. This was their final concert under W. G. Whittaker. Cuthbert, however, continued to play with the choir under Sidney Newman, J. A. Westrup and Chalmers Burns. His final concert with the choir was in February 1947.

In 1939 Cuthbert published (in French) his seminal work on Mozart's piano concertos, *Mozart et ses concertos pour piano*.

Cuthbert's father died in 1941 and his mother in 1953. They had spent much of their retirement living in the south of France, where they owned properties in Biarritz and, at the time of their deaths, in Cannes.

In the summer of 1940 Mrs Girdlestone and their two daughters, Magdalen and Edith, were staying in what they thought was a safe part of France, when they received a telegram from the authorities advising them to evacuate because of the deteriorating political situation. They undertook a 250-mile taxi ride to a south coast port before escaping the country on a liner.

From about 1948 to 1961 Cuthbert and Anne Marie were living at 41 Sandhill in the quayside area of Newcastle. Nos. 41–44 Sandhill, better known as Bessie Surtees House, are two five-storey sixteenth- and seventeenth-century merchants' houses with fine Jacobean domestic architecture, now in the care of English Heritage. Their daughter Magdalen was also living there in 1948, and their other daughter, Edith, in 1960 and 1961.

In 1957 Cuthbert published (in English) his second famous book, *Jean-Philippe Rameau, His Life and Work*, which was later translated into French and published posthumously in 1983.

Cuthbert retired from his post as professor of French in 1960. A subscription list to a book (*Medieval Miscellany* 1965, ed. Whitehead *et al.*) reveals that he lived in retirement at 1 Parc de la Bérengère, Saint-Cloud (SO) France. He died on 10 December 1975 in Saint-Cloud, aged eighty.

James Thomas Griffiths, ARCM (1870–1944)
Violoncello 1915, 1916 and 1917

JAMES THOMAS (JIM) GRIFFITHS, third of four children of Thomas Griffiths and Ellen Jenkins, was born in Swansea. His parents were born in Carmarthenshire, his father in Llandeilo Fawr and his mother, the daughter of a land agent, in Llangunnor, a suburb of Carmarthen. His father was a boot- and shoemaker. James was brought up in the nonconformist (Calvinistic Methodist) tradition. Although his parents were bilingual Welsh/English, James spoke only English. At the time of his birth the family lived at 24 Vincent Street, Swansea, but by 1891 they had moved to 2 George Street, where his parents were still living in 1901.

In 1891 James was living at home and working as a grocer's assistant. By 1901, however, he had moved to Newcastle upon Tyne and was living in digs at 230 Westgate Road in the city's West End. His occupation is given as 'violoncellist and grocer'.

He married Mary Agnes McMaughan in 1901 in Tynemouth. Agnes was born in Middlesbrough, the daughter of Peter McMaughan, a waterman, who was originally from Gateshead. At the time of her marriage she was living at 13 Albany Gardens, Whitley Bay, and working as a domestic help for a Mrs Hedley. They had four daughters, Nina Winifred (b.1902), Muriel Laura (b.1903), Iris (b.1905) and Sylvia Frances Agnes (b.1907), who were baptized into the Roman Catholic Church.

James began playing the cello in the Newcastle Philharmonic Orchestra in 1910 and continued to do so until about 1923.

In 1911 the Griffiths family were living at 3 Gallalaw Terrace, South Gosforth, at which time James was recorded as a 'teacher of violoncello'. From around 1914 until 1921 he taught the cello from rooms at 17 York Street. Newcastle. In 1929 he was teaching at 12 Sunbury Avenue, Jesmond, and in 1938 at 42 Valley View, Jesmond, not far from Jesmond Dene.

James first played the cello with the Bach Choir at its inaugural concert in November 1915. During his time with the choir he played in five concerts wholly or partly devoted to Bach cantatas and in one performance of the St John Passion. His final concert with the choir was in March 1917.

In the 1930s he played the cello in the Newcastle Theatre Royal piano quartet with Leo Beers (second violin) and Karl Livock (piano) under the leadership of Hermann McLeod.

In the 1930s James and Agnes moved to live at 17 Forest Avenue, Forest Hall. James died on 10 May 1944 at the Preston Hospital, North Shields, aged seventy-three.

Thomas Walton Hardy, ATCL (1863–1946)
Violin 1915–20

THOMAS WALTON HARDY, first of three children of John Hardy and Sarah Thompson, was born in Poplar, London. Both his parents were born at Middleton in Teesdale. His father, John Hardy, began his working life as a lead-miner in Teesdale. By 1871 the Hardy family had moved to London, where John worked as a lead crystallizer. The family returned to the North East to live in the village of Eston, near Middlesbrough, where John Hardy worked as a labourer in an iron works. Thomas was only fourteen when his mother died in 1878, aged thirty-nine. Later that year his father married Hannah Sempers, a mineral clerk born in Poppleton, Yorkshire, and they had one daughter.

In 1881, at the age of seventeen, Thomas was working as a shop boy in the village of Eston. He seems to have taken an interest in music and was clearly talented. He obtained the ATCL, became a violin teacher and frequently played in theatre orchestras.

Thomas married Elizabeth Ruth Wilkinson in Newcastle in 1892, and they had two daughters, Amy (b.1894) and Elsie (b.1898). The family lived at 7 Park Avenue, Whitley Bay.

Thomas first played the violin with the Bach Choir at the inaugural concert in

November 1915. During his time with the choir he played in five concerts wholly or partly devoted to Bach cantatas and in one performance each of the St John and St Matthew Passions. His first six concerts with the choir spanned November 1915 to February 1917. Elizabeth died in 1918, aged fifty. Her death prevented him from performing again with the choir until the concert of February 1920, which was his final concert with them.

In 1933, at the age of seventy, Thomas married Ellen Marianne Thompson, the 37-year-old daughter of Adam Brown Thompson, an organist and music teacher from Whitley Bay, but they had no children. They lived at 54 Park Avenue, Whitley Bay.

Thomas died on 12 November 1946 at the Victoria Jubilee Infirmary, Tynemouth, aged eighty-three. Ellen died in 1982, aged eighty-six.

Alice Hayes (b.1900)
Violin and viola 1919–25

ALICE HAYES, the elder of two daughters of Joseph Jobson Hayes and Martha Wilson, was born in Heworth, County Durham. Both of her parents were born in or near Gateshead, County Durham. Her father was a coal miner. Her mother had previously been married to a Richard Robinson, but he had died and the marriage had been childless.

No marriage record has been found for Alice's parents, but her birth certificate shows that at the time of her birth on 22 December 1900 they were living at Crow Hall Cottages, Sunderland Road, Heworth. The family surname was recorded as Hay. A second daughter, Martha, was born in 1902.

In 1911 Joseph Hayes and his two daughters were living at 2 Back Holly Hill, Heworth. The census also reveals that by this time Joseph was a widower, but his wife's death record has not been found. Also living with them was Margaret Ellen Arnell, who was a daughter from Joseph Hayes's father's second wife's first marriage. (She was incorrectly referred to as a sister of Joseph Hayes.)

The earliest reference to Alice's musical abilities is a report in the *Yorkshire Post* from January 1912 in which it was reported that she was awarded first prize in a violin contest at an eisteddfod for the Cleveland and Durham District at Middlesbrough town hall. She repeated her success in the 1914 eisteddfod, winning the violin solo competition for competitors aged 14–21 years, attaining 91 marks; her nearest rival had 81 marks. In September 1915 she played the violin in a concert for the Gateshead Temperance Council in the grounds of the Gateshead rectory.

Joseph Jobson Hayes died on 9 July 1917 at the family home in Back Holly Hill, Heworth. It is not known where Alice and her sister lived after this date.

Alice first played the violin in orchestras accompanying the Bach Choir in May 1919. During her years with the choir she played in four concerts wholly or partly devoted to Bach cantatas and in one performance each of the St John Passion and the B Minor Mass. She played in performances of the Brandenburg Concerto No. 3 and in concerts with music by Holst (the *Ode to Death*, *The Cloud Messenger* and the *Fugal Concerto*).

She played with the Newcastle Symphony Orchestra in the 1919 season and with the Newcastle Philharmonic Orchestra from 1920 to 1924. In 1923 she performed a violin solo on local radio Newcastle 5NO. In 1924 she was in a quartet alongside J. H. Thompson, Rosina Wall and Arthur J. Bull, playing music by Cecil Armstrong Gibbs in a concert organized by him in Newcastle. Marjorie Amati and Arthur Lewis were the vocal soloists at that concert.

The author has been unable to trace any records of Alice from after 1925.

Mark Hemingway (1880–1971)
Trumpet 1919–26

MARK HEMINGWAY, ninth of ten children of William Hemingway and Hannah Rayner, was born in Dewsbury, Yorkshire, where his parents were born. Census records give contradictory information about his father's precise place of birth, but his mother is known to have been born in Earlsheaton, a suburb of Dewsbury. William Hemingway worked as a cloth fuller, and the family lived in Dewsbury for many years. In 1871 they were at the Co-operative Society building at 88 Commercial Street; in 1881 at 208 Spring Road Terrace; in 1891 at 4 Clarence Place; and finally in 1901 at 113 Soothill Terrace.

Little is known of Mark's early life and education, but in the 1901 census his occupation was given as 'musician and teacher'. The earliest newspaper reference to him is from 1902, when he was solo trumpet in a performance of Handel's *Messiah* for the Nottingham Sacred Harmonic Society. In 1905 he was already being described as 'the famous Dewsbury trumpeter', and in 1907 a concert announcement proclaimed him 'the finest trumpeter in the world'. In the years around 1905–8 he was playing in the Harrogate and Leeds municipal orchestras.

In 1904 Mark married Martha Wolstenholme, the daughter of Henry Wolstenholme, a hairdresser from Dewsbury, at the Wesleyan Centenary Chapel, Dewsbury. They had a daughter born in 1908 and a son born in 1911.

Between 1902 and 1924 Mark appeared in performances of Handel's *Messiah* on at least fifteen occasions, with choirs such as the Aberdeen Choral Union, the Cupar Choral Society, the Derby Choral Union, the Hull Vocal Society, the Newcastle and Gateshead Choral Union and the Nottingham Sacred Harmonic Society. His performances of the obbligato to 'The trumpet shall sound' were universally acclaimed. Mark also featured during those years in several performances of Handel's *Samson*. Such was his reputation that he was the only local orchestral player contracted to play at the Leeds Triennial Festival in 1913.

Mark first played the trumpet with the Bach Choir in May 1919. During his years with the choir he played in six concerts wholly or partly devoted to Bach cantatas and in two performances of the B Minor Mass. He played in one concert that featured two works by Holst (*The Cloud Messenger* and the *Fugal Concerto*) and two of Bach's secular cantatas. His final concert with the choir was in February 1926.

He played in the Newcastle Philharmonic Orchestra in the 1924 season and with the Newcastle Symphony Orchestra from 1919 to 1924. Mark also played with the Hastings Municipal Orchestra, under Sir Henry Wood in Queen's Hall concerts and in concerts for the BBC. Sir Henry had 'a high opinion of his tone and technique'.

From 1932 Mark and Martha lived in Edgware, Middlesex, at a house called Glenariffe on the Watford bypass.

In 1935 Martha died at St Columba's Hospital, Swiss Cottage, Middlesex, aged fifty-five. In that year Mark was appointed first trumpet in the Bath Pump Room Orchestra.

Mark was still living at Glenariffe in 1937. He died in 1971 in Scarborough, aged ninety-one.

Adolphe Hervé, LBC (BRUSSELS) (1878–1935)
Viola and violin 1917, 1919 and 1920

ADOLPHE HERVÉ, son of Napoléon Hervé, a merchant, was born in Belgium in about 1878. Little is known of his early life, and it is uncertain when he moved to live in the United Kingdom. However, it seems that he trained at the Brussels Conservatoire, obtaining the LBC. The earliest reference to him in this country is an advertisement dated August 1903 for a concert at the Victoria Hall, Sunderland.

In 1907 he married Maud Hepworth Coxon, daughter of William Coxon, a draper from the city of Durham. At the time of their marriage he was living at 56 Bolingbroke Street in the Heaton district of Newcastle.

In January 1915 he played alongside James Mark at a concert in aid of the Belgian Relief Fund at the Empire Theatre, Newcastle.

Adolphe first played with the Bach Choir in February 1917. During his years with the choir he performed in three concerts wholly or partly devoted to Bach cantatas and in one performance each of the St John and St Matthew Passions. In May 1917 he played in the Bach Choir's first performance of Holst's *The Cloud Messenger*. In December 1917 he played in performances of music by Hubert Parry (*Lady Radnor's Suite* for strings), Frank Bridge (*Two Old English Songs* for string quartet) and Percy Grainger (*Room-Music Tit-Bits*).

In 1919 Adolphe began to advertise himself as a teacher of violin and viola at 3 Jesmond Dene Terrace, Newcastle. In that year he played for the Newcastle School Concert Society in a quartet with Alfred Wall, Elsie Pringle and James Griffiths. In another concert later that year, at the Newcastle Laing Art Gallery, he played in an octet with Alfred Wall, J. Young, Elsie Pringle, Flo Gavin, J. Hood, James Griffiths and Fred Smith.

Adolphe's Bach Choir appearances continued with the May 1919 concert, which was mostly devoted to Bach cantatas but also featured the Brandenburg Concerto No. 3. In December 1919 he played in performances of music by Walford Davies (*Six Pastorals*), John Dowland (*Lachrymae, or Seaven Teares*), William Boyce (the Suite in E), Holst (the *St Paul's Suite*) and Vaughan Williams (the Fantasia on Christmas Carols). In that concert there were also performances of carols for solo voices and strings. Adolphe's final concert with the choir was in May 1920.

Around 1923 Adolphe and Maud moved to the south coast of England, where Adolphe had taken up a post as a teacher of violin at the Hastings and St Léonard's School of Music (one of whose patrons was Lord Eustace Percy, the MP for Hastings and son of Henry, seventh Duke of Northumberland). For a number of years he played with the Compton Quartet (alongside John Davies and Fred and Harold Mayall), which frequently appeared on the pier at St Léonard's. In 1926 he played in a concert at the Eastbourne Music Festival under Sir Thomas Beecham.

For some years Adolphe and Maud lived at 6a Lascelles Mansions, Eastbourne. Adolphe died there on 19 August 1935, aged fifty-seven. Maud returned to the north of England and died in Redcar in 1961, aged eighty-nine. They had no children.

Florence Kate Hetherington (1880–1954)
Viola and violin 1915–17

FLORENCE KATE CROSS (known as Kate), the elder of two children of Henry Cross, a ship chandler's clerk, and Emilia Bell, was born in Newcastle upon Tyne. Her father was born in Newport Island, Guernsey, and her mother in Newcastle. His family came originally from Dorset, and the majority of his siblings were born in the Dorset coastal town of Lyme Regis. The Cross family moved from Guernsey to Newcastle between 1861 and 1871 to live at 7 St Thomas Terrace, which his father, Benjamin, a clothier by trade, ran as a lodging-house. Kate's mother died in 1882, aged twenty-two, at the time of the birth of her second child. In 1889 her father married Mary Emma Thompson, from the Northumberland town of Alnwick, and they had one child, a daughter, who was born in 1897. They first lived at 22 Summerhill Terrace, Newcastle (near Westgate Road), but by 1901 they had moved to 14 East Parade in Elswick.

Kate studied the violin and by 1897 was teaching the instrument privately.

Kate married Henry Hetherington, a marine engineer, in Barnet, Middlesex, in September 1907. Henry, who was born in Islington, London, had moved to Newcastle to take up an engineering apprenticeship in about 1900. In 1901 he was in lodgings in the West End of Newcastle, not far from the Cross household. His father, a grocer and tea dealer of Woodford Green in Essex, died suddenly in March 1907. Kate's father died the following year. Kate and Henry had two daughters, born in 1908 and 1911. In 1911 the family were living at 50 Croft Avenue, South Shields.

After 1911 Kate and her family moved to live in Newcastle. From 1912 to 1914 Kate was a visiting teacher of the violin at St Anne's Convent in Summerhill Grove, at Beechgrove Road Girls' School and at the Convent of the Sacred Heart. From 1914 onwards she played in chamber concerts with the Oppenheim Musical Society under the direction of their leader and pianist, Sigmund Oppenheim. She continued with her private teaching.

Kate first played with the Bach Choir at its inaugural concert in November 1915. During her years with the choir she played in four concerts of music wholly or partly devoted to Bach cantatas. They included other Bach works in which she played: the Violin Concertos in A minor and E major, the Clavier Concertos in D minor and F minor, the Concerto in C minor for two claviers and the *Italian Concerto*. The concert records do not make it clear whether, in three of these concerts, she played viola or violin, but in the programme for the December 1916 concert she is known to have played the viola. She was due to play in the March 1917 performance of the St John Passion, but her name is crossed out on the archive copy of the programme.

Fig. 147 Family photograph, *c.* 1894.   Fig. 148 Family photograph, *c.* 1905.

There was a hiatus in Kate's teaching career between 1915 and 1920, after which she resumed private tuition. She became a member of the Incorporated Society of Musicians. In 1921, when she registered with the Teachers' Registration Council, her professional address was 95 Elswick Road, Newcastle.

Merchant Navy records show that Kate's husband, Henry, served as a second engineer from 1918 to 1921 and was awarded the Mercantile Marine Medal. In 1921 the family were living at 25 Lonsdale Terrace in the Newcastle suburb of Jesmond.

In the mid to late 1920s Kate was also a member of the Newcastle Philharmonic Orchestra, which often accompanied the Newcastle and Gateshead Choral Union.

Henry travelled widely in his career as a marine engineer, taking up posts on a number of ships. It seems that his relationship with Kate broke down, and he disappeared from her life. Merchant Navy records of him exist until the early 1940s. He died in Liverpool on 2 February 1953, aged sixty-nine.

Kate went to live at 8 Leazes Terrace (close to the Royal Victoria Infirmary and the St James's Park football ground), where she ran a 'music studio' with her eldest unmarried daughter, who lived with her in her later years. Kate died in 1954 in Newcastle, aged seventy-three.

The author acknowledges the collaboration of Maxine Young with this biography.

Constance Maria Leathart (1871–1932)
Double bass 1915–27

CONSTANCE MARIA (CONNIE) LEATHART, eighth of the thirteen children of James Leathart and Maria Hedley, was born in Gateshead, County Durham. Her father was born in Alston, Cumberland, and joined the Newcastle firm of Locke, Blackett & Co., lead manufacturers, as a fourteen-year-old apprentice. He studied chemistry and metallurgy in his own time and eventually worked his way to the top, becoming a joint managing partner of the firm. His new-found wealth enabled him to become an art collector, commissioning works by local artists such as William Bell Scott and by many of the Pre-Raphaelite school such as Dante Gabriel Rossetti and Arthur Hughes. Eventually, owing to increasing foreign competition, the firm's financial health and his personal fortune declined, obliging him to sell his collection of paintings. He died in 1895, aged seventy-four, his wife having predeceased him in 1899, aged fifty-eight. The Leathart family lived for many years at Bracken Dene, a large house in Low Fell, Gateshead.

Constance's mother, Maria, was the daughter of Thomas Hedley, a wealthy soap manufacturer who had been lord mayor of Newcastle. Hedley's firm is best known for its product, Fairy Soap. The firm was eventually taken over by Procter and Gamble. Maria Leathart was a society beauty, and features in portraits and family group paintings commissioned by her husband. Constance (then aged seven) is almost certainly among those portrayed by Arthur Hughes in his 1878 painting *A Christmas at Bracken Dene*. Otherwise not much is known of Constance's childhood. It is likely, however, that she was educated privately.

Some of Constance's sisters married well, and many of her brothers had successful business or professional careers. Her brothers Thomas Hedley Leathart and James Gilbert Leathart took over the management of Locke, Blackett & Co. Her niece Constance Ruth Leathart, named after her, was the daughter of Thomas Hedley Leathart and became a famous pioneer aviator in the 1920s.

In 1895 Constance performed the launching ceremony of the schooner *Grenadier* at the Wigham Richardson yard in Walker for the Tyne Steam Ship Company, of which her father was a director.

HONORARY MEMBERS.

NOTE.

All lovers of orchestral music are invited to join the Society by becoming Honorary Non-Playing Members. A subscription of One Guinea entitles Members to two tickets for each Concert, and also to admission to Rehearsals; half that amount (10/6) entitles to one ticket. These tickets may be obtained by applying to the Honorary Secretary,

Miss LEATHART
20, Brandling Park,
Tel: 121 Jesmond.   **Newcastle-on-Tyne.**

Fig. 149 From a Newcastle Symphony Orchestra programme, 1925. *Courtesy Newcastle City Libraries.*

Constance first played the double bass with the Bach Choir at its inaugural concert in November 1915. During her year with the choir she played in seventeen concerts wholly or partly devoted to Bach cantatas, in three performances of the St John Passion and in one performance each of the St Matthew Passion and the B Minor Mass. Some of the cantata concerts also featured other works by Bach, including the Violin Concertos in E major and A minor, the Clavier Concertos in C minor, D minor and F minor, the *Italian Concerto* and the Brandenburg Concertos Nos. 3, 5 and 6. She played in concerts with music by Holst (*The Hymn of Jesus*, the *Ode to Death*, *The Cloud Messenger* and the *Fugal Concerto*) and Vaughan Williams (the Fantasia on Christmas Carols). She appeared less frequently with the choir from 1924, and her final performance with it was in April 1927.

She also played the double bass with the Newcastle Symphony Orchestra from 1917 to 1927 and was its membership secretary for many years.

Other members of the Leathart family played in the Newcastle Symphony Orchestra. Janet Ruth Grant Leathart (formerly Tennant), the wife of Thomas Hedley Leathart, played the viola (and occasionally the violin), and their daughter Constance Ruth, the aviator, was even co-opted to play the timpani in the 1923/4 and 1924/5 seasons. Violet Leathart (formerly Noble), the wife of James Gilbert Leathart, VC, played the cello.

At one time Constance shared a home with her brother James Gilbert Leathart in Low Fell, Gateshead, but after his marriage in 1911 she moved to Newcastle, where she lived at 20 Brandling Park, Jesmond, from about 1914. She died on 4 April 1932 at Drummond's Nursing Home, 5 Saville Place, Newcastle, aged sixty, and is buried in St John's Church, Low Fell. She was unmarried.

James Mark, LRAM, ARCM (1882–1955)
Violin and viola 1915–29

JAMES (JIMMIE) MARK, the second of four children of Robert Thomas Mark and Mary Loudon Thomson, was born in Dennistoun, Glasgow. His father, who was born in Salford, Lancashire, was initially a journeyman wire-drawer but eventually became an electrical storekeeper. His mother was born in Milton, Glasgow.

The family moved from Dennistoun to Newcastle between 1891 and 1901 and set up home in the Heaton area, first at 53 Tynemouth Road and later at 16 Eversley Place. James studied music and obtained the LRAM and ARCM.

The earliest record of James Mark performing in public was at a People's Concert in the Theatre Royal, South Shields, in 1901 in which 'Master James Mark gave a pleasing violin solo.' In 1914 he performed at a concert given by the Newcastle Musical Society at the Grand Assembly Rooms, playing alongside Edgar Bainton and Alfred Wall. In January 1915 he performed with his friend Adolphe Hervé at a concert in the Empire Theatre, Newcastle, in aid of the Belgian Relief Fund.

James married Lillia Isabella Dean in Newcastle upon Tyne in the summer of 1915. His wife was the daughter of Edward Dean, a pharmaceutical chemist who had a shop in Copland Terrace, Newcastle. James was described by contemporaries as 'a popular man of short stature' but who was 'quiet and retiring'. They had a son, James Kenneth, born in 1916 and later described as tall and handsome, and a daughter, Mary Gwyneth, born in 1917.

James first played with the Bach Choir at its inaugural concert in November 1915. He sometimes played the violin but more frequently the viola. During his years with the choir, all under the conductorship of W. G. Whittaker, he played in twenty concerts wholly or partly dedicated to Bach cantatas, in three performances each of the St John and St Matthew Passions, and in two performances of the B Minor Mass. Additional items in some of the cantata concerts included other works by Bach, such as the Clavier Concertos in D major and F minor, the Concerto in C minor for two claviers, the Violin Concertos in A minor and E major, the Brandenburg Concertos Nos. 3 and 5, the *Italian Concerto* and the Suite No. 2 in B minor. In addition he played in concerts with music by Holst (*The Cloud Messenger*, *The Hymn of Jesus*, the *Ode to Death* and the *Fugal Concerto*) and Vaughan Williams (the Fantasia on Christmas Carols and *Sancta Civitas*). In the May 1916 concert he and Annie Eckford played in performances of violin and keyboard sonatas by Henry Purcell and William Babell. A contemporary press report recorded that they 'showed great sympathy and unity of artistic idea' in their treatment of the works. James was also a soloist in the February 1917 and May 1917 concerts, and played the violin obbligato in the April 1928 performance of the St Matthew Passion. His final concert with the choir was in November 1929.

James was also a violinist in the Newcastle Philharmonic Orchestra from 1911 to 1924 and later principal violinist and leader of the Newcastle Symphony Orchestra from 1919 to 1946. In the 1923 season of the Newcastle Symphony Orchestra he played under the conductorship of Sir Henry Wood at a charity concert at the King's Hall in Newcastle. In the 1920s he performed regularly on the local radio station Newcastle 5NO. In the early 1940s he played with the Newcastle String Orchestra under Hermann McLeod.

James and Lillia lived until their deaths at 445 Chillingham Road in the Newcastle district of Heaton. James died on 2 February 1955 at St Nicholas's Hospital, Newcastle, aged seventy-two. Lillia died on 6 March 1962 at Walkergate Hospital, Newcastle, aged seventy-five.

The author acknowledges the collaboration of Mrs Lorna Rosner, daughter of Hermann McLeod, with this biography.

Ethel Ada Page (1876–1960)
Violin and viola 1915–28

Emily Hetty Page, LRAM (1881–1973)
Violoncello 1919–30

THE personal and professional lives of the Page sisters were so closely linked that a composite biography is appropriate.

Emily Hetty Page (known as Hetty) and Ethel Ada Page (known as Ethel), two of six children of Alfred John Edward Page and Emily Ann Robbins, were born in London, as were their parents. Their father and maternal grandfather were watchmakers and jewellers. In 1881 the family were living at the home of their paternal grandfather in St George's Square in Westminster. By 1891 the family had moved to 12 Tenth Avenue in Heaton, Newcastle. Some time before 1901, Alfred and Emily, Hetty and two of their other surviving children moved to live at 27 Fowler Street, South Shields. Ethel, however, remained in Newcastle, living at 1 Percy Terrace in Jesmond. Their mother died in 1905 and their father in 1909.

Ethel became a pupil of the Newcastle pianist Samuel S. Wiggins, and gave an early public performance in one of his concerts at the Central Masonic Hall in

Newcastle in 1896. She also received singing training from Miss Kate MacGregor. Ethel was a versatile musician, and by 1902 was becoming established as a violinist, pianist, accompanist and vocal soloist; she had a forte for singing humorous songs. In 1903 she was honorary accompanist to the South Shields Choral Society. She was a frequent performer in concerts arranged by the local Newcastle singing teacher William McConnell-Wood, appearing with the violinist Alfred Wall. She performed at concert parties at Wynyard Hall, County Durham, hosted by its owner, the Marquis of Londonderry.

Hetty was predominantly a cellist. In the late 1890s she undertook concerts at the South Shields Empire organized by Snowdon and Downey. In the early 1900s she was a regular member of the Sunderland Chamber Music Society, in which she played with the violinist Alfred Wall and the pianist Oscar Cohen. By about 1907 the sisters were performing together in concerts; for example in 1919 they both played at a St David's Day gathering for the Newcastle Cymmrodorion (a Welsh-speakers' gathering) at the famous Tilley's Tea Room in Market Street. For many years Hetty gave cello lessons at her home in Brandling Park. She was principal cellist with the Newcastle Symphony Orchestra from 1917 to 1931.

In 1911 Ethel and Hetty were living with their younger brother, Harold King Page, at 21 Brandling Park, Jesmond, in Newcastle. Harold later studied arts at the University of Durham and became an Anglican clergyman.

Their next-door neighbour at 20 Brandling Park was Constance Maria Leathart, the amateur double-bass player whose biography appears earlier in this chapter. In 1914 Ethel and Hetty hosted a Schumann–Brahms lieder recital at their home in Brandling Park. The soloists were Doris Woodall and Mostyn Bell; Ethel was the accompanying pianist.

Ethel first played with the Bach Choir at its inaugural concert in November 1915. In the majority of concerts she played the viola. In her years with the choir she played in seven concerts wholly or partly devoted to Bach cantatas, in three performances of the St Matthew Passion, and in one performance each of the St John Passion and the B Minor Mass. Some of the cantata concerts contained other music by Bach, including the Violin Concertos in A minor and E major, the Clavier Concertos in D minor and F minor, the Concerto in C minor for two claviers, the *Italian Concerto* and the Brandenburg Concertos Nos. 3 and 5. Ethel played in concerts with music by Holst (the *Suite for Strings*), Vaughan Williams (the Fantasia on Christmas Carols), Walford Davies (*Six Pastorals*), Dowland (*Lachrymae, or Seaven Teares*) and Boyce (the Suite in E). She took part in the March 1924 concert that featured the concert pianist Harold Samuel. Her final concert with the choir was in April 1928.

Ethel was also a violist with the Newcastle Symphony Orchestra from 1917 to 1922.

Hetty was principal cellist in the Newcastle Symphony Orchestra from 1917 until about 1931. She first played with the Bach Choir in May 1919. During her years with the choir, all under the conductorship of W. G. Whittaker, she played in eight concerts wholly or partly devoted to Bach cantatas, in two performances of the St John Passion, in three performances of the St Matthew Passion (playing the cello obbligato in two performances), and in three performance of the B Minor Mass. Some of the cantata concerts contained other music by Bach, such as the Brandenburg Concertos Nos. 3 and 5 and the Suite No. 2 in B minor. Hetty played in concerts with music by Holst (*The Hymn of Jesus*, the *Ode to Death*, *The Cloud Messenger*, the *Fugal Concerto* and *The Golden Goose*) and Vaughan Williams (*Flos Campi* and the *Concerto Accademico*). Her final appearance with the choir was in April 1930.

Throughout the 1920s and early 1930s the sisters broadcast on local radio as soloists, occasionally together and sometimes with the Northern Studio Orchestra. Neither of them played in the Newcastle Philharmonic Orchestra.

In about 1936 the sisters moved to 2 Crawborough Terrace, Charlbury, Oxfordshire, to be near their brother Harold, who was living not far away in Cheltenham.

Ethel died at their home in Charlbury on 11 November 1960, aged eighty-four. After her sister's death Hetty moved to residential accommodation at Saintbridge House, Gloucester, and died at the Royal Hospital, Gloucester, on 27 March 1973, aged ninety-one. Neither of them was married.

Elsie Pringle (1895–1980)
Violin 1915–28

ELSIE PRINGLE, youngest of eight children of John Blagdon Pringle and Elizabeth Weddell, was born in Newcastle. Her father, a joiner by trade, was born in the mining community of Longhirst, Northumberland, the son of Thomas Pringle, a hind (a skilled agricultural labourer). Because of the ephemeral nature of Thomas's work, the family had to move frequently around the county, but they eventually settled in the village of Belsay, around 1861. Elsie's mother, Elizabeth, was born in the rural Northumberland hamlet of Simonburn, where her father was a farmer and joiner. The Weddell family lived for many years at Low Park End, Simonburn.

Fig. 150 Family photograph, *c*. 1915. Fig. 151 Family photograph, *c*. 1910.

John and Elizabeth Pringle set up home at 208 Hamilton Street in Elswick, Newcastle. After John Pringle's death the family moved to 29 Darnell Street, in the Arthur's Hill area.

Elsie was trained at the Newcastle Conservatoire of Music, where she was a pupil in 1915, and played a violin solo in the Conservatoire Pupils' Concert that year. She first played violin with the Bach Choir at its inaugural concert in November 1915. During her years with the choir, all under the conductorship of W. G. Whittaker, she played in twelve concerts wholly or partly devoted to Bach cantatas, in three performances each of the St John and St Matthew Passions, and in two performances of the B Minor Mass. In some of the concerts she played in performances of other music by Bach, including the Violin Concertos in A minor and E major, the D minor and F minor clavier concertos, the Concerto in C minor for two claviers, the Brandenburg Concertos Nos. 3, 5 and 6, and the Suite No. 2 in B minor. In the February 1921 concert Elsie and Florence Gavin were the soloists in Bach's Concerto in D minor for two violins and string orchestra. One contemporary press report recorded that they were 'warmly applauded' for their performances, and another that they had received 'well-deserved applause for their excellent work'.

In addition Elsie performed in concerts with music by Holst (the *St Paul's Suite*, *The Hymn of Jesus*, the *Ode to Death*, *The Cloud Messenger* and the *Fugal Concerto*), Vaughan Williams (the Fantasia on Christmas Carols), Parry (*Lady Radnor's Suite* for strings), Frank Bridge (*Two Old English Songs* for string quartet) and Percy Grainger (*Room-Music Tit-Bits*).

Elsie also played first violin with the Newcastle Philharmonic Orchestra from 1920 to 1930.

Elsie worked for a number of years as a senior clerical assistant in the Newcastle Central Post Office, where she met a young contract officer called Louis Bennett Stott (formerly Swales), whom she married in Newcastle in 1931. Louis was born in Darlington. After the death of his father, Louis's mother, Emily, had married Matthew Richard Stott, and Louis subsequently adopted the Stott surname. The Stott family eventually moved to live in Hexham, Northumberland.

Louis was called up in 1915 and enlisted in the Royal Army Medical Corps, attaining the rank of staff sergeant. He developed pericarditis in 1916 and spent the remainder of his military service in Curragh Camp near Dublin attached to the 5th Battalion the Royal Irish Rifles, acting first as chief clerk and later as a hospital steward.

In 1931 Louis was appointed sales supervisor for GPO Telephones in Brighton, where his and Elsie's son, also Louis, was born in 1934. In 1936 the family moved to Glasgow, where Louis senior became area sales manager and was later promoted to sales superintendent. In 1938 he was appointed senior sales superintendent in Lancaster, and the family went to live in Morecambe. That year Elsie became organist at the recently built Anglican church of St Christopher in Bare, Morecambe. In 1952 Louis was appointed chief sales superintendent in London, a post he held until his retirement in 1956. During this period Elsie continued to live in Morecambe, and their son was sent to a boarding school. At first the family lived at 71 Broadway, Morecambe, but eventually they moved to 2 Beaufort Grove.

Elsie took an active part in her community, and was treasurer of the local Workers' Educational Association. Among her other pastimes she was an enthusiastic fell-walker and an avid reader.

In retirement, Louis returned to Morecambe, and acted as a part-time teacher of German to adults in nearby Preston for a number of years. He died at the Royal Infirmary, Lancaster, on 6 February 1979, aged eighty-two. Elsie died at the family home in Beaufort Grove on 18 December 1980, aged eighty-five.

The author acknowledges the collaboration of Louis Stott with this biography.

Stephen Proctor (1873–1939)
Violoncello 1919–30 and 1936

STEPHEN PROCTER, second of four children of Edmund Procter and Alice Watson, was born in Newcastle. His father, who was born in Willington, near North Shields, Northumberland, was a flour miller. His mother, who was born in Newcastle, was the daughter of James Watson, a Newcastle mercer and draper. The family lived at 2 Otterburn Villas South in the Newcastle suburb of Jesmond. Edmund Watson died in 1895, aged fifty-five.

Stephen and his elder brother, Alan, worked for the family business. Stephen was at first apprenticed to his father but later worked as an office clerk. In 1911 he was working for the firm as a commercial traveller.

Stephen was a cellist, and was a member of the Newcastle Chamber Music Society from about 1914. The society included among its performers Hermann McLeod, ARCM, C. F. B. Hutchinson, G. M. Hutchinson, J. C. Robson, S. M. Spoor and J. E. Hutchinson, Mus.Bac., FRCO, and Stephen's brother, Alan, who was a pianist.

Stephen first played with the Bach Choir in November 1919. He was consistently entered in concert programme notes as 'Stephen Proctor'. One can only assume that he preferred this spelling of the family surname. During his time with the choir, under the conductorship of W. G. Whittaker, he played in ten concerts wholly or partly devoted to Bach cantatas, in three performances of the St John Passion, two performances of the St Matthew Passion (playing the cello obbligato in one), and two performances of the B Minor Mass. He played in concerts with music by Holst (the suite for strings now known as the *St Paul's Suite*, *The Cloud Messenger*, the *Fugal Concerto*, *The Golden Goose* and *The Hymn of Jesus*), Vaughan Williams (the Fantasia on Christmas Carols, the *Fantasia on a Theme by Thomas Tallis*, *Sancta Civitas*, *Flos Campi* and the *Concerto Accademico*) and Bax (*Of a rose I sing a song*). In the Orlando Gibbons Tercentenary concert of November 1925 he played in works by Gibbons (fantasias for strings) and Bach's Violin Concertos in A minor and E. In the February concert of 1928 he was in a performance of Bach's Suite No. 2 in B minor. His final concert under Whittaker was in April 1930, but he played once more with the choir, in the April 1936 performance of the St Matthew Passion under the conductorship of Sidney Newman.

He was also a member of the Newcastle Philharmonic Orchestra from 1920 to 1927 and the Newcastle Symphony Orchestra from 1933 to 1936.

Stephen never married, and lived all his life at the family home, 2 Otterburn Villas South, with his mother, Alice. She died on 26 June 1935, aged eighty-nine. Stephen died on 6 February 1939 at Gresham House, Park Terrace, Newcastle, aged sixty-five. One of the executors of his will was Basil Douglas (1914–1992), ho worked for the BBC until 1950 and later ran Benjamin Britten's English Opera Group.

Alfred Michael Wall, ARCM (1874–1936)
Violin and viola 1915–36

ALFRED MICHAEL WALL (known as Alf), sixth of the seven children of William Henry Wall and Rosina Reynolds, was born in St Pancras, London. His parents were also born in London. His father was a musician (a professor of music), and his paternal grand-father, John Edward Wall, was a 'lyrical and dramatic author'.

Fig. 152 Alfred Wall, 1920. *Courtesy Newcastle City Libraries.*

Alfred studied as an honorary scholar at the Royal College of Music in London from April 1891 to June 1892. His first study was the violin and his subsidiary subjects were piano and composition. He was awarded a testamur (certificate of completion of studies) on 5 October 1892. At a concert given by the students of the college in June 1891 he was said to have 'played with much spirit and . . . musicianly style'. In 1893 he was awarded the ARCM in violin playing as an external candidate.

He moved to Newcastle and by 1898 had formed the Central School of Music at Heath Chambers in Blackett Street with the pianist M. De Wilden.

In 1902 he married Emily Constance Forster, a singing teacher and contralto soloist, who was born in the Northumbrian coastal town of Blyth. Their first daughter, Rosina Constance Forster Wall, was born in 1904. In 1911 the Wall family were living at 45 Clayton Road, Newcastle. A second daughter, Dulcie Mary Wall, was born in 1914. Both daughters became musicians. Rosina played the viola and Dulcie the cello. More can be read about them in Rosina's biography later in this chapter.

Alfred joined Edgar Bainton, W. G. Whittaker, George R. and Herbert Yeaman

Dodds and William Ellis at the Newcastle Conservatoire of Music. He first played with the Bach Choir at its inaugural concert in November 1915. In almost all the concerts he was principal violinist and leader of the orchestra, and was a frequent soloist. In his years with the choir under the conductorship of W. G. Whittaker, he played in twenty-three concerts with music wholly or partly devoted to Bach cantatas, in four performances of the St John Passion, and in three performances each of his St Matthew Passion (playing the violin obbligato in two concerts) and the B Minor Mass. In the December 1916 concert he played Bach's Violin Concerto in A minor with an interpretation that had 'the classic touch and ring'. He played in concerts featuring other works by Bach, such as the Concerto in E major for two violins, the D minor and F minor clavier concertos, the Concerto in C minor for two claviers, the Brandenburg Concertos Nos. 5 and 6, the *Italian Concerto* and the Suite No. 2 in B minor. In addition he played in concerts with music by Holst (*The Cloud Messenger*, the *St Paul's Suite*, *The Hymn of Jesus*, the *Ode to Death*, the *Fugal Concerto* and *The Golden Goose*) and Vaughan Williams (the Fantasia on Christmas Carols, *Sancta Civitas*, *Flos Campi* and the *Concerto Accademico*). In the Christmas concert in December 1922 he was the soloist in a performance of Arnold Bax's Violin Sonata No. 1 in E with the composer at the piano.

He played in a number of other concerts with music by British composers. In the May 1917 concert he was violin soloist in trios for piano, violin and viola by Arnold Bax and Thomas Dunhill. In December 1917 he played in performances of music by Hubert Parry (*Lady Radnor's Suite*), Frank Bridge (*Two Old English Songs* for string quartet) and Percy Grainger (*Room-Music Tit-Bits*). In February 1918 he was in performances of violin and piano sonatas by John Ireland (the Sonata No. 2 in A minor) and Joseph Gibbs (the Sonata in D minor). In the December 1919 concert Alfred played in music by Holst (the *St Paul's Suite*), Walford Davies (*Six Pastorals*), Dowland (*Lachrymae, or Seaven Teares*), Boyce (the Suite in E) and Vaughan Williams (the Fantasia on Christmas Carols). The string orchestra, of which he was the leader, was described as playing the *Lachrymae* 'artistically'. In the January 1922 concert he gave a first performance of his own Sonata in A for violin and piano, accompanied by Annie Eckford. A contemporary press report recorded that 'Mr Wall showed him himself not only as a master executant but as a capable and pleasing composer.'

Alfred's last performance with the Bach Choir under Whittaker was in April 1930. He continued to play with the choir under the conductorship of Sidney Newman. His final appearance was in the April 1936 performance of the St Matthew Passion, a few months before his death.

He was also principal violinist with the Newcastle Philharmonic Orchestra from

1911 to 1927. He developed a strong working relationship with Edgar Bainton, deputizing for him as conductor of the Philharmonic Orchestra while Bainton was interned in Germany. He played in a trio with Bainton (piano) and Carl Fuchs (cello) which broadcast regularly on the radio in the late 1920s and early 1930s.

Alfred began composing as a student at the Royal College. His works included orchestral and chamber works. His concert overture *Thanet* was performed at a Henry Wood Promenade concert. He was much in demand throughout his professional life, not only in the North East of England but nationally.

In 1934 he became leader of the Birmingham Philharmonic String Orchestra and moved to live in Tirril Moor, Barton, Westmorland. He did not live long enough to enjoy his new professional experience, for he died on 8 October 1936 at the Eden Mount Nursing Home, Stanwix, Carlisle, aged sixty-one. Eventually Emily Wall moved to live with her daughter Rosina at Combe-in-Teignhead, Devon, and died in Newton Abbot Hospital on 15 December 1959, aged eighty-three.

Rosina Constance Forster Wall, ARCM (1904–1986)
Viola 1924–44

ROSINA CONSTANCE FORSTER WALL, the elder of two daughters of Alfred Michael Wall and Emily Constance Forster, was taught by her father and became an exponent of the viola. She first played with the Bach Choir in February 1924. During her years with the choir, under the conductorship of W. G. Whittaker, she played the viola in all but one concert. She played in five concerts with music wholly or partly devoted to Bach cantatas, in two performances of the St John Passion, and in one performance each of the St Matthew Passion and the B Minor Mass. She played in concerts with music by Holst (*The Cloud Messenger*, the *Fugal Concerto*, the *Ode to Death* and *The Golden Goose*) and Vaughan Williams (*Sancta Civitas*, *Flos Campi* and the *Concerto Accademico*). In the concert in November 1926, at which Harriet Cohen was the guest pianist, she played in two works by Bach, the Clavier Concerto in D minor and the Concerto in C major for two claviers. She was the violin soloist in a special concert given in April 1927 for the Workers' Educational Association (Ashington branch), playing a sonata by Handel and a number of eighteenth-century pieces arranged by Moffat. Her last concert under Whittaker was in May 1930.

After Whittaker's departure she played occasionally under Sidney Newman and J. A. Westrup. Her final performance with the choir was in April 1944. She also played the viola with the Newcastle Philharmonic Orchestra from 1923 to 1927.

From 1936 she was principal viola with the Newcastle Symphony Orchestra, in which she played from 1923 until about 1939.

Rosina moved to live and work in Dorset, and in 1953 was living at 15 Parkstone Road, Poole. After her husband's death Emily Wall went to live with Rosina and died in Newton Abbott Hospital on 15 December 1959, aged eighty-three.

By 1964 Rosina had moved to the Devon village of Combe-in-Teignhead, situated between Newton Abbot and Shaldon. At first she lived at a house called Linden Lea. She founded the Linden Orchestral Players, which she led and conducted for many years until rheumatoid arthritis prevented her from playing.

Her sister, Dulcie Mary Wall, who was a cellist, had an eventful personal life. She was married three times. Her second marriage, in 1941, was to the actor John K. Bryning, who appeared in the films *Rembrandt* (1936), *Caesar and Cleopatra* (1945) and *Trilby* (1947). She married her third husband, Jean Salder, at the age of forty-eight, and the marriage lasted for twenty-nine years. Dulcie and Jean lived in Exeter. All three of the marriages were childless. Dulcie took over conducting the Linden Players from her sister and renamed them the Newton Abbott Orchestra. The orchestra is still in existence and now numbers about forty players.

Rosina moved to Flat 1, Church House, Combe-in-Teignhead, where she died on 14 March 1986, aged eighty-two. She was unmarried.

Mary Gillies Whittaker, ARCM (1906–2003)
Violin 1928 and 1930

MARY GILLIES WHITTAKER, the younger of two daughters of William Gillies Whittaker and Clara Watkins, was born in Newcastle upon Tyne. Her father was the founder of the Newcastle Bach Choir and her early family history life is recorded in Chapter 1.

Mary and her sister Clara Margaret (known as Clarrie) attended the Newcastle Central High School for Girls, where their father held a part-time teaching appointment.

Mary's first concert with the Bach Choir was in the March 1920 performance of the St Matthew Passion. In the archive copy of the programme her name and that of her sister Clara were added, in their father's handwriting, to the list of members of the ripieno choir that had been provided by Rutherford College Girls' School.

Mary attended the Royal College of Music in London between 1923 and 1928, qualifying as an ARCM. She studied the violin (under Achille Rivarde), piano (under Lillian Gaskell), German, French and, 'extra piano' (under Freda Swain). She later revised the bowing for several of her father's arrangements of string orchestral pieces by Handel and Purcell.

She played the violin with the choir on only two occasions, first in the April 1928 performance of the St Matthew Passion and then in the April 1930 performance of the St John Passion. After her father's appointment in Glasgow she moved to London, where she taught music.

On 21 August 1936 Mary married Edward Percy Pollitzer at the register office in Willesden. Edward was a wharfinger (a keeper or owner of a wharf who was responsible for the custody and delivery of goods). Edward came from a distinguished London Jewish family of merchants. The patriarch of the family was Sigismund (Sigmund) Pollitzer, who was born in Vienna about 1842 and came to London at the age of fifteen. In 1863 he and John Beck founded the well-known firm of Beck & Pollitzer, a general carrier and warehousing partnership at 211 Upper Thames Street, London. The firm still operates under this name but is now a large, diversified, multinational company.

On 13 March 1864 Sigismund Pollitzer married Rebecca Coleman (described as a 'professor of music' and the daughter of an artist and illustrator) at Portland Street Orthodox Synagogue in Marylebone, London. Sigismund became a naturalized British subject in 1874. He was president of the London Austro-Hungarian Chamber of commerce, and was awarded several honours by Emperor Franz Joseph for services to the trade of his native country. He was a Freemason of London, a master of the Montefiore Lodge, and a member of the Common Council of the City of London. He and Rebecca had four children, Julia Adelina Miriam (b.1865), Violetta Eugenie (b.1867), Joseph Frank Coleman (b.1869) and William Percy (b.1873). Joseph, known as Frank, was a partner in the family business until 1930. He had a very distinguished career; he was an alderman (1933) and sheriff (1936) of the City of London and a justice of the peace in the County of London, and was knighted in 1937.

William Percy Pollitzer was a partner in the family business until 1937. On 27 June 1905 he married Caroline Rachel Rozelaar at Hampstead synagogue. They had three children, Bella Rebecca (b.1907), Edward Percy (b.1911) and Arthur Sigmund (b.1913). Arthur Sigmund, always referred to as Sigmund, became a famous artist renowned for his figural landscape paintings and portraits inspired by ancient Greece, several of which were engraved on glass. He was unmarried and died in 1982.

Mary's husband, Edward Percy Pollitzer, was a partner and director of the family business. He was a keen amateur musician and an accomplished violinist.

He became a trustee of the London Symphony Orchestra along with Edward Heath, then Lord Privy Seal and later prime minister. Percy was involved with the London Opera Centre and was eventually appointed chairman. The Centre's life-span was short: it closed in 1977, relocating to the Royal Opera House, Covent Garden. Among its most famous former students was the soprano Kiri Te Kanawa (from 1966 to 1968). Edward Percy became honorary treasurer of Save the Children, a patron of the Bach Society and chairman of the International Orchestra Employers' Association. He was a generous patron to many artists and became an OBE in 1976.

Edward and Mary had three children, Jonathan Piers (b.1941), Sebastian Charles (b.1943) and Caroline Clare (b.1946). Edward Pollitzer celebrated the birth of their firstborn by commissioning the world-renowned sculptor Jacob Epstein to produce a bronze of William Gillies Whittaker's head. Epstein named it *The Viking*, and it presided over the family dining-room for many years. Jonathan pursued a career in publishing, editing and criticism and eventually became a writer.

Sebastian read history at St Catherine's College, Oxford, and after a sabbatical year in Tibet studied medicine at the Royal Free Hospital, London, qualifying in 1973. After house officer posts he and his new wife, Melanie, spent a year sailing around the Mediterranean. It was during the final stages of this voyage that he was tragically lost at sea between Gibraltar and the UK, after a collision during the night of 11/12 November 1975. He was only thirty-one.

Jonathan recorded that his sister Caroline pursued a career in ballet and married in 1979.

Edward Pollitzer was highly successful in the family business and retired in 1959 at the age of fifty-two. He devoted himself to many cherished causes. His and Mary's long marriage ran into difficulties and was eventually dissolved. Edward then married Claude-Andrée Benoît on 13 July 1970. Mary did not marry again.

In 1976, the centenary of the birth of W. G. Whittaker, members of the family established the Whittaker Centenary Fund. As part of this venture Jonathan Pollitzer created Viking Publications, which he ran from 3 Pembroke Gardens in London, where he lived with his sister, Caroline, and his mother. A number of concerts took place in Newcastle and Glasgow to celebrate the centenary year.

Edward Percy Pollitzer died on 6 December 1988, aged seventy-seven. Mary Gillies Pollitzer later moved to The Oast House, Goddards Green, Cranbrook, Kent, where she died on 2 April 2003, aged ninety-six. Jonathan died suddenly of a ruptured aortic aneurysm seven weeks later on 22 May, aged sixty-one.

The Windram Family

THE Windram family had three consecutive generations of military service. Two of its members, James Causley Windram and his younger brother William Charles Windram, played in orchestras accompanying the early Bach Choir. Their grandparents, William Windram and his wife Harriet, were born in Leicestershire, William in 1828 in Wigston and Harriet in 1829 in Hinkley. William was a regimental sergeant major in the 5th Dragoon Guards, and military records show that he served in the Crimean War from 1854 to 1855. William and Harriet had four children between 1854 and 1866. In 1861 they were living with their first two children at the headquarters of the 5th Dragoon Guards, Preston Barracks, Brighton. In 1871 William was still in military service and living with his wife and all four children at 26 Barnes Hill, Paignton. By 1881 they were living at 2 Palace Gate in Exeter.

William Charles Windram, second of the four children of William and Harriet, was born in Steyning, Sussex. He joined the Army, serving in the 3rd King's Own Hussars, and by 1881 he was at the Royal Military School of Music, Kneller Hall, Twickenham, training as a trumpeter. In 1885 he married Katherine Causley, a farmer's daughter from Gittisham in Devon. Their first child, James Causley, was born in Chorlton, Lancashire, in 1886, and their second child, Harriet Sidwell, in Tipperary in 1889.

In 1891 William was appointed bandmaster of the 2nd Battalion the Gordon Highlanders. Their third child, William Charles Jun., was born in Portsmouth in 1899. In 1901 William became bandmaster of the Royal Marines, based at the Royal Naval School of Music, Eastney Barracks, Portsmouth, with the rank of warrant officer (Class 1). In keeping with the delightful idiosyncrasies of Royal Naval custom, his posting was assigned to HMS *Excellent*, the Navy's name for the Royal Naval School of Gunnery, a shore-based complex on nearby Whale Island. In that year the family lived at 24 Angerstein Road, Portsmouth, but by 1911 they had moved to 53 Wadham Road. In 1919 William was promoted to commissioned bandmaster. He retired in 1921.

In retirement they lived at 14 Northwood Road, Tankerton, near Whitstable. William played an active part in his community, conducting, composing and producing musical shows; he was also involved with the Whitstable Operatic Society, for which he designed and painted stage scenery. Katherine died in 1935, aged seventy-seven, and William in 1936, aged seventy-five.

Major James Causley Windram, LRAM (1886–1944)
Trumpet 1916

JAMES CAUSLEY WINDRAM, eldest child of William Charles Windram and Catherine Causley, was born in Chorlton, Lancashire. In 1901, aged fourteen, he was serving as a boy soldier with the Gordon Highlanders at Aldershot Military Barracks in Hampshire. By 1911 he had been promoted to lance sergeant and was training at the Royal Military School of Music, Kneller Hall. While he was there his talents were discovered by the composer Gustav Holst, who dedicated his new composition, the Second Suite in F minor for military band, to him. While still at Kneller Hall he became an LRAM.

Fig. 153 James Causley Windram. *Courtesy the Regimental Archivist, Coldstream Guards.*

In 1913 he married Ida Earl, a music teacher; she had been born in Devonport, but by that time her family had moved to Portsmouth. That year James was appointed bandmaster of the 1st Battalion the Northumberland Fusiliers with the rank of lieutenant.

After the outbreak of war in 1914 the band was largely involved in efforts to maintain local public morale and promote recruitment. It was also involved in charitable fund-raising for the armed forces. In 1915 they played at a garden party in Jesmond Dene, Newcastle, and in the grounds of St Nicholas's Hospital, Gosforth, which had been designated the Northumberland War Hospital for the care of wounded soldiers. In November that year they took part in a fund-raising parade through the streets of Newcastle.

Gustav Holst may have recommended James to W. G. Whittaker, for James was recruited to play the trumpet in the February 1916 concert of the Bach Choir, which featured three Bach cantatas and his Clavier Concerto in D minor. He played in the November concert of that year (in which his brother, William, also played), which featured three Bach cantatas, the Brandenburg Concerto No. 5 and the Second Suite in B minor. James did not play again with the choir.

The year 1916 saw the band continue its public activities at garden parties in Jesmond Dene Hall, Ravensworth Castle (the County Durham home of Lord and

Lady Ravensworth), and at the Northumberland Bowls Club in Gosforth. In June 1917 they played at the War Memorial, Barras Bridge, Newcastle, for the King and Queen and wounded soldiers from the Northern General Hospital, which had been set up in the nearby King's Hall of Armstrong College. In July of that year they played in a concert at the bandstand on the Newcastle Town Moor. After the cessation of hostilities the band entered into a more settled regime of performances, including several concerts in the summer seasons at Folkstone and Hastings.

In 1930 James was appointed director of music for the regimental band of the Coldstream Guards at Wellington Barracks, London. Under him the band frequently performed on the radio, in addition to its ceremonial duties and public engagements. In 1936 the band performed at the proclamation of King Edward VIII, and, after his abdication, for that of King George VI. The band visited the New York World's Fair in 1939. The band also made many gramophone recordings, some of which are still available.

In the 1930s James and Ida lived at 12 Cecil Court, Kensington. Ida died in 1937, aged fifty, and James moved to Regents Park Barracks in Albany Street. In 1939 he married Olive Atkinson Carruthers, the daughter of an accountant, who was born in Rock Ferry, Cheshire. There is a record of their sailing on RMS *Aquitania* that year from Southampton to the United States of America, with diplomatic status.

On Sunday, 18 June 1944, while the band was playing at the Guards' Chapel in Wellington Barracks, the building was struck by a German V1 flying bomb. Some 120 people were killed, including James Windram and five band members. At the time of his death his residential address was 21 Sloan Court, Chelsea. James is buried at St Pancras Cemetery, London.

Major William Charles Windram (1899–1965)
Oboe 1916, 1917 and 1919

WILLIAM CHARLES (BILL) WINDRAM, the youngest child of William Charles Windram and Catherine Causley, was born in Portsmouth.

Bill followed the family tradition and joined the army. He trained at the Royal Military School of Music, Kneller Hall. On 4 May 1914 he joined the 1st Battalion the Northumbrian Fusiliers in Portsmouth and served in the regimental band, of which his elder brother, James, was the bandmaster. He served with the 14th and 19th Battalions of the regiment during the First World War in France and

Fig. 154 W. C. Windram (centre), 1949. *Courtesy the Inniskillings Museum.*

Flanders, attained the rank of lieutenant corporal, and was awarded the Victory and British War Medals.

He played oboe d'amore with the Bach Choir in the November concert of 1916 (an all-Bach programme), which featured three cantatas, the Brandenburg Concerto No. 5 and the Suite No. 2 in B minor. His brother also played in that concert. Bill next played with the choir in the December concert of that year, in another Bach programme, which featuring two cantatas, a motet, the Violin Concerto in A minor and the Clavier Concerto in F minor. In March 1917 he played in a performance of the St John Passion. His last appearance with the choir was in the May concert of 1919, which featured three Bach cantatas and the Brandenburg Concerto No. 3.

Bill married Jessie Frances Hadland, a nurse, in Blean, Kent, in 1925. That year he was appointed bandmaster of the 1st Battalion the Royal Inniskilling Fusiliers, then stationed at Shorncliffe, Kent. In 1926 the regiment moved to Ulster. Bill was described by a contemporary as 'an accomplished instrumentalist and . . . quite at home with any musical instrument, possibly excelling in the violin'. In August 1925 and October 1926 the band gave concerts at the Marine Gardens Pavilion, Folkestone. In August 1928 they took part with the 6th Battalion the Gloucestershire Regiment in a 'torchlight tattoo' in Cheltenham.

Bill and Jessie's daughter, Frances Patricia, was born in 1929. In July, August and September that year the band toured England, performing in Bradford, Sunderland, West Hartlepool, Darlington, Ripon, Cleckheaton, Barnsley, Norwich, Great Yarmouth, Lowestoft and finally Morecambe.

In addition to his musical skills Bill was also a keen sportsman. He won the Battalion tennis tournament (playing 137 games on the final day), and also captained the Battalion hockey team.

In 1933 the 1st Battalion moved its base to Aldershot. In 1934 it was posted to Shanghai and in 1936 to Singapore. In 1937 Bill took the unusual step of relinquishing his appointment as bandmaster to take up the commissioned post of battalion quartermaster, with the rank of major.

In 1939 the Battalion was posted to Wellington, Madras, where they remained until about 1943, when they were flown to Burma to fight the Japanese advance. The Battalion returned to India, and Bill Windram spent some time at the British Base Reinforcement Camp north-east of Bombay. A passenger list of the merchant vessel *Capetown Castle* dated 30 March 1945 shows Jessie Windram and her daughter returning to the UK from Bombay. Their country of last permanent residence was recorded as India, and it would seem that they had been living there for some time since the definition of 'permanent residence' was 'residence for a year or more'.

The Battalion spent several months in Malaya, hunting insurgents, before returning home in 1949. On 1 March 1949 Bill was seconded to the ERE (extra-regimental employment) list. That year Bill's daughter, Frances, joined the Women's Royal Naval Service, in which she served until 1962, eventually attaining the rank of first officer.

Bill officially retired on 10 February 1954. From about 1957 he and Jessie lived at Richmond, Oteley Road, Shrewsbury. Bill died on 17 April 1965 at the Royal Salop Infirmary, aged sixty-six, and Jessie in 1980 in Shrewsbury, aged eighty-two.

The author acknowledges the collaboration of Natasha Martin of the Inniskillings Museum with this biography.

Chapter 11
Honorary Officials
Philip Owen

Walter Shewell Corder, JP (1861–1933)
Secretary of Guarantors 1918–24   Chairman 1924–9

Fig. 155 From the 1922 choir photograph.

Fig. 156 Obituary photograph
from *Archaeologia Aeliana*, 1934.

WALTER SHEWELL CORDER, second of four children of Alexander Corder
and Lucy Watson, was born in Sunderland, County Durham. His father,
who was a silk weaver descended from an old Essex Quaker family, was born in
Widford, Essex, and his mother in Gateshead, County Durham.

Walter was educated at the Friends' School in Wigton, Cumberland, and then
studied chemistry at the College of Physical Science (later Armstrong College)
in Newcastle. He was apprenticed to his uncle Octavius Corder, who was a chemist
in Norwich, and then became an assistant to the famous London chemist, William
Martindale. From 1883 to 1885 he practised as a chemist in Kendal. He settled in
North Shields and established a chemical works at Low Lights. Later he went into
partnership with Robert Williamson, founding the firm of Williamson & Corder,
which manufactured glue and gelatine at its factory in Walker. The firm eventually
amalgamated with British Glues and Chemicals Ltd.

He married his second cousin, Margaret Lindsay Watson, in Middlesbrough in 1891, and they had a son and a daughter. They lived at 4 Rosella Place, North Shields.

Walter Corder was a great music lover, and the Newcastle Bach Choir was one of a number of musical societies that benefited from his advice and financial support. He was secretary of guarantors of the Bach Choir from 1918 to 1924, and its chairman from 1924 to 1929. But he was a man of many other interests. His years at Wigton School gave him a passion for mountain walking and rock-climbing. He served on the committees of the Newcastle Society of Antiquaries and the Newcastle Literary and Philosophical Society. He had a large collection of graphic prints, a subject in which he was an acknowledged expert. He was a skilled photographer and became president of the Northumberland and Durham Photographic Societies. He was an ardent supporter of the Liberal party. For a number of years he served as a justice of the peace in North Shields.

Walter died at his home in Rosella Place on 24 July 1933, aged seventy-one. Margaret died at Western House, Darlington, on 20 July 1940, aged seventy-five.

Francis John Culley (1857–1935)
Vice-Chairman 1924–9   Chairman 1929–35

FRANCIS JOHN CULLEY, eldest of seven children of John Culley and Ellen Mary Blakely, was born in Costessey, Norfolk. Both his parents had been born in Norfolk, his father in the village of Ringland and his mother in Norwich. His father was a farmer and the son of Henry Utting Culley, a wealthy miller who owned Costessey water mill, one of the largest water mills in Norfolk until it burned down in 1924. His mother died in 1869, when he was twelve. His father then married Katherine Dexter and they had three children.

Little is known about Francis's early education, but by 1881 he was working in Hartlepool, County Durham, as a commercial shipping clerk. Some time after this date he moved to Newcastle.

In 1886 he married Mary Constance Angus, the daughter of Jonathan Angus, a Newcastle woollen merchant who had been mayor of Newcastle in 1880 and 1881. In 1890 Francis was working for C. S. Swan & Hunter, a local shipbuilder, as a cashier, and he and Mary were living at 34 Heaton Road, Newcastle. Their only child, Olive Mary, was born in 1895. By 1901 the family had moved to 4 Northumberland Terrace, Tynemouth, where they remained until about 1911. From about this time on they lived at 'Ringland' (named after his father's birthplace), which was in Jesmond Park Road, Newcastle, where they remained for the rest of their lives. Francis's career progressed, and by 1910 he had become company secretary to the enlarged firm of Swan, Hunter and Wigham Richardson Ltd, who were major shipbuilders on Tyneside.

Francis was vice-chairman of the Newcastle Bach Choir from 1924 and chairman from 1929 until his death. He was elected chairman at a difficult time in the choir's history after the departure of W. G. Whittaker in 1929. His fellow committee members included Isaac Winter (secretary), W. Deans Forster (treasurer), Joseph Robinson (assistant conductor) and Ernest Robinson (auditor). It was owing to the efforts of this small team that the choir survived.

Mary died at the family home of Ringland on 13 February 1934, aged eighty. Francis also died there, on 24 February 1935, aged seventy-seven.

William Deans Forster, FRSA (1870–1941)
Treasurer of Guarantors 1920–34   Chairman 1935–c. 1939

Fig. 157 Deans Forster in 1930. *Courtesy the Newcastle Rotary Club.*

WILLIAM DEANS FORSTER (known as Deans), eldest of eight children of James Forster and Margaret Jane Scott, was born in Hexham, Northumberland. Both his parents were also born in Hexham. His father was trained as a stonemason. The Forster family initially lived in Hexham but by 1891 had moved to South Shields, County Durham, and by 1911 to North Shields, Northumberland, where they lived at Washington Terrace East. Edward Travers Forster was the only child to follow in his father's footsteps, and he became a monumental mason, operating from Queen Alexander Road, North Shields.

Deans began his working life as a solicitor's clerk, first in Hexham and later in Gateshead. In 1898 he married Catherine Dowson Robson in Gateshead. At the time of their marriage she was working as a telegraphist. In about 1901 Deans began working for Lloyds Bank, and by 1911 was manager of the Northgate branch in Darlington. He eventually became manager of the Lloyds Bank branch in Collingwood Street, Newcastle.

Deans and Catherine had a daughter and three sons. Their daughter, Dorothy, married Charles Edward Hickman of Ackleton Manor, near Wolverhampton, who was a wealthy ironmaster. Their first son died in infancy. Their second son became a company representative and settled in the Norwich area. Their third son, William John, joined the Royal Artillery in the Second World War, attaining the rank of captain, but he was killed in action, aged thirty-two, on 31 May 1942, while serving in Libya.

Fig. 11.4 The officials of the North of England Musical Tournament at the house of Deans Forster on 14 July 1929, meeting to discuss the programme for the following year. *Back row, left to right*: Dr J. E. Hutchinson, Ernest Potts, Herbert Yeaman Dodds, Alfred Wall, Robert Peel. *Front row*: Edgar Bainton, Deans Forster, George Dodds. *Author's collection.*

For many years the family lived at The Cottage in the hamlet of Dalton near Ponteland.

Deans was a keen and talented musician. At one time he was choirmaster and organist at the Hebron Memorial Church in Hexham, and later became honorary director and president of the North of England Musical Tournament.

He was treasurer of the guarantors of the Newcastle Bach Choir from 1920 to 1934 and, after the sudden death of Francis Culley in 1935, was chairman until about 1939. He was also treasurer of the Newcastle and Gateshead Choral Union from about 1921 to 1931. To commemorate his contributions to the musical life of the North East his friends and admirers set up the Deans Forster Trust to support local musical activities.

In 1927 he was appointed a land tax commissioner for the county of Northumberland. In 1930 he was president of the Newcastle Rotary Club. He retired in 1934.

Deans died at 10 Osborne Villas, Jesmond, on 23 June 1941, aged seventy-one. Catherine died in the village of Thorpe-next-Norwich on 21 July 1953, aged eighty-five.

Mowbray Thompson (1874–1945)
Member of the Management Committee from 1925   Vice-Chairman 1929–34

MOWBRAY THOMPSON, eldest of five children of Thomas Thompson and Mary Mowbray, was born in Sunderland, County Durham. Both his parents were born in Bishopwearmouth near Sunderland. His father was originally a hot water engineer, but changed his career to become a whitesmith (a person who makes and repairs things made of light-coloured metal, particularly tin).

Mowbray Thompson began his working life in Sunderland as an office boy and then became a clerk to a flour miller. As a young man he joined the local YMCA, becoming secretary and later chairman. Several newspaper articles from 1901 record him singing solos at YMCA meetings. He was also devoutly religious, a member of the Bethesda Church. An article in the *Sunderland Echo* from 1902 records him giving a lecture to the YMCA bible class entitled 'Every Christian has a Mission'. That year he was elected chairman of the Sunderland YMCA football club, whose club strip was black and amber stripes. In 1903 he was elected to the committee of the newly-formed local YMCA debating society, and in 1904 gave an address at the anniversary service of the Ocean Road Congregational Sunday School, South Shields.

Mowbray Thompson married Henrietta Cluley Alderson in 1908, in South

Shields, and they had three daughters. Henrietta's biography will be found in Chapter 5. The family lived at The Briery in the Newcastle suburb of Fenham before moving to the affluent Newcastle suburb of Jesmond, first to live at 30 Eslington Terrace and finally at 7 Lindisfarne Road.

By 1911 Mowbray was working at Caledonian Buildings, 145 Pilgrim Street, Newcastle as a chartered secretary for Leverson's Wallsend Collieries Ltd. Despite its name the firm owned the Usworth mine in Washington, County Durham. Mowbray remained with the firm for the rest of his working life, eventually becoming a director. In September 1911 he gave an illustrated lantern lecture entitled 'Down Among the Dutch Men' to the Morpeth YMCA camera club, and in November that year gave a lecture at the Queen Street church in South Shields, at which Cluley sang solos.

In 1915 Mowbray was elected to the committee of the Newcastle City Mission. In January and February 1917 he gave talks to factory workers in Newcastle to encourage them to contribute to the newly-established War Loans. At one such meeting he exhibited his temperance beliefs by urging that 'waste caused by the amount expended over alcohol be done away with' and that 'the number of ships at present required for conveyance of brewing materials to the exclusion of food should be very much reduced'.

In 1924 Cluley joined the contralto line of the Newcastle Bach Choir and Mowbray joined its management committee.

Mowbray became President of the Free Church Council, and in June 1925 was involved in a civic welcome to the Wesleyan Methodist Local Preachers' Mutual Aid Association in Newcastle.

He became vice-chairman of the Bach Choir in 1929, during the difficult time in the choir's history after W. G. Whittaker's departure for Glasgow. He was vice-chairman until about 1934.

In the early 1940s he was chairman of the Newcastle Higher Education Committee, and with the Pilgrim Trust was responsible for supporting British prisoners of war who were studying for degrees while they were interned abroad. By 1942 Mowbray was deputy lord mayor of Newcastle and had become national president of the Chartered Institute of (company) Secretaries.

During the Second World War his eldest daughter, Helen, served with the Women's Royal Naval Service, attaining the rank of third officer in 1942. She was listed as a first officer in the Women's Royal Naval Reserve in 1948.

Mowbray died at the family home in Lindisfarne Road, Newcastle, on 30 November 1945, aged seventy-one, leaving an estate worth £45,956 18s. 9d.

After Mowbray's death Henrietta went to live with her daughter Alison at

Alpenrose, Kennylands Road, Sonning Common, Reading, where she died on 27 April 1950, aged seventy-two.

Beatrice Mary Turnbull (1884–1956)
Honorary Secretary and Treasurer 1915–18

BEATRICE MARY TURNBULL, elder of two daughters of William Turnbull and Jane Helen Laidlaw, was born in Newcastle upon Tyne. Her father was born in the remote Northumberland village of Elsdon and her mother in Yarrow, Selkirkshire. Both parents had had previous marriages that ended with the deaths of their spouses. William's first marriage produced about eight children, but Jane's first marriage was childless. William Turnbull began his working life as an agricultural labourer in the Northumbrian village of Rochester. By about 1867 he and his first family had moved to live in Newcastle, where he worked as a wine and spirit merchant. His first wife died in 1880. In 1881 he was landlord of the Trafalgar Inn, 84 New Bridge Street. He married Jane Laidlaw in Edinburgh on 5 February 1884. At the time of their marriage William was based at Bridge of Allan, Scotland, and Jane was living at 5 Brunswick Place, Newcastle. They returned to Newcastle, where Beatrice was born in 1884 and Edith in 1887. By 1891 the Turnbull family were living at Meadowfield House, Chillingham Road in the Newcastle suburb of Heaton. William Turnbull died on 25 January 1897 when Beatrice was only three years old. He is buried at All Saints Cemetery, Newcastle.

Beatrice showed an aptitude for music. There is a contemporary press report from 1901 recording that she 'successfully took honours in the literary and theoretical part of the professional diploma' at the examination held in Newcastle for the Incorporated Society of Musicians.

In 1911 Jane Turnbull, Beatrice and Edith were living at 57 Highbury in the Newcastle suburb of Jesmond. Beatrice was working as a secretary at the Newcastle Conservatorium of Music, where the principal was Edgar L. Bainton and W. G. Whittaker was one of the staff members.

When the Newcastle Bach Choir was founded in 1915, Beatrice was its first administrator, acting as honorary secretary and treasurer until mid-1918.

Jane Turnbull died on 31 August 1927 at 7 Moorfield, Newcastle. Beatrice was one of the executors of her estate.

Edith Turnbull, Beatrice's sister, married in 1935 at the age of forty-nine and continued to live in Newcastle until her death.

Edgar Bainton relinquished his directorship of the Conservatoire in 1934 when he left to take up the post of director of the New South Wales Conservatorium of Music in Sydney. Dr Leslie Russell took over the directorship of the Newcastle Conservatoire, but it struggled financially and closed in 1938. It is uncertain whether Beatrice was still working for the Conservatoire at the time of its demise, when she would have been fifty-four.

In 1944 Beatrice lived at 15 Victoria Square in Newcastle, close to the Conservatoire's first premises at 72 Jesmond Road. She continued to live there until about 1953, when she moved to 116 St George's Terrace, Jesmond. She died there on 23 February 1956, aged seventy-one. She was unmarried.

PART THREE

After Whittaker and Beyond

Chapter 12
Building on the Heritage (1930–1984)

Roy Large

1930–1940
Conductor: Sidney T. M. Newman (1906–1971)

Fig. 159 Sidney Newman. *Courtesy the Library of the University of Edinburgh.*

WHEN W. G. Whittaker resigned from Armstrong College and his conductorship of the Bach Choir he was fifty-four years old and had a national reputation as a scholar and promoter of the works of Bach. His successor, Sidney Newman, was thirty years younger and had an impressive musical background, but was otherwise unknown, and it must have been daunting to step into such distinguished shoes.

307

Whittaker had established the choir's repertory as 'Bach and British', and this was emphatically endorsed in Newman's first concert with the choir in December 1930, when they sang Bach's motet *Jesu, priceless treasure* and Arnold Bax's motet *Mater ora filium*. The concert produced enthusiastic reviews: the *Musical Opinion*, in particular, was gratified to find that 'the same high standard of choralism was forthcoming under Dr Whittaker's successor', and noted that Newman's 'youthfulness of years was offset by a mature artistic judgment'. A performance of the B Minor Mass in 1931, however, provoked criticism of Newman's conducting style, which the reviewer found 'very distracting'. The performance used a small orchestra, including wind players from Glasgow, Edinburgh and Leeds, and a piano, which 'played uncommonly well – the best we have ever heard a "scratch" band do'. Whether this ensemble would have appreciated the epithet 'scratch' may be open to speculation; its leader was Alfred Wall, a composer and violinist who had been described by one critic as 'one of the finest Bach players' and had performed with Whittaker from the founding of the Bach Choir.

At a 'soirée musicale' the same year, Newman asserted his intention 'to uphold the traditions of the society' as far as possible and 'not only to revive but to retain in their repertory the works of Bach and other composers of real value'. In pursuit of the hint implicit in these remarks, programmes the following year included Mozart's Requiem, music by Schütz and Caldara, and the Dies Irae from Lully's *Prose des Morts*, the performance of which was referred to in the programme as 'certainly the first in England since the eighteenth century'. One reviewer was prompted to pay tribute to Newman 'for the privilege of hearing works which have so long suffered a quite undeserved neglect'. This was certainly in the Whittaker tradition of not only bringing unfamiliar or unknown works to light but also extending the repertory more widely. Another tradition was maintained – that of repeating unfamiliar works at the end of a concert, though one critic suggested that this was done 'because of their novelty and beauty' rather than 'because of the strange musical language in which they are expressed', as he claimed had been the case under Whittaker.

In 1932 another unfamiliar work, Purcell's Ode for St Cecilia's Day, *Hail! Bright Cecilia!* was performed. Of two local reviews, one found the ode 'disappointing' and not worth 'the time or the talent expended on it'; the other thought the performance 'unsatisfactory' and complained that 'the wind department was often out of tune'. More valued was a concert in February the following year, featuring English madrigals and a group of madrigals by Monteverdi. Rudolph Dolmetsch played both virginals and harpsichord in a range of pieces by Byrd, Farnaby, Rameau, Purcell, Bach and Scarlatti. This was the first appearance

of a member of the Dolmetsch family, another of whom, Carl, would be a frequent performer during Chalmers Burns's time as conductor.

In February 1933 the second half of a programme of madrigals and works for
harpsichord and virginals, played by Rudolph Dolmetsch, was broadcast by the
BBC. Broadcasts by the choir had been made in Whittaker's time and were to
continue during the 1930s, though infrequently in later years. The most striking
departure from traditional repertory was heard the following month, when Kodály's
Psalmus Hungaricus was performed. This called for a much bigger orchestra,
including tuba, harp and celesta. The *Newcastle Journal* reviewer seemed to have
been quite overwhelmed by the performance: 'at times the choir gave us waves
of sound of almost terrifying power and insistence – the cry of destruction and
remorseless judgment'. Descending from these heights, the reviewer concluded
by declaring that it was a concert 'of immense educational value'. The programme
included Bax's *Walsingham*, which was repeated at the end of the concert.

At the annual general meeting later in the year, Newman, who had now been
with the choir for three years, came in for a good measure of praise; he had
'kept up the prestige of the society and [had] shown a valuable knowledge of the
type of music with which it was identified', a type that, as we have begun to see,
was gradually developing from its earlier tradition to embrace a wider range of
composers.

The singing of the choir at an all-Mozart concert in December led one reviewer
to observe that the choir had 'now reached the standard at which Mr Newman
aimed'. The programme, however, failed to attract a good audience, prompting the
Yorkshire Post reviewer to complain that 'Newcastle yet again proved itself utterly
unworthy of such magnificent performances'. This was a continuing complaint
throughout the choir's history. In another review of the concert, the *Newcastle
Journal*'s music critic, while praising the Bach Choir, took a side-swipe against
other larger choirs: 'Until there comes a readjustment of forces, or alternatively
a great accession to the male ranks of our big choral societies, the Bach Choir will
always achieve triumphs foreign to choral battalions massed without regard to
relative strengths and numbers.' At this concert there were sixty-four singers in
the choir, a comparatively small number, but it showed that the choir was increasing in size, with the danger that it might find itself allied with the very 'choral
battalions' that the reviewer railed against.

We may glean a hint of Newman's mercurial temperament from an information
sheet issued to the choir for this concert. 'Anyone', wrote Newman, 'who looks at
their copy for a moment more than is necessary will be shot at dawn!' As we have
seen, his conducting style had already come in for some criticism, and one choir

member recalled his extravagant gestures when taking a rehearsal, often causing his collar to come awry.

The November concert in 1934 was given as a memorial to Gustav Holst, who had died the previous May. It was a demanding programme, including his *A Choral Fantasia* and, appropriately, the *Ode to Death* as well as Vaughan Williams's *Sancta Civitas* and *Five Mystical Songs*, settings of poems by English poets. Most of the reviewers were full of praise, one writing of 'hearing music so difficult and abstruse rendered not only with surpassing delicacy and refinement, but with such a real endeavour to interpret the spirit at once of the poems and the inordinately difficult musical idioms in which they are expressed'. The final concert of the year consisted mainly of Christmas music, though it included two Bach sonatas for violin and piano in which Newman was the pianist. Newman would spend much time at rehearsal to achieve exactly the right shading of sound. His care for delicate phrasing and shaping of a melodic line may have been behind one reviewer's observation that the choir sang 'with a perfection of tone, balance and expression that only a well-prepared choir can produce'.

The following April the choir promoted a Bach festival to commemorate the 250th anniversary of the composer's birth. This included the motets *Jesu thou my treasure* (sung in memory of F. J. Culley, chairman of the Society, from 1929 to 1923; see Chapter 11), *Come, Jesu, come* and *Sing to the Lord*, as well as the St Matthew Passion. At the concluding concert, given in the Cathedral on Palm Sunday, Cantata No. 182, *King of heaven, be thou welcome* (*Himmelskönig, sei willkommen*), and No. 139, *Happy is the man, who to his God* (*Wohl dem, der sich auf seinen Gott*), formed the centre of what in some ways had the character of a service, with hymns, readings and the blessing, and beginning and ending with organ music. Referring to the performance of the St Matthew Passion, 'Even the audience', wrote one critic, 'realised that they were not taking part in a mere musical performance, but were sharing in the reverent presentation of the most tragic event in the history of the world.' The reviewer's condescending 'even the audience' and his idea of 'a mere musical performance' both jar; his view diminishes the whole concept of musical performance, which stands or falls by its fidelity to the music and not whether it is a 'reverent presentation' of an historical event no matter how significant it may be in religious terms.

At this performance the girls of Rutherford College sang the ripieno chorale in the opening chorus, participation which was particularly appropriate, first because Whittaker had taught at Rutherford College and second because girls from the school had sung this chorale at the first complete performance of the work given by the Bach Choir in 1920. The tradition was by now well established that local church choirs or schools would provide voices for this chorale – and for such choruses as, for example, Vaughan Williams's *Sancta Civitas* demanded. The reviewer who wrote: 'Bach's turn has come, and the world of music hears him gladly' neatly summarized the place Bach that had at last taken in the journey of rediscovery from the early nineteenth century to the present day, a journey in which Whittaker and the Newcastle Bach Choir played a significant part.

A characteristic of the Bach Choir was identified by the *Northern Echo*'s music critic when he wrote:

> There is something unique about the organisation of the [Bach Choir] in that it always provides a programme of music that we have little chance of hearing elsewhere. The average choral society seldom gives miscellaneous concerts and rarely includes the smaller types of choral work that modern composers are producing in increasing numbers.

This observation was prompted by a programme that included Arnold Bax's *This worldes joie* and his carol *Of a rose I sing a song* for choir, harp, cello and double bass, Vaughan Williams's *Flos Campi*, his part-song *The Turtle Dove* and setting of Psalm 100, Holst's part-song *I sowed the seeds of love* and three part-songs by Ravel.

In February 1936 the choir joined the Newcastle Philharmonic Orchestra in a concert in the City Hall that presented a significant departure from the kind of programme with which Bach Choir audiences were familiar, for it included Constant Lambert's *The Rio Grande*, a setting of the poem by Sacheverell Sitwell. The programme shows that it was performed twice.

It is evident from the reviews of about this time that the choir, first under Whittaker and now under Newman, had become well disciplined and experienced in the performance of Bach's music. As one reviewer wrote: 'The choir has, through long study, made Bach's method of using the voices perfectly familiar and they now sing with a fluency of technique that would have been impossible a generation ago.'

The same reviewer also suggested that the audiences had 'become familiar with the Bach idiom and are capable of following the untold beauties of his score'. If these reviews reflect the situation accurately we recognize in this a signal achievement, for in Newcastle until 1915 the only regular experience that Newcastle audiences would have had of the choral music of Bach would have been large-scale performances of a handful of his works performed in the romantic tradition.

The Lord Mayor and Lady Mayoress held a 'reception and conversazione' at the Laing Art Gallery in March to meet the Berlin College of Music Singers, who had been on a tour of Scotland and England, and members of the Bach Choir. During the evening the Berlin singers sang German folk songs, and the Bach Choir English madrigals. Later in the year the choir performed for the first time one of the major works by a nineteenth-century composer, Brahms's *A German Requiem*, which, in the opinion of one of the reviewers, was sung, with the exception of the opening chorus, 'as finely, probably, as it has ever been sung'. The performance was given in memory of two people who had been closely associated with the choir for many years – Ernest J. Potts, a bass soloist and choir member, and Alfred M. Wall.

The choir gave their own first concert in the City Hall in January 1937, with a performance of the Christmas Oratorio. Though one reviewer thought that 'effects of detail and phrasing failed to tell because of the vastness of the hall and because the choir is essentially a chamber choir', another quoted a visiting organist as having found the performance 'wonderful, and quite as good as anything we ever hear in London'. At the annual meeting in June, Newman announced that the coming season would begin with a 'conversazione' and there would be a 'carol party', which would be free to members. Although carols had been sung at a Christmas concert as early as 1917, and Newman had included a few in his Christmas concerts, the carol party, essentially a recital or concert entirely devoted to carols, was an innovation, and one that Newman took with him to Edinburgh.

The choral music of Handel had become almost the prerogative of the large choirs such as the Newcastle and Gateshead Choral Union, who regularly performed *Messiah* and *Israel in Egypt*, as well as some of the other oratorios. Now the Bach Choir was to enter this territory, with a performance in 1937 of *Israel in Egypt*. But this was to be a very different performance from that offered by the Choral Union. Newman set out the rationale for his approach in a foreword to the programme. It is worth quoting from the opening paragraph, not least because it gives a flavour of his distinctive style:

> With whatever feelings of sentimental regret one may reflect upon the destruction of the Crystal Palace, one may be permitted to hope that the 'Handelian Inanity' of megalomania has perished for ever in the conflagration. Saul may have had his thousands, but Handel was given a bodyguard equal to the hosts of David – with the consequence that he was hardly ever visible to his humble devotees.

Having referred to the 'additional accompaniments' added to Handel's oratorios in the nineteenth century he then wrote of the 'conscientious movement to restore the original orchestration'. He also justified a number of cuts:

I cannot here make a reasoned defence of all the omissions made in this performance. Some may deplore the fact that I have forbidden the frogs to hop into Pharaoh's palace and make their unmentionable messes there. But the frog like the mouse is ridiculous whatever Pharaoh or Sennacherib might have to say to the contrary, and there is no place for his antics in the vindictive succession of plagues which sweep across the stage.

Newman's account demonstrates that the Bach Choir's approach to music, especially of the period up to the death of Bach and Handel, largely retained its commitment to what has come to be known as 'historically informed performance'. In this, from its foundation by Whittaker as a small choir, it had been among the pioneers. There were compromises, unfortunately but perhaps necessarily, in the use of the piano as a continuo instrument. A harpsichord had been used occasionally at concerts by the choir, but it did not regularly replace the piano until later, and it was later still that a chamber organ appeared as part of the instrumental ensemble for music of the seventeenth and eighteenth centuries. By that time, however, the choir had considerably increased in size, and was therefore a less 'authentic' instrument for this early music.

An all-Mozart programme, including the Piano Concerto in D minor, K466, with Arthur Milner as the soloist, prompted the *Northern Echo*'s critic to draw attention to the wider 'educative quality' of the choir's concerts: 'We get the chance of hearing many of the works of the great masters in their original form, which seems not to attract the attention of choral societies in general.' This interest in the educative value of the choir's repertory had been noticed before. The following month the choir sang Palestrina's *Stabat Mater*, a motet for double chorus, at a concert that also included Pizzetti's *Messa di Requiem* and three Easter carols. The Pizzetti *Messa* was a significant new departure, as it was the first modern Italian work the choir had performed. Composed in 1922–3 in memory of King Umberto I, it made strong demands on the choir's resources, notably in the Sanctus, which called for three four-part choirs, one of sopranos and contraltos, the other two of tenors and basses. With only eleven tenors and eleven basses this must have been quite challenging for the men. 'It would tax any choir', the *Northern Echo* commented, 'to sustain it throughout with the degree of excellence that the Newcastle choir achieved.'

A major event in the spring of 1938 was the visit of the choir to London and Oxford, which, as it turned out, was to be the last of the choir's tours away from Newcastle. It extended from Thursday, April 28, to Sunday, May 1. Many choir members travelled to King's Cross on the Silver Jubilee express train, arriving at

2 p.m., joining the rest of the choir for a rehearsal at the Royal College of Music, followed by tea and then an illustrated lecture by Newman on Bach's motet *Sing ye to the Lord*. The choir then changed into evening dress before having a meal, followed by the concert in the Parry Theatre at 8.15 p.m. The concert began with English and Italian madrigals and concluded with *Sing ye to the Lord*. Altogether this must have been an exhausting day.

The RCM concert attracted the notice of *The Times*, whose reviewer applauded the madrigal singing, which

> showed that the choir maintains that thoroughness in the study of its music by which its reputation was made when Dr Whittaker was its conductor, and Mr Newman showed both his taste and scholarship in the choice of works, which he introduced with appropriate comments, and his skill in getting a vital performance of them.

In a review for the *Daily Telegraph*, J. A. Westrup, who was to succeed Newman in Newcastle, found Newman's treatment of *Sing ye to the Lord* to be 'lively and expressive, and in the chorale section he did not hesitate to use rubato – a device which half-educated purists imagine to be foreign to Bach's period'. Although he thought that 'in quality of tone the choir seemed inferior to our crack London singers', he admired the choir's musicianship, saying that it 'responds readily to the conductor's strenuously enthusiastic guidance'. Next day the choir travelled to Oxford to give a recital in New College Chapel, staying overnight. The following afternoon they returned to London for a recital at St Margaret's, Westminster. The choir had given the first complete London performance of Byrd's Great Service at St Margaret's in 1924, and returned now with a programme that included Palestrina's Stabat Mater and Caldara's *Crucifixus*.

The last three performances of the year began with a mainly orchestral concert in October that opened with Bach's Cantata No. 50, *Now is the salvation* (*Nun ist das Heil und die Kraft*), and included the Piano Concerto No. 17 in D minor by C. P. E. Bach, conducted by Clifford Harker (the choir's assistant conductor) with Newman as the pianist. The following month the choir gave a challenging 'modern choral concert' offering works by Kodály and Vaughan Williams.

A concert of Bach cantatas was performed in February 1939. The first of these, No. 116, *Thou prince of peace, Lord Jesus Christ* (*Du Friedefürst, Herr Jesu Christ*), must have been singularly appropriate for the year in which the Second World War began, for a programme note referred to its theme as 'a prayer for peace and guidance in a time of danger and anxiety'. The programme for an afternoon

performance of the St Matthew Passion in the King's Hall in March 1940 included
the instructions:

> In the event of an Air Raid Warning being sounded during the afternoon,
> the performance will be stopped immediately, and *all* members of the public
> and performers will be required to leave the Hall and College buildings for
> the Shelters which are provided in the College grounds and in the immediate
> neighbourhood (if the Warning were of short duration the performance would
> be resumed as soon as possible after the *all clear* signal). Full instructions pro-
> viding for such an emergency will be announced from the platform before the
> performance.

The instructions ended with an assertive 'WALK QUICKLY BUT DO NOT RUN'. Fortunately they did not need to be followed.

In June Newman married Joy Pickering. Greta Large, herself a member of the
Bach Choir, recalled that the night before the wedding in the Cathedral there were
five air raids, 'so some very tired choir members turned up to sing at the ceremony
the following morning'. The service included the hymns 'St Patrick's breastplate'
and 'The King of love my shepherd is' and the anthem *Rise, heart, thy Lord is
risen*, a setting of George Herbert's poem by Vaughan Williams. The following
year Newman was appointed to succeed Sir Donald Tovey as Reid Professor of
Music at Edinburgh, and so left Newcastle after just over ten years as conductor
of the choir.

1941–1944
Conductor: Jack A. Westrup (1904–1975)

JACK WESTRUP was appointed to succeed Newman as lecturer in music at King's
College in 1941. His time in Newcastle coincided with the Second World War,
and it is perhaps because of this that fewer records seem to have survived of his
concerts with the choir, though that they continued to be given is shown by a letter
launching an appeal to establish a guarantee fund, in which we read that 'the
Concerts continued throughout the War, despite the lack of the invaluable support
given by the subscribers in the town and neighbouring counties'. The absence
of press reviews during these years may perhaps be explained by the restrictions
on paper production produced by the war; printed programmes also were usually
reduced to a single double-sided sheet.

The choir sang in the Church of the Divine Unity in April 1942 with George
Sutcliffe as the organist, though there appear to be no details of the music

performed. It was reported, however, that 'Mr Westrup conducted a fine programme'. The November concert of that year, though it opened with Schütz's *Our
Father*, remained largely true to the 'Bach and British' theme, including Bach's
Cantata No. 161, *Come, sweet hour of death* (*Komm, du süße Todesstunde*), as well as
music by Bax and Vaughan Williams. The recently established 'carol party' tradition was observed in December.

Fig. 160 Jack Westrup. © *National Portrait Gallery,
London.*

Elgar's *Four Part-Songs* were performed the following February, the first performance of his music by the choir. It is possible that they were chosen as fitting
at a time of war, as the first of the songs opens with the lines:

'Dishevelled and in tears, go, song of mine,
To break the hardness of the heart of man'.

The concert, which included motets by Byrd and Bach's motet *Come, Jesu, come,* also offered Mozart's Sonata in D major for two pianos, K448, and the Suite No. 2 for two pianos in C minor by Rachmaninov.

In April the choir performed the St John Passion, and in October, for the first time, Parts 1 and 2 of *Messiah*. (Westrup omitted Part 3, as he thought a complete performance would be 'too long for the habits of a modern audience'.) Newman's performance of *Israel in Egypt*, as we have seen, broke fresh ground by moving into territory closely associated with the Choral Union and other large choirs. Westrup's approach to *Messiah* echoed Newman's to *Israel in Egypt*. Apart from using a piano to replace both the harpsichord and organ,

> the conditions of performance are, as far as possible, those for which Handel wrote. Choir and orchestra are roughly the same size, and the many parts for additional instruments which well-intentioned but misguided people have added to the score have been discarded. The result may be different from what most listeners are accustomed to, but it is much nearer to what Handel intended. . . . It is a simple duty to assume that the composer knew what he wanted and to try to realize his intentions in performance.

A tradition that Westrup attempted to put a stop to was that of standing for the Halleluiah Chorus: 'It is one thing to rise from one's seat in uncontrollable enthusiasm; it is quite another to do so from deference to custom.' Whether or not he was successful in this aim at this performance history does not relate.

In November, 1943, a concert of choral and instrumental music was given in the Church of the Divine Unity, at which Westrup played the organ in Bach's Sonata No. 2 in D major for cello, and in two pieces from *Lambert's Clavichord* by Herbert Howells. The choir sang motets by Tomkins and Purcell, accompanied on the organ by Chris Dodds. A concert of English music the following February included Arthur Bliss's *Pastoral*: '*Lie strewn the white flocks*', composed in 1928 for chorus, mezzo-soprano, solo flute, drums and strings, and Purcell's Cecilia's Day ode, *Welcome to all the Pleasures*. This was not the ode so much disliked by a reviewer in 1932 but an earlier one, which Westrup, in his book on Purcell, had referred to as 'one of the best of Purcell's earlier works'.

Bach's B Minor Mass was performed in the King's Hall in April followed in June by a 'motet recital' in Durham Cathedral. Westrup having been appointed to the Peyton and Barber Chair of Music at Birmingham University, his last concert with the choir was in July 1944 for a 'special music course for Canadian troops' arranged by the British Council and the Canadian Legion Educational Services. The programme comprised English madrigals and part-songs by Rubbra and Stanford, Westrup's own *Weathers*, an arrangement by Vaughan Williams of 'The spring-time of the year', and one instrumental work, Elgar's Sonata for violin and piano in E minor.

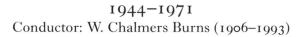

1944–1971
Conductor: W. Chalmers Burns (1906–1993)

Fig. 161 Chalmers Burns. *Courtesy the Newcastle Evening Chronicle.*

WESTRUP was essentially a scholar and academic, disciplined and perhaps rather austere. His successor, W. Chalmers Burns, could hardly have been more different. A witty raconteur, with a self-confident manner that concealed an underlying sensitivity, Burns brought a much more relaxed manner, possibly at times too relaxed, to his conductorship of the choir. He had read music at Cambridge and subsequently studied conducting under Sir Henry Wood at the Royal Academy of Music. He had been an assistant to Whittaker at Glasgow and also organist at St Mary's Cathedral. Whittaker, apparently, had said, 'Burns is the man for Newcastle, and Newcastle the place for Burns'. Burns was to remain with the Bach

Choir for twenty-seven years, the longest period of any of the conductors until Eric Cross, the present conductor. As we shall see, these years were to show the greatest changes and challenges the choir had experienced since it was founded; and when Burns retired the choir had become a very different instrument from that envisaged by Whittaker.

Burns began traditionally enough with a performance in November 1944 of Bach's Christmas Oratorio, followed the next month by a 'carol concert' in St Thomas's Church. British music was the theme of the choir's contribution to the February 1945 concert, with Tudor motets and the 'Leroy' Kyrie by John Taverner (c. 1495–1545), no doubt to commemorate the 400th anniversary of his death, and seven unaccompanied part-songs by Gerald Finzi. The programme the following spring included the first performance of *Preparations* for chorus and orchestra by Ernest Bullock, conducted by the composer. Bullock had been organist of Westminster Abbey and had subsequently been appointed to succeed Whittaker in Glasgow.

The first challenge Burns faced, and one that was to remain with him through most of his time with the choir, was that of the choir's finances. Financial support had diminished at the start of the war, and it was largely due to the Carnegie Trust and the generosity of choir members themselves that concerts continued to be given. A 'conversazione' was arranged for September 1945, when the financial position was explained and plans were announced for the revival of an earlier subscription scheme. Even the ending of the war was prayed in aid: 'The Society sincerely hope that it may count on you for support in this Victory Season.'

In November the choir performed Vaughan Williams's *Thanksgiving for Victory*, which calls for a soprano solo, speaker and a choir of children's voices. Vaughan Williams had stipulated that 'the children's part must be sung by real children's voices, not sophisticated choir boys', leading to the appearance of children from the Heaton, Whitley Bay and Monkseaton Grammar Schools. The choir was also enlarged by members of the King's College Choral Society. The choir's long-standing association with Vaughan Williams was given special recognition this year when he was invited to become the Society's first president. In acknowledgment of the invitation he wrote, 'I would be proud, if elected, to become president of the Newcastle Bach Choir Society, a body which has such a fine tradition.'

In October 1945 a piano recital had been given by Louis Kentner, with another the following January by the Russian pianist Nicolas Orloff. These performances signalled a return to the practice in Whittaker's time when, for a number of years, programmes included chamber music and instrumental solo recitals promoted by the Bach Choir Society as distinct from the choir itself. Recitalists included the pianists Joan and Valerie Trimble, Frederic Lamond, 'the only surviving pupil of Liszt', Clifford Curzon, a former pupil of Wanda Landowska and, some years later, Myra Hess. A recital by Harriet Cohen in 1947 included two arrangements of Bach chorales in memory of Dr Whittaker, who had died in 1944. This late tribute was a reminder that it had been he who, in 1921, first invited Cohen to perform in Newcastle.

A concert in February included Vaughan Williams's Concerto in D minor (the *Concerto Accademico*) and the Concerto for solo oboe and string orchestra, with Léon Goossens as the oboist, as well as Thomas F. Dunhill's *Chiddingfold Suite* for string orchestra. The choir sang two groups of madrigals and a group of modern English part-songs. A note in Burns's hand shows that the Oboe Concerto (of which this had been the first performance in Newcastle) was repeated at the end of the concert, following a practice established by Whittaker 'when producing new and important works'. In May the choir gave a second performance of *Messiah* (with a number of omissions to allow all three parts to be performed), which had been advertised as 'with original orchestration'. In the printed programme was an appeal from Burns for additional singers, confirming his intention to enlarge the choir further, and thus marking a distinct move away from Whittaker's belief in 'the imperative of using a small choir'.

A performance of the St Matthew Passion in the City Hall in March 1947 established another precedent, in that for the first time the Bach Choir was joined by another choir, in this case the Blyth Oriana Choir, whose conductor was W. R. James, secretary and assistant conductor of the Bach Choir, as well as a few singers from King's College Choral society. The main combined choral forces for the performance amounted to eighty-two singers, of whom fifty were Bach Choir members. Girls from the Church High School and Rutherford High School sang the ripieno chorale in the first chorus. (A newspaper report referred to 'some 100 girls . . . who sang tunefully and unanimously'.) Among the soloists were Margaret Field-Hyde and Kathleen Ferrier. The musical forces employed contrasted markedly with Whittaker's in 1920, which used a choir of forty (excluding the ripieno group), with twenty-two strings and 'the requisite wood-wind'. Performances of the Passion were given regularly throughout Burns's years as conductor, the forces remaining much the same, and always with children from local schools for the ripieno chorale. An invitation to let the conductor leave the platform before applauding reflected a long-standing view that performances of this and similar music had the character of a religious event rather than primarily a concert.

In November 1947 the choir had performed Bach's B Minor Mass in an English version that had been prepared by Vaughan Williams while fire-watching in 1943.

One reviewer of the choir's performance thought that this version led to 'some impairment of the sonorous effect of the old language in concert with the majestic music'. A choral and orchestral concert in May, using a section of the Northern Philharmonic Orchestra as well as a number of local players, comprised music by Mozart and Vaughan Williams.

Low audience numbers at Clifford Curzon's recital and the choir's recent concert in the City Hall (attended by only 500 or 600) provoked a strong attack in *Palatinate*, the Durham University newspaper, which referred to the 'sickening confirmation of the suspicion that Newcastle must many times over multiply its audiences for real music, if it wishes to claim any reputation as a centre of culture in the north'. In addition to concerns about the size of audiences, the choir was once again experiencing financial difficulties. One activity that was arranged to mitigate the loss of nearly £200 on the past season was a bring-and-buy sale – an entirely new venture in the life of the choir. This was to be held in St James's Congregational Church Hall in October, to be opened by Lady Noble. There were to be 'side shows, stalls and competitions'. Another fund-raising event was a garden party organized by one of the members. An event of a different character in aid of funds was a concert by the Jarrow Choral Society in Ellison Street Methodist Hall, Jarrow, at which Burns spoke about the work of the Bach Choir Society. In May the following year the Bach Choir gave a concert at the church, perhaps by way of thanks for the Jarrow Choral Society's support.

Meanwhile, the November programme of 1948 ushered in a series of concerts that affirmed a commitment to early music presented with a regard for historical precedent. The first of these featured Alfred Deller, the first appearance at a concert by the choir of a countertenor, in a programme devoted entirely to the music of Bach and Handel. Deller sang the Agnus Dei from the B Minor Mass and two of Bach's solo cantatas, No. 53, *Strike, then, longed-for hour* (*Schlage doch, gewünschte Stunde*), and No. 54, *Stand firm against sin* (*Widerstehe doch der Sünde*). (Cantata No. 53 is now attributed to Melchior Hoffmann.) The choir performed the motets *Come, Jesu, come* and *Jesu, priceless Treasure*. The strings of the Bach Choir orchestra played three of Handel's Concerti Grossi, Op. 6. The next concert continued this approach to early music by presenting a programme for descant, treble and tenor recorders, treble and bass viols, viola da gamba and virginals played by Carl and Nathalie Dolmetsch and Joseph Saxby. Some of the instruments would have been unfamiliar to many in the audience, so informal demonstrations of them were given before the music was played. The first half of the concert alternated madrigals from *The Triumphs of Oriana* with instrumental works chosen to demonstrate the possibilities of the instruments, either as solo instruments or in consort. Three motets by Byrd opened the second half of the concert, followed by a set of Elizabethan 'bird' pieces (surely a deliberate pun): *The Goldfinch* for descant recorder (Benjamin Cozyns), *Robin* for treble recorder (John Mundy), *Wooddy Cock* for tenor recorder (Giles Farnaby) and *The Lark with Divisions* (also by Farnaby). The concert concluded with Arnold Bax's motet, *This worldes joie*, and Vaughan Williams's motet *Valiant for Truth*. A fulsome review asserted that there had been 'no more delightfully instructive and enjoyable concert in the long annals of the Newcastle Bach Choir than that of last night'.

In 1950 the choir commemorated the bicentenary of the death of J. S. Bach with the St John Passion on Good Friday and on Easter Sunday two cantatas and the Easter Oratorio. For these performances in, appropriately, St Thomas's Church, the choir and orchestra were placed in the west end gallery on either side of the organ, following common practice at the time of Bach. The choir was smaller and better balanced for these performances, and more nearly corresponded to the numbers used by Whittaker in his later years with the choir. The Bach Choir Society Orchestra was joined by Desmond Dupré, who played viola da gamba and guitar (substituting for the lute) in the St John Passion, and Norman Ashcroft, a former member of Harton Colliery Band, who led the trumpets in the Easter Oratorio and Cantata No. 31, *The heavens laugh* (*Der Himmel lacht! Die Erde jubilieret*).

In December, a concert given in the City Hall provoked the familiar complaint about 'row upon row of empty seats', though the *Northern Echo* reviewer blamed poor publicity for the low attendance. Whatever the reason, one of the problems was that the City Hall, with a seating capacity of more than 2,400, was too large for the type of audience that the Bach Choir's repertory tended to attract, and for some concerts the King's Hall, then holding 500–600, was too small.

A rehearsal for a concert in February 1951 was opened to 'parties of school-children and training college students', the concert itself proving popular, as the King's Hall was 'packed to the doors'. Arthur Milner wrote that the music was 'either played on the instruments for which the music was conceived or sung to the accompaniment of a small orchestra, which allowed Bach's closely-knit texture to be clearly heard'. Taking part in the concert were Carl Dolmetsch (recorder) and Joseph Saxby (harpsichord), who by now were becoming closely associated with the Bach Choir and increasingly appreciated by audiences both for their musicianship and their geniality. They were to continue this association until 1960, returning, after a break, in 1965.

The following year the choir sang *Israel in Egypt* without cuts and therefore including the frogs that had been expelled by Newman. A report in the *Evening*

Chronicle compared the performance of the oratorio sung by a thousand voices in the Royal Albert Hall the previous year as part of the Festival of Britain with the present performance, observing that 'The smaller numbers of the Bach Choir resemble those which Handel had at his disposal.' The annual general meeting in October heard that the season just ended had been a financial success; a bank overdraft had been cleared, leaving the Society with a small profit. Although grants for the coming season had been promised by the joint committee of the Arts Council and the National Federation of Music Societies, Burns warned the meeting against relaxing their efforts, either financially or in performance standards. The same meeting agreed that the Society should sponsor a series of six recitals by the London String Quartet, at which all the Beethoven string quartets would be played. In the end, two series were arranged, in 1953 and 1955. These led to the establishment of the annual series of recitals by the Aeolian String Quartet, which became known as the Annual Festival of Chamber Music, sponsored by the Society until 1968.

The 1952/3 season had begun with a challenging programme, the choir singing both Byrd's Great Service and Rubbra's *St Dominic Mass*. The Great Service was performed, as it had been under Whittaker in 1924, in sections interspersed with instrumental music, in this case with two groups of lute solos by John Dowland, played by Desmond Dupré. The coronation of Queen Elizabeth II was celebrated in a concert in February that included two coronation anthems, Purcell's *My heart is inditing* and Handel's *Zadok the Priest*. The rest of the programme was devoted to instrumental music, with Carl Dolmetsch (recorder), Joseph Saxby (harpsichord) and Beryl Kimber (violin). This was clearly a popular programme, as Arthur Milner reported that 'extra seats had to be brought in to accommodate the very large and enthusiastic audience'. The coronation theme continued in November with a performance of *A Garland for the Queen*, which had been commissioned by the Arts Council of Great Britain to mark the coronation. It comprises ten poems by British poets, each set to music by a British composer. The choir also sang a group of north-country folk songs arranged by W. G. Whittaker, and there were piano solos played by Celia Arieli.

In February 1954 Carl Dolmetsch and Joseph Saxby played music by Vivaldi, J. S. Bach and Loeillet, the choir performing two cantatas, No. 118, *O Jesus Christ, light of my life* (*O Jesu Christ, meins Lebens Licht*), and No. 50, *Now is the salvation* (*Nun ist das Heil und die Kraft*). An unusual appearance in the orchestra for the first of these cantatas was the appearance of cornet and trumpet players drawn from the Sunderland Police Band. The concert opened with Arnold Bax's *This Worldes Joie*, which was repeated at the end. Arthur Milner thought the choir's interpretation of this work was its 'outstanding achievement', displaying a 'sensitive appreciation of the many beauties of the music'. Carl Dolmetsch, in a tribute to Burns's conducting, had said he thought it was 'as difficult to handle a baton correctly as it is to use a violin bow.' A performance of the St Matthew Passion in the City Hall the same year led Arthur Milner to touch on the matter of the venue, expressing the view that the work should be performed in a church, allowing for a better disposition of the choral and orchestral forces and where 'the jarring effect of applause would be impossible'. He thought that in a hall 'the mundane atmosphere wages continual war with the spiritual beauty of the music'.

The November 1954 concert included what was thought to be Bach's earliest setting of the Magnificat (now considered to be spurious) for solo soprano, the score of which had disappeared in the mid nineteenth century and been rediscovered by Whittaker in 1938. Among the performers were Carl Dolmetsch and Layton Ring (recorders) and Joseph Saxby (harpsichord). Once again, for a concert of this character 'the hall was packed by a generous and musical audience'. In the same month the choir gave a carol concert in Hexham Abbey in aid of the Hexham and District Music Society's piano fund, prompting an enthusiastic review that referred to 'superb unaccompanied singing perfect in pitch and beautifully controlled'. A similar concert was given the following year.

As well as the Abbey performance there were the usual two carol concerts. As we have seen, Newman introduced carol parties in the late 1930s. The tradition had been maintained by Westrup and continued under Burns, though with a change of name. At first there was a single annual performance, and then from 1951 there were usually two. Although they were given originally in the King's Hall or the Durant Hall, Burns and subsequent conductors gave them in churches. These recitals offered a wide range of traditional carols, but also a number of modern settings, including a carol written for the Bach Choir by David Barlow, *The world's desire*. In the 1960s a dispute arose between the Bach Choir and the Performing Rights Society over charges for some of the music sung at one of the Christmas performances. What was at issue was whether it was a religious service. Dr Burns had apparently claimed that it was, though the PRS argued that the programme looked more like the kind of carol recital which, even if called a carol service, would not be regarded as such and would therefore be subject to the usual charges. The matter was resolved in favour of the choir, the PRS accepting Burns's assurance that the carol performance was 'in fact and in spirit a religious service and nothing else'. The PRS also agreed to offer the same exemption each Christmas, provided that the circumstances remained the same.

The February concert in 1955 was devoted to British music, including a performance of Whittaker's setting of Psalm 139, encouraging the *Northern Echo* reviewer to comment that Burns maintained the tradition (established by Whittaker) that the choir's purpose was 'to sing the music of Bach and British composers'. A further performance of the St John Passion was given in March, with the Newcastle Bach Choir Orchestra and additional performers including Léon Goossens (oboe) and Desmond Dupré, now playing the viola da gamba and the lute instead of the guitar that he had used previously. Arthur Milner drew attention to the 'unexplained omission of the final chorale'; the explanation was simply that Burns forgot it.

Although 'Bach and British' remained at the core of the choir's repertory, Burns, especially, had very much extended this repertory, as was exemplified in the November concert, which offered a wide range of music, beginning with a work by the sixteenth-century composer Léonhard Lechner, *Das Hohelied Salomonis*, and concluding with Poulenc's *Quatre motets pour un Temps de Pénitence*, of which the *Northern Echo* reviewer wrote, 'the music is very difficult to sing and the choir deserved warm congratulations for a performance which seemed to get at the heart of the music as well as being technically very efficient'. The choir also sang motets by Brahms. The rest of the programme comprised music for cello and piano by Brahms and Martinů and Reger's *Air and Variations* for unaccompanied cello.

The choir returned to its traditional repertory the following February, performing three Bach cantatas and instrumental works by Bach, Telemann and Rubbra. Carl Dolmetsch (recorder), Christine Ring (flute), Layton Ring (recorder) and Joseph Saxby (harpsichord) were the soloists, playing with members of the Bach Choir Society Orchestra. Although she did not play on this occasion, the concert marked the retirement of Muriel Plant, who had been the Bach Choir's accompanist, and frequently the continuo player, for thirty years. She recalled that the late Arnold Dolmetsch thought the modern grand piano 'an infernal machine', and had taught her how to play the much more expressive and musical spinet. Muriel Plant was succeeded by Sheila More, who continued as accompanist until 1967.

Under Burns the choir had sung both *Messiah* (in 1946) and *Israel in Egypt* (1952); now, in 1956, they performed Handel's oratorio *Jephtha* semi-dramatically, which elicited a lukewarm response from Tom Little of the *Northern Echo*, who found it 'only partially successful'. This performance established Burns's commitment to Handel's choral music. During the rest of his time with the choir he conducted the quasi-opera or secular oratorio *Semele*, the oratorios *Belshazzar*,

Solomon, *Saul* and *Samson*, the masque *Acis and Galatea*, *Alexander's Feast*, Psalm 109, *Dixit Dominus* and a third performance of *Messiah*, with the Free Church Choir Union and the Cathedral Choral Society, as well as some smaller works.

The November 1956 concert again demonstrated the choir's extensive repertory when the music chosen ranged from Heinrich Schütz, born a hundred years before Bach, to Kodály and Copland. The curious mixture of unaccompanied items included music by Samuel Wesley and E. W. Naylor, both associated with cathedral repertory, and a motet by Naylor's son, Bernard. These were followed by works by Stravinsky and Kodály, concluding with Aaron Copland's *Las Agachadas* (the Shakedown Song). A programme note on this last work explained that the main melody was given to a small group 'who must sing with robust and unpolished freedom in the peasant style', a requirement that must have presented an unusual challenge to those chosen to form the small group. Arthur Milner, however, was dismissive of it, regarding it as 'not worth the trouble obviously taken with its preparation'.

At the annual general meeting in September 1957, the death of the Society's chairman, Dr A. Charlton Curry (a former lord mayor of Newcastle) was announced. He was to be succeeded by Alderman Violet Grantham, JP. It was also reported that the Society was in a healthy financial position; encouragingly, there had been capacity audiences at two of the concerts. Burns pointed out that recent programming had tended to follow a pattern that was 'worthy musically' and evidently acceptable to audiences. This basic pattern offered a November concert of unaccompanied choral music with one or more solo instrumentalists; December brought two carol concerts; in February there was a choral and orchestral programme, often including Bach cantatas and sometimes with Carl Dolmetsch and Joseph Saxby; in March there was a major work by J. S. Bach, but increasingly there were works by Handel. To this pattern should be added the series of chamber music recitals in January, promoted by the Bach Choir Society.

The 1957/8 season exemplified this. The November concert included music by the London Alpha Trio and unaccompanied choral music by the choir; there were two carol concerts in December; the Aeolian String Quartet gave a series of recitals in January; in February, Carl Dolmetsch, Joseph Saxby and Layton Ring played in a programme including Bach cantatas; and the season ended in March with the St Matthew Passion. Of the performance of the Passion, Burns was reported as saying that the combined choirs would come to nearly 300 singers. By this time, although Burns used small-scale orchestral forces that had some historical validity, when it came to the ever-increasing size of the choir this sense of historical appropriateness seemed to have been lost, and with it one of the distinctive features of the choir. However, apart from the now familiar reservation about the use of the City Hall rather than 'some vast cathedral', as one reviewer wrote, the critics were at one in their praise of the performance. There was also praise for the 'excellent audience' and gratification for the 'evidence of the cultural climate of the area as of the reputation which Dr Burns and the Newcastle Bach Choir have earned for themselves in the difficult post-war years'. Despite this, the question of attendance at concerts would be a continuing issue.

In August 1958 Vaughan Williams died. He had been associated with the Bach Choir from its earliest years, and the choir had performed most of his choral music as well as a number of his smaller instrumental works. In a letter of sympathy to Mrs Vaughan Williams, W. R. James, the choir secretary, wrote of the lively and practical interest that Vaughan Williams had taken in the choir, and the honour he had brought to it as its president. At the annual general meeting the following month, Burns spoke of the 'several occasions on which RVW had shown his real interest in the work of the Society, & of his meticulous courtesy & freely-given encouragement'.

The new season began with Vaughan Williams's motet *Valiant-for-truth*, which, with its text from John Bunyan, concluding with the words, 'So he passed over, and all the trumpets sounded for him on the other side,' undoubtedly served as a commemoration of the Society's late president. The season also saw a further appearance of Carl Dolmetsch and Joseph Saxby and another venture into semi-dramatic performance with Handel's *Semele*.

At the September 1959 annual general meeting, the treasurer again reported an improved overall financial result. Burns stressed 'the need for regular attendance at rehearsals & for work at home. Given that, the choir should continue to perform good music, without which one could not expect support from the public.' For the coming season he intended to change the order of the November and February concerts. This would introduce some variety and, in particular, would allow more time to prepare the music for the unaccompanied concert. He also reported that Dr Edmund Rubbra had accepted an invitation to become the Society's president, and partly because of this he had chosen to perform three works by Rubbra at the second concert and hoped that Rubbra would be able to attend.

Following the new programme pattern, the November concert offered two Bach cantatas as well as Handel's cantata for two voices, *Apollo e Dafne*, and instrumental music by Purcell. Although Tom Little wrote that he could not remember the choir 'singing so splendidly for several years', he drew attention to the weakness in the tenor line, a weakness that he said was shared 'with most choirs in the north'. At the concert of unaccompanied choral music in February three works by Edmund Rubbra, the Society's new president, were sung, the season ending with a performance of Handel's *Belshazzar*.

Two issues came to the fore during the 1960s. The first was concern about the choir's standards of performance, the second its relationship with the recently-formed Northern Sinfonia Orchestra. Much of the concern about the choir's standards emerged through the criticism of reviewers, notably from Tom Little of the *Northern Echo* and Arthur Milner and John Healy of the *Newcastle Journal*. Although by no means consistent, and sometimes contradictory, the criticism found its echo in the reports of meetings of the choir or the committee. At the 1960 annual general meeting there were signs of concern about standards, Burns acknowledging that the choir's balance may not have been ideal. He may have been thinking in particular of the depleted tenor line, but there may also have been some slackening of choir discipline, for Burns exhorted members 'to endeavour to attend all rehearsals, be on time, and to do as much work at home as possible'. It was agreed that in future members should have to attend a certain number of rehearsals in order to be eligible to sing at the concert being rehearsed. It was also agreed that the committee should meet at least once a month, suggesting, perhaps, that a firmer line was to be taken over the management of the choir. Outlining the programme for the 1960/61 season, Burns said there would be two rather than three concerts, plus the Christmas concert. In March, however, the choir would also sing at two of the Northern Sinfonia's concerts, to be conducted by Burns.

The November 1960 concert offered a programme of Bach cantatas, and instrumental music by Alessandro Scarlatti and Bach. The orchestra was the Bach Choir Orchestra, strengthened by the Edinburgh String Quartet. Of this performance Tom Little wrote that 'few concerts in the North-East, for sheer musical interest, can equal those given by [the Bach Choir]'. He praised Burns for maintaining the achievements and traditions established by Whittaker, and also enlarging them. Significantly, he referred to the 'dividends of a minor reorganisation of the society', which were 'evident in the improved standards of performance'. This improvement was noted by Arthur Milner after the next concert when he wrote that the choir 'have never sung better than they did on Saturday'.

The concert with the Northern Sinfonia Orchestra in the City Hall in March 1961 offered Vaughan Williams's *Flos Campi*, with Cecil Aronowitz as the viola soloist, and Brahms's *Nänie*, as well as his *Academic Festival Overture*, and Berlioz's symphony *Harold in Italy*. Praising Burns's command of the orchestra, Tom Little found this 'a quite outstanding concert'. He referred to 'the superb work' of the choir in *Flos Campi*, which he thought 'would have won the whole hearted approval of the former president of the Bach Choir, Vaughan Williams himself'. Burns's report at the annual general meeting in October said that the 'standard of singing during the previous season had been as high as ever before'. He welcomed new members, hoping that they would soon catch 'the infectious attitude of the choir', though he regretted the lack of tenors and urged members to recruit new singers. He also stressed 'the need for a "Don Cossack" bass or tenor to rumble down in the nether regions'.

A performance in November 1961 of Purcell's *The Fairy-Queen* was 'full of many delights', Tom Little wrote, while John Healy especially praised Sheila More for her 'alert playing' of the harpsichord. The centenary of the birth of Delius was commemorated the following year in a concert that included three of his works as well as music by Palestrina and Vaughan Williams, prompting Arthur Milner to refer to it as 'one of the most interesting programmes the society has yet presented'. In March the choir sang those sections of Mozart's Requiem that were known to have been composed wholly or substantially by Mozart. Tom Little thought the choir 'sang with real assurance and mastery and produced a splendid choral tone' that he found 'very welcome after some tentative singing which they [had] offered earlier this season'.

About the same time a delicate matter was raised to do with rooms for choir members. Apparently men and women had shared the same room in the Armstrong Building, which had led to some embarrassment when the men of the choir had needed to change before a concert. It was agreed to ask for separate rooms for women and men so that 'if the latter needed to change their trousers, the sensibilities of the former would not be outraged'.

The annual general meeting in October 1962 heard that there had been 'an enormous loss' on the past season's concerts, largely owing to the heavy expense of using the Northern Sinfonia Orchestra. Burns acknowledged his anxiety about the expense and his awareness of the attitude of some of the players, but remained committed to the Sinfonia, emphasising 'how lucky the Society [was] to have such an enthusiastic body of players at its disposal'. Burns also expressed his concern about the choir's membership, for he referred to the resignation of about a dozen singers, and suggested that 'this might act as a spur to recruitment'.

Handel's *Acis and Galatea* and a Bach cantata were performed in November, with the participation of the Northern Sinfonia. This concert prompted Tom Little to write powerfully in praise of the choir's contribution to the music of the region, describing it as 'a monument to the sterling achievement which is possible for amateur forces when they are directed by really outstanding musical personalities', by whom he meant Whittaker and Burns. Both Little and Arthur Milner, however, were critical of the Sinfonia's playing, the latter referring to playing that 'sounded sometimes perfunctory or under-rehearsed'.

A concert in February 1963 produced the first serious criticism of the choir's quality from the pen of Tom Little. He wrote of 'the unlovely sound of much of the singing', adding: 'Dr Burns must do something to improve the quality of the sound of this choir. What I think it needs is a very large blood transfusion. But it is most important that it should be young blood.' This criticism is curious in that it occurs only a year after Little had observed that the choir 'produced a splendid choral tone' and three months after he had written that 'the choral tone itself was also very pleasant'. It is hard to believe that from being 'splendid' and 'pleasant' it was now necessary to 'improve the quality' of the choir's sound. These reviews suggest a certain inconsistency of judgement, and it is difficult to say whether any hint of the later criticism had any impact on either Burns or the choir committee. Certainly in considering the 1963/4 season, Burns mentioned 'the importance of recruiting new voices', but that was a frequently expressed demand, and the view that 'if we sang well enough, people would come to our concerts and clamour to join us' did not obviously reflect a concern about the choir's tonal quality. At the same time, reservations about the choir's quality continued to be made in reviews for the rest of the decade.

Reference to a reduction in the size of audiences raised the question among the choir committee as to whether the choir performed 'the right kind of music to attract audiences'. Burns, defending the choir's repertory, observed that the choir 'had never tried to play safe, throughout its long history'. Drawing attention to a programme to include music by Debussy, he argued that 'it [was] our job to sing such things, and if we stopped doing so, who would take our place, especially with new and unfamiliar music?' This view echoed that expressed by a reviewer in the *Northern Echo* in 1935, who wrote of the Bach Choir that 'it always provides a programme of music that we have little chance of hearing elsewhere'.

Referring to financial loss during the year, Burns acknowledged that it was largely owing to the cost of supporting the Sinfonia by engaging them. At the 1963 annual general meeting he explained that he had discussed with the orchestra manager the high cost of using the orchestra and that both were aware of each other's financial problems. But he urged the Society 'to appreciate the cost of running such an orchestra'. It is clear that Burns was strongly committed to the Sinfonia even when it was to the Society's financial disadvantage. The following month the treasurer spoke of the 'alarming state of the Society's finances', and in December the situation was seen as casting 'the shadow of bankruptcy over the Society'. The cost of the Sinfonia remained an issue, Burns defending the cost of £200 for the November engagement as 'a generous charge, in view of the augmented orchestra and the extra rehearsal'. He admitted, however, that the financial problems once again raised the question, 'Can we afford the Sinfonia?' The Rev. John Chalmers raised an ethical issue when he asked whether the Society could expect the City Council, 'using ratepayers' money', to continue to subsidize the choir. A pressing concern was the need to raise funds for the coming Jubilee season, and after various suggestions had been considered, it was decided to launch an appeal 'to a limited number of local bodies and firms'.

The November concert had taken place the day after the assassination of President Kennedy, and as a tribute the Northern Sinfonia played Bach's *Air on the G String*, with the audience standing. This was followed by Britten's *Hymn to St Cecilia*, performed in honour of the composer's fiftieth birthday on 22 November. Burns, according to his successor Percy Lovell, had an aversion to Britten's music, and seems to have given only two performances of his music with the choir, both of the *Hymn to St Cecilia*. We gather from John Healy's review of the main work performed at this concert, Handel's *Solomon*, how the semi-dramatic performance was presented. In the centre was 'a small stage on which the characters made their entrances and exits when required'. The choir was divided into two choruses, one on either side of the stage, and the orchestra was in front. It may be surmised that this was substantially how the other semi-dramatic performances were given. Tom Little in his review made the point that Burns had 'done his best to repair the musical deficiencies of those who believe that to know the *Messiah* is to know the oratorios of Handel'. As to the singing, he noted 'a marked improvement in what I heard a year ago. The choral tone was very pleasant and homogeneous; the singing generally was alive and interesting.'

Despite the concern about its cost, the Society continued to employ the Sinfonia, giving a performance in February with the orchestra that included John Blow's coronation anthem, *God spake sometime in visions*, followed by the masque in *Dioclesian* by Purcell. In the second half of the concert the Northern Consort sang a selection of modern works by Thomas Pitfield. The final work was Sir Arthur Bliss's *Pastoral: Lie strewn the white flocks*. The concert, and especially the use of the Northern Sinfonia, 'raised some important questions of musical policy for the region', according to Tom Little, who was concerned that local choral societies should have to 'beggar themselves' in order to employ the orchestra. He argued that the orchestra should hire the choirs, and recognize the advantage of performing in an area where there were choirs of the calibre of the Bach Choir.

The Golden Jubilee Season 1964/5

THE Golden Jubilee opened with a celebratory dinner in the Co-operative Society Hall in October 1964. Toasts were made to the Queen, the City and County of Newcastle upon Tyne, the University of Newcastle upon Tyne, to the guests and past members, and finally to the Newcastle upon Tyne Bach Choir Society itself, proposed by the former conductor Sir Jack Westrup, with a response from Dr Burns. In the toast to the University, George Brownlow encapsulated the characteristics of Whittaker and the three conductors who were present. Whittaker was notable for his 'commanding eye and discipline', Newman for his 'intensity and fire', Westrup for 'the wonderful élan' that he brought to the choir's singing, and Burns for his 'persuasive cajolery'. Mr James, proposing the toast to the guests, recalled that one description of the choir's singing was 'celestial treacle ladled out with a golden spoon', but added that other criticisms had been 'much more astringent'. In his own speech, responding to the toast to the Society, Burns recollected that the choir was 'the first to be formed in Britain using the same number of singers as Bach was accustomed to handle, and achieved an international reputation'. He thought that the choir's greatest contribution to the future could be 'to spread the gospel of personal satisfaction and the enrichment of life which followed active music-making'.

In November the first concert of the Jubilee season, at which the Northern Sinfonia Orchestra played, began with Telemann's Concerto for Viola and Strings, with Cecil Aronowitz the soloist. The choral items, all by English composers, were Purcell's coronation anthem *My heart is inditing*, Holst's *Ode to Death* and Vaughan Williams's *Flos Campi*. Of the Holst, Arthur Milner wrote, 'the choir has never done anything more convincingly'. The February concert saw a return of Carl Dolmetsch and Joseph Saxby in a programme that offered some of the most characteristic elements of the choir's repertory from the time of Whittaker onwards. It began with the Magnificat and Nunc Dimittis from Byrd's Great Service, first performed by Whittaker in 1924. Then, after instrumental music by Handel, K. F. Abel and Telemann, the first half of the programme closed with Bach's motet *Sing ye to the Lord*. The second half began with a sonata for treble recorder and harpsichord by J. H. Roman, a contemporary of J. S. Bach, after which all the music was modern and British. Two works for solo harpsichord by York Bowen were followed by three works for recorder and harpsichord by Edmund Rubbra, the Society's president. The choir then sang Stanford's *Three*

Motets, Op. 51, followed by Bax's motet, *This Worldes Joie*. The next choral work was the first performance of Edmund Rubbra's *Bonny Mary O!* (a work for choir and piano written the previous year), with Sheila More as the pianist; this was received so enthusiastically that it was given an immediate encore. The concert closed with two north-country folk songs arranged by Whittaker, 'The Willow Tree' and 'Sir John Fenwick'. Rubbra had been unable to attend the concert, owing to pressure of work, but asked whether he could borrow a tape-recording of *Bonny Mary O!* On the day of the concert he sent a telegram wishing Burns 'great success tonight'.

The final concert of the Jubilee Season was the St Matthew Passion, performed in the City Hall. For this the Bach Choir was joined by both the Blyth Oriana Choir and the Newcastle University Choir, with the chorale in the opening chorus sung by children from the Church High, Dame Allan's, Manor Park and Pendower Technical High Schools. Members of the Manchester Mozart Orchestra provided the first orchestra and the Bach Choir Orchestra formed the second. Léon Goossens played the oboe and oboe d'amore. The continuo section was provided by Desmond Dupré (viola da gamba), Layton Ring (harpsichord) and John Edwards (organ). In a review, Andrew Grimes was critical of Burns's 'over-reverential' handling of the music, complaining of becoming 'exhausted by the sheer Gothic weight' of the performance, though he noted 'some flashes of illuminating brilliance'.

At the annual general meeting in October the treasurer was able to report that, largely owing to the generous response to the Jubilee appeal, the year had ended with a profit. In his own report, Burns thanked everyone for their response during the season; with the St Matthew Passion as the 'unquestioned highlight' it had been 'a happy and memorable year'. Referring to the coming season, he said he had just auditioned several new members who, he hoped, would contribute to an improvement in the balance of the choir. He urged members to maintain the choir's reputation by applying themselves 'conscientiously to studying and practising their music at home [and] to punctual and regular attendance at rehearsals'.

There had been some recent criticism of the choir's attire, especially that of the men. After rejecting the idea of a referendum on the subject among the whole choir, it was thought that a strong recommendation on standards from the committee might be better, 'as compulsion was out of the question'. At about the same time there had been discussion about 'suitable dress for the ladies', with the suggestion 'that "Black and White" be dropped'. Unlike the decision for the men, this matter was to be the subject of a vote among members.

The Final Years with Burns

THE 1965/6 season opened with a programme of music by Bach and Handel, including three Bach cantatas and Handel's setting of Psalm 109, *Dixit Dominus*. Again, the orchestra was provided by the Northern Sinfonia. Tom Little described this concert as 'one of the most outstanding post war achievements' and noted that Burns had now assembled 'perhaps the best collection of voices [he had] ever heard'. 'Much of the dead wood in this famous choir has been removed,' he wrote, 'and the freshness of the singing was one of the notable gains from this ruthless pruning.' However, he found the orchestra's playing 'perfunctory'. Although Burns at the previous annual general meeting had accepted some new members and acknowledged that more were needed, there had been no reference to 'pruning'. As the names of choir members were no longer listed in the programmes it is not possible to identify who may have constituted the 'dead wood'.

In March the choir sang the B Minor Mass in the King's Hall with the Manchester Mozart Orchestra. Arthur Milner reiterated his previous observation about the numerical weakness of the men's voices, and found them 'wanting in unified blend of tone'. What was astonishing, however, were the comments of Tom Little, who only the previous November had found in the choir 'perhaps the best collection of voices [he had] ever heard', was now able to write that we were 'not living in the greatest days of the Bach Choir', adding that the B Minor Mass performance 'made it clear that an overhaul is needed if the choral tone is to be improved and the singing invested with vitality'. Praising Dr Burns as 'a practical musician of great resourcefulness, experience and accomplishment', he added that 'ruthlessness' was also needed to maintain high standards. He also took up a familiar theme, observing that the 'performance is as much a spiritual as a musical exercise. Criticism is largely silent and subdued before such musical magnificence'; though in this instance it appeared to have been neither silent nor subdued.

Despite the recent contradictory views of the choir's choral tone, there may have been some justification for Little's recent remarks; for Burns, in his report to the annual general meeting, emphasized that 'the vital importance of getting fresh vocal blood', adding that the previous season 'was encouraging in this respect', but that it had had 'the inevitable consequence of making performances less spontaneous'. Because of this he intended to give another performance of the B Minor Mass in 1967.

The first concert of the 1966/7 season was a performance of Handel's *Saul*, with the Northern Sinfonia Orchestra. It is apparent that there had been some infusion of 'fresh vocal blood' into the choir, for both the *Newcastle Journal* and the *Northern Echo*'s reviewers alluded to it. The choir, 'with much new blood in it, was in splendid form', John Healy wrote. Tom Little became almost lyrical: 'The singing was the best I have heard from this choir for longer than I care to remember and at times I wondered if I was witnessing the renaissance of a choir which in its greatest days was one of the musical glories of the land.' He also noted the presence of more young singers, and praised both the balance of the choir and the 'pleasant tone' it produced.

The repeat performance of the B Minor Mass was given in St Thomas's Church, again with the Northern Sinfonia, and produced markedly conflicting views as to both the performance and the venue. As might have been expected from his earlier comments, Little thought the location contributed to a much improved perform-ance, and recognized signs of the choir's 'moving surely back to its former great-ness'. A totally contrary view was taken by John Healy, who clearly thought the choir would have performed better in the King's Hall, as he felt they were un-comfortable in the choir stalls with the orchestra in between. He was also critical of the tonal blend and weak attack at the beginning of choruses, and thought there was 'a general lack-lustre about everything'.

The choir's finances were once again of pressing concern, especially because of the cost of hiring an orchestra, and it was agreed to ask the Cultural Committee of the City Council and the North East Association for the Arts to meet an overdraft of £300, advising them that the choir's very existence could be threatened by this debt. The annual general meeting in October heard of the resignation, because of the demands of other work, of Sheila More, who had been the choir's accompanist since 1956; she was succeeded by June Reed. At the same meeting John Edwards, the organist, also resigned; but on the suggestion of Burns the position of organist was left vacant and has never subsequently been filled on a regular basis, organists being chosen as and when required.

Handel's *Samson* was performed in November 1967 with the Lemare Orchestra, and the following February 'Bach and British' was emphatically the theme, though with the distinctive difference that it included six motets by three of the Bach family – Johann Michael, Johann Christoph and Johann Sebastian. There were four works by Holst, and the programme concluded with Whittaker's *Lovelady Shield* and a group of north country folk songs. Tom Little praised Burns for his 'efforts at choral renewal in the last two or three years. His sopranos and altos are nearly all young and the dividends in fresh, bright choral tone are there for all to hear.' A similar view was expressed by him the following month after the choir sang Haydn's *The Seasons* for the first time, for which they were joined by the

University Musical Society Choir. The 'liberal infusions of fresh young blood' contributed to a choir that had 'never sounded more beautiful or sung as expressively within my 30 years adult musical memory'.

In the same month, March 1968, choir members met to consider what might be done to raise funds to alleviate the Society's debts. They decided to hold a jumble sale in Wycliffe Baptist Church Hall, Elswick Road and a more up-market bring-and-buy sale in St James's Congregational Church Hall in the city centre. This seems to have been only the second time that events of this character had been arranged to raise funds, the first having been in 1948. At the annual general meeting in October it was revealed that some members of the choir had apparently made interest-free loans to the Society, some of which had been converted into gifts. Because of the Society's financial position, Burns said that the next season was to be organized on 'economy lines', with only two concerts apart from the annual carol recitals. He also reported that the annual chamber music festival by the Aeolian String Quartet, which had for some years been promoted by the Society, would next year be taken over by the University.

The two concerts in the new season offered, in November, a wide-ranging programme that included Bach's motet *Come, Jesus, come*, written for a funeral service in Leipzig, and Samuel Wesley's *Carmen Funèbre*, composed for a funeral in 1827, as well as works by Brahms and E. J. Moeran. Owen Wynne, countertenor, sang music by Purcell and Peter Dickinson. The performance of two of Bach's harpsichord works provoked John Healy to write, 'I, for one, longed for a grand piano', a view that was markedly at odds with the tradition established at the Society's concerts, notably by Joseph Saxby, in the performance of keyboard music of the baroque era. The main work at the following concert in March was Handel's *Acis and Galatea*, performed with the Bach Choir Orchestra.

A much healthier financial position was reported at the annual general meeting in October 1969, when the chairman paid tribute to the individual and collective efforts made in overcoming the 1967/8 deficit. Despite this financial improvement, the programme for the coming season would again be on 'economy' lines, Burns announced, with only two concerts, as before, in addition to the Christmas music recitals. The meeting heard of the impending retirement of Dr Burns, and approved a proposal to give a performance in the City Hall of the St Matthew Passion, joining with the Newcastle and Gateshead Choral Union, of which Burns was also conductor, to mark his final appearance with the two choirs.

Two works only were performed at the November concert in 1969, Beethoven's Mass in C and *An Oxford Elegy* for speaker, chorus and orchestra by Vaughan Williams, which was performed in memory of Professor Peter Ure, the professor of English, who had recently died. The speaker in the *Elegy* was the local poet Basil Bunting, who, unfortunately, was said to be 'often inaudible'. The concert in February 1970 saw the return of Carl Dolmetsch and Joseph Saxby in a programme of choral and instrumental music from the Renaissance to the late twentieth century. Among the instrumental works performed was a toccata by David Barlow dedicated to Joseph Saxby.

The November concert of 1970 was devoted to two works: Bach's Cantata No. 180, *Adorn yourself, beloved soul* (*Schmücke dich, o liebe Seele*), and Handel's *Alexander's Feast*. Apart from the Christmas recitals and the combined performance of the St Matthew Passion planned for the following year, this was Burns's last concert with the choir, and it prompted Tom Little to write appreciatively of Burns, 'who has greatly extended [the choir's] musical repertory, and at a time of difficulties for choirs has kept the flag flying and preserved standards'.

The valedictory performance of the St Matthew Passion was given in the City Hall the following March by the Bach Choir, the Newcastle and Gateshead Choral Union, the University of Newcastle Choral Society and the Blyth Oriana Choir, with children from Ashington Grammar, Dame Allan's, Heaton Grammar and Newcastle Church High Schools and with the Northern Sinfonia and another, unspecified, orchestra.

The presentation dinner in Burns's honour was held in the university refectory in May 1971. The were no toasts, only the presentation of a tape recorder to Burns by Mrs V. H. Grantham, JP, the chairman of the Society, in 'a felicitous speech in keeping with the very happy atmosphere of the occasion'. In his reply Burns 'touched on high lights of the Choir's music-making during his 27 years' regime, and wished it well in the future'. At the annual general meeting in October Dr Burns was elected an honorary vice-president of the Society 'in recognition of his 27 years of invaluable service to the Choir as its Hon. Conductor'.

A Successor to Burns

WITH the departure of Burns, the Society turned to the question of his successor. Denis Matthews, the concert pianist, had been appointed to the first chair of music at the University, and it was agreed to invite him to take over the conductorship of the choir, thus continuing what had become a tradition that the head of the Music Department should become the conductor of the Bach Choir. However, it was intended to ask Percy Lovell to take this on should Matthews decline. In his letter to Matthews inviting him to become the conductor, William James, the choir secretary, set out the relationship of the choir to the University, which the choir valued highly.

In his reply, Matthews said that he was honoured to receive the invitation and thought the association with the University 'excellent' and that it should continue, but that he did not wish to commit himself to the conductorship during his first year, explaining that he needed to discuss the work of the Music Department and music-making generally, and had also to consider his commitments as a pianist. He offered, however, to conduct one of the concerts during the coming season.

What emerged from the ensuing correspondence between James and Matthews was that Percy Lovell would take the rehearsals during the autumn and conduct the November concert, and that James himself, as assistant conductor, would conduct the Christmas carol recitals. We detect, however, an increasing sense of exasperation on James's part over Matthews's indecision over the arrangements for the rest of the season. Matthews had thought he might conduct the March 1972 concert, and we find James advising him that he 'would need to take at least half' of the eight rehearsals. Matthews evidently remained undecided about this concert, for James wrote to him to say that if he were not to take it then Lovell would be asked to, and that 'the sooner he knows and can give it thought the better'. It became clear that Matthews would, indeed, conduct it, but then problems emerged over his choice of music and his delay in selecting it. Matthews had originally proposed Schubert pieces for unaccompanied male voices, but James discouraged these because of the shortage of tenors and their weakness of quality. In another letter to Matthews, James wrote that he did not want to appear to be 'hustling' him but asked whether he could have his choice of music by September. By October, however, although a programme to include choral music by Bach, Brahms and Bruckner had been agreed, there was still no final decision about the specific items to be performed, which caused James some anxiety over the ordering of music in time for the first rehearsal in January.

Matthews was not able to take all the rehearsals for the March concert, so James took two of them, reporting on what he had done. Perhaps his concluding remark in his report pointed to a lack of confidence in Matthews's ability to take a firm enough hand with the choir: 'I'm afraid I'm something of a task-master & slave driver at rehearsals – but time is precious,' he wrote. After taking one or two rehearsals, Matthews complained about the seating arrangements for the choir during rehearsals in the King's Hall, which James attempted to improve. Despite all the difficulties and problems that had arisen, Matthews did eventually conduct the concert, in a programme of Schubert piano duets played by himself and his wife, Brenda McDermott, and the unaccompanied choral music.

It had become apparent that Matthews was reluctant to take on the conductor-ship of the choir, and that he seemed unfamiliar with the responsibilities that such a position would call for. Moreover, the rehearsals he had taken showed that he was not a natural conductor, and his direction of the choir was unclear. Indeed one person said of him that he 'hadn't a clue about how to conduct a choir'. It was not surprising, therefore, that at a meeting called to discuss the conductorship the secretary reported, perhaps with a sense of relief, that Matthews 'did not wish to be nominated'. As had been expected, Lovell was invited to conduct the 1972/3 season 'with every expectation of re-appointment for subsequent seasons as with all the choir's former conductors'. Now in a magnanimous mood, the members agreed to invite Matthews to be a president of the Society, along with Dr Edmund Rubbra, a position that Matthews was happy to accept.

1972–1984
Conductor: Percy A. Lovell (1919–2004)

Fig. 162 Percy Lovell. *Courtesy Jonathan Lovell*.

PERCY LOVELL was formally invited to become the choir's conductor in October 1972. In accepting the invitation he said that the choir had 'a great chance at the moment to be a leading exponent of choral music in the City'; he sensed 'liveliness and enthusiasm among members', noting that there had been 'a nice influx of younger singers and the direction of the Society [was] firm and forward-looking'. We also see from his acceptance letter something of his characteristic tact and sensitivity in ensuring that Matthews was included in initial discussions about immediate and long-term plans for the choir. As to Lovell's choice of repertory, the previous November's concert with music by Monteverdi, Giovanni Gabrieli and Bassano gave some indication of future programming. The November 1972 concert, however, presented a more traditional programme with music by Thomas

Fig. 163 Lovell conducting the final Bach Choir rehearsal on 28 November 1981 for the Monteverdi Vespers. *Courtesy Philip Owen.*

Tomkins, marking the 400th anniversary of his birth, and his near-contemporary Heinrich Schütz, as well as Vaughan Williams. Tom Little had previously described Lovell as 'an unassuming but thoroughly musical director'; in his review of the present concert he wrote that Lovell 'directed with distinction', adding that 'fresh young voices put a bloom on the choral tone.'

For the first concert of 1973, the choir, which had now reached nearly 100 members, performed the B Minor Mass with the Bach Choir String Orchestra and the Edinburgh Wind Players. The concert was given in the University Theatre, whose acoustics, the *Journal* reviewer wrote, 'did not seem to favour great masses of sound of complex and intricate gesture'. He also thought the singers might have had difficulty hearing those 'other than that in their immediate vicinity', leading in some rapid passages to 'a pleasant and enthusiastic scramble'.

The Bach Choir had never had a formal constitution, but it had become necessary to have one when claiming exemption, as a charity, from income tax. The annual general meeting of 1973 formally adopted one, based on a model obtained from the NFMS, adapted to suit the particular circumstances of the Bach Choir. The matter of the programmes of the Christmas recitals was also considered at the annual general meeting, as some members thought they should include more familiar carols and offer more for the congregation to sing. For a few years five congregational carols were sung, later settling down at four.

Fig. 164 Percy Lovell conducting the final Bach Choir rehearsal on 28 November 1981 for the Monteverdi Vespers. *Courtesy Philip Owen.*

The November concert, performed with the Durham Sinfonia, was devoted to Kodály's Missa Brevis and works by Mozart. Reiterating a familiar theme, Tom Little wrote that the choir was now 'getting back to its old form after a period in the doldrums. On Saturday no one could fail to be impressed by the beauty of the choral tone, the general security of the singers and the buoyant vitality of the rhythm.' Commenting on the appearance of the Durham Sinfonia, he added that 'the Northern Sinfonia, in its quest for international recognition, has priced itself out of the market it was created to serve'.

The year 1974 began with a concert of music by Bach and Vivaldi, with the Bach Choir Orchestra, but the main event of the season fell in May when the choir gave a 'commemoration concert' celebrating the fiftieth anniversary of the first modern performances of Byrd's Great Service given by the choir in Newcastle Cathedral and St Margaret's, Westminster, in 1924. That performance was conducted by the choir's assistant conductor, W. R. James, who had sung in the first performances. In 1924 the separate sections of the Great Service had been interspersed in Newcastle by organ music; in a performance with Burns in 1952 instrumental works had separated the various sections. Now, the Venite and Te Deum were followed by instrumental music by Avison and Boyce, after which the Benedictus, Kyrie and Credo were sung. The second half of the programme began with modern instrumental music, the concert ending with the final sections of the Great Service, the Magnificat and Nunc Dimittis.

Inevitably, after the major celebrations of the Golden Jubilee, the Diamond Jubilee was celebrated on a smaller scale. It began with a concert given with the Bach Choir Orchestra in November. In addition to music by Charpentier, Handel and Tippett, two works by Denis Matthews were performed, his *Suite for Greys*, for string orchestra, and the first performance of *The World of Light*, a setting of words by Henry Vaughan for chorus and strings, written for the Bach Choir. Tom Little wrote that Matthews 'scored a personal triumph' in directing *The World of Light*, though he thought the music 'sounded curiously out of its time' suggesting that it 'might have been written by one of Vaughan Williams's pupils 40 years ago'.

The complete St Matthew Passion was performed in the King's Hall in March, with the Bach Choir Orchestra and the Tyneside Chamber Orchestra. No other choir took part, except that of Newcastle Church High School. Both John Healy and Tom Little praised the performance, Little asserting that the choir remained 'one of the region's great cultural forces'. Of the orchestra, Healy wrote that it 'showed how well our local musicians can cope with great and exacting music'. The Diamond Jubilee year ended with a 'serenade concert' with the Bach Choir and the Tyneside Chamber Orchestra in a programme, given in the University Theatre, comprising items from Purcell's *The Fairy-Queen*, Britten's *Serenade for Tenor, Horn and Strings*, the Élégie from Tchaikovsky's *Serenade for Strings* and music from Handel's *L'Allegro*.

At the 1974 annual general meeting it had been agreed to hold a social evening, 'as there was little opportunity at rehearsals for members to get to know one another'. Although a committee was later set up to arrange social functions, the first report of one was in 1979, when a successful social evening was held at the Novocastrians Rugby Football Club, at which the 'excellent cuisine and friendly atmosphere' suggested that there should be a similar event in the following season. In the end several such events were held over the next few years.

There had been a number of new applicants in 1974, and the committee felt that with about ninety members the choir was large enough, and that new admissions should be only to fill vacancies, though it was recognized that there should not be a hard-and-fast rule. Lovell believed that the choir could give 'valuable experience to students of the Music Department' and that some return was owed to the University 'for the generous facilities put at the choir's disposal'. A compromise allowed Lovell to choose 'a limited number of students' to sing in the forthcoming performance of the St Matthew Passion. The discussion showed some tension between the need to maintain the choir as a balanced, highly trained instrument, and the need to make it a useful training facility for the Music Department and an asset to the University as a whole. At the annual general meeting the following year it was reported that the chairman of the Bach Choir Society, Councillor Mrs V. H. Grantham, JP, who had been chairman since 1957, now wished to stand down. The members, while reluctantly accepting her resignation, thought it would be 'a serious loss to the choir'. Prof. David Newell, the chairman of the choir committee, was subsequently elected to replace her.

The 1975/6 season opened with a group of unaccompanied pieces by David Barlow: *Salve me*, composed in 1971 but only recently discovered and now given its first performance, *Behold, and see* (1973), and the Christmas carol, *The World's Desire*, written for the Bach Choir in 1958. Although it was not specified in the programme, these were undoubtedly performed as a tribute to Barlow, who had died earlier in the year at the age of only forty-eight. The rest of the concert was devoted to music by Mozart and Haydn.

The choir, with the Tyneside Chamber Orchestra, of which Lovell was conductor, performed Bach's St John Passion in March. Ken Darling, for the *Journal*, congratulated Lovell 'on his ability to grasp and exploit all the capabilities of this big choir of around 100 voices and of the Tyneside Chamber Orchestra'. The final concert of the season, given in St John's Church, Grainger Street, began with Fauré's Requiem followed by instrumental music by Vivaldi and Dag Wirén and concluding with unaccompanied choral music of the Elizabethan period.

The centenary of the birth of W. G. Whittaker was commemorated in November 1976 with a concert that included his own setting of Psalm 139. The concert, given with the Tyneside Chamber Orchestra, was conducted by Lovell and Chalmers Burns. The choir also contributed to a 'centenary festival' the following summer, arranged in association with the Newcastle Festival, when Burns returned to conduct the choir in a programme including a further performance of Whittaker's Psalm 139. In March that year the choir and Bach Choir Orchestra had performed Monteverdi's Vespers of 1610 for the first time. Tom Little wrote that Lovell, 'a devoted Monteverdian, presented the work as a great musical masterpiece inspired by religious feelings'. A second performance of the Vespers was given as part of the 1,300th anniversary of St Andrew's Church, Corbridge, this time with the Tyneside Chamber Orchestra.

Lovell, in his report at the 1977 annual general meeting, spoke of the excellent performance of the Vespers, paying tribute to 'the fine work of the Tyneside Chamber Orchestra'. He concluded his remarks with 'the slight admonition that [he] would like to be able to start rehearsals punctually and asked members to make this possible'. The meeting agreed to launch an appeal 'to raise a capital sum for future years, to allow the Committee flexibility on expenditure on concerts when soloists, orchestral players or other costs exceeded the estimates'. The appeal letter was sent to local firms and businesses as well to present and retired University staff, mainly to professors and heads of department. The total raised was £350.

In March 1978 the choir gave a performance of Handel's *Messiah*, in the Watkins Shaw edition, which had been published in 1958. It followed a talk given the previous evening by Dr Shaw on the origins of *Messiah*. A note written by Lovell on the performance is instructive: 'The recent popularity of "scratch" performances of *Messiah* has tended to obscure the plain truth that any really good interpretation of this work demands concentrated hard work and practice from all concerned whether amateur or professional, singer or player.' Referring to the present performance, he went on to say that the aim had been 'to get as close as we can to the style of the first performances under the composer's direction. We hope, in so doing, to allow the power and spiritual beauty of the work to speak to us afresh.' Although the choir was now greater in number, Lovell's approach appeared to have reflected that of Westrup in 1943, which aimed to be 'nearer to what Handel intended'. It may also be noted that each of the performances was a reaction against a prevailing tradition: in the first case that of performances with markedly unbalanced orchestral and choral forces and additional instruments, and in the present case that of 'scratch' performances. Ken Darling, reviewing this concert, recognized the aims and achievements of the performance when he wrote that

> The choir and the orchestra managed to bring some new freshness to the great work, which has become overlaid with unnecessary conventions over the years. . . . The performance was a nice example of 90-plus singers working as one, rather than battling against each other, which has too often become the hallmark of Northern oratorio.

Just as Burns had espoused Handel's choral works, it was becoming apparent that Lovell was promoting Italian music. A number of works by Italian composers had already been performed, and the 1978 season began with a further concert entirely devoted to Italian choral music. There were three works by Monteverdi, followed by Vivaldi's seven-part *Beatus Vir* and Cimarosa's Requiem.

In March 1979, a Porters' Union strike at the University caused a planned performance of the St Matthew Passion in the King's Hall to be transferred to St Thomas's Church. The work was recorded by Radio Newcastle, which subsequently broadcast extracts. Performing with the Bach Choir were members of the University Choral Society, the junior choir of Dame Allan's School, the Tyneside Chamber Orchestra and the Bach Choir Orchestra. For this performance the audience was invited to join in the singing of the chorales, for which copies of the words were provided. Tom Little, rather predictably, found it 'one of [the choir's] finest performances', approving the transfer to St Thomas's Church, and describing it as 'more an act of devotion than a musical performance'.

In June, the choir offered a 'festival concert' in St Nicholas's Cathedral, performing two nineteenth-century works, Puccini's *Messa di Gloria* and Liszt's setting of Psalm 13 for tenor solo, choir and orchestra, alongside the Andante Con Moto from Suk's *Serenade for Strings*. Referring to the choir's choice of 'syrupy settings of the liturgy', Ken Darling, for the *Journal*, found it 'quite a pleasant change to hear the choir . . . launch into the high drama of the *Messa di Gloria* by Puccini'. He complimented the orchestra for their 'racy backing to the choir in Quoniam Tu Solus from the *Gloria*, a performance worthy of any Italian opera house'.

The 1979/80 season opened with a programme of English music of the seventeenth and twentieth centuries for choir and orchestra, including Purcell's Funeral Music for Queen Mary (1695) as a tribute to Canon John Chalmers, who had died in September, having been a member of the choir for many years and the chairman of the choir committee from 1960 to 1964. The second half of the concert was devoted to music by Holst and Britten. The choir returned to an all-Bach programme in March, performing three of the cantatas as well as the Missa Brevis in F. For the final concert of the season the choir made a significant departure from their usual repertory by performing Mendelssohn's *Elijah*. Again they performed with the Tyneside Chamber Orchestra, though with the addition of guest woodwind and brass players.

The Society's financial position continued to be a matter of concern. Expenses of the concerts were not matched by income, and the choir remained dependent on grants, including those from Northern Arts, to meet its costs. In March 1980 the music officer for Northern Arts was invited to talk to the committee, and his advice was that the choir should attempt to increase its income by 25 per cent. It was subsequently agreed to increase membership subscriptions and the price of season and individual tickets. It was also decided to reduce the cost of printing programmes by using a 'do-it-yourself' method.

In April 1981 the choir recorded fifteen short works to be broadcast as part of Tyne Tees Television's Epilogues. They had been asked to provide 'hymns, songs, motets, etc. suitable for mass viewership'. Contemplative secular music was said to be acceptable, 'but not in Latin'. The programme eventually chosen included four hymns, Bach chorales, extracts from Mendelssohn's *Elijah* and Fauré's Requiem, music by Tallis, Purcell, Vaughan Williams and Britten, two spirituals and 'Brother James's Air'. A 'summer serenade' was presented in June with music by Vaughan Williams and Elgar.

There had been some adverse criticism about the dress of the women in the choir, some members of the audience finding the multi-coloured dresses 'too visually distracting'. After a questionnaire had been sent to choir members on the matter, it was reported that by a majority of one the choir preferred the dress to remain as it was. At some subsequent stage this decision was changed, and for many years the women of the choir wore black skirts and white blouses. The choir's finances were now seen to be in a much healthier state, largely owing to reduced costs for soloists, the reduced cost of producing posters and programmes, the increase in subscription charges and a donation of £150 from Tyne Tees Television for the Epilogue music.

At the annual general meeting in 1981 a slight drop in the total membership of the choir to eighty-nine was reported. Among those elected to office was Dr Eric Cross, as an assistant conductor to W. R. James. Cross was a lecturer in the Music Department, and would later succeed Lovell as the choir's conductor. The choir were told of the intention of the University Senate, 'on instructions from the University Grants Committee', to close the University Music Department, and it was unanimously agreed that a letter 'expressing the choir's concern' should be sent to the dean of the Faculty of Arts, Prof. John Cannon.

In November the choir gave a further performance of Monteverdi's Vespers, using the Tyneside Chamber Orchestra and a 'consort of winds and sackbuts', these latter appearing in the form of trombones. The B Minor Mass was performed in March, again with the Tyneside Chamber Orchestra and 'wind soloists'. The final concert of the season included Bach's Fantasia in G for organ, played by Stephen Cleobury on the King's Hall organ, which had been built in 1978. Among other works, the choir sang Stephen Dodgson's *The Tower*, which, according to a note in the programme, had been 'commissioned by the Arts Council of Great Britain at the instigation of tonight's baritone soloist', Mark Rowlinson. After Duruflé's Requiem for choir and organ, a presentation of books was made to W. R. James to mark his retirement. James had been a member of the choir for more than fifty years, and a former secretary and assistant conductor.

The 1982/3 season was unusual in presenting three major choral works: Handel's *Israel in Egypt*, Bach's St Matthew Passion and Mendelssohn's *St Paul*. Tom Little, noting that Lovell had considerably widened the choir's repertory, referred to the performance of *St Paul* as an 'illuminating experience'. Reg Taylor, writing in the *Journal*, regretted the small audience but praised the choir for singing 'with unflagging vivacity throughout the long performance'.

The question of attendance was again raised at the 1983 annual general meeting, when members were reminded that failure to attend a sufficient number of rehearsals would debar a member from taking part in the relevant concert. Two significant events concerning the NFMS were reported. The first was the Federation's annual conference, which was to be held in Gateshead, with a concert in Queen's Hall, Hexham, which the choir had been invited to provide. The jubilee year of the establishment of the Federation would fall in 1985, and a regional concert to mark the occasion would be presented in the City Hall in which the choir would participate. Reporting on the past season's concerts, Lovell referred especially to the performance of *Israel in Egypt*, saying that it had taken place 'at a particularly poignant moment in time, almost like a political comment'. He did not elaborate on this observation, but it is possible that he had in mind the release from internment of Lech Wałęsa, the leader of Poland's Solidarity movement, earlier in the month. As he was retiring from the University in 1984, he would offer for his valedictory performance 'a pageant of English music, with works particularly associated with himself'. Particular thanks were expressed by the chairman for his work both with the choir and with the Tyneside Chamber Orchestra. It was agreed that Eric Cross should be invited to prepare the programme for the ensuing season.

The concert given in the Queen's Hall Arts Centre, Hexham, for the NFMS conference included Vaughan Williams's *Dona Nobis Pacem* and Mozart's Kyrie in D minor. As expected, Lovell's last concert with the choir was devoted to English music for voices and strings, under the title 'Byrd to Britten'. It was given in the Brunswick Methodist Church, Newcastle, with the Tyneside Chamber Orchestra, and included music associated not only with Lovell but with the choir as a whole: Byrd, Vaughan Williams and Holst were among the composers represented. Although this *was* Lovell's valedictory concert, it was not the last time that he conducted the choir, for he shared in a concert with Eric Cross a year later, at which the choir sang the final chorus from Bach's St John Passion as a tribute to W. R. James, who had recently died.

Lovell had a gentle approach to conducting, expecting that members would learn their parts at home rather than having to be drilled in them. Sometimes this led to a less than accurate performance, but at its best the quality was very high. 'In singing one is always on a knife-edge,' he said; 'achieving and maintaining truly focused attention is so easily disturbed.' At the annual general meeting in 1985 it was agreed to invite Lovell to become a vice-president of the Society, an invitation that he accepted.

It was now more than fifty years since Whittaker had resigned from the choir he founded. The legacy he passed on to his successors was not locked away like the family silver but was developed under four very different conductors. The choir that Eric Cross was to inherit was larger and its repertory wider than the one that Sidney Newman had taken over, but it remained true to its guiding principle: 'Bach and British'.

Chapter 13

After 1984: A Personal Reflection

Eric Cross

THE previous chapters of this book have examined the history of the Newcastle upon Tyne Bach Choir and the way it has developed chronologically during the reigns of its various conductors. Unlike that of many choirs, the directorship of the Newcastle Bach Choir has been remarkably stable. Apart from Denis Matthews's very brief tenure and Jack Westrup's short appointment at Newcastle (which lasted only three years before his departure to take up the chair of music at Birmingham), the other five conductors have filled the remainder of the century, Sidney Newman's being the shortest period at just over a decade. It came as something of a shock when I realized that I am the longest-serving musical director, having the privilege of holding the post for more than thirty years. I don't know who finds this the most unnerving – myself or the sizeable number of the choir who have lasted the course! However, this seems a good point at which to reflect on the last three decades. Rather than taking a standard chronological journey through the years, I hope that you will indulge me in a slightly more personal approach, looking at the choir from different perspectives and suggesting what I see as some of the fundamental aims and issues that we have been tackling together.

The Bach Choir has always been an important part of my life. I arrived at Newcastle University to take up the post of lecturer in music on the retirement of Dr Frederick Hudson in September 1978. This was my first job, and I arrived with a half-completed Ph.D. thesis on Vivaldi's operas and more experience as an orchestral and operatic conductor than a choral one. My wife Lindsay and I both joined the Bach Choir immediately. (Fortunately for me, Percy Lovell – always the gentleman – declined to audition a colleague, otherwise my career might well have turned out rather differently!) The very first concert I sang in was a mix of Italian choral music: Percy's beloved Monteverdi coupled with Vivaldi and Cimarosa; and a couple of years later we performed the Vespers of 1610 with a mix of leading professionals (in this case tenors Rogers Covey-Crump and Leigh Nixon) and local soloists, some of them drawn from the choir, which was a feature of many concerts from that period. Rogers Covey-Crump became a frequent visitor to Newcastle, as his high flexible tenor and stunning musicianship made him an ideal Evangelist and a first choice for the Bach Passions, both for Percy and for me in

Fig. 165 The Newcastle Bach Choir at Sage Gateshead, March 2009.

the 1980s and early 1990s. He was, of course, memorable as much for his name as for his singing. I remember him guffawing one night while we were waiting in the green room to go on stage about a concert programme in which his hyphen had been misplaced and he was listed as 'Rogers Covey (Crump-tenor)', a truly medieval sounding version of a countertenor!

Those first six years at Newcastle singing under Percy's direction (I remember Tom Little, the *Northern Echo* critic, aptly describing his conducting style as 'genial') provided an ideal way of getting to know the choir. At the same time I was getting more experience as a choral conductor with Cappella Novocastriensis, whose directorship I took on after my first Christmas here. My time as a singer in the midst of the choir meant that a number of my scores have circles around certain notes in the bass line, and I often know, before they have sung a note, where they are going to go wrong – hence perhaps the fact that my gentle sarcasm tends to be directed at the basses rather more than at any other part. I also became assistant conductor in succession to William James; though in reality this was a largely honorary role, so I was only too delighted to accept the offer of taking over the conductorship when Percy retired from both the University and the Bach Choir in the autumn of 1984.

University Music Department

THE conductorship of the Bach Choir had always been connected with the University Music Department, and until Percy took over from Denis Matthews it had always been held by the head of music. This was a period when the department was a very small family affair – between eight and ten single honours students a year and a handful of postgraduates, a far cry from the current intake of around one hundred students a year. These were turbulent times, and twice – when Percy and Denis retired together in 1984 and then again in 1986 when Denis's replacement as chair of music, David Greer, moved down the road to Durham – Music was nearly closed. Indeed, it was only the outcry about the impact on the musical life of the city, the hundreds of letters to the Vice-Chancellor from 'Disgusted of Gosforth', and not least from many members of the Bach Choir, that got the decision reversed.

Committee Chair

ANYONE who has been music director of a choir or orchestra will know how important an effective committee, and particularly the chair, is to the efficient functioning of the organization. I cannot speak for my predecessors, but I have certainly been very fortunate in this regard. Professor David Newell was chair when I took over from Percy, and he provided stability during the changeover with his customary friendly efficiency, and indeed still takes an interest in the choir's fortunes from the opposite side of the globe. He was followed by Maurice Bone, a great supporter of both the Bach Choir and the University Concert Series, who worked tirelessly to place the choir's finances on a more secure footing, bringing in corporate members to supplement choir subscriptions with a further regular income stream. Maurice, to whose memory our performance of the St John Passion in March 2012 was dedicated, was succeeded by John Smith, who continued the strategy, building up the choir's resources further and allowing us to perform regularly in expensive venues like Sage Gateshead (see fig. 165) and to work with some of the UK's leading soloists and instrumentalists, taking risks from time to time with unfamiliar repertory without fear of impending bankruptcy. John recently passed on the role to Jenny McKay, who like her predecessors has strong support from a hard-working group of officers and committee members.

Accompanists

THE other critical role for any choir is that of accompanist. Here again the choir has been very lucky to have talented individuals who have undertaken long-term commitments. Roy Large mentions in his contribution to this volume that Sheila More replaced Muriel Plant, who had accompanied the choir for more than thirty years, in 1956. Sheila in turn served the choir for more than a decade, playing the piano and harpsichord in concerts as well as accompanying rehearsals. Her replacement in 1967 was June Reed, although the post of organist, vacant at the same time owing to the resignation of John Edwards, was never reinstated. (In recent years John Green, former organist of Hexham Abbey, has been the choir's most regular organist and harpsichordist for concerts.) June vied with Muriel Plant for the long-service award, remaining accompanist until her eventual retirement from the role in 2009, after a similar extraordinary period of more than three decades. June had an amazing facility and could get round the most challenging Lisztian vocal score arrangements. Her successor and current accompanist is Dr Alison Shiel, a fine musician who had already sung in the choir for many years, often taking smaller soprano solos. For many years, too, one of our long-serving secretaries, Rose Haslam, has agreed to act as reserve accompanist, as did Bryan Cresswell in the past. I count myself as very fortunate to have had pianists of this calibre throughout my time as conductor, for I know only too well that an inexperienced or incompetent accompanist can effortlessly wreck a rehearsal.

The Size and Make-up of the Choir

MUCH has been said earlier in this volume about Whittaker's aims in founding the Bach Choir and his desire to create a crack choir of twenty-four singers that would be close to what was then believed to be the size of choir that Bach himself may have worked with. We now know, of course, that Bach often worked with much smaller forces, and indeed there is substantial, albeit not uncontroversial, evidence that he often had just one singer per part. To modern ears, then, accustomed as we are to the many recordings of works with smaller groups of singers and period instruments that recreate the sonorities of an eighteenth-century orchestra (or what we believe they would have sounded like), Whittaker's forces, with the use of a Steinway piano for the continuo and modern wind and string instruments, might make his claims seem rather misguided, but that rather misses the point. His aim, and that of his successors, was to present a then largely unknown repertory of Bach cantatas in all their wonderful variety, in a way that he sincerely believed reflected the composer's intentions: performances imbued with a strong educational purpose befitting a university-based organization. And that was, and still is, very much my aim too.

Roy Large has drawn attention to the way in which the choir has grown over the years. Indeed, even under Whittaker it grew from the original twenty-four to around forty. Newman soon saw it increase to sixty-four, although reviewers still praised its small size and more even balance between the parts, allowing it to 'achieve triumphs foreign to choral battalions massed without regard to relative strengths and numbers', as the *Newcastle Journal*'s music critic put it in 1933. Chalmers Burns continued to grow his forces, as did Percy Lovell when he took over, so that I inherited a choir that numbered around ninety. Now one could take a relatively purist line and say that a Bach choir should be less than half that size, and many other Bach choirs, such as the Yorkshire Bach Choir, are indeed much smaller, although of course the best-known, the London Bach Choir, is actually more than double our size. However, to reduce the size significantly would mean a rather inhumane and lengthy process of re-auditioning everyone (unless one were simply to draw lots!) and would also then make the choir too small for much of the later repertory. So I have always worked with a compromise: to accept that the size of the choir is an anomaly in terms of the number of singers that Bach would have used, but to attempt to recreate the style in which I believe the music would have been performed, with a lightness and clarity of articulation that mirrors that of period instruments – a challenging goal that during some rehearsals seems futile but which I believe we frequently achieve, even if only on the evenings of performances when for once there is something approaching 100 per cent concentration from all members.

Another recurrent issue is the balance of the choir. The last fifty years have seen the Era of the Alto – this has always been the biggest section, at times threatening to outnumber the rest of the choir put together. This is not helped by the tendency for sopranos to graduate downwards as they get older, and this raises the thorny problem of ageing singers. Some choirs have a policy of jettisoning members as they get older, but I have always been reluctant to go down this road. Apart from the time commitment needed to audition 100 singers regularly, is it right to say to someone who has served the choir faithfully for forty years, perhaps for a considerable period as secretary, treasurer or chair, 'Sorry, but we no longer need you'? As well as an educational purpose akin to an evening class, the regular rehearsals also provide an important social element for many members. The choir has had members from their mid-teens to their late eighties; it provides an important gateway to the choral repertory, especially but not only for the younger, less experienced members, and an important – indeed sometimes perhaps the only – regular weekly social event for older ones. And of course the physical benefits of singing to older people are well documented. So, although the Bach Choir is not perhaps the most social of organizations, I see it as having an important duty to provide for its members as well as take from them. This is another reason why I have not sought to reduce the number of singers – it is much easier to hide the occasional problematic older voice in a larger than in a smaller section!

Venues

ANOTHER advantage of a larger choir, of course, is more ticket sales, so reducing the size would also make balancing the financial books more challenging. Maintaining audience numbers has been a recurrent challenge throughout the choir's history, as it is indeed for most amateur choirs. Newcastle and Gateshead are not blessed with a variety of good concert venues: the King's Hall works very well for smaller-scale programmes that are unlikely to bring in an audience of more than four hundred, and its ambience is not completely inappropriate for sacred works. Newcastle City Hall was for many years the only large concert venue in the city, but its capacity of 2200 has always made it a challenging venue to fill: an audience of several hundred still looks pitifully small there; and its very dry, revealing acoustic does amateur performers no favours. In the late 1980s and 1990s this was the only option for large-scale concerts, and our joint performances with Durham Choral Society of the Verdi Requiem and Britten's *War Requiem* had perform- ances there as well as in Durham Cathedral. This was a welcome opportunity to perform a programme more than once: ideal after weeks of hard work preparing a programme but generally impossible for most of our programmes with orchestra and soloists, when each performance loses a substantial amount of money.

Hall One of Sage Gateshead is the North East's most prestigious concert venue, though it is very definitely a concert hall and therefore even further away from the ambience of an eighteenth-century Lutheran church. Its capacity of 1650 is also a considerable challenge, as often is pinning down an available date that suits the pattern of our concert season, with its primarily end-of-term concerts. It is also a very expensive venue to hire, which means that the costs of an orchestra and high-quality soloists makes it difficult not to make a loss unless we can attract an audience in four figures. This we have achieved for some programmes (our first *War Requiem* there, for example, aptly timed for Remembrance Weekend, was a sell-out), but none of our Bach programmes (or our recent Mozart Requiem, for that matter) has ever attracted more than around 800 people, so they all require a significant subsidy rather than breaking even. This, of course, is not a unique problem; many current Royal Northern Sinfonia concerts are poorly attended, and it was also a challenge to the Bach Choir in earlier decades. Many press reviews over the century have drawn attention to the undeserved sparseness of the audience, and there were certainly times during Chalmers Burns's reign when the choir was in a parlous financial state. I have regarded myself as very fortunate that, throughout my time with the choir, I have never really had to worry about tailor- ing programmes to bring in money; there has always been sufficient money in the reserves to underwrite any potential financial disaster.

What of course Newcastle has always lacked is a suitable concert venue that holds around 800, something that many local choral societies covet. Over the years we have used certain local churches to fill this gap, most notably St Nicholas's Cathedral and St George's, Jesmond (which holds nearer 600), though the cathedral has presented problems of balance when using a large orchestra; and both are problematic from the point of view of staging and sight-lines. We have nearly lost more than one concert manager over the years as a result of the logistical challenges presented by some of these 'away matches'.

Programming

EACH of the choir's musical directors over the years has had his (and of course we have not yet had a female conductor) own approach to programming. Often this has involved a series of instrumental concerts alongside the choral programmes, with artists connected to earlier repertory, such as the Dolmetsch family, who were frequent visitors in Chalmers Burns's time, or simply well-known musicians such as the pianist Clifford Curzon. These additional concerts reflected the separate constitutional existence the Bach Choir Society as opposed to the Bach Choir itself, a historical formal distinction that has long disappeared.

Despite the personal differences in conductors' approaches to repertory – Whittaker, for example, placed considerable emphasis on new or recent works, often written by his friends such as Holst and Vaughan Williams, while Burns included many Handel oratorios – the fundamental core of 'Bach and British' has remained throughout, as I believe has the concept of educational value. For Whittaker I think that this meant two main things: performing the music of Bach, especially the largely unfamiliar cantatas, in a way that took into account the composer's original intentions, and providing a platform for recent works that were often too challenging for the average choral society.

For me it has meant embracing Whittaker's first aim, and I have tried to encourage a performance style that reflects the huge changes in historically in-formed performance over the last few decades, even though the number of singers means that it can never be regarded as 'authentic', as well as alternating the 'big works' (the two main Passions, the B Minor Mass and, latterly, the Christmas Oratorio, which I confess for a long time I never really appreciated, not least because of the way it combines six originally independent cantatas unidiomatically into a single evening) with programmes in alternate years that explore the wonderfully varied cantata repertory. After more than thirty years I still feel that we have only scratched the surface, and there must be some 150 cantatas that I have never performed: plenty to keep the choir going for another century!

Another important decision in performing Bach's works is that of language. Early performances of the cantatas and Passions – and sometimes even the B Minor Mass – were invariably in English, and this has much to commend it in terms of understanding the meaning of the texts. But it frequently goes against the rhythms and phrasing of Bach's music, and one of the changes I instituted very early on was performing the works in their original German, which, so long as the audience has a full printed translation in their programme that allows them to follow closely the meaning of the words, allows the full appreciation of Bach's sensitivity to his texts.

As to Whittaker's second aim of promoting new works, while I have tried to include recent, primarily British, repertory, including a handful of special commissions, the choir is not skilled enough to cope with a lot of contemporary music, which requires a more professional make-up of singers. So I have tried to take a broader educational mission, particularly presenting music from earlier centuries that is rarely heard and in some cases has never been performed in the North East. This has included several works by Michael Haydn, edited by a long-term member of our soprano section and now accompanist Dr Alison Shiel (the *Missa Trinitatis*, the *Missa Sanctae Theresiae* and the motet *Ave Regina Coelorum*), as well as Joseph Eberlin's Requiem and various operatic arias and overtures by Vivaldi (my own particular research interest). Other works, if not first performances in the region certainly very rarely heard works, include C. P. E. Bach's colourful Easter oratorio *Die Auferstehung und Himmelfahrt Jesu*, William Boyce's *Solomon*, Michael Haydn's Requiem, Cherubini's Mass in C minor, Handel's *Belshazzar* and, most recently, Zelenka's *Litaniae Lauretanae*, ZWV151, and Miserere in C minor, ZWV57, while later repertory has included Delius's Requiem, Howells's *Hymnus Paradisi*, Janáček's *Otčenáš*, Arvo Pärt's *Beatitudes*, and John Joubert's *South of the Line* and *An Hymn of the Nativity* (the latter a special commission for another local choir, Cappella Novocastriensis).

As mentioned earlier, when the Newcastle Bach Choir was founded, Whittaker's aim was predominantly an educational one – to provide an opportunity for modern audiences to hear Bach's works and particularly the cantatas; and this didactic element has continued with later musical directors. (Roy Large quotes the *Northern Echo*'s reviewer in 1935, who said that the choir 'always provides a programme of music that we have little chance of hearing elsewhere'.) I believe that this is a really important aspect of the choir's mission: to give both singers and audience a chance to get to know works that they would never otherwise have an opportunity to sing or to hear live. Of course this can also be a challenge: how do you get audiences to come to hear unfamiliar music and to trust that the choir would not programme a work if it were not worth listening to? This is a challenge to any concert promoter, and one that an organization like Sage Gateshead has to deal with every week. The answer is not necessarily to default all the time to the tried and tested music of Mozart and Beethoven but to mix programmes regularly during a season to offer both familiar and unfamiliar works. It is certainly a major challenge, however, for any musical director, and while audiences will come to listen to *Messiah* in their droves, they will not necessarily do the same for another

Fig. 166 Will Todd and Eric Cross in the King's Hall, June 2015, for the first performance of Will Todd's new work *Songs of Magical Creatures*.

Handel oratorio such as *Belshazzar*, *Saul* or *Jephtha*, even though the music is just as good if not better. So over the last thirty years I have tried to provide a reasonably eclectic mix of the well-known and the relatively unknown, hopefully building a reasonably regular core to our audience that has a degree of curiosity, something that I believe is appropriate to a choir based at a university.

I said earlier that the choir was not as adept as Whittaker's original creation at performing new works, but that does not mean that we have avoided this aspect completely. We have commissioned three new works during my tenure. The first was Wilfred Josephs's *Tenebrae* in 1990, for the seventy-fifth anniversary. Then came two works by Will Todd: first in 2006 there was *Let us be true*, a setting of Matthew Arnold's *Dover Beach*, written in memory of Percy Lovell (who was a great admirer of Will's music), and most recently *Songs of Magical Creatures*, settings of Shakespeare to celebrate the centenary in June 2015 (see fig. 166). We have also been involved in two joint commissions by multiple choirs through Making Music and its predecessor the National Federation of Music Societies:

Geoffrey Burgon's *Revelations*, performed by several North East choirs with the Northern Sinfonia under Richard Hickox to a near-empty City Hall in 1985, and Peter Maxwell Davies's *The Kestrel Road* (June 2005). Interestingly, the latter work shows the difficulties of writing for amateur choirs: the first work that Maxwell Davies produced was considerably more difficult and would have been too challenging for many of the participating choirs. Rather than trying to tinker around with his original piece, the composer provided a new one, pitched at just the right level of challenge yet practicability for choirs like ourselves and one that proved very rewarding to perform.

Orchestras

WHEN the choir first began exploring Bach's music under Whittaker, it faced a significant problem: some of the instruments that Bach wrote for were not available. The distinctive lower member of the oboe family, the oboe d'amore (pitched a third lower than the ordinary oboe), was not generally available, although the oboe da caccia (pitched a fifth lower) could be replaced by the similarly pitched cor anglais. Some of the very high trumpet and horn writing was particularly challenging to players in those days who were unfamiliar with such stratospheric writing; while the cornett, a throwback to the Renaissance that had become somewhat anomalous by this time, was pretty well unknown. And then, of course, the harpsichord had been replaced long ago by the piano, and it is interesting to observe that, as the former became more and more common over the decades, sometimes conductors still preferred a modern Steinway. Whittaker clearly brought together players with both the skill and the interest in tackling this often challenging repertory, sometimes not just drawing his players from the North East but bringing them up from London too. For example, the name of the great oboist Léon Goossens appears several times over the years, and he later played concertos for Chalmers Burns.

The Burns era saw the foundation in 1958 of the Northern Sinfonia by Michael Hall, a graduate of what is now Newcastle University (then King's College, Durham). Although originally formed in part to play for regional choral societies, the Sinfonia soon became too expensive for the Bach Choir to afford, and this remained the case in following decades. The only time I have used players primarily from the Northern Sinfonia was for my first St Matthew Passion in 1990, when I booked the players as individuals to reduce the cost. Percy Lovell began using the Tyneside Chamber Orchestra, a primarily string-based group of which he was also conductor, as the regular instrumentalists to accompany the choir, bringing in wind players as necessary, and I took over this convention in 1984. While it had decided administrative advantages, it could mean that the strings were rather unbalanced, with a sometimes very large cello section; and, at the suggestion of one or two members of the orchestra, in February 1989 we started using a rather smaller, select group of players instead. This had the benefit of both improving the balance and, very swiftly, raising the general standard of playing, and for much of the remaining period I have booked players individually rather than using an existing group or employing a separate 'fixer' to book players, which can sometimes lead to variable standards.

The biggest single policy change, much more significant than the decision to abandon the Tyneside Chamber Orchestra, was the move to use period instruments for our programmes of Bach and other baroque composers. I had first used a period band for a *Messiah* performance with Cappella Novocastriensis, for whom I was also musical director from 1979 to 2010. This was, as far as I am aware, the first time that a choir based in the North East had used a period instrument orchestra, and the benefits were immediately apparent. Rather than spending rehearsal time on cajoling players on modern instruments to use baroque articulation and phrasing, shortening bow strokes and lifting upbeats, this all happened automatically, making it realistic to bring the players in just on the day of the concert without jeopardizing performance standards.

Although the costs of a period band are significantly more than those of a modern orchestra, we first brought in period instruments for our Bach cantata programme in November 1994. This was the Avison Baroque Ensemble, a group founded by two local musicians, trumpeter George Parnaby (a regular in the Bach Choir's orchestra) and cellist Gordon Dixon. Gordon had founded the original modern-instrument Avison Ensemble to promote the music of the Newcastle-born composer Charles Avison, but had recently decided to convert to period instruments. The Avison Baroque Ensemble (see fig. 167) provided the orchestra for our baroque programmes until 1998, when George and Gordon parted company and George formed Newcastle Baroque. Whereas the Avison Baroque Ensemble brought most of their players up from London, Newcastle Baroque had the laudable aim of developing a nucleus of locally based players. While there were a few common players, the two groups rapidly developed distinctive profiles, and Newcastle Baroque became our regular partner. Although the line-up has varied over the years, it has formed a core of regular members. Many of the string players are based in the North East, several of them in the Newcastle area, while others are closer to York and a few near Edinburgh. Wind players are less easy to

Fig. 167 The Newcastle Bach Choir and the Avison Baroque Ensemble with soloists Mhairi Lawson, James Bowman, Charles Daniels and John Bernays in the King's Hall, March 1996. The concert, entitled 'Not the B Minor Mass', included Bach cantatas sharing musical material with the B Minor Mass, along with the Mass in G major, BWV 236. This was one of the earliest Newcastle Bach Choir concerts to involve period instruments.

source locally; although George Parnaby and his colleague Mike Walton have often provided two-thirds of the trumpet section, and there are several sackbut players within a 100-mile radius, oboes and bassoons are more challenging and frequently have to be brought up from London and Manchester.

One of the greatest pleasures for me of our concerts over the years has been the opportunity to work with some of the finest instrumental players in the UK and, indeed, the world. We have been fortunate to have Crispian Steele-Perkins, one of the finest baroque trumpeters of his generation and still on fine form as he turns seventy, playing for many of our Bach programmes, most recently in the B Minor Mass in March 2015; while Tony Robson, for years principal oboe with the Orchestra of the Age of the Enlightenment but who always enjoys returning to his native North East, has been a regular member. To perform one of the Passions or a cantata programme with the likes of Tony, coupled with perhaps James Eastaway (oboist in that very first Cappella *Messiah*), is an unforgettable privilege. For those of us brought up on those early Harnoncourt recordings with strident, slightly out-of-tune oboes, the warm tone and perfect intonation of players like Tony and James (and the various other younger wind players whose standards seem to rise all the time) adds hugely to the performance and lifts the choir's standards.

I have been fortunate with many of our other regular players, too. Edwina Smith has always been our principal flautist: a wonderful York-based musician who has delivered some memorable obbligatos and never seems to recognize quite how good she is. As I have said, the strings have some more local players, and cellist Deborah Thorne and organist John Green have formed a consistently reliable, flexible and versatile continuo section for countless performances. Our leaders have been more varied and have normally come from further afield: Simon Jones, leader for that first *Messiah* with Cappella, has led on several occasions and always contributes so much to detail of articulation and phrasing, while for several of the earlier concerts Adrian Chandler provided a more vigorous and Italianate interpretation of the music in keeping with his dedication to the music of Vivaldi. Duncan Druce has also been a regular member of Newcastle Baroque; he was one of the early pioneers of period performance in the UK, as well as being the editor of the Novello edition of Mozart's Requiem that we have used for all our recent performances of that work.

Since March 2004 we have also ventured into the realm of period instruments for classical repertory. Originally this option had been too expensive, with the increased costs of larger forces, but the 2004 concert that included Mozart's C Minor Mass proved what a difference the subtler sonorities of the wind can make in this repertory. For me this has been most noticeable in performances of Mozart's Requiem, where the dark tones of period basset horns, bassoons and sackbuts make a huge difference to the orchestral palette.

I mentioned that I have been fortunate to have many fine players as regular members of our orchestra, but it is also important to stress what nice people they all are to work with. While players like Crispian Steele-Perkins and Tony Robson work regularly with the likes of Roger Norrington and John Eliot Gardiner, there is never any self-importance in the way they approach our dates. When they play for us they are always charming to deal with and every bit as professional in the performances they provide for us as they would be if they were playing in the Royal Festival Hall. An additional bonus was to welcome Catherine Rimer to the cello section for our B Minor Mass in March 2015. She is a native of Gateshead and is principal cello for John Eliot Gardiner. Her family has a long connection with the Bach Choir, her grandfather Eric Rimer having sung under Whittaker.

Soloists

As well as the privilege of working with some of the UK's finest instrumentalists, I have been extraordinarily fortunate in having the opportunity to work with some wonderful singers. This is partly the result of the choir's stronger financial footing that developed during the late 1980s and early 1990s. Looking back at the lists of soloists in earlier eras, there were some very famous names such Kathleen Ferrier, Alfred Deller, Wilfred Brown and Owen Brannigan. These artists were at the top of their profession but often shared the platform with local soloists. Percy Lovell frequently mixed singers like Martyn Hill or Rogers Covey-Crump with local singers or members of the choir. I have tried to achieve a more consistent level of professionalism for our main concerts, and our stronger bank balance has allowed me to compile much more even teams of soloists than were often heard in the past.

Given the remit of the choir, many of our soloists are specialists in earlier repertories (and sometimes overlap too into contemporary music, where the elements of musicianship and sight-reading ability are more important than a big operatic-style voice). It is perhaps a bit unfair to single out too many individuals, but I have gone back regularly to certain soloists because they are not only extraordinary artists with a profound understanding of eighteenth-century performance styles but also a joy to work with. We have been lucky enough to work with many of the finest tenors of the last few decades, including Martyn Hill, Rogers Covey-Crump, Charles Daniels, James Gilchrist, Mark Padmore, John Mark Ainsley, Thomas Walker and James Oxley. Two fine Bach basses, Peter Harvey and Stephen Varcoe, have been regular visitors, along with sopranos Lynne Dawson, Catherine Bott, Lynda Russell, Gillian Keith, Joanne Lunn and Mhairi Lawson. Mhairi is a Newcastle University alumna, and I have always tried where appropriate to invite such home talent. Both Mhairi and Chris Foster have been regulars with us, while other alumni have included Elizabeth Roberts, Amanda Pyke, Alasdair Baker and Robert Murray. Portraits of Mhairi, Chris and Rob appear in fig. 168, and of Rogers Covey-Crump, Charles Daniels, Peter Harvey and Joanne Lunn in fig. 169. Although I generally prefer male altos to contraltos for Bach's music, I have worked with Catherine King, Kitty Whately and Catherine Wyn-Rogers, along with countertenors James Laing, Chris Royall, Russell Missin, Robin Blaze and James Bowman.

Fig. 168 Newcastle University alumni. *Clockwise from left*: Christopher Foster (baritone), Mhairi Lawson (soprano), Robert Murray (tenor).

Along with the emphasis in our programmes on Bach and British, I have also tried to include bigger works by combining with other choirs, and this has enabled us to work with some larger-scale operatic voices, including Claire Rutter, Jean Rigby, Anne-Marie Owens, Ian Storey, Matthew Best and, of course, the choir's distinguished President, Sir Thomas Allen, who is pictured in fig. 170.

Initially these larger-scale programmes involved the Durham Choral Society for a memorable Verdi Requiem in both Durham Cathedral (conducted by their director, Richard Brice) and Newcastle City Hall (conducted by me). The final rehearsals, which we shared, turned out to be a fascinating lesson in the need to tailor one's interpretation to different acoustics. Rehearsing the Sanctus in

Fig. 170 *Clockwise from top left*: Rogers Covey-Crump (tenor), Joanne Lunn (soprano), Peter Harvey (baritone), Charles Daniels (tenor).

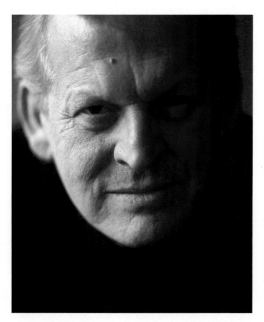

Fig. 169 Sir Thomas Allen, CBE, current
president of the choir.

Durham offered wonderfully dramatic moments as the big chords echoed around
the tower and nave for several seconds, but all the detail in the double-choir
counterpoint and filigree orchestral writing got completely lost in the wash.
Performing in the City Hall was exactly the opposite: a very dry acoustic in which
all the detail was clear (occasionally a bit too clear!), but the big moments were
somewhat underwhelming. Our second collaboration with Durham was memorable in a very different way: in the run-up to the concert the Cross family
gradually went down with chickenpox; I carried on unconcerned, having already
contracted it in my youth, but discovered on the Monday evening before the
concert that it was possible to catch it, in rare cases, more than once. It became
horribly clear by the middle of the week that I would never be able to conduct
anything at the weekend, let alone the *War Requiem*, and I had to call in a favour
with one of my colleagues in the Music Department, David Clarke, to take over
my role. I think that weekend was just about the most miserable one of my life –
not only was I missing out on the opportunity to conduct a work that I admire
hugely, and which we had been saving up for years to afford to put on, but I was in
agony from the spots. Not a good combination.

One of the challenges of working with singers is that, like animals and young
children on stage, they can be remarkably unpredictable. In particular, I seem to

work with soloists who suffer from weak bladders. In the days when I was head of music, I used my extraordinarily large university office (long since converted into a seminar room as student numbers increased and put pressure on accommodation) as a green room. The route from there to the King's Hall ran past the lavatories, and I always seemed to lose at least one of the four soloists *en route* before we got near to entering the hall. More serious than that, however, has been my ability to lose singers altogether through last-minute cancellation. Although for one Bach programme in King's Hall in November 1994 we actually had two late replacement soloists, the most memorable such occasion was the Verdi performances with the Durham Choral Society already mentioned. On the Saturday night, when I was in the audience and Richard was conducting, all went smoothly and tenor John Mitchinson was on fine form. Unbeknown to any of us, however, he was due to go into hospital later that month for a gall bladder operation. On the Sunday morning his condition flared up, and at midday I had a call from his agent to say that he was writhing around on his hotel room floor in agony. Now, trying to find a soloist for the Verdi Requiem on a Sunday afternoon is quite a challenge! It's not the kind of work you can just ask a choir member to take over – something that we did discuss quite seriously in the remarkably long interval of one concert in Hexham Abbey when the baritone soloist for the Brahms Requiem, Graeme Danby, failed to show up by the time we were due to restart. (He did, I'm glad to say, eventually appear, nonchalantly walking up the aisle having had problems finding somewhere to park.) Mercifully for the Verdi, an appropriate replacement was sourced by the agent: John Treleaven, a lead tenor with Scottish Opera and Opera North. There were, however, two problems: firstly he lived in Glasgow and secondly it was his son's twelfth birthday that day. The first was solved by the fact that he had a large, very fast car (and fortunately there were no speed traps that day, as he must have averaged around 100 m.p.h.); the second required an addition to the fee. By the time he finally arrived at the City Hall we had long finished rehearsing with the orchestra, so there was only a chance to talk through a bit of detail about tempi etc. Fortunately he had studied the work with John Mitchinson and as a result their interpretations were almost identical.

The other similarly nail-biting substitution was for *Elijah* at St George's, Jesmond, in March 1999. The baritone Peter Savidge was taking the title role, and for once I had the luxury of a piano rehearsal with him the night before. He was in splendid voice and it all went very smoothly; come the morning, however, I had a whispered phone call from him – he had been struck down with laryngitis and had completely lost his voice. An excellent replacement was found (once again the agent earned their fee, which is not, I have to say, always the case) in the late

Robert Poulton, who just managed to catch the afternoon flight from Heathrow. He was met at the airport and driven straight to our house in Fenham, where at about 6.15 p.m. we had half an hour round the piano with Bryan Cresswell before heading off for the church. We were fortunate that in this case it was a familiar work in any self-respecting baritone's repertory, but that is not always the case. Much more recently mezzo Beth Mackay lost her voice between the afternoon rehearsal and the concert. She struggled bravely through the first piece but was devastated that her voice had completely disappeared by the interval. Fortunately for us, however, tenor James Oxley is, like many specialist early music singers, a marvellous reader, and in the soprano and alto duet in Bach's Cantata No. 36 he sight-read the lower part, changing gear effortlessly into falsetto for the higher sections with an assurance that made it sound as though he had been practising it for months.

Christmas Music

As we have seen in earlier chapters, over the century the choir has dipped in and out of carol concerts, which were sometimes referred to as 'carol parties'. Percy Lovell revived a tradition of two concerts of Christmas music, one generally in St Andrew's, Corbridge and one in Newcastle. One of the challenges of a choir like the Bach Choir is that its members are busy people who cannot all commit to extra concerts. I soon found that it was often a problem to get a balanced choir willing and able to commit to the three rehearsals necessary as a minimum to prepare a Christmas programme that was not simply recycling well-known, straightforward carols. So for a number of years, after a couple of events in which standards were not really good enough and audiences seemed unseasonally uninterested, we stopped trying to put on carol concerts, except for a few occasions when Bryan Cresswell kindly stepped in to conduct. Recently, however, the membership has regained its enthusiasm, and the last couple of seasons have included programmes of Christmas music that happily have been closer to the choir's usual standard.

Highlights

So what, then, have been the highlights that I remember most strongly from the last three decades? That is not an easy question. I have very fond memories of so many evenings, even though there are more rehearsal evenings that I am happy to forget! Frequently they are the concerts in which the guest soloists and instrumentalists have raised the bar and encouraged the choir to reach standards they have never come near to in rehearsal. I have already mentioned some of the outstanding orchestral players who can help change the gear of any performance, and the same is true even more of some of our vocal soloists.

My first *Messiah* with the choir in March 1997 included Catherine Bott, James Bowman, Martyn Hill and Henry Herford, and the privilege of performing the work again ten years later with the legendary Emma Kirkby along with Catherine King, Charles Daniels and Peter Harvey made it a really memorable night. The last few performances of the Bach Passions have, for me, been outstanding: Charles Daniels's wonderfully sensitive Evangelist in the St Matthew Passion in March 2009, and the powerful momentum that the St John Passion achieved towards the close in 2012 through stunning arias from Mhairi Lawson and Robin Blaze still loom large in my memory. To share a platform with our president Sir Thomas Allen is always a joy, and I have had the good fortune to conduct him on three occasions: in Walton's *Belshazzar's Feast* in December 1995, in Vaughan Williams's *Dona Nobis Pacem* and the *Five Mystical Songs* in March 2000, and most recently in Britten's marvellous *War Requiem* in November 2014.

But despite these memorable high points, the singer I have probably most enjoyed working with is James Bowman (see fig. 172). I have always admired him as a peerless interpreter of Handel, from the times when as a student I saw him with the Handel Opera Society at Sadler's Wells or as Julius Caesar in the eponymous Barber Opera at Birmingham; but I didn't really know him as a Bach singer. I knew that he had grown up in Jesmond and had been a chorister at St Nicholas's Cathedral, but it had never occurred to me that we would be able to afford someone of his calibre and reputation. However, I heard at second hand that he was disappointed that no one from Newcastle ever asked him to sing here – he had sung with the Bach Choir once under Percy Lovell back in November 1971 – so I thought we should do something about that. He became quite a regular visitor from his B Minor Mass in March 1993, and, as well as the Agnus Dei from that work, which I shall always associate with him, I especially remember his performances of two of Bach's solo alto cantatas, Nos. 54 and 170. His ability to shape a phrase and to add an edge of emotion to a single note puts him, for me, in a class of his own; and the innate musicality, as well as the raw power, of his voice made many evenings very special ones. And then there was the sheer entertainment value of working with him, from the tales of fellow musicians and their mishaps with which he would regale us, to hoots of laughter, in the green room just before we went on, to the unexpected occurrences on the platform, particularly his invective against Hobnobs when an interval biscuit caused him to

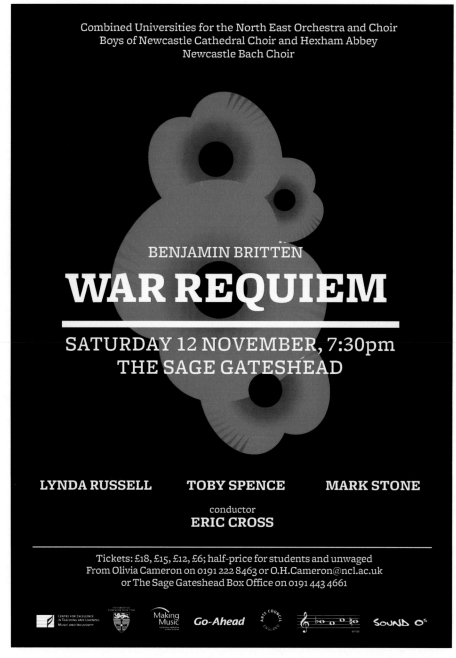

Fig. 171 Poster for Britten's *War Requiem*, November 2005. This was the choir's first concert in Sage Gateshead, which combined forces with the Newcastle University Symphony Orchestra and Choir.

Fig. 172 James Bowman (countertenor).

cough just before his first entry of the second half, or the time that his shirt stud flew off into the front row of the audience, from which he insisted on retrieving it immediately before continuing.

The other highlights have to be the large-scale concerts, especially those over the last few years in which we have combined with singers and players from the University, bringing together two important strands of my career at Newcastle, sometimes with soloists drawn from the formidable ranks of Samling scholars. Since 2005 this has enabled us to give two memorable performances of Britten's *War Requiem*, as well as *The Dream of Gerontius* (all three of these involving Newcastle alumnus Robert Murray, who displayed an extraordinary sensitivity to the text in his delivery of both works), a Verdi Requiem with a wonderful quartet of Samling soloists (see fig. 174), and, most ambitious of all, Mahler's Eighth Symphony. The poster for the *War Requiem* performance appears as fig. 171. It has to be said that there is an element of megalomania in most conductors – why else would you want to impose your ideas about a piece of music on hundreds of hapless performers? I will certainly own up to getting a huge buzz from the opportunity to direct a choir of 200 and a big orchestra in Hall One of Sage Gateshead (see fig. 173), as well as a sense of achievement and pride in the extraordinary standard that the Newcastle University Symphony Orchestra has

Fig. 173 The Newcastle Bach Choir and the Newcastle University Choir and Symphony Orchestra rehearsing Mahler's Symphony No. 8 in Hall One of Sage Gateshead, April 2008.

achieved on each occasion we have performed there. It is always a gamble planning a programme in a new academic year, when you know that you are losing your most experienced players who have just graduated but have no idea what the new first year will bring. So far the gamble has paid off, and I think the Mahler was probably the most satisfying of all, as it demands so much from its huge orchestral forces. The almost professional standard that the students achieved on this occasion is one of the moments of which I am most proud – something enhanced by the fact that the orchestra was ably led by our elder son, Ed, who has played for many of our concerts over the last decade on both modern and baroque violin. For me, this type of opportunity to assist amateur musicians from all kinds of different backgrounds and ages to come together and reach standards of performance that they would not have imagined possible, especially in works that they would otherwise never engage with, is what has been most important in my directorship of the Bach Choir (as indeed it was during my years as director of Cappella Novo-castriensis).

Fig. 174 The Newcastle Bach Choir and the Newcastle University Choir and Symphony Orchestra rehearsing Verdi's Requiem in Hall One of Sage Gateshead, April 2013.

Conclusion

WHEN Whittaker founded the Bach Choir a hundred years ago it was to fulfil a very specific purpose: to make the works of Johann Sebastian Bach, and especially the cantatas, better known to the general public. A century later, despite the daily availability of a vast range of music through YouTube, Spotify and the like, this fundamental aim still stands, for the average music-lover will still only have heard probably a handful at most from the vast repertory of cantatas. Our knowledge about the way in which Bach's works were originally performed has changed enormously, although there are still many unanswered questions. But some of the fundamental objectives of the Newcastle Bach Choir and its promotion of 'Bach and British' remain remarkably unchanged. I feel immensely privileged to have had the opportunity of working with so many members of the choir over the last thirty years – years that have encompassed hugely rewarding musical experiences as well as fostered many lasting personal friendships. The present choir, assembled

Fig. 175 The Newcastle upon Tyne Bach Choir in the Robert Boyle Lecture Theatre in the Armstrong Building of the University of Newcastle upon Tyne on 12 October 2015. *Photograph by Mark Savage.*

for the centenary photographs, may be seen opposite. As we embark on the next hundred years, I think the choir's role will remain just as important, and that critical experience for both performers and audiences of live music-making will never be replaced by recordings. I look forward with anticipation to this next phase of the choir's history.

Index

The scope of this index is restricted to choristers, conductors and officers of the Newcastle Bach Choir past and present and to others who are or were closely associated with it, including vocal and instrumental soloists whether visiting or indigenous. The names of former married women choristers are given in the forms by which they were best known within the choir.